GEORGIAN RIDER CHRONICLES

THE ADVENTURES OF GEORGIAN RIDERS IN AMERICA

RICHARD ALEXIS GEORGIAN

Barringer Publishing, Naples, Florida
www.barringerpublishing.com
Cover, graphics, layout design by Lisa Camp

Front Cover Artwork:
Data Kadjaia and Georgian riders, ca. 1902
Buffalo Bill's Wild West
Courtesy, Denver Public Library, Western History Collection, NS-174

ISBN: 978-0-9908209-9-4

Library of Congress Cataloging-in-Publication Data
Georgian Rider Chronicles / Richard Alexis Georgian

Printed in U.S.A.

DEDICATION
To the Georgian performers,
their families and countrymen

Georgian riders, ca 1902
Standing left to right: Joseph Simon Imnadze, Luka Nanikos Chkhartishvili, David Kadjaia,
Ushangi Kvitaishvili, Miron Chkonia, Alexander Khukhunaishvili, Pavle Rostom Makharadze.
Middle row left to right: Karman Maqsimelis Imnadze, Ivane Magsimelis Jorbenadze, Irakli Tsintsadze,
Nikoloz Antadze. Front row left to right: Porfile Ivane Kantaria, Konstantine Nanikos Chkhartishvili,
Teophane Kavtaradze, Ivane Dianosis Baramidze, Simon Oragvelidze
Author's Collection
Plate No. 1

CONTENT

LIST OF ILLUSTRATIONS

Chicago World Fair, ca 1893
Left to right: Walks-under-the-ground (?) and Kishvardi Makharadze
Courtesy, Denver Public Library, Western History Collection, NS-141
Plate No. 2

PREFACE

People by the hundreds of millions have trod this planet, forgotten and unrecorded by historians. Our ancestors laid the foundation of our societies. We can never be sure what impact one human life centuries ago might have on our own, even when separated by time and distance. Georgians from 1801 to May 1991 had felt the heavy foot of the Russian empire on their necks. The men and women in this book felt that foot. In 1993 Abkhazia with the connivance of Russia carried out "ethnic cleansing," in 2008 the Russian empire used separatists to invade South Ossetia, and in 2014 we again watch the Russian empire welding power over its neighbors. As we observe historians continuing to record humanities conflicts, what of the individual? In this book it is the individual and their stories and what they observed that I have exposed.

Ask yourself, where did I come from? You might be surprised at the answers. In my case, I uncovered an entire unknown history of a lost generation. It was my paternal grandfather's story, which started out as interesting and developed into perplexing questions. Why was my grandfather called a "Russian Cossack" when he was neither an ethnic Russian nor a Cossack? Why did he change his name from Gogokhia to Georgian? Where did he come from and how did he become involved with American western icons such as Buffalo Bill, Annie Oakley, Pawnee Bill, Frank James and Cole Younger?

The answers were found in the United States and Georgian National Archives, the Library of Congress, historical newspapers, and documents from American and Georgian museums and personal records. I uncovered a marketing ploy perpetrated by Buffalo Bill's organization that led to the loss of the identity of the Georgian riders. This is the story of Georgian men and women who rode in American tent shows as "Russian Cossacks," as revealed through primary sources such as historical documents, letters, photographs and newspapers.

As I reconstructed this history, a problem arose with names and dates. The spelling of the Georgian riders' names used in this text is based on current transliteration of Georgian into English. Their names in the original documents are problematic because the spelling was determined by the individual writing the document. In those cases where the correct interpretation of a name could not be determined, the original remains and is annotated. The original Georgian documents were dated based on the czar's Julian *(old style)* calendar, which by 1890 was 13 days behind the Gregorian calendar. In this book, Russian documents are annotated *(old style)* if the dates are not converted to the Gregorian calendar.

Reconstructing the culture of American tent shows between 1890s and 1920s requires an understanding of the language used by those of this period. Languages evolve, and people revise the intent and meanings of words; thus I have dealt with a century of change by keeping the characters and language within their period. Their word choices may not be acceptable today. You will view their world as seen through their eyes and their time period. The controversial use of the "N" word to identify African Americans is one such case; or "redskins, squaws, and savages" for Native Americans. Another might be the use of Constantinople instead of Istanbul, which may prick the sensibilities of the Turkish people. The characters in this history would have referred to Istanbul as Constantinople, since the name was not changed until 1930 by Kemal Ataturk.

The *Customs List of Passengers* from the United States archives and the *Form of Passenger List* from the British Public Records Office contained useful information as to which Georgians traveled the Atlantic and when they embarked/disembarked. These forms often listed the ages of the passengers. I discovered, however, that during the various years, the ages reported did not remain consistent. I have included the ages of the riders as reported, but the reader may, with reason, be suspicious of their validity.

I record events as they were observed by the riders, in chronological order, for each show they performed in. I also include in these chapters, where available, information on their voyages to the United States. I have taken the liberty to infuse a touch of shipboard life the Georgian riders might have observed. The Georgian riders in the last two chapters were no longer star performers, and details about them became more limited each year.

I have taken the liberty of changing the word Cossacks to Georgians in most quotes. The replacement word *Georgians* is in italics. A quotation from *The Knight in the Panther's Skin* precedes the prologue to each year. It is a Georgian national epic written by Shota Rustaveli during the reign of Queen Tamar (1184-1213), and is a literary poem, consisting of 1,576 4-line stanzas, that has seeped into the collective consciousness of the Georgian people. A specific feature of this poem is the aphoristic thinking of Rustaveli. His short, pithy, instructive sayings have become popular and widespread in the folklore of the Georgian people. Those readers unfamiliar with the Georgians' strong cultural heritage of chivalry, code of honor and hospitality may be enlightened by Rustaveli's aphorisms.

For more photographs and the dates the Georgians were in each city please visit my website www.GeorgianRiders.com

ACKNOWLEDGMENTS

This book reveals the experiences of men and women who over a hundred years ago came to America to support their families. I wish to thank the people and organizations that helped make this possible. As you pull back the curtain on time and read the exploits of Georgians in Wild West shows and circuses here are some of those behind-the-scenes actors.

Those in the Republic of Georgia that contributed to this project deserve special attention. Manana Lomadze at the Ozurgeti museum was a gracious host and supporter providing documents and insight. I could not have succeeded without the translation and communication assistance of Tamar Ghlonti, vice-president, Youth Resource Center of Guria. Georgian documents were also translated by Maia Natroshvili, Nana Khizanishvili, and Mariam Esebua. My guide and translator while visiting Guria was Maia Tavadze. Irakli Makharadze provided invaluable photographs, documents, translations, and insight into Georgian culture. I visited Professor Amiran Tsamtsishvili in Georgia. He wrote historical documents concerning the Georgians in America. My visit with him was inspiring.

Any historian owes gratitude to librarians all over the world. I spent years in the Library of Congress researching newspapers, microfilm, and books. I traveled the United States, England, and the Republic of Georgia, visiting historical societies, State archives, museums, and unique Wild West show and circus archives. I am indebted to them all.

Every writer owes a debt to the editor, and I wish to thank Carole

Greene and Lisa Camp. On the home front, my appreciation goes to my brother-in-law, Bill Burch, and to my indispensable Glen David King, who kept the home fires burning.

Richard Georgian

Ivane Makharadze, ca 1892
Author's Collection
Plate No. 3

CHAPTER 1
THE GRAND REVIEW: 1890 TO 1894

The equestrian director, the supreme boss inside the arena, clapped his hands. Sweeney's cowboy band struck up the *"Star-Spangled Banner,"*[1] and the Buffalo Bill Wild West exhibition was on. The "Rough Riders of the World" always opened the exhibition in a grand review. With a shrill cry, a horde of dark-skinned, almost-naked Indians rode into the arena. Straight and swift like a feathered arrow, the group shot across the arena, taking their flight to where the applause was swelling. With a swoop, they curved at the end, spread like an opening fan, circled, stretched across the arena, and ended their flight in a dust cloud, motionless, facing the reserved seating. Another tribe of Indians followed on their painted ponies, and then another group brandishing tomahawks. Each entered, rode around the whole enclosure at a gallop, and then aligned themselves with the others. Following the Indians, rode the Irish Lancers by fours, leaning almost perpendicular to their saddles as they turned in a splendid sweep on galloping horses; they fell in behind the Indians. Buffalo Bill, hiding behind the entrance canvas and peering through a peek hole, signaled the next troupe to charge. The announcer introduced the czar's wild Cossacks who rushed headlong into the arena, riding like madmen. The Georgians straddled strange saddles that elevated them two-feet above the plunging steeds. With long whips swinging wildly, sabers

---

[1] William Sweeney from 1882 to 1913 opened every Buffalo Bill show with the Star-Spangled Banner. This may have influenced the public's acceptance of the Star-Spangled Banner as America's National Anthem in 1931.

glistening in the sun, the stampeding Georgians suddenly stood on their saddles, bringing gasps from the crowd. Towering over the Indians and Irish, they slashed the air with the sabers as if cutting off the heads of enemies. Making their last turn around the arena, the Georgians plopped back onto their saddles, accompanied by a collective groan from the males in the audience, and stopped in a cloud of dust next to the Irish. The whooping cowboys, the Arabs with their streaming draperies, the Mexicans with wide sombreros and flapping trousers, the heavier Germans, the gallant Frenchmen, and then the U.S. cavalry horsemen arrived to complete the Grand Entrance. After the performers assembled there came an extra flourish by the cowboy band, and Buffalo Bill, clad in a picturesque garb of buckskin and mounted on a splendid horse, Duke, dashed in and introduced his riders. "Allow me to introduce a Congress of Rough Riders of the World," Buffalo Bill bellowed.

William Frederick Cody, known as Buffalo Bill, created the "Congress of Rough Riders of the World" for his Wild West exhibition. Cody included a contingent of "genuine Don Cossacks" in every show starting at the London 1892 Horticultural exhibition until his death in 1917. The press release was a colorful literary marketing ploy that set in motion more than a century of misinformation about these men and women.

The Buffalo Bill Georgians came from a land immersed in myth, wine and blood. Georgian kings and queens ruled their kingdoms and principalities for centuries before Czar Alexander I and his Russian bureaucrats, aristocrats, and priests took over the country. The czar's colonial policies from 1801 to 1917 gradually suppressed the Georgian culture and language, subordinating them to Russia. The plain truth is Cody's "Russian Cossacks" were neither ethnic Russians nor Cossacks, but were Georgians, and the impact of working with the shows and being in America is revealed in these pages.

The Georgian's homeland is an ethnically diverse, ancient culture and civilization. It is a land blessed by temperate weather, fertile fields, sunny beaches, and snow-capped mystical mountains. One Georgian rider compared his homeland to southern California but without the smog. The Georgians were tribal and did not wander far from their small piece of paradise. Nevertheless, for more than thirty-three years, between 1892 and 1925, Georgian men and women stood before their doors and turned several times to the right, a Georgian way of calling for favorable omens before starting a journey. They came to America.

They left home for the oldest reason. As quoted in a London paper, "we get more money here than we can earn at home." They came to work for Buffalo Bill and other American Wild West shows. Their reasons for leaving home over the years differed; some were economic, some political, some to escape criminal prosecution by the czar's police. We explore their common experiences as Georgians in America's Wild West shows and circuses as they toured on America's railways. During these years, they witnessed the spectacular growth and the decline of American tent shows.[2] As the threads of their lives wove between the culture of their homeland, America, and life in tent shows, these Georgians also observed the rise and fall of Georgia's aspirations for independence from Russia. They endured the personal suppression of their Georgian heritage for the sake of putting food on their families' tables.

The Georgian riders took umbrage at being called "Russian Cossacks," but with limited English language skills, they were unable to clarify their true identity to the public. The Gurian riders were angry being called Cossacks and used to say: "It's real death to call us as Cossacks and we couldn't make them understand that we are the sons of Georgia." They learned to live with the curse of being called "Cossacks." In 1917, Alexis (Gogokhia) Georgian, one of these riders wrote about his feeling toward "Cossacks," saying:

> "An indisputable fact is that the masses of the Russian nation and of other nationalities belonging to Russia are filled with a deep-felt hate toward the Cossacks. This hatred is not limited to the masses in the labor movement; it is deeply rooted throughout the nation. All classes of the small nationalities, heretofore belonging to the Russian empire, speak of the Cossacks in terms of hatred and loathing.

> "The history of the Cossacks is such that these nations look upon a Cossack as upon a man ready to perform any act of utter brutality; a man who mercilessly will flog women and children

---

[2] Wild West shows and circuses were called "tent shows" in the business, but to the American public they were all circuses.

with his knout; a man who, just for the fun of the thing, will trample under the feet of his horse innocent people, as so often did happen in the long and dark years of the Russian absolutism. The very name of the Cossacks recalls in the minds of the people bitter memories of the cruel days of Russian oppression.

"The Russian people know the Cossack as the archenemy of all that is human. The Cossack was the cruel tool of czarism, a flogger, a torturer, a brutal violator of womanhood, a savage."[1]

More than 100 years later, the curse is still upon them. American circus and Wild West Show histories continue to identify these magnificent riders as "Russian Cossacks." From the beginning, these few Georgian men and women rode, danced, sang, made love, and died without leaving an accurate historical account of their passing. They traveled more than 8,500 miles from Batumi to New York. These particular men and women left a legacy to the world of horse riding skills that evolved into American rodeo, as noted by the historian Dee Brown: "Trick riding came to rodeo by way of a troupe of Cossack daredevils.... Intrigued by the Cossacks' stunts on their galloping horses, western cowboys would soon introduce variations to the American rodeo."[2]

Here, then, are the stories of these forgotten few who were raised in a province called Guria. Although these horsemen began as landlords, peasants, bakers, jewelers, farmers, and family men, they learned the skills of Georgian riding. The Georgians' identities were purposely distorted, first by entertainment moguls to commercialize their talents, and then by their communist masters to hide the riders' capitalist success.

Georgia is rarely a traveler's destination, but rather a place where a variety of nationalities have wandered. Greeks, Romans, Turks, Persians, and Russians, to name a few, have each possessed this small enclave of mountains and valleys. Now, at the beginning of the twenty-first century, it is oil that causes interest in Georgia.

The Georgians, over the centuries, have depended on their cavalry for survival. These cavalry fighters learned the craft in their youth through riding passed down by their forefathers. The boys, adolescents, and men of Georgia played more than 365 different horse-racing games, and these games became an essential part of Georgian life.

The Georgian horsemanship of the late nineteenth and early twentieth century, as seen by millions of Americans, can be traced to exhibition riding in the days of the Roman Empire. An early accounting of Georgian riding is recorded in the time of Parsman (Farsman) II, The Good, King of Iberia (A.D. 116-140), which today is in the easternpart of the Republic of Georgia. The Romans dominated Georgia in this period so they could build roads between their Eastern Empire and Rome. Parsman II was King during the Roman Emperor Hadrian's reign (A.D. 117-138), and like his predecessor, allied himself with the Romans. To solidify his alliance, Parsman II visited Rome with his son, Radamisti, accompanied by a large retinue. He received a royal welcome, and the Georgians were granted the right to offer sacrifices to the gods in the capital. During Parsman's visit, Hadrian held a grand military horse race dedicated to the god of war on Mars square. Parsman II and his son participated in this horse race. Dio Cassius, who witnessed the events, wrote:

"The Roman citizens admired Parsman's racing. In fact they were so enchanted by how the Georgians rode their horses that they erected a statue of King Parsman on the Emperor's orders on the Mars Square."[3]

Thus began a Georgian tradition of sports riding to entertain friends, allies, and conquerors.

■ ■ ■

William Frederick Cody (1846-1917) was born February 26, 1846, on a farm near Leclair, Iowa. Bill Cody's first job was herding cattle for the freight wagon trains of Russell, Majors and Waddell. His early career included trapping, prospecting for gold, and riding for the Pony Express. Cody became a buffalo hunter for the railroads, to feed the construction crews. He was recruited as an Army scout stationed at Fort McPherson, Nebraska; then, fate intervened by way of a novelist.

Ned Buntline, whose real name was Edward Zane Carroll Judson, is best known for dime novels and a pistol called the Colt Buntline special. Buntline came out to Fort McPherson on a hunting trip, and to collect stories for his novels. Ned found Cody, suffering from a severe hangover, under a wagon at Fort McPherson. Buntline created Buffalo Bill from stories the twenty-three-year old Cody told. He transformed William Cody's tall tales into the adventures of *Buffalo Bill Cody – King of the Border Men*. Over the next fourteen years, 1869 to 1883, the Buffalo Bill dime novels became popular, and Cody took on the Buffalo Bill persona. William (Buffalo Bill) Cody's acting career started in 1872 with a Buntline play, *Scouts of the Prairie*. Cody continued on the stage until 1883, when his life took another dramatic change.

The first Cody wild west show was titled "The Wild West, Rocky Mountain and Prairie Exhibition," held on May 17, 1883, at the Omaha, Nebraska, fairgrounds. During 1883, in collaboration with William Frank (Doc) Carver, a Wild West show toured the country. In 1884, Cody separated from Carver and, in conjunction with new financial backing from Nate Salsbury, Milton E. Milner, Frank C. Maeder and William D. Guthrie, organized "Buffalo Bill's Wild West." Six years later, 1890, Cody was touring Europe with genuine bull-punchers, scouts, Indians and frontiersmen in his "Buffalo Bill's Wild West Show." Upon Cody's return to America in 1893, he changed the name of the exhibition to "Buffalo Bill's Wild West and Congress of Rough Riders of the World," and the name remained until the show declared bankruptcy in 1913.

▪ ▪ ▪

The change in the composition of the Wild West exhibition from Plainsmen to Congress of Rough Riders started after events in 1890. First, American Indians in Dr. Carver's Wild West show died while touring Russia. Painted Horse, one of the Indians with Dr. Carver's show, said, "The Indians were cruelly treated by the showmen, and while given plenty of whiskey, received little else." Then a disgruntled contingent of Buffalo Bill's Indians—Eagle Horn, Blue Rainbow, Little Lamb, Blue Cloud, Running Creek, and Kill-His-Pony—arrived in New York in June, 1890, and told stories of maltreatment. Kill-His-Pony, an eighteen year old, died from consumption *[tuberculosis]* shortly after his arrival. In July, three Indians—White Horse, Bear Pipe, and White Weasel—arrived in New York and told General O'Beirne, a special Indian agent, stories of maltreatment. Bear Pipe said, "Their acting chief and interpreter treated them very cruelly, the food they received was not fit for dogs, and they had to strip to the waist and come out in war paint even in the cold weather. Buffalo Bill would not let them wear shirts." The Indian commissioner, Thomas Morgan, reading these newspaper accounts, asked his Indian agents to deliver reports showing the effects the shows had on the Indians. Some of the letters received by Commissioner Morgan described such bad conditions that the statements were unfit to print, even in the government report. The report indicated the young Indians were ruined morally and physically on the tours, having come into contact with the most vicious elements. Many Indians died, and those who returned to the reservations brought with them low estimates of white men's morals and religion. The returning Indians were often in such poor physical condition they were a menace to the tribe and sowed the seeds of ailments that were never eradicated from the community. Referring to the Indian school in Carlisle, Pennsylvania, the Commissioner's 1890 report read: "The influence of these shows is antagonistic to that of the schools. The schools elevate, the shows degrade. The schools teach industry and thrift, the shows encourage idleness and waste. The schools inculcate morality, the shows lead almost inevitably to vice." These reports resulted in the Secretary of the Interior, Mr. John Willock Noble, issuing an order in September, 1890: "No more Indians will be permitted to leave their reservations to take part in any shows, either here or abroad."[4] Buffalo Bill still had two more years to tour in Europe and foresaw a financial disaster. The American Indians were the staple of his show; without them he had no show. He rushed back to Washington, D.C., to plead his case.

Nate Salsbury, Cody's business partner, anticipated a debacle and sent his agents throughout Europe to find replacement acts for the Indians. He sent Joe Hart to Moscow to find Russian Cossacks. Salsbury and Cody were aware of Russian Cossack riders after an 1887 exhibition in Russia that received American press coverage. Cody wrote an article in July of 1888, for a Philadelphia publication, comparing Cossack riding to cowboy riding. Mr. Hart came back empty-handed because "Cossacks" were the czar's personal military force and not allowed to leave Russia. However, Nate Salsbury gathered enough riders from Germany, England, and Mexico to replace the Indians if necessary.

The American Indians were experiencing a spiritual revival, thus precipitating the second reason Cody required new acts. The Indian

"Messiah" craze reached a fever pitch by late 1890. Whites viewed the Indian outbreak as a fanatical religious crusade against them.

The Pine Ridge, South Dakota, Indian agent who believed the Indians were out to kill all the whites frantically pleaded with the Army for help. The Eastern press stories and the Indian agent's stupidity resulted in Sitting Bull being shot by the Indian reservation police, and the U.S. Army's 7th Calvary massacring the Sioux at Wounded Knee Creek in December of 1890. Kicking Bear and other remaining Sioux Ghost Dance leaders finally surrendered on January 15, 1891. The U.S. Army sent Kicking Bear, Short Bull, Lone Bull, Bright Star, High Eagle, Know-His-Voice, One Star, Revenge, and Wounded-With-Many-Arrows to Fort Sheridan for a two-year incarceration. But their fate took a surprising twist. Buffalo Bill hired the rebellious leaders, with the Secretary of War's approval, and took them to Europe for two years, a show business tour that turned out to be the best solution.

Buffalo Bill's Wild West toured Germany, Belgium, England, and Wales during the 1891 season, with the rebellious Ghost Dance Indians as his headlining act, along with his newly-recruited riders from all over the world. Upon Cody's return to the United States, the Sioux Indians found themselves practically prisoners of war at Fort Sheridan. These Sioux would not return home until April, 1892, except for Kicking Bear and Short Bull, who remained at Fort Sheridan.

The final puzzle piece of how Georgians wound up riding for Buffalo Bill occurred during the winter of 1891-1892. Mr. Charles Malden Ercolè, called "The Baron," was a Parisian impresario. Ercolé was the European talent agent for the Barnum & Bailey organization for many years. His office was in Paris at 60 rue Caumartin. Mr. Ercolè sent his agents to the obscure Russian province of Georgia in search of a troupe of Georgians to work for Buffalo Bill during the 1892 season in England. Why Mr. Ercolè sent his agents to Batumi can never be fully explained. Thomas Oliver, who apparently was one of these agents, lived in Tbilisi as a youth, spoke Russian, and was a circus acrobat. Thomas Oliver may have crossed paths years earlier with a Georgian rider in the closely knit tent show community.

William Cody opened the door for Georgians to ride in American Tent shows; however, two other organizations helped perpetuate their years of performances. James Anthony Bailey, who became a monarch in the tent show business, gained control of P.T. Barnum's organization after Barnum's death on April 7, 1891. The Ringling Brothers of Baraboo, Wisconsin, were actively challenging Barnum & Bailey in "Billing Fights." These two organizations, Bailey and Ringling, would have a significant effect on the Georgian riders.

■ ■ ■

The beginnings of the Georgian riders in American Wild West exhibitions can be traced to Ivane Rostom Makharadze. Ivane, described as the man who carried the whip, led the original troupe of ten riders in Buffalo Bill's Wild West that performed in London, England, in 1892. We shall explore the origins of how Ivane Makharadze and his Georgian riders became involved with Buffalo Bill.

Ivane's father, Rostom, lived in the central part of the village of Bakhvi, a few kilometers from the town of Ozurgeti, Guria. He had four sons: Silibistro, Alexander, Pavle and Ivane. Rostom's house was near the river Bakhvis Tskali. They lived in a typical wooden, square, two-room Gurian house, built on high stone piers, thus providing a bright and dry dwelling despite the humid climate. The well-aired house had a large roofed porch with a bench built into the railing surrounding it. The ceilings were not flat and smooth, but designed in relief, slanted and rising toward a center beam like the popular cathedral-type ceilings in modern American homes. Rostom liked the number "nine," and he put nine great red pots in the yard for wine storage, planted nine ash trees, and nine acacias or thorn trees. A Makharadze family story places a Georgian rider in American exhibitions earlier than 1892, but this has not been confirmed. Vakho, a grandson of Ivane Makharadze, relates a family tale as told by his grandmother, Nino Makharadze. This story explains how Ivane entered into the American tent show business.

GRANDMA'S TALE

Here are Professor Vakho Makharadze's memories of Grandma Nino telling this story during cold winter nights.

"There was, there was always Makharadzes in our village of Bakhvi. Your ancestors were famous for their superb riding and hawk training.

Your great-grandfather, Rostom, sang folk songs at the table; he rode the fastest horses, and hunted with his trained hawks. He especially liked riding games[5] such as 'Tarchia.'[3] Rostom taught his sons his love of singing, riding, and hunting throughout their childhood. Three of his sons, Ivane, Silibistro and Pavle, became riders, and Alexander became a singer.

"One day, late in the reign of Czar Alexander II, around 1880, Rostom sent his 14-year-old son, Ivane, to Bakhmaro[4] to visit with relatives and escape the summer heat. In those days, we could all go to Bakhmaro whenever we wanted.

"Bakhmaro, God's touch of heaven, is in our backyard. You follow our river into the mountains, through the great gorge. I've told you about the high plateau in the mountains where the air is cool, clear, where the pine trees touch the clouds, where the great horse races are held.

"'Yes, tell me about Bakhmaro,' I asked.

"The devil does his work even in God's great creations as he can do in you. It happened high in the herdsmen's great plateau before we called it Bakhmaro. Turks came by ship and overland to invade our land, to steal our food, and capture our young women as their concubines. The Turks on one of these raids captured several young maidens including Maro. They headed up our river Bakhvis Tskali, the one you play in each summer. They say Maro fought her captors and in the valley now called Bakhmaro these Turks slit her throat, mutilated her body, and wrote on her chest in Turkish, in her own blood, 'Now see Maro.' So, we still call this place Bakhmaro, 'Bakh' meaning to see, and 'Maro,' Mary in Turkish.

"Rostom saddled his favorite horse and told Ivane he could ride him to Bakhmaro to race. Ivane so honored, rode the trail along the river, proud

---

[3] "Tarchia," one of Georgia's oldest riding games, is a game of gallantry. The riders chosen to play in this game are normally men who wish to gain the attention of a young lady. The lady in question chooses one of the riders and fastens on his right arm or collar a colored hat. The man who receives this hat is called "Tarchia," and it becomes the goal of the other riders to try to take it away. The Tarchia's duty is to try and bring the hat back to the lady. The game begins with the Tarchia and his pursuers separated from each other and the lady at a distance of 100 meters. The lady signals the beginning of the contest. If the Tarchia can reach the young lady with the hat, he becomes the winner and is rewarded by the lady. If the hat is taken away from the Tarchia, the game is stopped and the rider who took the hat becomes the Tarchia himself. He fastens the hat on his arm and the game is continued from the place where it was stopped. The riders must give the new Tarchia a distance of 50 meters, and the game is continued. The game goes on until someone gives the young lady her hat.

[4] Bakhmaro is approximately 50 km [30 miles] from Bakhvi.

his father trusted him with his horse. Ivane stopped at Baisuri, a bend in the river gorge about a kilometer below Bakhmaro, to rest his horse, let it drink, and so he could clean up before arriving to meet his friends.

"Ivane paid no notice when his horse started pawing the ground or stretching out as if to urinate without doing so. Ivane became concerned when the horse repeatedly started lying down and getting up and rolling, especially violent rolling. He first worried about his father's saddle, and then became more concerned with his horse's rapid respiration, flared nostrils and lip curling. Ivane's stupidity and inattention in allowing an overheated horse to drink its fill of the cold mountain water caused a slow painful death from colic.

"Ivane struggled to remove the saddle, blanket and bit, and loaded them on his shoulder to return home. Ivane's fears rose with each step on the long, lonely walk home. What would his father do or say?

"Rostom, seeing his son walking into the yard with his saddle and gear draped over his shoulder, worried his son might be hurt. As Ivane told his story, Rostom became angry. He became furious and struck Ivane with his hand. Ivane, shamed, ran away from home.

"The port of Batumi was called Porto-Franco (Free Port) in those days. Ivane traveled to Batumi, about sixty km [thirty-eight miles], and after some days of wandering he met two Rachian sailors.[5] These sailors worked on a ship as firemen. They took Ivane to the ship's captain, who liked the smart boy and took him on as a fireman. Next day the ship left Batumi and after 50 days sailing came to New York. The young boy was so tired of his hard labor he refused to continue to work on the ship. His sailor friends took him to a Rachian baker in New York. Ivane worked hard for the baker, since he had no other way to make a living. He had to work to earn enough to live and learn English. Once he learned enough English, he ran away and joined a New York Arabian circus as a sweeper.

"Ivane, fond of horses from his childhood, soon caught the attention of an Arabian rider in the circus. He noticed the young man's ability to handle horses and hired him as a hostler. Ivane saved his money and

---

[5] Racha is a part of Georgia, in the mountains northeast of Guria.

eventually was able to buy an Arabian horse. The Arab rider gave Ivane a position as a rider in the show. Ivane in his Georgian dress (Chokha), would pick coins thrown on the ground while riding at a gallop.

"The spectators liked the show of this smart boy with a mustache and applauded him. The Arab increased his wages, allowing Ivane to buy a second horse, and then Ivane left the Arab's show. He created his own separate circus show with his two horses, and soon made more money. With money in his pocket, he wrote to his parents and told them his address and promised to come back home soon. In 1885, Ivane returned to his father's home here in Bakhvi.

"There's your grandfather's story; now you must finish your chores."

Vakho Makharadze knew the family history; and after Ivane's return, Rostom Makharadze gave each son a separate place to live on the hill overlooking Bakhvi. Today they call this place "The hill of the Makharadze's." Ivane decided to build a new American-style house with eight rooms on his plot of ground. Rostom moved in with Ivane and they tore down the old family homestead. Ivane married Nino Kalandarishivili at the end of 1886.

There are three Georgian sources that chronicle Ivane Makharadze's 1892 entry into American Wild West show history. First, Amiran Tsamtsishvili, a professor of Georgian history in Tbilisi, interviewed the last known rider survivors in 1958.[6] The family records of Kirile Jorbenadze are a second source, and the third is a dispatch from the port city of Poti, printed in the Tbilisi newspaper, *Iveria*. Each source provides insight into how Ivane Makharadze and his troupe of riders arrived in London in May of 1892.

The survivor's story began with a ship arriving in Batumi from America in 1887. Mr. Thomas Oliver, a representative of a large circus company, came to bring Cossack riders from Russia. Thomas Oliver stayed with the American consul, Mr. James C. Chambers. There Oliver met Kirile Jorbenadze, Mr. Chambers' butler. When Kirile Jorbenadze learned why their guest had come all the way from the United States, he promised to help Oliver find excellent Georgian riders. Vice Consul Harry R. Brigs and Thomas Oliver obtained permission to travel to Lanchkhuti, and took Kirile Jorbenadze along. Their first stop was at the Makharadze family home in the village of Bakhvi, where they talked to Ivane Makharadze, who was already a well known rider in Guria. This account, transcribed in 1958 by old men whose memories either faded or were only second or third-hand information, has a flaw in the date of the ship's arrival.

Alika Jorbenadze, Kirile's son, provided documents with these facts about his father. In 1887, Kirile, age eighteen, went to work for James Chambers, the American Consul in Batumi. He worked for Chambers until November 1, 1895. He received a letter from Mr. Chambers, praising his eight years of service. Chambers described Kirile as a calm and attentive person who performed his jobs accurately. Kirile arrived in Batumi as a wood cutter, but through his hard work, first became Chambers' butler then his secretary.[7]

The evidence from these two sources confirms the 1887 ship arrival date was most likely in error. Thomas Oliver probably arrived late in 1891. Kirile, an eighteen-year-old woodcutter in 1887, could expect promotion to butler by 1891.

A contemporary newspaper account from the port city of Poti printed in the Tbilisi newspaper *Iveria*, issue 124, Tuesday, June 16, 1892, binds together the Kirile family history and the memories of the survivors.

> "Some Georgian riders are in London, and they amused the frowning and reserved people of England with their show and songs. It's interesting who these Georgians are. Since your newspaper has its eye on Georgians all over the world, I considered it necessary to inform you about the Georgians who left for London six months ago. They are from Guria, namely from Chibati and Lanchkhuti. They belong to different levels of society, but the majority of them are landlords. You might be surprised imagining Gurians in London. But there is nothing surprising: two months ago the Consul of England in Batumi hosted a rich man from abroad. This person was called "an English Lord" in Georgia. The guest was fascinated by the appearance and clothes of the Gurians, which were present at the meeting. He asked his Gurian host to find 12 handsome fellows, good riders and singers, in order to take them to England. The promise was to pay 50 rubles each, per month, and cover all travel expenses to and from England. They

obtained the permission from the Governor, and two months ago they left for abroad."

Whether or not one believes the Makharadze grandma's tale, the old riders' reminiscences, or the newspapers, the fortunes of Ivane, his relatives, and his friends in Guria were changed forever. Ivane Makharadze and companions were about to ride onto the world stage in American tent shows as a result of a tragic calamity which befell a tribe of American Indians in 1890. The Georgian riders' benefactors were Buffalo Bill and Sioux warriors from the Pine Ridge, South Dakota, reservation.

Georgians in Buffalo Bill's Wild West, ca 1892
Right, Luka Chkhartishvili, Left Ivane Makharadze
Courtesy, Denver Public Library, Western History Collection, NS-451

Plate No. 4

"Fate, like the weather, is fickle; sometimes it smiles upon us, Sometimes it whirls down like a tempest straight from wrathful heaven."

Shota Rustaveli

1892 PROLOGUE

The year 1892 is the historical beginning of three decades of sustained participation by Georgian riders in the American tent show business. The year began in Georgia with a terrible catastrophe when a bridge over the Kura River in Tbilisi collapsed during a blessing ceremony. Two days later, on January 22, a disaster on the Trans-Caucasian railway occurred when two trains carrying petroleum rammed into each other. The Russian government disclosed its intention to construct a harbor for commerce at Poti, leaving Batumi as a strongly fortified point for military purposes only. Cholera reached Georgia by June. Georgian political leaders, nationalists, socialists, and future communists formed a political alliance in 1892, founding their social democratic organization as a literary and political group known as the Mesame-Dasi (Third Group). These revolutionaries wanted to keep Georgian culture alive, throw off the Russian czar's shackles, and remove his Cossack enforcers. Alexis Gogokhia, one of these forward thinking revolutionaries, would eventually ride for Buffalo Bill in the Wild West shows.

Luka Chkhartishvili would begin his career as a "Russian Cossack" rider this year. His career ended in 1914. As a youth, he was a goldsmith apprentice to his father. He loved to ride horses. He would make the deliveries for his father, and was known as the best rider in Lanchkhuti.

BUFFALO BILL'S WILD WEST (1892)

Leave it to the English to turn a garden show into a cultural event. The Bishop of London blessed it, and the Duke of Connaught furnished the pomp and ceremony befitting the Horticultural Exhibition opening at Earl's Court, London. Even the weather cooperated on May 7, 1892. America may not have lords, dukes, and queens, but it had a popular authentic western hero named Colonel William F. Cody, who, as an exalted gentleman and a spectacular entertainer, brought his Buffalo Bill's Wild West to the exhibition.

Ivane Makharadze , Luka Chkhartishvili, Dimitri Mgaloblishvili, Vaso,

Data, and Irakli Chkonia, Levan and Klement Jorbenadze, Mose Gigineishvili, and Besarion and Meliton Tsintsadze left their homes and families in early May.[8] They descended from the hills and valleys of Guria and traveled the thirty-eight miles [sixty km] to Batumi, a fortified town with a considerable Russian garrison. It had a deep harbor with a western jetty, but the country was said to be unwholesome, owing to the marshy nature of the surrounding area. There was a vivid odor of petroleum from the refineries.

Buffalo Bill's Wild West, London, ca 1892
Standing Left to Right: Besarion Tsintsadze, Mose Gigineishvili, Vaso Chkonia, Data Chkonia, Meliton Tsintsadze. Sitting left to right: Luka Chkhartishvili, Klement Jorbenadze, Levan Jorbenadze, Dimitri Mgaloblishvili. Reclining left to right: Irakli Chkonia, Frederic Remington,, Ivane Makharadze.
Plate No. 5
Courtesy, Buffalo Bill Ranch State Historical Park, Nebraska Game and Parks Commission

Ivane's instructions were to collect their tickets and itinerary from the shipping company, Navigation Paquet & Cie, in Batumi. The ticketing agent gave them their second-class tickets, valued at 175 francs ($35.00), and escorted the ten countrymen to the Russian administrative building to gather their passports. Each in turn stood before the administrative clerk, presented his papers, and furnished his name, age, and village. The clerk recorded the passport information in Georgian, Russian, and French. He demanded payment, and made an impressive show of stamping the documents before handing them over. The men hustled to the docks, where they boarded a steamship sailing between Batumi and Marseilles, with a stop in Constantinople for passenger pickup.

Their first overnight sea voyage resulted in a few seasick Gurian farmers. After two days, they arrived at the Bosporus Strait. The Gurians leaning on the ship's railing stared at thousands of ships and boats as they slowly moved down the strait to Constantinople. The shores were alive with human activity. The clatter, whistles, and city noises carried across the water. They arrived at the harbor called The Golden Horn, where they could see the city of seven hills that had a mosque on top of each. The exotic aroma of cooking herbs and spices mixed with manure, burning coal and wood wafted across the harbor. The brilliant red minarets of the Hagis Sophia and Topkapi Palace punctuated the skyline. New passengers boarded the ship and it continued across the Marmara Sea into the Aegean and Mediterranean Seas. Nine days sailing brought them to Marseilles. The first-time voyagers were now sea-hardened travelers.

The Gurian country boys discovered their wobbly sea legs after disembarking at the Quai de la Joliette in Marseilles. The intercontinental passengers collected their luggage, passed through Customs, and boarded a special train at the Garè Maritime for their trip to Paris. The train to Paris arrived May 20, at the Garè de Lyon. They visited the offices of C.M. Ercolè, and soon found themselves on the French coast. A packet steamer took them to England. The Georgians, newly dubbed "Russian Cossacks," arrived at Earl's Court on May 26. Ivane Rostom Makharadze found himself now titled in the English press, "Prince Makharadze."

Ivane, Luka, and their comrades discovered their accommodations at Earl's Court were tents, a city of white tents, laid out in neat rows. A wide street separated tents from tepees. English ladies, gentlemen, and children meandered along the streets while peering into the Georgians' private living quarters. Buffalo Bill called his tent the "Pahaska Tepee."[6] The arena was a large, open rectangle with covered bleachers on three sides and a canvas curtain along the fourth.

The first recorded discussion of Buffalo Bill's Georgian riders newly arrived to London occurred in the publication The *Oracle* printed May 28. A reporter had a chat with Nate Salsbury, the Wild West general

---

[6] Pahaska is the Lakota word for "long hair," what the Sioux fondly called William F. Cody, "Buffalo Bill."

manager and business brains:

"I understand you have got a troupe of Cossacks in Camp, Mr. Salsbury?"

"Yes, they arrived last night. They come from beyond Tbilisi, near the extreme of the Caucasus Mountains. They are headed by Prince Ivan Makharadze, and are under the charge of an interpreter called Tom, whose life is a romance in itself. He (Tom) was of English parentage and was born in London. He was kidnapped when less than three years of age and taken to Russia. He was adopted by a French family, and has lived in the Caucasus ever since. These are genuine Don Cossacks, and we claim they are the first of their class who has ever left their country except in a war. The Cossack is different from a cowboy in as much as he is really a soldier and a part of the Russian Army. Their riding consists mainly of tricks on horseback, and I am very anxious to see what they can do in that line. We cannot try them yet, as their wiry little horses need rest after their long journey. These men were brought over by the energy and enterprise of Mr. Ercolè, the great Parisian agent, who was nearly in prison half a dozen times over his job. We have had to guarantee the return of these men to the Russian government, our Ambassador in St. Petersburg being the guarantor. We shall probably get these men to ride next week.

"As Mr. Salsbury spoke, several *Georgians* approached. They were apparently sauntering around the camp out of curiosity, and presented a picturesque appearance with their astrakhan caps and long, dark red coats and top boots. They are small, undersized, but wiry-looking men."[9]

For more than thirty years, this single exaggerated interview set the fantastic storyline of Georgian men and women riding in Wild West shows. Its elements can be found in newspaper articles ten and fifteen years later.

The Georgians were from around the Gurian towns Ozurgeti and Lanchkhuti. They were not "Don Cossacks." The "Don Cossacks" are from the Donets Basin and Don River north of the Kuban lowland and North Caucasus Mountains. The czar's Cossacks would savage the peasants of Guria over the next two decades.

Thomas Oliver's fellow performers nicknamed him "Cossack Tom." He was born a British subject on May 9, 1867, in Toronto, Canada. *The New York Clipper*, a show business magazine, published this account of Tom Oliver on April 20, 1889: "Tom Oliver is re-engaged for Locke's circus. He closes with A. S. Palmer's Specialty Company at Calvert, Texas, April 26, 1889."[10] He had known Nate Salsbury earlier in his career when he was called Tommy Oliver. *The London Daily News*, on June 2 published additional information about Thomas Oliver:

> "Not being able to speak English, the visitors have brought an interpreter with them, who spoke English, French, Russian, and Tartar. A romantic, though pathetic, interest attaches to this man. He is a native of Manchester, and his name is Thomas Oliver. His parents came to London when he was five years old, and joined the Manly circus, which was starting for the Caucasus. By some accident, he got left behind at Tbilisi, and has since earned his living amongst the various circuses traveling in that part of the world, Russians being extremely fond of that kind of entertainment. He now returns to his native land after an absence of eighteen years. He is trying to find his parents, but knows nothing about them beyond the fact that his Mother's name was Mary Lizzie and that he had a sister."

Major John Burke, Buffalo Bill's press agent, authored these newspaper accounts. He embellished the Georgian riders' tales, much as Ned Buntline did in creating the Buffalo Bill image. The Georgian riders' press coverage fell into two types: those articles written and planted in the newspapers by the press agents such as Major Burke, and the articles written by reporters after interviews with the Georgian riders. The early press stories told the Londoner "Every one of them is said to be of noble blood, and they certainly have the commanding figure and lofty bearing." Neither Ivane, a landowner and considered wealthy, nor any of his countrymen were from the aristocracy. The poetic descriptions of their heroism, "the medals which several of them wear for coastguard service," were a complete fabrication. These were farmers, and none are known to have ever been in military service. A quote, "never before been out of our own country," attributed to Ivane, casts doubt on the family tale of his travels to America as a youth.

Major Burke's liberal use of literary license has created a number of historical conflicts. One of these concerns the horses used by the Georgians.

His planted stories praising their "lithe steppe horses, as fierce and active as the riders" implied they rode Georgian horses. Fortunately, we have quotes from reporters disputing Burke's fairy tale: "The fact is the *Georgians* have not been able to bring their own horses, the Russian government preventing even so limited an export of horses." Another quote: "Then you have not brought your own horses?" a reporter asked. "Our horses? Oh, no, they could not stand the journey of thirteen days. We ourselves were very ill on the Black Sea; how would our horses have fared? But we brought our saddles, our whips, and everything else," Ivane replied.

The London press trailed the Indians and Georgians wherever they went. They were sighted in St. Paul's Cathedral at a Sunday morning service. The press also raised doubts about the Russian Cossacks' legitimacy. No one doubted they came from Russia, but the question remained, "were they Cossacks?" *The Army & Navy Gazette* on June 11 published a letter to the editor from Alex Kinloch. This letter found its way into several newspapers in the next few weeks. Mr. Kinloch said he spent many years with Cossacks and he could say Buffalo Bill did not have Cossacks. He declared them from a wild tribe in the Caucasus and probably they were Caucasian Jews.

Earl's Court, London, ca 1892
Left to right: Melitons Tsintsadze, John Nelson, Maj. Burke, Unknown, 2 Indians
Courtesy, Denver Public Library, Western History Collection , NS-397
Plate No. 6

The Georgian riders themselves tried to educate the public as to their true identity, but they never succeeded. It was the Wild West manager's desire to create the image of Georgians as fierce, dangerous, bloodthirsty killers, battle-hardened warriors of the czar.

Several times, Ivane answered the controversy over whether they were true Cossacks. Ivane, asked by reporters about the language he spoke, replied with a slight, contemptuous smile, "We talk our own language— the Georgian dialect." Another reporter asked Ivane how he liked London. His reply gave clues to their true identity.

"We like it. The railway running under the earth is strange, and the town is large. Ordinary railways we know. There is one at home, at Batumi, which we have seen when we came from our village."

Major Burke's press materials implied the Georgians were released from military service by the Russian government. But Ivane tells us their reason for joining the Buffalo Bill Wild West. "We came because we get more money here than we can earn at home, but we have only come for six months. Then we go back to our wives and children." When asked about their families, Ivane replied:

"No, our women would not come. Not for anything. They have remained behind to look after the grapes, the maize, the horses, the old people, and the children, while we are away."

Despite doubts cast as to whether the Georgians were Cossacks, the Georgians found themselves invited to many society functions. Members of "The Savage Club"[7] invited Col. Cody, Major Burke, two Sioux Indian Chiefs, Ivane Makharadze, and Tom Oliver to a house dinner, an event covered by many newspapers.

The press described the Georgians' picturesque entrance into the arena. "The performance began with what perhaps had best be termed a musical ride, the horsemen cantering slowly round the ring while they sang a strange, weird refrain, which was at once harmonious and barbaric. The strain they lifted was touched with a Chopinesque melancholy, and to the imaginative ear clearly suggested the sadness of the illimitable snow-covered steppe."[11] Their riding technique was described in many articles. An example published in the *City Press*, June 22:

---

[7] The Savage Club was founded in 1857 as a Bohemian Gentleman's club. A 'Savage' must be a real toiler in the field of literature, science, or art. In 1892 they met in Lancaster House, site of the Old Savoy Palace.

"The last novelty introduced at the latter entertainment comprises a company of *Georgians*, whose evolutions render a second visit a necessity. Their dismounting is a marvel of rapid executions, and their terpsichorean performances—for they do dance, in spite of their long costumes—are equally astonishing. The movements of the men are electric, and their very legs are provocative of sentiment; now compelling your admiration by whirl and poise; now by rapid inversion of knees and toes, producing an indescribable grotesqueness. Their feats of horsemanship are amazing for pace and skill. One member of the troupe flies along sitting astride in reversed position, another rides upon his shoulder, and a third upon his head; these topsy-turvy adventures called forth a storm of plaudits; and the leader, not to be outdone, makes the circuit of the arena, alighting and remounting a dozen times while his horse is at full gallop."

Frederic Remington wrote in the *Harper's Weekly* the most literary description of the Georgians' riding performance. Remington's colorful Georgian riding description, shrouded in the myth of the cutthroat "Cossack," helped set the stage for thirty years of literary license in the popular press.

"The Cossacks will charge you with drawn sabers in a most genuine way, will hover over you like buzzards on a battlefield—they soar and whirl about in graceful curves, giving an uncanny impression, which has doubtless been felt by many a poor Russian soldier from the wheat fields of Central Europe as he lay with a bullet in him on some distant field. They march slowly around over imaginary steppes, singing in a most dolorous way—looking as they did in Joseph Brandt's paintings. They dance over swords in a light-footed and crazy way, and do feats on their running horses, which bring the hand clapping. They stand on their heads, vault on and off, chase each other in a game called "chasing the handkerchief," and they reach down at top speed and mark the ground with a stick. Their long coat tails flap out behind like an animated rag bag, while their legs and arms are visible by turns. Their grip on the horse is maintained by a clever use of these stirrups, which are twisted and crossed at will. They are armed like "a pincushion," and ride on a big leather bag, which makes their seat abnormally high."[12]

Buffalo Bill craved the attention of high society and the kings and queens of Europe, and received it when Queen Victoria's equerry, General Sir Henry Ponsonby, sent a message to the "Pahaska Tepee" at Earl's Court, stating, "Her Majesty will be highly honored if the Wild West managers could make it convenient to let their Cossack riders come to Windsor and show their wonderful proficiency on horseback to Her Majesty, members of her family and the Royal household."[13]

Buffalo Bill's Wild West, rehearsal, ca 1892, Georgian riding performance
Courtesy, Denver Public Library, Western History Collection, NS-176
Plate No. 7

Other than Annie Oakley, the Georgians were the only Buffalo Bill act known to have spawned a command performance. Queen Victoria's request became a singularly important moment in the long history of these Georgian riders. Buffalo Bill would use this command performance to his advantage throughout his remaining career. Thus, the Georgians became as indispensable to Buffalo Bill as his Indians, and would always be integral to his shows.

COMMAND PERFORMANCE

Buffalo Bill's command performance on Saturday, June 25, 1892, was reported in two sources: Nate Salsbury's memoir,[14] and a *correspondent's*.[15] These accounts are intertwined to give one version of this historic Georgian riders' event.

"This polite request was construed, as it always is in England, to be a mild sort of command. As the *Georgians* only consumed about twelve minutes in their performance, I concluded that, no matter how startling it would be, it would hardly compensate for all the trouble of getting them down to Windsor, so I determined to take the whole outfit, and do something worthy the occasion. To this end, I engaged a train of cars, and loaded enough of our outfit to give a representative performance, leaving enough members of the company in London to satisfy the public, which was easily done, when it was explained to the afternoon audience that Colonel Cody had gone to Windsor by Royal command.

When Buffalo Bill's troupe arrived at Windsor they were greeted by a great crowd which had gathered about the railway station and lined the streets along which the procession passed. The party was lustily cheered throughout its progress to Windsor Castle.

I preceded the company by one train and, repairing to the Castle, found Colonel McNeill, the Equerry for the day, awaiting my coming. He told me that I had carte blanche to use any part of the ground on the east side of the castle, and at once the servants of the castle began to environ the lawn with sheep fold fences. These fences are movable, and readily adjusted themselves to the purpose, which was to create a complete oval, inside of which we were to work. At the lower end of the lawn, a large tent was erected, in which was spread a splendid luncheon for the company when they should arrive. On the battlements of the castle wall was placed the canvas pavilion for the queen and her immediate household. A carpet was spread over the rough stones, and a number of comfortable chairs were placed upon it. In due course, the train bearing Cody and the rest arrived and they were escorted to the castle ground, and after the company had lunched and otherwise refreshed themselves, I sent word to the Equerry-in-Waiting that we awaited Her Majesty's pleasure. The Queen (Victoria) indicated her desire to have the performance begin at once, and so her pony carriage was driven around to the state apartments and from there to the pavilion on the wall. The walls of the castle at that point are not less than fifteen feet wide. Her Majesty alighted from the carriage with difficulty, and was assisted by her Scotch Gillies to her chair in the pavilion.

On entering the archways, Mr. Cody and Salsbury were received by Major General Sir John C. McNeill, K.C.B., who said that the Queen was anxious to view from her window the entry of the troupe into the arena, so Buffalo Bill

37

at the head of the motley procession of cowboys, Indians, Georgians, and South American Gauchos paraded under the Queen's windows and after performing several maneuvers proceeded to the place selected for the exhibition.

The arena, which faced the east terrace, was a large open space of beautiful turf. The grounds had been enclosed with hurdles trimmed with red bunting and in the center of the terrace a small pavilion, surmounted by the Royal arms, had been erected. The spaces on either side were crowded with aristocratic personages, a special train having brought a number of the Queen's guests to the castle. Promptly at the hour fixed for the show to commence the Queen came forth from the castle, attended by Princess Beatrice and her children and Princess Christian. She entered a little pony carriage, led by a groom and attended by two gillies and some Indian servants, and the party then proceeded to the pavilion.

The Queen was attired in a black dress of the plainest description and wore a queer looking straw bonnet.

Arriving near the pavilion, the Queen was carefully lifted from her carriage and walked, with the aid of a stick which she carried, to the seat which had been prepared for her in the center of the pavilion. When the royal party had settled in their places, a signal was given and the entertainment was at once begun.

Major Burke let his hair down, and we knew the afternoon was bound to be a success, for whenever the Major let his hair down the world stood in awe. Her majesty requested that someone connected with the Wild West should be with her to explain to her anything that she might not understand, and I nobly threw myself into the breach, and was escorted with much ceremony to the pavilion. Don't suppose for an instant that I look back on that experience with any but feelings of respect and admiration, for the methodical conduct of the whole affair. While there was much ceremony, there was also much courtesy shown to us. As I entered the pavilion, I removed my hat, as any gentleman would do in the presence of ladies in an enclosed place. After I was introduced to the Queen, I gave the signal to begin the performance and took my place beside the Queen's place as Scout, Guide and Interpreter for the occasion. Noticing that I was standing and uncovered, her majesty said, "Mr. Salsbury, please put on your hat, as I feel a strong draft here, and please take a chair."

"Your Majesty," said I, "I am very comfortable."

"But I would be more comfortable if you would take a chair."

All this is very commonplace, I know, and I would not record it here except that it struck me at the time as being very thoughtful on the part of a woman who is not obliged to consider anything while in the pursuit of pleasure. Being an American, I followed the etiquette of such an occasion by addressing the Queen as Madame, after the first acknowledgment of her imperial title. An Englishman would have been required to address the Queen constantly as Majesty.

The performance consisted of the introduction of the different bands, a race between cowboys, Indians, and Mexicans, Indian sports and an Indian dance, horsemanship by the Gauchos, a fight between cowboys, Indians and Georgians, riding and taming bronco ponies and fancy rifle shooting by Buffalo Bill. Nate Salsbury, the manger of the Wild West show, was introduced to the Queen and stood by her side, explaining each act as it was performed.

Our performance lasted the better part of an hour and a quarter, and during that time the Queen evinced the utmost interest in all she saw, and plied me with questions innumerable regarding the people in the show. And withal, she displayed a nice discrimination in her inquiries, which were all of a sensible, information seeking sort. As for instance: while Cody was shooting glass balls, she turned to me and said, "Mr. Salsbury, what arm is Colonel Cody using?"

"He is using the Winchester rifle, Madame," I responded, "an American firearm."

"Ah," said she, "a very effective weapon, and in very effective hands."

At a point in the performance when the *Georgians* were doing their horseback work, Prince Henry of Battenberg, who was standing in the rear of the pavilion, said to the Queen in German, "Mamma, do you think they are really Cossacks?" Before the Queen had time to reply to him, I said, "I beg to assure you, sir, that everything and everybody you see in the entertainment are exactly what we represent it or them to be."

Her Majesty turned to the Prince and said, "Prince, I think we had better speak English for the rest of the afternoon." Princess Beatrice, who was sitting beside the queen, was much amused at her husband's discomfiture, and smilingly said to him, "Monchere, vous averz recu' votre preiere lecon Americaine."[8] I immediately replied, "Oh, Madam, J'espere non."[9] At this there was a general laugh, which I wish Burke could have heard, for he could have used the incident in his own way in his description of the affair.

---

[8] My Dear, you have just received your first American lesson.
[9] Oh Madam, I hope not.

The Queen was in the best of humor and appeared to be greatly interested in the many strange sights which she witnessed. She asked Salsbury many questions and said that it was a wonderful show. She admired the daring and brilliant riding of the cowboys best of all, and was especially delighted with their work on the mettlesome bucking ponies. She was most impressed by the wonderful ménage and informed Salsbury that she had never before seen such horsemanship. At the end of the performance she requested that Buffalo Bill and Major Burke be presented to her. She complimented Buffalo Bill very highly, and presented him with a large gold seal containing her monogram, surrounded by the words of the royal motto: "Honi Soit Qui Mal y Pense,"[10] the whole being surmounted by the imperial crown. She gave Mr. Salsbury a handsome scarf pin, consisting of her initials studded with diamonds and also surmounted by the imperial crown.

When the show was over, the Queen requested that Cody be presented to her, and after thanking me for assisting her to enjoy the Wild West, she arose and was escorted to her carriage by her ever-present body guard of Gillies. I sent for Cody, who came in his buckskins, and he was presented to the Queen, just before she started on her afternoon drive around the grounds of the castle. *Colonel Cody, before leaving, was introduced by Sir Henry Ponsonby to her Majesty, who told him she had been extremely gratified with the marvelous horsemanship exhibited by his troupe, and that the performance was excellent in every way.*[16] Her Majesty was very gracious to Cody, and complimented him very highly for the delightful afternoon she had enjoyed, and wished him good luck for the future.

Cody and I were then invited to the Equerry's apartments, where we were urged to partake of a lunch. We compromised by another act of self-sacrifice on my part, for as Cody did not drink anything that summer, I did duty for both of us in a glass of wine. The whole thing was delightfully informal, and wound up by our each being presented with a memento of the occasion in the Queen's name. Cody received a beautiful watch charm, and I was complimented with a scarf pin, set in diamonds, and bearing the Royal Monogram.

The entire show went without a hitch; in fact, all who took part in the exhibition performed their various feats better than usual.

After Buffalo Bill and his party had departed from the castle and were already seated in the special train which was to bear them to London, Sir

---

[10] Shamed be he who thinks evil of it.

Henry Ponsonby, private secretary to her majesty, and Sir John McNeill arrived at the station to again convey the Queen's compliments to Buffalo Bill and his companions and to assure them that the Queen was highly pleased with the entertainment which they had provided for her pleasure."

Queen Victoria[17] wrote in her evening journal:

> "We went on to the East Terrace, & watched from a tent, open in front, a sort of "Buffalo Bill" performance, on the lawn below. It was extremely well arranged, & an excellent representation of what we had also seen five years ago at Earl's Court. There were Cowboys, Red Indians, Mexicans, Argentinos taking part, & then a wonderful riding display by Cossacks, accompanied by curious singing, & a war dance by the Indians. There were extraordinary buck jumping horses, shooting at glass balls by Col. Cody, & display of cracking huge long whips. The whole was a very pretty wild sight, which lasted an hour. At the conclusion of the performance, all advanced in line at a gallop & stopped suddenly. Col. Cody was brought up for me to speak to him. He is still a very handsome man, but now got a grey beard."

Dinners honoring Cody, Salsbury, Major Burke, Ivane Makharadze, and his riders filled the last weeks in London. The International Academy of Horsemen presented Ivane Makharadze with expensive presents and medals that had the form of galloping horses. He also received a book, rumored to contain the signatures of 25,000 English gentlemen.

The season at Earl's Court closed to great cheering on October 12, after the evening performance. The Grenadier Guards band played at the International Horticultural Exhibition, marching around the arena playing *"The Star-Spangled Banner."* Cody chartered the *SS Mohawk* to convey his outfit to America, and they sailed on October 15, arriving in New York on October 24. The Georgian riders also sailed for home on October 15, but in the opposite direction, returning home to the vineyards and maize fields of their villages: Bakhvi, Lanchkhuti, and Ozurgeti. The Georgians who undertook this first journey to London could hardly imagine that more than 150 other Georgians would travel the same route during the next three decades.

1892 EPILOGUE

A cholera epidemic began in Mecca, Saudi Arabia, during hajj, the annual Islamic pilgrimage, and spread through the Muslim world in 1892. Cholera was headline news in England and America. The United States Customs office in New York even refused entry of licorice root from Batumi in August 1892.[18] The epidemic ravaged the Georgian cultural mix of Muslims and Christians. The Georgians arriving at the port of Batumi from England in mid-November probably were apprehensive as to whether cholera had stricken their families.

Ivane Makharadze and Luka Chkhartishvili were the only Gurian riders who returned to America in 1893 to ride again for Buffalo Bill. Dimitri Mgaloblishvili signed a contract with the Barnum & Bailey organization and rode for the Adam Forepaugh circus in 1893. The Besarion and Meliton Tsintsadze brothers and Levan Jorbenadze, never again rode in Wild West shows; however, other Tsintsadze and Jorbenadze family members would one day join troupes of riders in America. Data and Vaso Chkonia stayed home in 1893, but Dimitri enticed them to join him the following year in the Barnum & Bailey circus.

KIRILE JORBENADZE BIOGRAPHICAL SKETCH

Kirile Jorbenadze, born in 1869, is considered by Georgian historical records to be the conduit between Ivane Makharadze and Buffalo Bill's agents. A wood cutter in 1887, he came under the influence of Spiridon Gurgenidze, a merchant, who took the eighteen-year-old boy to Batumi. Kirile married a Lanchkhutian woman, Tamar Chkonia, in 1901. When first married, they lived in rented apartments, and after two daughters were born, they moved to their own house with a private yard and five rooms next to the Women's Gymnasium on Beibutovi Street. Kirile maintained a close relationship with James Chambers over the years. Mr. Chambers would send his son to Batumi to stay with Kirile during holidays. Kirile operated his own restaurant, "Florida," and became a shareholder in the hotel "London" in Batumi. He owned plots of land, but in 1922 the revolutionaries confiscated all his properties. Kirile Jorbenadze died in 1938.

Over half of the horses Ivane and the others rode during the season were sold at auction in the arena on October 13 before their human companions left town.[19] The auctioneer said there was no guarantee of soundness and kindness in the horses, and their temper was seriously questioned. The prices realized, on the whole, were very low. Cody was disgusted at the suspicions of the bidders and the smallness of the bids, and expressed his feelings. When a bidder retorted, Cody had the bidder ejected. Some seventy-five of the horses in the sale were bred by Colonel Cody himself on his ranch at North Platte, Nebraska.

Harper Weekly, Vol XXXVI, No. 1863
Saturday, September 13, 1892
Frederic Remington drawing of
Georgian Riders

Plate No. 8

"But like a rock stand firm amidst all misfortunes and troubles."

Shota Rustaveli

1893 PROLOGUE

Buffalo Bill's Georgians were not the first Georgian riders to arrive on United States soil. The 1892 press coverage and hype generated by Cody's Georgians caught James Bailey's interest. Bailey's corporation was headquartered in London. James A. Bailey owned the Barnum & Bailey and Adam Forepaugh circuses. He arranged to have Georgians in his Adam Forepaugh show. The Adam Forepaugh manager was Joseph Terry McCaddon, whose sister, Ruth Louisa, was married to James Bailey. For many years, Georgian riders came under the influence of Bailey and McCaddon. Joseph McCaddon was described as "a man of a liberal collegiate education and refinement, and ambitious to the end that the circus shall not only be popular, but also refined and fashionable."[20] The Adam Forepaugh contingent of Georgian riders beat Cody's Georgians to the North American continent by eleven days.

Two inventions created in 1893 eventually caused repercussions for the tent show business. Thomas Edison introduced the Kinetoscope, a new device for showing motion pictures, which later dethroned the American Wild West shows. Henry Ford tested his first gasoline-powered automobile, which ultimately uncoupled tent shows from their dependence on American railways.

William Cody applied for a concession at the World's Columbian Exposition, known as the Chicago World Fair, but the Committee on Ways and Means turned him down. Cody then secured the rights to a parcel adjacent to the park's main entrance. Mr. Ferris' wheel made its debut at the Chicago World Fair. One wonders if the daredevil Georgian riders of Buffalo Bill's entertainment found this new contraption, the Ferris wheel, as exciting and thrilling a ride as their horses.

Two other events in 1893 impacted tent show business, the first helping and the second hurting. Tent shows gained an advantage with the completion of the Great Northern Railway to the Pacific, opening new access to Utah, Oregon, and California. Business became depressed from an economic panic caused by a drop in the U.S. gold reserve. Gold plummeted, due to an obligation to purchase large amounts of silver, which led to a depression resulting in unemployment of more than twenty percent.

Monsieur C.M. Ercolè, the Parisian impresario (address: 16 rue de la Chausee D. Antin, Paris) acting as Forepaugh's agent, secured a contract with Dimitri Mgalobishvili to provide twelve riders for the Forepaugh circus and a contract with Ivane Makharadze for ten riders with Buffalo Bill. He surely was pleased to have two groups of Georgians in American tent shows. Ercolè arranged an interview with the "Petit Journal" for the Georgian riders as they passed though Paris on their way to America. A Tbilisi newspaper in Georgia printed an extract from the interview:

> "Our editorial department hosted fifteen Caucasians. All of them are excellent and brave riders. These people are heading to Chicago. The leader of this team looks like his friends; he has a black leather hat, gown, and red costume with ornaments. He is armed with pistols and saber. The saber is ornamented and has a black leather sheath. The riders are from Georgia and they served in the Russian army, but they don't speak Russian. These fellows are extraordinary in appearance, calm; long beards, and black eyes add a very strange effect to their faces. These savages from Asia, boasting with their handsome appearance and arms, were behaving like children at the opening of champagne bottles, and are far different from our nation."[21]

ADAM FOREPAUGH'S CIRCUS (1893)
Saturday, March 18, 1893, Southampton, England (in transit)

Twelve Georgians were on their maiden voyage to North America. Their passage and hotel accommodations from Batumi to New York were arranged by Forepaugh's shipping agent in New York, Mr. Edwin H. Low. Those accommodations included second class cabin fare, 175 francs (approximately $35 USD), on the *SS Mingrelie* for their journey from Batumi to Marseille, the train from Marseille to Paris, then on to the French coast and the packet steamer to the shores of England. They enjoyed a stay in London and then had one more short train trip to Southampton. The intercontinental passengers assembled at Waterloo station, London, at 9:40 a.m., to catch the special train the shipping companies ran to the Empress docks in Southampton. The passengers milled about waiting to board the *SS Chester.*

The ship's Captain, Arthur W. Lewis, had extra ceremonial duties to perform since he took command of a renamed ship put into service by the American Line Steamship Company. The *SS Chester's* maiden voyage from Southampton to New York required Lewis to waste time dealing with excited company officials. His crew spent long hours stowing gear, greeting Company officials, and making last minute preparations for sea. Captain Lewis did not notice the eleven men and one woman who walked up the gangplank in unique garb. They did, however, attract the attention of the other passengers and the purser. The strangely dressed passengers, having finished two other sea voyages on the Black and Mediterranean Seas, carried themselves with more confidence then the other landlubbers. The *Chester's* cabin-class purser collected their tickets, and attempted to read off their names: Eristoff, Alexander Tsintsadze, Andro Iorashvili, Mikhako Kobaladze, Lewis Staditze, Giorgi Makinelishvili, Samuel Zitlitzi, Charles Baikini, Raphael Tvaladze, Gaston Matitashvili, Dimitri Mgaloblishvili, and Frida Mgaloblishvili. The Georgians, together with the other 165 cabin-class passengers, settled in for the twelve-day crossing. Prince Eristoff, who led these Georgians, was informed an Adam Forepaugh circus representative would meet them in New York.

Typically, a ship's captain only wants fair winds and following seas, and no other surprises. Eight days out, the *Chester's* passengers and crew sighted the *SS Strassburg* in distress. The *Strassburg* broke her shaft and bobbled dead in the water. When *Chester* hove in sight at 2:30 p.m., the *Strassburg* Captain asked, "Will you tow me to New York?" "Yes," replied Captain Lewis. Two eight-inch manila hawsers were sent aboard *Chester,* and at 5:30 p.m. she put on steam. The hawsers snapped like twine. The *SS Chester* stood by until 7:00 a.m., Monday, when two more hawsers connected the vessels and they finally were underway. The *SS Chester* towed the *Strassburg* at a steady ten knots into New York.[22]

WEDNESDAY, MARCH 29, NEW YORK CITY (ARRIVAL)

The *Chester* docked late at pier forty-three, at the foot of Christopher Street; at 5:30 p.m. Reporters crowded the pier following the word of *SS Chester's* rescue of the *SS Strassburg*. Arriving late, the passengers missed their connections. The Daily Tribune printed a conversation overheard between Dimitri Mgaloblishvili and Prince Eristoff:

> "'Me thinks,' said the proud Prince Eristoff, as he wrapped his fur-lined overcoat about his manly form, 'the inhabitants of this village have not accorded unto us a royal welcome.'
>
> "'Why should it be so?' quoth Dimitri, pensively. 'It must need be a cold day when such a welcome is accorded. Do you observe that to-day is not especially chilly?'"[23]

Several Adam Forepaugh executives met the ship. The ship's late arrival caused the men to spend Wednesday afternoon rearranging transportation and accommodations for their newest circus act. These men were experts at making last minute arrangements. They booked rooms for the Georgians at the Astor House, 225 Broadway, and notified the press a prince and princess would tour the city. The prince and princess were Dimitri and Frida Mgaloblishvili.

On Thursday, the Forepaugh executives were eager to show the sights to the Georgians and to introduce them to the press. They visited the Pulitzer building where from the dome they viewed the lower bay to Harlem. Later, they called on Mayor Gilroy. The Mayor shook hands with each man and with the princess, and then examined their weapons.[24] Thursday afternoon, the Georgian riders crossed the North River to Jersey City and boarded a train for Philadelphia. The story given to the press was that Dimitri and Frida were husband and wife, but in reality, they had quite a different relationship.

Frida's parents were Maka Dolidze—nee Chkonia, and Simon Dolidze from the town of Ozurgeti. Frida's father died in her youth, leaving her mother with four children. Maka married Giorgi Mgaloblishvili, a wealthy widower living in the village Onchiketi, and the father of Dimitri. Maka left her three sons with the family of Dolidze and took her daughter, Frida, to Onchiketi. Giorgi, one of the area's best riders, loved his horses. His ability to ride on the steep mountain slopes and up some church stairs amazed the people. Dimitri and Frida learned the skill of riding from their father in the mountains of Onchiketi and Erketi.

Giorgi, a progressive man, wanted his step-daughter to receive an education. Giorgi's brother Ilarioni, a priest, had sent his children to a monastery in France for their education. Giorgi took Frida to France and left her in the monastery. After reuniting in France, Dimitri and Frida rode together for two years in American tent shows. As the protective older step-brother, Dimitri assumed the role of husband to assure Frida's safety and chastity.[25]

The next two weeks consisted of rehearsals at Forepaugh Park, with a full dress rehearsal on Friday, April 14.[26] The 1893 season, Forepaugh's thirteenth, opened in Philadelphia on Saturday, April 15. "One of the most important features with the Forepaugh shows this year is the Cossacks, whom Manager McCaddon has brought all the way from Southern Russia to give exhibitions, under the Forepaugh canvas, of their superb skill as riders."[27] The Georgian riders were advertised as the "Royal Russian Cossacks, The Wild Warriors of the Czar."

The Georgians' working conditions in the Forepaugh circus were much different from the large open air arena of Buffalo Bill's Wild West. The Adam Forepaugh circus worked under canvas, using three rings and a hippodrome track. The riders raced around the track, executing their trick riding and using one ring to exhibit Georgian dancing. The Adam Forepaugh circus traveled across the U.S. in twenty-two cars with four sleepers, while the Georgians attached to Buffalo Bill remained in Chicago for the season. Show people measure how important a circus is by the number of cars, as a stockbroker measures companies by the price per share.

Their initial newspaper reviews must have pleased them greatly.

"The much discussed *Georgians* were disappointing in an agreeable sense; much has been expected of them and they surpassed by far everything that had been expected. They are truly the greatest riders in the world. Their performances almost surpass belief. They seem to defy every law of gravitation and to be simply inseparable from their horses. They cling to them as a needle does to a magnet, no matter what position they may assume. Riding backwards, standing in their saddles and picking coins from the ground and similar feats are done while their horses are galloping about the race course, and this is done with astounding ease, grace and dexterity. They were frequently cheered and made a most emphatic hit."[28]

The Georgians visited the White House and were introduced to President Grover Cleveland on Monday, April 24.[29] The *Washington Post's* Monday edition ran an interesting interview with Frida Mgaloblishvili, and one wonders if the President read it before their meeting. The article read in part:

"Of all the groups in the big lighted supper tent, the most striking was that of the *Georgians*, who under their leader, the prince Dimitri, have come over to America for a season of sightseeing beyond the iron handed sway of the czar.

"The prince is accompanied by his wife, the Princess Dimitri (Frida), who is the only one of the *Georgian* troop who speaks English. She was educated in Paris and speaks with a French-Caucasian accent that is bewitching, but scarcely possible of reproduction in cold type. The princess is patriotic in support of the *Georgian* rough riders as the greatest horsemen of the world.

"'I have seen Buffalo Bill in Paris and in England, and the American, what you call Cowboy, they ride well, but you give our *Georgian* a bucking horse and he can sit him as well as the cowboy, even better, and he can do also many other things which the cowboy he does not do,' she said.

"The arms of the *Georgian* soldiers are quite rich in ornament, all of their daggers, swords, and old fashioned horse pistols being embellished with chasing of gold and silver. The men, besides being centaur-like riders, are expert swordsmen as well, and affect razor-edged sabers with which they can snuff a candle while going at a full gallop or dissect an enemy's head at the axial vertebra with equal facility.

"The *Georgians*," said the princess "had only come to America for the sake of seeing the country. They travel on passports from their government that have to be carefully visaed by all the consuls through whose stations they pass, in order that they may return to their fatherland with an official record of all their proceedings since leaving there."[30]

These Georgian riders became the first to exhibit their riding style in the United States capital city. A *Washington Post* reporter described the Georgians' riding exhibitions as seen by the political elite of The United States:

"The dancing and singing of the terra cotta coated riders was as unique as their horseback exhibition, and their part of the day's programme concluded with a running fight for a pocket handkerchief, which the princess and the stalwart Sgt. Andre Kcincatzi *(sic)* (Alexander Tsintsadze) succeeded in carrying off from the rest of the rough riders in a break-neck race around the hippodrome track."[31]

Dimitri and Frida can be forgiven if they felt like a real prince and princess. They were introduced to the President, sought after for interviews, given top billing in the newspapers, and they led the daily parade. These spirited riders appeared to be living a fantastic life.

In reality, however, they were circus performers who lived a life on the road which was not always comfortable, nor were they always treated as aristocrats. Take for example an incident recorded in Frederick, Maryland, on April 28. "A Negro insulted Frida Mgalobllishvili, but was promptly and effectually chastised by Dimitri Mgaloblishvili, who tapped him on the head with a riding whip, felling the Negro to the ground like an ox." The next day the circus arrived in Martinsburg, West Virginia, in a driving rain. Since the show must go on, McCaddon decided to conduct the parade. However, shortly after it started, the Georgians and cast floundered in the mud.[32]

Joseph McCaddon felt obliged to allow the Georgian riders to attend divine services on Sundays. The show would not reach Pittsburgh until Monday morning as a result of Saturday's rain and mud in Martinsburg. McCaddon sent the Georgians in advance to Pittsburgh to allow them to attend divine services. Their arrival attracted much attention and caused quite a stir at a cathedral.

"The Princess Dimitri is a bright, interesting and attractive young lady. She speaks five languages and can make herself understood in English. Prince Eristoff, one of the leading members of the troupe, is almost a giant in strength. He wears several medals and decorations that were presented to him by the czar for bravery during the late Turko-Russian war.

"The costume worn by the *Georgians* is a picturesque one and each carries upon his person numerous swords and daggers all richly inlaid with gold and silver. Princess Dimitri dresses in a costume like that worn by the men, though it is much richer in quality and in its gilt ornamentation. Most of the troupe being of the Russian church which resembles the Greek Church. A few, however, are Roman Catholics, among them the Princess."[33]

Frida's many newspaper interviews provided fodder for the reporters to describe Frida and her retinue. "She is a comely woman, whose superb figure and healthy color give evidence of her hardy outdoor life at her home. Her education embraces French, German, Latin and English and her conversation shows cultivated tastes for art, music and all the higher things of life, which we are apt to imagine, are only appreciated in the fashionable world."[34]

The interviews provided details of her life and the lives of those who followed for the next twenty-five years. History, however, overshadowed these details of their heritage. She informed us, "she was twenty-two years old, and her native town was a wee village nestled in among the mountains, rejoicing in the name of Ozurgeti." She told the reporters "from her infancy the horse was her plaything and comrade. To ride was her chief amusement and the long journeys of many days' duration, together with wild dashes over the steppes, gave her the wonderful physique that is one of her greatest attractions today."

Frida provides us insight into her childhood. "A little needlework, the piano and mandolin were taught by various instructors, and when but twelve years of age the youthful Princess left the odd little province bordering on the Black sea, and went to Paris to be educated as befitted her rank, but as she quaintly observes: 'I preferred the riding all the time.'"

Frida's pleasant chats with reporters eventually turned to a description of her uniform that was unlike anything women had seen in America.

"This garb consists of full trousers met at the knee by boots of black patent leather, a gay petticoat over these, and a surtout[11] confined with a gay plaid sash and trimmed with gold braid. Her cloak is of pure white astrakhan, fine and silky."

Each of Frida's interviews revealed additional information about the Georgian riders' lives, and separated truth from fiction. Strangely, while in St. Louis, Missouri, on Thursday, May 25, McCaddon engaged Mr. Moriz Berger as the interpreter for the Georgians.[35] Frida, who spoke for the Georgians, was suddenly cut off from the Press, and the mystery of why an interpreter was required remains unclear. The Forepaugh's next engagement was a week later in Chicago, Illinois, where they set up a lot on the lake front.

The Forepaugh 1893 route book, a sort of year book for the staff and crew, was printed a few weeks before the season's close. The route book listed where the show performed each day and described unusual incidents. One such event occurred Sunday, June 11, in Chicago: "All the Georgian riders packed their bags and stole away from the Forepaugh show, except for Frida and Dimitri Mgaloblishvili."[36] The lure of Chicago, its large Russian community, and the other Georgians working for Buffalo Bill tempted the Georgians with the Forepaugh show. One can imagine them talking about their experiences and lives on the road with Buffalo Bill's gang of Georgians. All-night parties, drinking, storytelling, and as sure as young men are men, sex with the loose women of Chicago, who whispered sweet nothings in their ears, might have drawn the Forepaugh Georgians to desert the show.

There are, fortunately, additional documents explaining the Georgian's behavior in the Forepaugh circus. In a small gossip column, the *New York Clipper* provided a more rational reason for the Georgians jumping the show. "A band of *Georgians* who have been touring with the Forepaugh circus last week entered a bill for two-thousand dollars, claiming a breach of contract. The matter was satisfactorily settled."[37] The Georgians, it appeared, were not paid during May. It also suggests a reason for management hiring an interpreter in May, since Frida Mgaloblishvili spoke too freely with the press.

Georgian old-timers interviewed in 1958 related more tales about some

[11] Surtout - A man's long, close-fitting overcoat.

of their exploits in Chicago:

- A story concerned one young married Georgian rider who fell madly in love with an American girl, but knew he could not marry her. He committed suicide.

- A yarn tells of a wealthy American lady who, feverishly in love with one rider, had a golden ring made to fit the young rider's penis.

Unfortunately, these stories, though titillating, are not documented.

The truant Georgians' activities in Chicago are speculative, but the age-old problems of money, shelter, and food eventually caught up with them. Their money ran out. Buffalo Bill would not hire them, food got scarce, or maybe the good ladies of Chicago lost interest in these virile, bankrupt men of Georgia. Food, board, one-dollar for each performance day, and thunderous applause in every town; what more could one ask? The Forepaugh route book states, "Thursday, July 6, Toledo, Ohio, five of the truant Georgians returned to the Forepaugh show, and appeared glad to get back."

The Cleveland, Ohio, newspaper, *The Cleveland Plain dealer,* reports all twelve Georgians were back with the show by July 10.

"While the reporter was in the tent, Prince Dimitri Mgaloblishvili entered with his troop of *Georgians,* twelve in number. This is the first time they have ever been out of their own country. They don't like America very well and are very homesick. An ironbound contract is the only thing which keeps them here."[38]

The story of the deserting Georgians and their return is still not complete. A reporter for the *New York Dramatic Mirror* happened to visit the office of Edwin H. Low of 947 Broadway, New York, on Wednesday, July 20, and saw four Georgians in his office. When the reporter asked about his strange visitors, Low replied, "I am transporting these persons from Chicago to a remote place in Russia. They are part of a band of *Georgians* that I brought to this country under contract with Forepaugh's circus. The main part of the troupe still remains in this country, but these four, for some reason that I do not fully understand, are recalled. I am required to see that they get back."[39]

The four Georgians boarded the *SS Rotterdam* the next day, Thursday, July 21, and at 10:30 a.m. were on their way to Boulogne-sur-Mer, France. They took a train from Boulogne-sur-Mer to Marseilles and a ship to Batumi. Edwin Low may not have known the reason for their being returned early, but judging by Mr. McCaddon's financial problems; it appeared he needed to reduce the number of performers in his circus.

The spectacular Georgian riders were overwhelmingly received by the towners for a good reason: their riding was dangerous. Every showman prayed for clear weather, large and sedate crowds, and no accidents. But after 193 performances, the first Georgian accident occurred. "Wednesday, August 2, Cedar Rapids, Iowa, Frida Mgaloblishvili was thrown from her horse and quite badly hurt during the evening performance."[40] One week later she returned to the saddle. There are no records of what happened to her and an article in Ottumwa, Iowa, simply stated: "Tuesday, August 8, Frida Mgaloblishvili made her first reappearance after her accident."[41]

The performers enjoyed a respite from traveling and living on a train with an occasional Sunday spent in a hotel. Circus or Wild West performers were not always welcomed at hotels as the Georgians discovered in Minneapolis, Minnesota. The *Minneapolis Times* on August 14 printed this story:

> "The *Georgians* connected with the Forepaugh show were denied hospitality in a Minneapolis hotel yesterday, for the only time since they landed in this country last spring. Manager Hoopes, of the National Hotel, made a contract to keep some of the circus people over Sunday. The agent of the show wrote upon the register, "Prince Dimitri and princess" and six other Cossack names of a more formidable appearance and sound. Manager Hoopes made no objection to the entries, thinking, perhaps, that the *Georgians* were ordinary United States mortals when not on view under canvas. Yesterday, after the arrival of the circus trains, the *Georgians* proceeded to the hotel, led by the princess, who is an accomplished linguist, speaking seven or eight languages, and therefore acts as interpreter. The hotel man then discovered that they wore the costumes of their native land, and he didn't like it.

He waved his hand in a gesture of repulsion, and exclaimed that the men couldn't stop in his house. He even refused to admit them to the dining room for breakfast.

"These *Georgians* are proud fellows, as they are all of the noble blood and high standing at home, and though they couldn't understand the language, they did comprehend the gesture. Hungry and chagrined, they proceeded to the circus grounds and laid their grievances, the princess acting as spokesman, before Manager McCaddon. Manager Hoopes arrived about the same time, and there was a somewhat animated conversation.

"'You don't have to take these men if you don't want to,' said Mr. McCaddon. 'There are plenty of good hotels that will. The Astor house, in New York, and the Continental hotel, in Philadelphia, made no objection to them, and I don't think your hotel is any better.'

"'I would take them if they wore American costumes,' said Mr. Hoopes.

"'That is just what they cannot do,' said Mr. McCaddon. 'Their contract with me compels them to wear their national dresses.'

"'Will you promise that they will not leave their room?'

"'No. If they go to your house they must have the right to do as other guests. These men are much above the average of our foreign population in character, and I would not insult them by such a stipulation as you ask.'

"Then Hoopes said he didn't want them, and Mr. McCaddon told him if he refused to keep them he must refuse the others on his circus contract, as it was all or none. Hotel agent Abbot was immediately dispatched to transfer all the circus employees to the Hotel Brunswick.

"What apparently troubled the *Georgians* most about the whole difficulty was that it prevented them from attending church. They are devout members of the Greek Church, and never lose an opportunity to attend service, usually going to the Catholic Church."

A reporter in Topeka, Kansas, intrigued by Frida's wardrobe, "Another dress reform idea which was found to have practical demonstration with the Forepaugh shows is the comfortable walking dress, reaching to the knee. This is worn by the princess Dimitri, the only woman with the *Georgians* who was found upon the show grounds after the parade returned. It is the regular costume of her native land, and it sets off her trim figure in a manner to cause all women to envy her. Besides it allows perfect freedom of movement, and so cultivates that natural grace which all women seek to acquire. The princess wears high top boots with her short skirts, and the most violent opponent of a change in woman's dress could find no suggestion of immodesty in it."[42]

The *Kansas City Star,* September 11, wrote the last important article concerning the Georgians in the Adam Forepaugh circus.

"The Cossacks are bona fide Cossacks and not Polish Jews with long coats on as they seem. They are from near the Caucasian mountains near the Black Sea. The men cannot speak any English, except to say whenever you address them on any subject from religion to free silver, 'Oh, yes, it's warm in Russia.' They are in the charge of a local chief, who is called a prince in the local official directory, and the other Cossacks are afraid of him. They throw salaams at him and he makes them sit at another table when he eats. He is accompanied by the Princess Dimitri…She says, and probably truthfully, that she had an English governess as a child…Her dress is peculiar and striking. Beginning at the feet, she is dressed in high topped boots, baggy plaid trousers of an oriental cut, a tan coat—after the blazer style—fastened with cords in front and covering a silk blouse waist made full in front… She says that she likes circus life because all the people about the show are so kind and thoughtful of her. She has taught the women a new lace stitch and appears to be moving in the smart set—as becomes her royal blood—in circus society."[43]

After traveling 10,332 miles in 159 days, giving 312 performances, visiting 131 cities in fifteen different states, and only losing six performances, the show closed the season on October 14, in Lancaster, Ohio. It is unknown if all the Georgians returned to Georgia at the season's end.

The Adam Forepaugh Circus under McCaddon's management lost money during the season. Owner James Bailey always blamed McCaddon for the financial loss. In reality, the financial panic of 1893 led to a depression, and many farmers, which was the community the Forepaugh Circus was trying to pull into the tent, were driven into bankruptcy.

BUFFALO BILL'S WILD WEST AND CONGRESS OF ROUGH RIDERS OF THE WORLD (1893)

Saturday, March 25, 1893, London, England (in transit)

One week after Dimitri and Frida left London to join the Forepaugh Circus, Ivane and Luka, who spent the previous year in London, were back to board a steamship for New York. Captain R.W. Bristow's passengers onboard his steamship the *SS Persian Monarch* were mostly Buffalo Bill's European artists destined for Chicago, Illinois.

Albert E. Sheible and Joseph Hart, Buffalo Bill representatives, were saloon passengers escorting their riders to Chicago. Among the sundry group of foreigners were ten Georgian men from Guria and the Englishman Thomas Oliver.

Buffalo Bill's Wild West Georgians, ca 1893, Chicago
Standing in white: Ivane Makharadze. Sitting from left: Paul Makharadze,
Luka Chkhartishvili, Solomon Dgebuadze, Kishvardi Makharadze, Giorgi Kalandarishvili. Standing from left:
Karman Kalandarishvili, Ivane (kid) Makharadze, Silibistro Makharadze, Joseph Talakhadze.
Author's Collection.
Plate No. 9

Ivane Makharadze, the leader, leaned on the ship's rail watching London drift past while the previous weeks floated through his memory. It was only five months ago he and Luka sailed down this river on their way home. They signed a contract with Buffalo Bill to return and perform in Chicago, and here he was sailing for America. Luka was the only one to return with him. Ivane spent the intervening months gathering a new troupe of riders and working with them. He recruited his brothers Pavle and Silibistro and his two cousins, Kishvard and Ivane (kid) Makharadze. It took a little more persuasion to enlist his brothers-in-law, Karaman and Giorgi Kalandarishvili. Joseph Talakhadze and Solomon Dgebuadze rounded out his outfit. They said their farewells in the last week of February and rode off to Batumi. The three-day voyage along the Black Sea coast to Constantinople was not as sickening as it was the first time. He could empathize with his relatives on their first sea voyage. The visual delights of Constantinople, the long passage to Marseilles, arrival on the French coast, and the train into Paris were all recalled from last year. Ivane and Luka could explain the Customs procedures to the newcomers as they crossed France and arrived again in London. As the landscape of England glided past, he knew the next two weeks at sea would be the last peace and quiet for several months.

MONDAY, APRIL 10, NEW YORK CITY (ARRIVAL)

The *SS Persian Monarch* arrived at the Bar at 6:00 p.m., April 10. "The Bar" is an anchorage at Sandy Hook between Coney Island and the New Jersey shore where ships wait their turn to be piloted through the Narrows and Upper New York Bay to the piers on the North River. The passengers spent the evening viewing the lights of New York from their anchorage. The immigration and Customs agents and pilot came out to the ship in the pilot's boat after 6:00 a.m. The agents carefully prepared the *Customs List of Passengers*,[44] listing each passenger by number, name, age, calling, native country, intended destination, space occupied, and number of pieces of baggage. The agents started processing passengers after breakfast. Dockside, Buffalo Bill's agents met the ship and helped arrange the payment of Customs duties on the European contingent's belongings. They gathered their gear and boarded a ferry for New Jersey where a train bound for Chicago departed. The Chicago Limited arrived the next day, April 12. Ivane and his troupe had two weeks to train the horses that made them famous.

• • •

Having been denied a lot on the Chicago World Fair grounds, Cody paid $180,000 for fourteen acres across the street from the entrance to the greatest attraction of its time and erected his grandstand along 62nd and 63rd Streets and Grace and Madison Avenues. The Buffalo Bill Wild West spent the entire season in Chicago, opening Wednesday, April 26, in a pouring rain, four days before the World's Fair opened. The arena had a seating capacity for twenty-thousand at a general admission cost of fifty cents per adult and twenty-five cents for children under ten. The reserved seats at the center of the action were an additional twenty-five cents per person. For ten cents, one could buy a copy of "Buffalo Bill's Wild West Historical Sketches and Programme."

After the lavish attention Ivane Makharadze and his riders received the previous year in London, they were under-whelmed by their American reception. There are no records of banquets in their honor, as in England. There were no full-page discussions of their heritage or personal interviews. On May 8 the *Chicago Times* published the longest piece of newspaper print about the Georgians in the Buffalo Bill show. It was a mere three sentences.

"A dozen *Georgians* mounted on yellow ponies paraded around the enclosure singing a weird native hymn which had all the swing and charm of 'Ta-ra-ra-boom-de-ay.' Many persons were inclined to believe the two airs (songs) were identical. At all events, the song of those red-gowned *Georgians* seemed to be the original version of the popular tune and before the gentlemen from the Caucasus had ended their musical ride the man who has been charged with having written 'Ta-ra-ra-boom-de-ay' was proven an impostor."[45]

A *Brooklyn Daily Eagle* article stated that "the czar of Russia ordered home all of his soldiers at the Chicago World's Fair." Major Burke seized the opportunity to tell the press, "The only men we have are Cossacks. They are reserve men of the irregular cavalry and liable to be called in case of war. I have heard nothing of the matter."[46] Nothing came of this report, but it did provide Major Burke a means to showcase his Georgian riders. Burke had another chance to strut his Georgians before the press when Spanish caravels arrived on July 7 at the World's Fair. Cannon fire and steam whistles saluted the caravels' arrival off the exposition grounds at 2:50 p.m. A contingent of Buffalo Bill's Indians, Bedouins, and Ivane Makharadze and his Georgian riders were arranged in a line on the terrace.[47]

Ivane and his troupe were witnesses to a disastrous fire at the World's Fair grounds on July 10. The fire started in the chimney of a warehouse used for storage of cold produce. Firemen climbed the exterior of the chimney to a platform and were in the process of hoisting a hose when the tower trembled, swayed, and fell with a crash. As the tower struck the roof, it crashed through, carrying into the interior of the building a surging mass of flames and the firemen. Members of Buffalo Bill's exhibition reinforced the guards and uniformed guides in crowd control and firefighting efforts. The only piece of luck that day was the wind blew in the right direction; otherwise, the entire World's Fair might have gone up in flames.[48]

Cody used his Georgians and other world rough riders for his benefit in Chicago, but then in July, United States Commissioner Hoyne said Cody's company had violated the "Contract Labor Law." The contract labor law was passed to protect the workingmen in the United States from the influx of foreign laborers brought in by employers in conflict with labor organizations. Cody's managers were brought before the Commissioner and threatened with $1000 fines per individual per day. Actors and singers were exempt from this law.[49] Cody escaped this fine, and in coming years the immigration status of Cody's riders would be listed as "Artists or Professionals."

On October 31, Buffalo Bill's Wild West exhibition closed after the night performance with an unequaled record of 378 open-air performances. Bad weather never caused a single omission of the twice-daily performance. The show closed one day after the World's Fair. William F. Cody and Nate Salsbury had the highest known profits in show business in 1893, estimated between $700,000 abd $1,000,000 (equivalent to $30,000,000 in year 2000 dollars).

Ivan Makharadze and his troupe of Georgians departed Chicago via train for New York on November 1. Buffalo Bill's management booked and paid their passage home on the White Star Line steamship *Majestic*. Their passage in the second class cost $45 per person, equivalent to a month's wage for the riders. The *Majestic* sailed from the White Star docks at the foot of 10th street, New York City, at 6:30 a.m. on November 8. The ship's captain, Capt. Parsell, cabled back to New York his Queenstown, Ireland, arrival at 4:40 a.m. on Thursday, November 16. Within 24 hours the *Majestic* sailed to Liverpool, England. From Liverpool the Georgians crossed the channel, the Mediterranean and Black Seas to arrive at Batumi, Georgia, during the first week of December. Ivane Makharadze returned to his home in Bakhvi, never to return to America.

1893 EPILOGUE
MAKHARADZE FAMILY BIOGRAPHICAL SKETCH

Ivane Makharadze, the original Georgian rider, lived near the Makharadze hill summit overlooking Bakhvi from 1894 to1917. In 1917 his house, built in the American style, burned to the ground. Nothing was saved. The fire was not an accident. According to a family member, a pile of wood placed at the only entrance to the house was set on fire. Ivane and his wife Nino barely escaped. They lost all the memorabilia from Ivane's Buffalo Bill riding career, including his medals and the British Society book with all the signatures. Ivane's sons, who by then were grown and working in Batumi, returned home to help their father build a four-room Gurian Oda (house).

It is said that Ivane traded some wood from the forest he owned to purchase a horse. They raised the horse like a child in the family. This horse was like a human being and could understand commands. For example, they would command the horse to lie down and then they would use him as a table, putting food on him, and the horse would remain lying until the dinner party was over. When the Bolsheviks came to power, the comrades asked Ivane to give them the horse. Ivane refused. As punishment, they arrested one of his sons and sent him to Siberia. Ivane Makharadze's grandchild was born in Siberia.

Ivane Makharadze died at the age of fifty-five in October 1921. He was buried in the church yard of Bakhvi. A few years later, the Bolsheviks tore down the church, stone by stone, planted rows of pine trees in the cemetery, and desecrated all the graves. Today, the overgrown church foundation, entrance steps, and neat rows of tall pines are all that can be seen. History has lost the grave of Ivane Makharadze, the "Russian

Cossack Prince," who brought the Georgian style of riding to America.

Ivane Makharadze, shortly after returning from America, reportedly came down with flowers disease, aka smallpox. He was never to venture abroad again. He remained in his native village, Bakhvi, as a landlord, farmer, and trainer of horses. Ivane and his wife, Nino, had six children: Ekaterine, Emeliane, Akaki, Elene, Grigoli, and Alexandre. Only one great-grandson, Akaki Makharadze, had a love of riding.

Ivane's cousins Kishvard and Ivane (kid) Makharadze never returned to America either. Ivane's young brother, Pavle Makharadze, rode for Buffalo Bill's Wild West during its tour of England and Europe from 1903 to 1906. Ivane's other brother, Silibistro, did not travel to America again. A tombstone belonging to an Ivane Makharadze remains in the old Bakhvi cemetery and it's presumed to be that of Ivane (kid) Makharadze. The inscription reads:

> I'm Ivane Makharadze raised into the Heaven prematurely. I have left my wife and children. I'm bidding farewell to friends of mine. I'm asking each of them to forgive me by that I'll be raised into the Heaven. Born in 1870, Died in 1914, May

KALANDARISHVILI BIOGRAPHICAL SKETCH

Ivane's brothers-in-law, Karaman and Giorgi Kalandarishvili, went home to their village, Kviriketi, about three KM from Ozurgeti. They did not revisit America. Karaman and Giorgi were peasants and cultivated approximately three hectare of land. Karaman's wife, Lissa, had one daughter, Mariami, nicknamed Zhiko by the family. Shortly after Karaman's return from America, Lissa contracted rabies (hydrophobia) and one winter day, Karaman fell asleep under a tree while preparing medicine for her. He caught pneumonia and passed away around 1895-1896. Lissa survived him. Her brother's relatives, Iagor Lominadze's family, supported Lissa and Mariami (five years old at the time). Mariami (1890-1981) married Vano Vashalomidze and they had four children: Simon, Arkadii, Tina, and Karaman. Karaman died in the Great Patriotic War, and in the year 2001 was survived by only one grandchild, Tina.

Few details are known about Giorgi Kalandarishvili's life after Chicago in 1893. He married, and one granddaughter, Suzi, is living in Tbilisi. Giorgi is buried in the church yard at Kviriketi and engraved on his marker stone is: "Born 1858, died 1906."[50]

SILIBISTRO (SIKO) MAKHARADZE BIOGRAPHICAL SKETCH

Siko Makharadze (1857/58-1909) was born in the village of Makvaneti, a part of the larger village of Shemoqmedi. He rode for one year in Buffalo Bill's Wild West. He moved to a bordering village, Kviriketi, where the Kalandarishvili brothers lived. Siko, a peasant farmer, cultivated hazelnuts and black apples, a species of apple growing only in Western Georgia that ripens in mid-winter. He had some bulls and oxen. Siko's grandson, Givi Mskhaladze, could only recall the story of Siko's death as told to him by his father Milorsi.

TALE OF SIKO'S DEATH

During the 1905 revolution, Czar Nicholas II sent the Russian General Alikhanov, nicknamed Avarski, to Guria to suppress the rebellious peasants. General Alikhanov with his punitive group of Ingushians, called the Black Army, was ruthless. They burned markets and villages, and raped and pillaged the countryside at will. The local Gurian "phirali," were quite different from ordinary outlaws. They would rob only the rich and give it to the poor, or their close friends, or the people in their village. Other outlaws, and often the authorities, would never approach a village where a phirali lived. For this reason, phiralis were always loved and supported by the people. The Black Army considered the phirali to be bandits. Melqisedek Guntaishvili, a rebel leader wanted by the czar's police, knew Siko Makharadze.

One day in 1907, Guntaishvili and five of his comrades were at the home of Sophio Tikanadze, his future bride, for a family feast. An informant notified the Black Army, and before they could catch them, the rebels devised an escape. They asked Siko Makharadze to help. They planned to hide the rebels in Siko's oxen cart and escape into the forest. Siko and the rebels reached the middle of the river Bzhuzhi when Black Army members approached the river bank. A small battle took place. Siko let his oxen free, the rebels slipped out of the cart into the river, found shelter in a nearby maize field and scattered into the forest. The Black Army leader's brother-in-law was killed in the skirmish. The army leader blamed Siko for everything that happened. Over the next year, Siko hid out in the forest and rarely visited his family. They arrested his eldest son in 1908.

One year later, Olia, Siko's eldest daughter, planned to get married. The neighbors advised Siko he could come home for the wedding since the army had forgotten about his part in the skirmish. As they prepared the wedding feast table, while Siko talked with neighbors, the local village head informed the Black Army group about Siko's presence. The army men came and Siko again tried to escape. When he opened the front door, they shot him. Siko died in his 52nd year.

Siko Makharadze left behind six children: Milorsi, Kakilo, Shalva, Olia, Vanichqa, and Giorgi. Milorsi, his oldest, was exiled as an anti-Soviet element to Karaganda in 1930. He spent nine years in exile and passed away in 1981. Giorgi, a social democrat, became a Guria committee deputy head. Giorgi, like other politicians, was arrested and dumped into the Metekhi prison. He became ill with tuberculosis and was released, but passed away within the year.[51]

ANDRO IORASHVILI BIOGRAPHICAL SKETCH

Andro Iorashvili was born in the village of Shemoqmedi-Gorisferdi into a gentry's family with a brother Vaso and five sisters. His father, Micheil, had been an officer in the King's army before Russian occupation. The family had huge land holdings in Shemoqmedi. Andro married Keso and they had two sons: Micheil and Serioja. Serioja was arrested in 1937 and passed away in exile. Micheil had two daughters and a son: Lulu, Nona, and Andri.[52]

REVOLUTION AT TBILISI SEMINARY

As the Adam Forepaugh and Buffalo Bill Georgian riders were returning from America, another group of Georgians embarked on their own history-altering adventure, at the only institution of higher education in Georgia, the Tbilisi Orthodox Spiritual Seminary. The Russian empire controlled the curriumlum and management of the institution. On December 1, 1893, the Georgian student leaders, Mikha Tskhakaia and Lado Ketskhoveli, presented the demands of the seminarians.

1. The Rector of the Seminary should stop abusing and humiliating Georgians. He should listen to our complaints and not shout at us or call bad names when we complain to him. The Rector should restore the tradition of

teaching the Geogian language and chanting in Georgian; give us right to read secular literature by Dostoevsky, Turgenev, and other writers, take all the measures necessary to stop teachers and supervisors from insulting and abusing us.

2. As N. Bulgakov, V. Ivanov and V. Pakroski supervisors will not change their ways, they should be dismissed.

3. Not to abolish the Georgian chants as they are no less beautiful than the Slavonic chants. Not to teach the Georgian language through Russian but as a subject in its own right.

4. To open the Georgian language department, because if we don't know Georgian language and literature we will not be able to carry out our duty in the Society.

5. To allow us leave the service in Church to go to the bathroom.

6. To abolish the system of spying in the Seminary. The practice is against Christian feelings and spoils an individual.

The student strike went on from December 1 to 5. The Seminary closed on December 7. The Seminary re-opened in March. 87 participants of the strike were expelled with a "Wolf's ticket," The active members of the strike were: Illarion Agladze, Simon Chelidze, Bessarion Meladze, Bartlone Museridze, Simon Chikviladze, Alexi Gogokhia, Mose Okropiridze, Gabriel Khundadze, Ivane Akhalshenov, Spiridon Gogiadze, Domenti Losaberiadze, Porpire Panjavidze, Toma Mchedlov, Capiton Trapaidze, Vladimer Tsagareli, Kapre Modebadze, Tarasi Trapaidze, Guiorgi Khutsievi, Petre Jalaganidze, Solomon Chachanidze, Vasil Chikvaidze, Ivane Margiani, Jakob Tsintsadze, and 62 others. One leader, Alexis Gogokhia, would become a Buffalo Bill Wild West rider in 1897.

"It is pleasant to gaze on beauty, and be near one's beloved."

Shota Rustaveli

1894 PROLOGUE

The influential tent show mogul James Anthony Bailey controlled the Georgian riders' careers and other performers for many years. Bailey was born July 4, 1847, in Detroit, Michigan, as James McGinnis, the youngest of Edward and Honora McGinnis' seven children.[12] He lost both parents by the age of eight and his eldest sister Catherine Gordon took him in. James was eleven when he ran away from his sister's home and supported himself as a bellboy and stable boy at Hodges House, a hotel in Pontiac, Michigan. A traveling circus visited the town, and the general agent, Col. Fred Bailey, took a fancy to young James McGinnis, who joined the circus. Later Fred Bailey adopted him. James McGinnis eventually took Bailey as his last name.[53]

In the fall of 1880, James Bailey formed a partnership with Barnum, Bailey & Hutchinson, which continued until 1885, when he sold his interest. After Mr. Hutchinson retired from show business in 1887, Mr. Bailey formed a partnership with P. T. Barnum, which lasted until Mr. Barnum's death in 1891. Subsequently, in the fall of 1894, he purchased the Barnum interest and the name of Barnum & Bailey from the Barnum heirs.

Mr. Ercolè had contracts with two groups of Georgians in 1894, one attached to Buffalo Bill and the other to the Barnum & Bailey's Greatest Show on Earth. Tom Oliver, still Buffalo Bill's Georgian interpreter, however, spent the winter season of 1893-94 with the Spark's circus that closed February 26 in Augusta, Georgia.[54] He rejoined the Georgian riders in London and accompanied them to America.

Meanwhile, in January 1894, Alexis Gogokhia, a student radical who became a Buffalo Bill "Russian Cossack" rider, was expelled from the Tbilisi Seminary along with eighty-seven other students for leading a strike. Alexis was unaware how his life would twist and turn among America's tent shows.

A mysterious lone Georgian walked into the Palace Hotel lobby in San Francisco, California, on January 22. He strode to the register and wrote his name in his native Georgian script. The newspaper described him as "six feet tall, wore a long black garment and had it not been for some other features of his costume he would have been taken for a priest; these were a knife and a sword." Shortly, the Russian Commissioner arrived and wrote in English under his name, M.T. Kotkoshvili. Kotkoshvili said he came from Chicago where he met some of his countrymen who were engaged last summer with Buffalo Bill's show. The translator reported, "He gave his countrymen special instructions in several of the most difficult performances."[55] M.T. Kotkoshvili is never further identified with any Georgian riders, and his significance and true identity in history remain a mystery.

BARNUM & BAILEY'S GREATEST SHOW ON EARTH (1894)
Saturday, March 10, 1894, Southampton, England (in transit)

Captain Fred Watkins stood on his flying bridge staring down at the mass of humanity scurrying back and forth on the pier at Empress Dock, Southampton. He attended to the preparations for getting underway, such as provisioning, the tide, and weather. He was not concerned with the passengers. His twenty-year-old steamship *Berlin* had more than 1500 tons of coal stowed below. The three booms were swinging back and forth loading merchandise, and the thirty-six furnaces with twelve boilers were being stoked in preparation for sailing on this gray Saturday morning. The *Berlin's* cabin-class purser double-checked his list of 200 passengers and directed the five foreign dressed Georgians to their staterooms: Data and Vasil Chkonia, Zosime Pataraia, Dimitri and Frida Mgaloblishvili. The Georgians were led, again, by Dimitri Mgaloblishvili and his step-sister, Frida. They left their homes in mid-February and were eager to get their two pieces of baggage stowed away. Like children, they roamed the passageways looking for the dining room, salons, and other pleasures that might be found onboard. Captain Watkins gave the orders, and officially at 11:30 a.m., the *SS Berlin* was underway for the 3,120 nautical mile trip to New York Harbor.[56] Dimitri and Frida found a comfortable spot along the railing to view the English Hampshire countryside; Calshot Castle, through the Solent, past Hurst Castle and the Needles.

TUESDAY, MARCH 20, NEW YORK HARBOR (ARRIVAL)

The *SS Berlin* arrived ten days later at the bar in New York Harbor at 3:18 a.m.[57] The cabin-class and third-class passengers assembled in their

---

[12] James Bailey's father Edward McGinnis died in October 1849 and his mother Honora, nee Kinney, died in Detroit on August 1, 1855.

appropriate dining saloons after breakfast. The cabin-class passengers were allowed to disembark at the pier in New York, while the third-class passengers would disembark onto barges and be taken to Ellis Island. The American citizens collected their trunks on the pier and proceeded through the inspectors.

A Barnum & Bailey representative met the ship pier-side to shepherd his artists through Immigrations and Customs. Dimitri, Frida, and the other Georgians knew the procedure from their experience the previous year. The Customs agents interrogated the Georgians: who are you working for, what are you bringing into the country, how many bags do you have, when do you expect to depart? Customs agents wrote their occupation as foreign artists and then stamped their passports. The show's agent paid the Customs and they were immediately taken to the training facilities to start breaking in their horses for the performance.

• • •

Barnum & Bailey's Greatest Show on Earth opened at Madison Square Garden, March 26. The Georgians were not scheduled to open until Monday, April 9. However, when a chariot race driver became ill, the little fluffy-haired princess, Frida Mgaloblishvili, volunteered to drive the chariot, and she thrilled the audience.

The Barnum & Bailey Program scheduled Georgian riders in two different parts of the show. They were in Circus Display No. 4: "Grand Pageant of the Strange and Savage Natives, Comprising the Ethnological Congress." This was part of The Greatest Show on Earth's traditional spectacular parade around the hippodrome track, consisting of all the different ethnological groups. The Georgians' real work came during the last program item: "Grand Hippodrome Races and other Thrilling and Interesting Contests." They performed in two of these events. The seventh event described a "Brilliant and Dashing Double Four Horse Tandem Hurdle Race, in which the daring originators ride one thoroughbred and rein three others in the lead driven at breakneck speed around the track and leaping high hurdles as they fly. Madame Castrioni & Madame Dimitri." The entire Georgian troupe performed in the twelfth event, "Wild and Thrilling Feats of horsemanship by the Renowned Cossacks. An unequaled and astonishing exhibition of all kinds of fearless and expert riding."[58]

The Barnum & Bailey advance organization gave away "Couriers," which were similar to small newspapers describing the various acts and performers in the show soon coming into town. The Barnum & Bailey Courier described the Georgian riders:

> "A people of very mixed origin from the Ukraine, the Lower Don, and first heard of in the tenth century. They are a most warlike race, and in physique, as in language and religion, they are mainly Russians. They have been employed as warriors by the Czar and the Kings of Poland to protect the frontiers against Nomadic races. Agriculture they eschew, self reliance and readiness at all times for defense or assault are their chief characteristics. Those we exhibit are the Zaparogian Cossacks dwelling near Parogi or Falls of the Dneiper, and have always been represented as little better than fierce savages. They are greatly superior in intelligence, refinement, and enterprise, however, to some of the people in Russia...."[59]

The Courier's misrepresentation of the Georgian riders perpetuated the false identity of these men and women as "Russian Cossacks."

Barnum & Bailey held the first payday on Saturday, April 21, while still at Madison Square Garden.

BARNUM & BAILEY'S 1894 CASH BOOK RECORDS OF PAYMENT TO GEORGIANS

Month	Place		Payment
21 April	New York City		$150.35
26 May	Oneonta, New York		$259.00
20 June	Salem, Massachusetts		$223.85
02 July	Rochester, New York	Trunk Money	$6.50
July	Unknown		$230.35
21 August	Appleton, Wisconsin		$224.40
21 September	St. Joseph, Missouri		$220.35
20 October	Radford, Virginia		$325.90
Total			$1640.70

The circus moved to Brooklyn, on Monday, April 23, and performed on two different lots during the week. Dimitri, Frida, and the others were now working in a circus tent (big top), which measured 445 feet *(135 meters)* in length and 245 feet *(75 meters)* wide. Their performances were on a large oval hippodrome track inside the big top between two rows of quarter poles. While in Brooklyn, one of the Georgians sprained his ankle during the act in the afternoon performance on Friday, April 27.[60] While the Georgian nursed a sore ankle, the Barnum & Bailey show moved to Philadelphia for a one-week stand. They left Philadelphia on Saturday evening and moved to Washington, DC, Sunday, May 6. The show set up on soggy ground, and seven tons of straw were thrown onto the track, making it like soft, spongy, fresh-risen bread.

The Ethnological Congress performers visited the White House on Monday, May 7. It was Dimitri and Frida's second visit. During their afternoon performance, "one of the Cossack riders' horses fell on the slippery track when his rider was in the act of picking a handkerchief from the ground at full gallop, but horse and rider appeared to have a mutual understanding on the subject and rolled in opposite directions, getting up to have another try at the handkerchief, which was captured without trouble."[61] "Madame Dimitri fell from her horse during the tandem race, dislocating her arm on Tuesday, May 8."[62] A small note in the program assured the general public that hurt performers were taken care of by the show. "The Travelers Insurance Company of Hartford Conn., insure the employees of this show against accidents through T.A. Richardson, district agent, South East Corner 4th and Chestnut Street., Philadelphia, Pennsylvania." However, this only applied to accidents outside their acts, such as train wrecks or other natural disasters. A performer hurt in the arena was liable for his or her own injuries.

Dimitri, Frida, and their three comrades continued the nightly trek along the East coast of the United States with the circus, traveling from Washington to Baltimore and into Pennsylvania. Management instructed them that in each town they would represent "The Czar" in the morning parade. Their Sunday stop in Reading, Pennsylvania, on May 20, turned into a three-day rest for the performers, but not for the crew. Rain and mud made it impossible to set up the show in Reading, and Bailey decided to skip Sunbury, Pennsylvania, and make their next lot in Wilkes-Barre.

The show closed Saturday, October 20, in Radford, Virginia. The season lasted (exclusive of Sundays) 180 days; during that time the show gave 350 performances and visited 187 towns, covering thirteen states. They gave 128 one-day stands, five two-day stands (Washington D.C., Baltimore,

Buffalo, Pittsburgh, and Minneapolis), three one-week stands (Brooklyn, Philadelphia, and Boston), and one four-week stand (New York City).

After this excruciating schedule, Dimitri, Frida, and their troupe returned to their homes in Ozurgeti, thankful for their health, experience, and money. Frida did not return to America. Step-brother Dimitri came back each year until 1900.

BUFFALO BILL'S WILD WEST AND CONGRESS OF ROUGH RIDERS OF THE WORLD (1894)

Saturday, April 21, 1894, Southampton, England (in transit)

The *SS Berlin* arrived from New York and spent the next twenty-four hours at the Southampton docks provisioning for the return voyage. The stewards cleaned the cabins; crews stowed supplies, checked merchandise invoices, stowed goods in the hold; and firemen bunkered the coal. Before sunrise on Sunday morning, they loaded fresh vegetables and other perishables such as ice, milk, and fruit. Porters scrambled to assist the passengers with their trunks, their practiced eyes on those who were big tippers. Amidst the cabin-class passengers were 161 members of Buffalo Bill's Wild West, representing all the great cavalry nations: forty men from German Kaiser Wilhelm's own regiment, the Gards Cuirassiers, under the command of Lieut. Von Natzener; forty French dragoons, commanded by Lieut. Alexander Bayard; forty men of the fifth Royal Irish Lancers of Great Britain, under Sgt. Major Murdoch; a group of Riffian Arabs and ten Georgians of the Caucasus proudly wearing their Chokhas, the traditional dress since the time of Catherine II. Luka Chkhartishvili led this group, which included Nikoloz Suguladze (Kazania), Kotia Zhordania, Kosta Chkhartishvili, Markoz Dzirtia, Alexander Kalavaladze, Leo Nakuadze, Teimuraz Tsuladze, Julius Von Katzmax, and Tom Oliver.[63] The porters knew these show people did not tip well, and they left them to carry their own trunks aboard.

Three blasts on the ship's whistle signaled to the stewards to traverse the passageways while ringing their chimes and stating "all ashore who's going ashore." This was the last warning that visitors must disembark. Capt. Fred Watkins passed orders to single the lines, lower the gangways, and slip the lines off the bollards and haul them aboard. The *SS Berlin* was underway at 11:15 a.m.[64]

TUESDAY, MAY 1, NEW YORK HARBOR (ARRIVAL)

Ten days later, on May 1,[65] the *SS Berlin* arrived at her berth at the International Navigation Company's pier fourteen at the foot of Fulton Street on the North River, New York City.

Albert Edward Sheible, business manager and Buffalo Bill's European agent, met the *SS Berlin*. Tom Oliver, who traveled with the Georgian riders, assisted Albert in his dealings with Immigration and Customs inspectors. Arrangements were made with the customs agents for all of Buffalo Bill's artists to disembark, but all did not go smoothly. Customs officers seized the large packed cases of uniforms, on the grounds foreign uniforms could not be worn in this country. All the men signed affidavits stating the uniforms did not belong to a foreign country, but were the personal property of the holders and were worn only for show purposes.[66] The cases were released the next day. Hackney transportation took the performers from the pier to the South Brooklyn Ferry landing, where they boarded a ferry that took them to the Ambrose Park dock.

• • •

During the winter of 1893-94, Cody and Salsbury, under the supervision of Lew Parker (actor, playwright, and set designer), built a magnificent grandstand and arena on their leased twenty-two acre Brooklyn lot. The builder's permit covered a grandstand 360 feet long by 45 feet deep and 38 feet high. It was one story in height and horseshoe shaped, the prongs reaching toward Second Avenue (facing Upper New York Bay) and thoroughly protected with every seat under cover. The arena was an immense space, 312 feet by 455 feet, shut in on three sides by the grandstand and backed by realistic scenery representing the Little Big Horn, where Custer made his last stand. Cody and Salsbury invested heavily to prepare the lot for the midway attractions from Chicago, but those contracts fizzled out. There was only a grandstand, arena and a white tent city built to last the season. Salsbury surrounded the lot with a ten-foot fence of corrugated steel to keep out boys with knives. He soon discovered the South Brooklyn youngsters had begun to attack it with chisels and drills.

The European artists and Georgian riders probably lined the ferry's railing as it approached the specially built Ambrose Park dock. The sight of an empty landfill with a ten-foot steel barrier in the middle of it was very different from the lot in Chicago. Luka and his men's impressions as they entered the great arched entrance—which contained three stuffed buffaloes atop the arch—were presumably reassuring. To the right of the entrance stood two pyramid-like headquarter tents separated by a platform where stood a large stuffed buffalo appearing to look toward the western plains. Two more stuffed buffalo appeared to be grazing near the entrance of each tent. The Georgians and Europeans were escorted around the grounds and shown the buildings.

The staff, performers, and crew comprised the 758 persons who lived in 140 white tents erected on the lot. The tents arranged in a dozen villages were scattered over the grounds. Each village housed a different Rough Rider troupe. The villages and tents had flower beds planted around them. Thomas Edison's small direct current electric power plant lit the tent city and arena at night. The walks and avenues were laid out after the fashion of a primitive western town. A log cabin dubbed "Scoop Shanty" served as a press headquarters. A peek into the tepees, where the braves and squaws reclined on blankets, might find the papooses tumbling about like young bears on the floor. Behind the arena were the stables for the 800 show horses, and the dining tent and kitchen.[67] Bakers union No. 75 succeeded in inducing Buffalo Bill to use none but union-made bread during the year. The performers found the eastern city savages would not only stare at them in a stony fashion for an hour at a time, but would walk into their tents or wigwams and figuratively look down their throats and handle everything they saw. Wire fences replaced the trampled flower beds by June.

A few Georgians saw the visitors from another point of view. A Georgian is quoted as saying, "I have just as much fun looking at the visitors as the visitors have looking at me; and as I get paid while they have to pay for it, I believe I have the best end of the affair."

On Wednesday, May 2, the performers who arrived on the *Berlin* had a day of rest and Thursday they commenced rehearsals. Every arena team member learned their cues for entrance and how long they had to perform in the arena. The Georgians had the added challenge of training their horses. A rehearsal viewed by the press noted the wonderful Cossack horsemanship, especially "considering they were riding horses strange to them and given to 'bucking.'"[68]

■ ■ ■

The Buffalo Bill exhibition opened on Saturday, May 12, at 3:00 p.m., under brilliant sunshine and balmy air refreshing to the 16,000 in attendance. The performance had not changed much over the years. The wild western sports opened with the usual grand entrance by all the different riders, followed by Annie Oakley (Little Sure Shot) and her sharp shooting. After Annie Oakley, came the horse races between Georgians, Mexicans, Indians, and cowboys. Buffalo Bill and his cowboys repulsed the Indians' attack on the immigrant train. A whirling Dervish gave his peculiar exotic religious exhibition. Johnny Baker shot glass balls and clay-pigeons. The Georgians showed their inimitable accomplishments as riders and executed a native dance. Buck riding, a military musical drill, and the attack on the Deadwood stage rounded out the show before the main event. General Custer's last stand on the Little Big Horn provided the historical spectacular event for this season. As always, Buffalo Bill's Wild West closed with a parting salute by the entire cast. Sgt. Bryan E. Lynn of the Fifth Royal Irish Lancers was stricken by a heart attack, and cast the only black cloud on opening day.[69] The sunny opening day turned into weeks of stormy weather, but the crowds braved the elements and went to Ambrose Park.

The *New York Times* of June 9 wrote: "Perhaps one of the best lot of riders are the *Georgians*, who seem to take delight in standing on their heads on their horses' shoulders, sitting on their horses' necks and riding backward, standing upright in the saddle and going like lightning, and other difficult feats."[70] The Georgian riders appeared to always receive the greatest praise in the press. The *New York Daily Tribune*, Sunday, July 22, ran a long article titled "A Day with the Wild West," which included a few details of the Georgian riders' performance. "The *Georgians'* riding takes your breath away. In spurred boots and long coats they stand on their horses' backs, lashing them furiously and inciting them to a madder speed with piercing cries, riding without check or rein. They sway far over and back, lean out, and bending low with a swift motion, catch an object and wave it wildly as they swing their bodies up again to the saddle. It looks like a delirium of riding."

While the industrial revolution ushered in electricity, telephones and other marvels, New York City's human essence remained the same. Life in South Brooklyn settled into a routine for all the performers. With no daily morning parade, the show people could use the mornings for chores, shopping, and sightseeing. The Georgians and other performers would scatter about, between the 3:00 p.m. performance and supper, visiting the saloons and stores which surrounded the show grounds. The Georgian riders, along with cowboys, Indians, Mexicans, and others, sought out the ladies and other forms of amusement after 10:30 p.m., once the spectators deserted the grounds. After paydays, when the showmen had dollars to spend, the shows on Monday or Tuesday noticeably lacked the bravado, spirit, and gusto which one might find later in the week before payday.

Each year the season's last day arrived with a flurry of activity. Indians struck down their tepees, Georgians spent the afternoon packing their trunks, and men embraced each other saying goodbye in many languages. The last performance went off with a vigor and enthusiasm that inspired the crowd of spectators to great applause. Buffalo Bill doffed his hat in salute to the audience for the last time this season on Saturday, October 6. Spectators deserted the grounds by 10:30 p.m. and at eleven o'clock the band marched down the white city main street and halted in front of Colonel Cody's tent, where they played the *"Star Spangled Banner"* and *"Auld Lang Syne."* By midnight, the foreign troops, including Luka and his comrades, were rushing into New York to board the *SS Maasdam* for a 4:00 a.m. sailing to Rotterdam.[71]

Buffalo Bill entertained more than 1.5 million people during the season, and the largest single day had 21,600 in attendance. There were 126 performance days. The weather was clear for fifty-five days, and the remainder ranged from cloudy to cyclonic. They missed one performance due to heavy rain on September 19. The high cost of leasing and building the lot plus the expense of feeding the cast, crew, and livestock resulted in Cody and Salsbury sustaining a financial loss on the season.

1894 EPILOGUE

Ioseb Tsetskhladze (Esopa), who rode with Ivane Makharadze in 1893 and with Luka Chkhartishvili in 1894, returned home to his village,

Likhauri, in the Ozurgeti district. He would not return to America.

Unbeknownst to the fearless riders from Georgia, subtle changes occurred over the winter in Buffalo Bill's Wild West management. James A. Bailey, who owned the Barnum & Bailey and Forepaugh organizations, came to the assistance of Cody and Salsbury after their financial disaster at Ambrose Park. James Bailey signed agreement articles with Cody and Salsbury on December 10 for a fifty-percent interest in the Buffalo Bill Wild West. Bailey would provide all the railway cars, wagons, horses, seats, canvas, and the experienced men to assemble it for the Buffalo Bill 1895 touring season. *The New York Times* in January 1895 reported the deal. Cody and Salsbury would retain management of the Wild West entertainment, while Bailey took over the business details, such as show routing and transportation.[72] Joseph T. McCaddon, as Bailey's right-hand man, became the Bailey agent attached to Buffalo Bill's Wild West. Now that Mr. Bailey was a part owner of the largest Wild West exhibition he had no more interest in a Wild West contingent in his Barnum & Bailey circus.

Georgian riders, ca 1894 Brooklyn, New York
Nikoloz Surguladze, Luka Chkhartishvili,
Konstantine Chkhartishvili.
Author's Collection
Plate No. 10

Luka Chkhartishvili, ca 1894
Courtesy, Denver Public Library,
Western History Collection
NS-629
Plate No. 11

CHAPTER TWO
THE BILL SHOW: 1895 TO 1899

B etween 1895 and 1899, the Georgians worked only for William Cody. In the business, Buffalo Bill's exhibition was known as "The Bill Show." What the public generally did not realize was that the James Bailey organization had management control. Joseph McCaddon, Bailey's brother-in-law, was the manager behind the scenes for several years. Mr. Bailey from 1895 onward controlled the routing for the Buffalo Bill Wild West and his own Barnum & Bailey Greatest Show on Earth. For example, the Bill Show would travel along the East Coast while Barnum's circus traveled through the Midwest.

Buffalo Bill's traveling Wild West exhibition was a big change for Luka and his troupe of riders. Those Georgians who rode for McCaddon in the 1893 Forepaugh Circus and in the 1894 Barnum & Bailey circus were familiar with life on the rail and living out of railway cars. Luka and his men were used to living in a white tent city during the season.

Joseph (Joe) McCaddon's unpublished memoir revealed the story of how Luka and the Georgian riders came under the management of James Bailey. "Nate Salsbury was ill at his New York home, *(winter 1894-1895)* suffering from an injury he met with in London two years previous."[73] McCaddon also mentioned that the arduous World's Fair season with the elaborate and expensive plant built at Ambrose Park, Brooklyn, in 1894 proved to be too much for Salsbury. Wishing to avoid the trials and tribulations of redesigning the show for traveling, Salsbury sent for

McCaddon to arrange an interview with Mr. Bailey. "Mr. Bailey came to New York, and an agreement was quickly arrived at for a period of one year whereby Cody and Salsbury were to provide a high class performance, all printing, portable electric light plants, also furnish food for Bailey's employees and horses, etc, McCaddon said." Bailey was to route the show, furnish the active manager, staff, all advance employees, and back the show with funds. Bailey also provided railway trains, canopy tents, baggage horses, wagons, and general paraphernalia. Bailey divided the shares 50-50 between himself, and Cody and Salsbury. McCaddon said he designed and made the canvas canopy that he stated was the first used by Wild West shows generally. McCaddon learned Cody placed great stress upon the unique Wild West character and it in no way was comparable to any other traveling exhibition. "Cody was very sensitive about being referred to as a circus performance, and yet in his final years he sold himself lock, stock, and soul to the unscrupulous firm of Tammen & Bonfils, who owned and operated the Sells-Floto shows, a Circus and Menagerie," McCaddon wrote.

McCaddon's personal account provides historians insight into Cody's character and business. "Cody was always very temperamental and difficult. The financial results the first year proved so profitable the agreement was renewed from year to year for seven years from 1895 to 1902 inclusive, and until the death of Salsbury caused the change in ownership, substituting Bailey for Salsbury. The three years 1895 to 1897 were under my personal management."

Luka Chkhartishvili and his troupe of Georgians discovered the management and travel arrangements had changed upon their arrival in the spring of 1895. The impact of the change meant their traveling by rail for the rest of their existence in the Wild West tent show business.

"A man must not yield to misfortune but meet it with unflinching courage."

Shota Rustaveli

1895 PROLOGUE

The Turkish, Armenian, and Kurdish conflict was the center of news in Georgia at the beginning of the year. A petroleum refinery in Batumi burned, with an enormous loss. The world press tried to gain access to the conflict area to report on the atrocities and massacres, but the Turkish government used a cholera quarantine to keep reporters out. A band of brigands sacked a railway station about the time Luka and his troupe of riders left their homes in March. The brigands were pursued by Cossacks—real ones—who killed five of the bandits. The czar, in response to the Armenian question, sent the Twentieth Caucasian army division to the frontier in Georgia. The nationalist Georgian movement's hopes and aspirations were dashed when Czar Nicholas II declared to all Russia he intended to protect the autocracy principles.

A common practice in the tent show industry was to reuse publicity materials designed and printed for one season at the beginning of the next. So when the 1895 Barnum & Bailey Greatest Show on Earth's early advertising said they had Cossack riders in their show, they, in fact, did not.

BUFFALO BILL'S WILD WEST AND CONGRESS OF ROUGH RIDERS OF THE WORLD (1895)

Saturday, April 6, 1895, Southampton, England (in transit)

Capt. Fred Watkins sat in his in-port cabin signing departure documents as Master of the *SS Paris*. The *SS Paris* at 10,669 tons with three masts and three funnels was twice as large as his last command, the *SS Berlin*. The *SS Paris* with twin-screws steamed at 20 knots, cutting the time between Southampton and New York to eight days. Hundreds of people wandered about the Southampton pier along Empress Dock after alighting from the special train, which completed the seventy-six mile trip from Waterloo Station, London. A keen observer could detect the fidgeting first-time passengers from those experienced ocean travelers. Ladies in their fashionable London hats and men in stiff high-collared shirts and suits meandered about, occasionally glancing at nine fierce-looking men in strange, menacing garb. Levan Shalikava and Klimenti Jorbenadze, being new to Southampton, stood guard over their baggage to keep the wharf rabble at bay, and nervously watched the boarding scene unfold. Luka and his brother Kosta Chkhartishvili, Giorgi and Irakli Tsintsadze, Kanatoyshvilii, Markoz Dzirtia, and G. Duratadze—those who made the trip before—relaxed, smoked their Turkish cigarettes, and watched the chic ladies, while passing the time before boarding. Tom Oliver was again along as interpreter.

Buffalo Bill's Georgian riders, ca 1895
Back row seated: Luka Chkhartishvili. Standing left to right: Levan Shalikava, Unknown, (Luka), Konstantine Chkhartishvili, Nikoloz Surguladze. Sitting left to right: Unknown, Unknown, Unknown, Markoz Jgenti. Known to be in photo: Giorgi Tsintsadze, Klimenti Jorbenadze, Irakli Tsintsadze, Duratadze, Kanatoyshvili.
Author's Collection.
Plate No. 12

Luka and his men wandered the second-class cabin passageways looking into the billiard, card, and bar rooms, walked through the library and found the dining room. Before the ship's bell struck noon, the last line was cast off and the turning screws roiled the Southampton mud. Sensing the turning screws and motion, Luka went on deck to watch the Hampshire landscape. From experience, he knew within the next two hours they would be out to sea and those in his group who tended to get seasick would be below decks wishing for an early death.

Capt. Watkins kept an eye on the strong currents created by the ebb and flow of the tides at the narrow entrance to the Solent, and he noted in the log his passing of Hurst Castle off the starboard at 1:50 p.m.[74] He knew a cable sent from the London office to New York would let the company know of his passage through the Solent.

The Georgians settled in for the eight-day voyage and their regular six meals a day. The ship served breakfast beginning at 8:00 a.m., bouillon and sandwiches at 11:00 a.m., a luncheon seating at noon, tea at 5:00 p.m., dinner seating at either seven or nine o'clock, and a midnight buffet.

Saturday, April 13, 1895, New York City, United States (arrival)

The *Paris* arrived in New York Harbor at 5:20 a.m., April 13.[75] The hustle and bustle around the wharf was no different in New York than it was in Southampton. The Georgians carried their own two pieces of baggage and kept close to their interpreter, Thomas Oliver. A representative from "The Bill Show" was waiting to escort them though Immigration and Customs. A bus took the Buffalo Bill artists to a ferry for the trip across the river to the New Jersey railway station. The afternoon train took them through New Jersey to Philadelphia, where their travel day terminated. Luka and his old troupers had one week to re-acquaint themselves with their horses, while the new members like Levan and Klimenti would use the time to become familiar with their horses and the show's routines.

■ ■ ■

The season opened Monday, April 22, in Philadelphia, the traditional winter quarters and opening city for the Adam Forepaugh show, whose equipment was now brightly painted with the logos and colors of Buffalo Bill's Wild West and Congress of Rough Riders of the World. Joseph McCaddon's newly designed arena, with a seating capacity of 12,200, was less than half filled for both the afternoon and evening performances. It rained the entire opening day.

The newspaper accounts of Buffalo Bill's adventures across America were generally of three types: advertising stories solicited with free tickets, dramatic news, and human-interest stories.

(1) The advertising stories were written by reporters who came out to the performance and gave a glowing show account using scripts supplied by the press agents.

Buffalo Bill's press agents supplied the Sunday newspapers with more extravagant advertising accounts and descriptions of their entertainment. A Sunday edition on April 28 printed an example of the hyperbolic language used by these agents:

> "It is not a show merely; it is not a circus. It is in no sense an aggregation of curios; but it is the gathering together in one sweep of the rough activities of five thousand years. It is a representation of the virility, the physical prowess, the speed and the daring of forceful men in all races from Abraham to Sheridan."[76]

Or, they might provide operational details such as:

> Around the arena on three sides, 2,000-candle-power electric arc lights dangled precipitously on high poles. These were placed about forty feet apart. Two Bail engines with boilers and steam connections, mounted on wheels, generated the power. Each engine connected to alternate lights in the arena, so in the case of a breakdown of one engine, the show could continue. The engines made 550 revolutions a minute, and the dynamos ran at 1,350 revolutions, generating direct current. The conductors were fine twisted wire cables, flexible and as easily handled as rope, and weighing not much more. The cables were sixty-six feet long, connected together by simple plugs in sockets easily pulled apart when the exhibition closed. The forty-six arc lights and two spot lights switched on, and the arena was flooded in an eerie glow using only sixty volts and thirteen amperes.[77]

(2) The American press occasionally provided insights into the daily drama of the traveling show:

> "The street parade in Wilkes-Barre, Pennsylvania, was abandoned owing to the Company and Stock being worn out by the shaking up they received at the hands of an engineer on the Central Railroad of New Jersey, who pulled them with a freight engine without air brake appliances."[78]

Negative dramatic press was another aspect of life on the road in Buffalo Bill's Wild West. Those stories, though occasionally untrue, revealed accidents, legal difficulties and human frailties. The Georgians learned about editorial errors in Poughkeepsie, New York, when the *New York Clipper* stated: "At Poughkeepsie, a boy was killed in the parade by one of the *Georgians* riding over him."[79] *The Courier*, a Poughkeepsie newspaper, had a correct version of the incident and the Georgians were not shackled for eternity with the death of a boy. "An unruly Mexican mustang with the Wild West Company nearly caused the death of a boy named Malkemus, aged seven. The boy with his mother was watching the animals when one of them broke away and plunged into the crowd. The boy was knocked down and cut badly on the head."

(3) A calamity was always a dramatic human interest story. On Tuesday, August 6, during the afternoon performance, the heavens opened and a cloudburst rained destruction on the Wild West show in Oswego, New York. The dressing tent was completely wrecked by the storm. The horses stampeded and several company members were hurt. This was all in full view of more than ten-thousand terror stricken towners in attendance. The east half of the grandstand was torn down next, with five-thousand patrons scrambling for shelter. Parents were separated from children, people were trampled in the mud and women fainted. With many injured, and more than half the audience having fled, the show continued.[80] This was the first of many recorded violent storms the Georgian riders were involved in on the road.

Georgians are among the most hospitable people on the planet, and as an expression of this they love to entertain guests with wine, women and song. In America, they sang their songs, chased women, but could never find a wine as good as that made back home. It did not stop them from trying to find a wine, brandy, or other liquor to satisfy their tastes. Over the years, Georgians were often discussed in newspapers because of their behavior in saloons, and here is one such story from Port Jervis, New York:

"After the performance of Buffalo Bill's Wild West in Port Jervis last Thursday (September 19) many of the Indians and others connected with the show wandered about town seeing the sights and making purchases. While the horses and paraphernalia of the exhibition was being placed on the Erie Railroad cars six Indians and three *Georgians* entered a saloon and drank freely. The convivial party was executing a war dance when in walked Mr. Cody. There is little ceremony about the measures taken by the leading spirit of the Wild West. He kicked the *Georgians* out of the place, it is said, and, drawing a revolver, ordered the Indians to leave; they left. Mr. Cody then reprimanded the barkeeper for selling liquor to the red men, calling his attention to its prohibition by the government."[81]

Sunday, the day of rest, was also the day reporters were escorted around the encampment to collect stories for Monday's newspapers. The reporters' stories occasionally provided enlightenment into the Georgian riders' character. However, on September 3, a different kind of story made headlines Monday evening in Paterson, New Jersey:

"Bernard Bernes, a Hebrew, eighteen years old, was severely lashed to-day in this city by a *Georgian*.

"Bernes was perched on an awning post watching the parade of Buffalo Bill's show when the affair occurred. In the parade was a *Georgian* mounted. As the *Georgian* passed the point where Bernes was, the latter shouted something at him. The *Georgian* reined in his horse, dashed into the crowd to a spot near the post, and began to ply his long, heavy whip across Bernes's back. Bernes was lightly clothed, and the heavy lash brought blood. A number of citizens interfered and forced the *Georgian* to cease beating the Hebrew. The *Georgian* has not been arrested."[82]

The czar's pogrom against the Jewish people, as executed by Cossacks, probably incited the young man to shout insults at the Georgian rider. The Georgian rider, who took the curses personally, lashed out against an innocent player in a clash of mutual misunderstanding.

The incident of confused cultural identity followed the next week with narrations in a more positive tone in Baltimore, Maryland, Sunday's edition of *The Sun*, September 29:

"The *Georgians* are headed by a real live prince, or "hetman," as he is called in his country. Prince Luka is a lithe, active chap, with the easiest, most gentlemanly manners that can be imagined. When he was introduced to some of the visitors, he grasped their hands with both of his and mustered up all the English of which he possessed any knowledge."[83]

A Baltimore American, September 30, reporter wrote:

"There are twelve *Georgians* and in charge is Prince Luka, a man of royal blood, and who, while he cannot speak much English, is as polite as a Chesterfield."[84]

A Georgian was involved in an accident in Washington, DC, on October 3. *The Washington Post* wrote:

"It was just as the *Georgians* were retiring on a run that one of their horses fell. He and his rider rolled in a cloud of dust under the feet of the others. One *Georgian* jumped his horse over the two fallen ones and the dismounted man springing to his feet was almost run down by another rider behind him. But apparently the Russians are made of rubber and whalebone, for the dismounted man, instead of being carried out to the hospital, jumped up and chased his horse out of the arena on foot and nearly caught him."[85]

These press reports provide insight into the disposition of the Georgian riders. They could be determined, feisty, and honorable. Luka's method of shaking hands and his being described as "a Chesterfield" provide insight into his diplomatic skills. "A Chesterfield" refers to Philip Dormer Stanhope Chesterfield's *"Letters to His Son,"* a book that became a bible for proper English gentlemen's manners. They also inform us there were twelve Georgian riders, not just the nine as recorded by the ship's passenger list. In all likelihood, three men stayed in New York during the winter season and met with Luka and his troupe upon their arrival.

James Bailey's organization routed Buffalo Bill's exhibition into the Southern states: North Carolina, South Carolina, Georgia, Alabama, and Tennessee. Mr. M. Coyle, the advance agent for Buffalo Bill, discovered a new problem in this region, now referred to as "The Bible Belt." The Attorney General of North Carolina was determined to classify the exhibition as a circus, which would increase the tax from

$20 to $200. More importantly, establishing the show as a circus in the State would discourage the attendance of the population of Baptists, Methodists, Church of God, and Presbyterians who would not attend an entertainment such as a circus. However, if it could be argued the exhibition was an educational experience, and other States viewed it as an educational exhibition, the citizens would attend. Mr. Coyle approached the local newspapers with certificates of payments from Washington, DC, Baltimore, Philadelphia, and Allegheny, Pennsylvania, which proved the show was not regarded a circus in those cities. This ploy proved successful, as many of the Southern cities had large crowds attending the exhibition. The religious morals of the towners did not preclude the Georgians from playing backgammon or stud-poker with cowboys.[86]

The season closed on October 28 in Atlanta, Georgia. The Georgians were on the road for 195 days, visiting 131 cities, giving 321 performances, and traveling over 8,980 miles [14,448 km]. There was one more death before the camp closed in Atlanta. James Doyle and Joe Emmett, two rough riders, quarreled, and Doyle shot and killed Emmett.

Buffalo Bill's organization provided the Georgians and the other Europeans transportation back to New York. Mr. Low, whose office was located in New York at 6 Bowling Green, arranged the shipping with the American Line. The performers embarked on the *SS Berlin* on Wednesday, November 6, at 11:00 a.m. for the voyage to Southampton. Capt. Lewis sighted Hurst Castle at 1:05 p.m. on November 16, and shortly thereafter his passengers arrived at the port of Southampton. The Georgians, now familiar with European travel procedures, continued their journey home.

1895 EPILOGUE

The Georgians were met with extensive flooding when they arrived home. The rail service between Batumi and Tbilisi was suspended.

LEVAN SHALIKAVA BIOGRAPHICAL SKETCH

Levan Shalikava, a singer and rider, returned home to his three brothers; Mikheil, Stephane and Solomon. The Shalikava family was known in their village, Mziani, as the best riders. When the surrounding villages' young men gathered in Nagomari for horse races they would always ask "Are the Shalikavas participating or not? If they are it is not worth participating." Levan Shalikava, who survived one tenting season in America, died a bachelor soon after his return from America.

Unknown Georgian rider
Courtesy Baker Album
Plate No. 13

"No one can force into being that which is not to be."

Shota Rustaveli

1896 PROLOGUE

The two worlds that the Georgian riders traveled between, the United States and Russia, were oddly experiencing similar socio-political turning points. America elected William McKinley as the twenty-fifth President. He would be assassinated in 1901. In Russia, Czar Nicholas and Czarina Alexandra were crowned in Moscow, and the entire family would be assassinated in 1918. The United States Supreme Court decision of "Plessy V. Ferguson: equal but separate accommodations" made segregation constitutional if those segregated enjoyed equal facilities. Russian censors were sent down from St. Petersburg to ban all Georgian language, literature, and libraries, thus suppressing Georgian culture. The reason given for abolishing the village libraries was that since everyone now was required to speak Russian, it was not necessary to trouble about the other languages.

Thomas Edison's Vitascope was used at the conclusion of a vaudeville program on April 26. This event was the dawn of commercial motion pictures in the United States, silently ringing the death knell of the Wild West exhibitions.

BUFFALO BILL'S WILD WEST AND CONGRESS OF ROUGH RIDERS OF THE WORLD (1896)

Saturday, April 4, 1896, Southampton, England (in transit)

Captain Watkins stood on his flying bridge observing one of the world's finest natural harbors at the confluence of the rivers Test and Itchen, the Port of Southampton. He was familiar with the two-knot tidal flow and the unique double tide the harbor enjoyed, giving it seventeen hours of rising water every twenty-four hours. His officers were reporting the status of the preparations for getting underway. His pursers were the welcoming committee, handling public relations, and answering questions from first-time passengers.

Luka age 28, Tom Oliver age 30, Nestor Khukhunaishvili age 29, Luka Ebralidze age 26, Alexi Murvanidze age 29, Dimitri Tsintsadze age 24, Alexi Tskvitishvili age 37, and Jimshet Lomadze age 31, viewed the *SS New York,* a sister ship of the *SS Paris.* It looked about the same: three masts, three funnels, and a steel hull. They wondered if the staterooms and saloons were similar. Deep in the boiler room, the firemen were stoking coal into the fifty-four furnaces, to bring the nine boilers up to steam pressure for getting underway. The Chief Engineer stood by the engine telegraph awaiting the signal bells to set in motion his triple expansion engines.

The Southampton morning air was thick with dampness that clung to one's skin and made the passengers eager to get aboard. Albert Sheible, Buffalo Bill's business manager, boarded via the first class ramp while Tom Oliver, Luka, and all the other Buffalo Bill employees boarded using the second-class gangway. The ship was underway before noon. After finding their cabin and stowing gear, Nestor Khukhunaishvili, Dimitri Tsintsadze, and the other new members of Luka's troupe went on deck to view the Hampshire landscape as the ship passed by. Capt. Watkins kept his eye on the tidal currents and noted his Hurst Castle passage. The American Line's New York City office received a cable "outbound passage at 1:45 p.m."

Georgians, ca 1896
Seated center in white: Luka Chkhartishvili. Sitting left to right: Dimitri Tsintsadze,
Nestor Khukhunaishvili, Konstantine Chkhartishvili. Standing left to right: Alexi Tskvitishvili,
Jimshet Lomadze, Alexandre Murvanidze, Luka Ebralidze.
Courtesy, Buffalo Bill Ranch State Historical Park, Nebraska Game and Parks Commission.
Plate No. 14

Saturday, April 11, 1896, New York City, United States (arrival)

After eight days at sea, the *SS New York* arrived at the bar at 6:40 a.m. The pilot maneuvered the ship to the International Navigation Company pier, fourteen, at the foot of Fulton Street, New York City.[87] Albert Sheible arranged the transportation to the New Jersey railway station for the trip down to Philadelphia. Saturday evening, Luka and his men were encamped on the lot at 11th and York streets. The Pine Ridge Sioux Indians arrived on Sunday, and Monday saw the arrival of Col. Cody, the Mexicans, and cowboys. Rehearsals began on Tuesday, April 14.

• • •

Opening day was Saturday, April 18, at a 2:00 p.m. performance with James Bailey visiting. The guest of honor was General Nelson Miles, a good friend of Col. Cody's. Buffalo Bill's Wild West stayed one week in Philadelphia, closing Saturday, April 25.

The preparations for the season's first jump began after the Saturday, 8:00 p.m. performance was underway. They left Philadelphia on Sunday morning at 3:00 a.m., and sustained a long, troubling day. Between Baltimore and Washington, the cookhouse canvas caught fire, destroying it. Coming into Washington, the journal box[13] on the rail car carrying the fire-damaged cookhouse wagon burnt off. This car had to be pulled out for a new pair of wheels. Because of the delays, both train sections stopped at Brunswick, Maryland, to water the livestock, and their day ended in Cumberland, Maryland, at 7:30 p.m.

Three weeks took them from Maryland to Missouri. The "Bill Show" employees anticipated a lazy week in St. Louis. All performers wanted to send out their laundry for a proper cleaning, or take a hot bath in a hotel, or find a saloon they could call home for a week. It would be a leisurely opportunity to repair saddles and equipment. The weather, unfortunately, did not cooperate. The St. Louis lot was miserable, full of mud, and caused a serious problem for riding. Instead of clean clothes, they fought mud, rain, and humidity. Rather than a joyful week, everyone was glad to get out of town, knowing after another week they would spend two weeks in Chicago.

On Sunday, May 31, a crowd of four to five thousand gathered outside the Chicago coliseum on 63rd Street to gawk at their arrival. Luka was familiar with the neighborhood because the coliseum was built on the site of Buffalo Bill's 1893 World's Fair encampment. The Georgians camped in the coliseum's upper balcony gallery. A reporter told his readers about the Georgians' laundry of colored garments drying on the upper balcony seats and railing,[88] and then quoted the chef: "We prepare 800 to 1,000 individual steaks every morning and serve them for breakfast. They are all done on this single range, over five griddle holes inside of twenty-five minutes by the watch. Oh, the boys are terrors on steaks!... The *Georgians* and Indians want 'em three times a day, and they get 'em too!"[89] In a related story another chef said: "The *Georgians* eat very much like they ride—at a gallop and without regard to the laws of health. Mastication cuts no ice with them; they could apparently digest rocks if necessary, after having swallowed them whole."[90] Monday they opened in Chicago with their usual performance. The crowd hooted and howled during the horse race between a cowboy, Indian, Mexican, and Russian. Their favorite was usually the cowboy, but the Georgian rider was the winner this opening day. The two weeks went by too fast for everyone, especially those like Luka, who had made friends in Chicago during the 1893 season.

The evening of June 14 was again a night of packing and preparing for the next stretch of one-day stands. Buffalo Bill's Wild West would crisscross Illinois, Indiana, and Ohio for the remainder of June and most of July.

Thomas Oliver and a group of side show bandsmen would not forget July 16 in Massillon, Ohio. During the parade, the wagon carrying the Italian side show bandsmen drove under the steel Fort Wayne railway bridge at Erie Street, which was too low for the bandsmen's high perch. They were scraped off their seats like ten pins. The wagon exited the other side with the only music being the screams and cries of crumpled men.

Later the same day, at the matinee performance, Thomas Oliver intercepted some unwanted buck shot. "Tom Oliver, known as Cossack Tom because he is the Cossack interpreter, was standing back of the back side wall while Johnnie Baker was doing his act. In shooting at the pigeons, one shot went through the side wall and struck Tom in the eye and another shot went through his left ear." Tom Oliver and those musicians who were not hospitalized crawled back into their train bunks at day's end to head for the next town. Tom walked around with a bandaged head for the next few days.

Bad luck plagued the outfit during August: there was much rain, broken equipment, arena accidents, and storms. The most damaging storm of their season occurred on Tuesday, August 11, at Muskegon, Michigan. Nestor and Dimitri, two of the Georgians riding with Buffalo Bill, finished their supper by 6:00 p.m., and were watching a Mexican teach a German trooper how to throw the lariat. The evening air was clear, the sky blue, with nothing to indicate the trouble about to befall the Bill Show. There were around two-thousand people already on the show grounds. The side show opened and many passed inside. Nestor and Dimitri were laughing at the German's sad attempts to throw the lariat, when a slight breeze sprang up. The clouds on the western horizon boiled upward, swelling into black thunderclouds within moments. Nestor gave Dimitri a punch on the arm as he pointed to the blackening skies. Few townspeople paid much attention, but all the show people started to scurry for cover and prepared for an emergency. Upon the peaceful scene, the storm suddenly broke in all its fury.

The wind blew a terrible gale and everything went before it. The refreshment stands went down first with pink lemonade scattered to the winds. The shelving boards were caught by the wind and carried through the air. The tents were easy marks for the wind, as they billowed out like sails, exerting an irresistible force against them. Those inside the side show tent heard the sound of straining ropes and flapping canvas as the big structure swayed in the clutch of the storm. Immediately, those who took part in the performance began to pack their belongings. The orator yelled at the audience, "Get out of here as quick as you can," but the order was unnecessary. The people broke for the side wall that was raised. The air filled with flying dust and everyone's eyes were soon red and swollen. Nestor and Dimitri raced for the dressing tent to gather their trunks and help bring down the canvas.

Within thirty seconds after the storm struck, every man attached to the Wild West was doing his duty. The first precaution taken was to run down (take down) the gaily painted announcement canvasses in front of the side show, and then everyone's attention turned to the big tents. The men rushed to the guys and added their strength to that of the stakes in holding the canvas as it bellied before the gale. In the meantime, the wind tore across the arena and struck the seats. The light boards lifted and were carried long distances, creating dangerous flying missiles. Rope after rope broke, stakes and poles snapped, until the arena canvas leaned badly before the wind. Buffalo Bill ordered the canvas taken down. There would be no evening performance in Muskegon that night.

Nestor and Dimitri, and all the other Buffalo Bill employees labored for the next two hours at corralling horses, finding seat boards in the adjacent corn fields, rolling up canvas, and searching for stakes, poles and personal possessions. The German, French, English, and Georgians, along with the cowboys, were drawn into military order. With Buffalo Bill in his carriage, they rode to the Ottawa Street depot where their two trains waited. The loss for Buffalo Bill's Wild West was about $300 in torn canvas, broken stakes and poles and other damage. About $3,000 in admissions was also lost. The trains were loaded and set off for the ninety-three-mile jump to Benton Harbor, Michigan, by 10:00 p.m.[91]

Luka and his troupe of Georgians had not seen the last of the rain and mud. Three days after the gale force winds of Muskegon, the Bill Show was in South Bend, Indiana, on Friday, August 14. A heavy rain at 4:00 p.m. disrupted an ordinary day. The evening performance had more accidents then ever before, due to the afternoon downpour. Luka and another Georgian rider were to experience the dangers of rough riding where water collected in puddles with soft muddy bottoms. The evening performance's excitement began with a French cavalry trooper falling forward and a horse falling on top of him. Soon afterward, a cowboy's horse made a complete somersault with his rider, and then an Indian fell and limped away leading his horse. A newspaper account recorded what happened as the Georgians took to the field.

> "The next to get a terrible fall was one of the wild riding *Georgians* and he painfully moved from the scene of his mishap, and did not again appear.
>
> There were several minor accidents of the same nature, but the climax was reached when Luka, the chief rider of the *Georgians*, a central figure at the World's Fair exhibition, and one of the best riders in the world, started at a mad pace along the east side of the arena at a place where the ground was supposed to be solid. He was

---

[13] Journal box - A journal is the axle supported by a bearing. The journal box is the housing enclosing the journal and its bearing. A hot box is a journal bearing that has over-heated.

mounted on the best horse in the outfit—a splendid animal that he had been riding at Chicago during the World's Fair and ever since, and a horse as intelligent and docile as the equine family affords. Suddenly near the northeast corner the swift running animal lurched and then fell headlong forward, his brave rider underneath. A groan of sympathy went up from the audience which but a moment before had been wildly applauding the rider. Both lay motionless and not a sound came from them. People as well as employees rushed to their aid and nearly two minutes were required before the horse was pulled from his rider, which he nearly completely covered and had entangled in the stirrups. The plight of the two had been observed by Mr. Cody himself, who came from his dressing room only partly dressed to look mournfully upon the gallant steed, which was found to have broken its neck. Luka was picked up unconscious by his fellow *Georgians*, and taken to the dressing room. Nearly everyone thought that he was dead, but when a *Times* representative, and Chief Cassidy, visited the dressing room a few minutes later, he was found to have recovered consciousness and was receiving necessary attention, being able to stand up. He is simply a mass of bone and muscle and in the best condition or it would have killed him. No ordinary man would have lived through it."[92]

The Georgians learned there were more hazards to traveling in a Wild West show than just arena accidents. The first train wreck in the two years since Buffalo Bill returned to the road occurred September 5, during the jump from Wausau to La Crosse, Wisconsin. Bill's outfit was traveling as a two-section train. The first train section was going up a grade between Centralia and Rudolph, when it stalled and could not climb the hill. The engineer cut his train in two and then took the first half up the grade to Rudolph. In the meantime, the second train found the other half of the first section along a siding, and this train conductor decided they should push the remaining first section cars up the grade to Rudolph. They had barely gotten underway when they met the first section engine coming back to retrieve the cars they left behind. They hit head on. Sleeping cars, flat cars and wagons were smashed. Incredibly, no one was hurt. This was the Georgian riders' first experience of a train wreck; however, there would be more.

The *Kansas Times,* October 19 printed a most unusual tall-tale generated by Buffalo Bill's press agents one week before the close of the season.

> "The Russians are a troupe of Cossacks of the Volga, headed by Prince Luka Chkhartishvili, about whom there is extant probably as pretty a romance as ever was written. The prince, who by the way talks English, French, and German, as well as Russian, is not of the blood royal, although of unquestioned birth and rank. But in his early day's he fell in love with Princess Stephanik, the morganatic[14] daughter of the present czar's father. She returned his love, and in secret they planned to flee to Poland and there live in disguises. Even the night for the elopement was set, and the Prince, who resided in a country palace some miles from St. Petersburg, had started for his bride-to-be, when arrested. The rigid system of passports prevalent in Russia had trapped him. He was banished to Siberia for life and drafted into the military service of the Cossack guards. He has proven himself a brave soldier, and has risen to rank and fame. The Princess died the month after he was banished. With him here are a dozen or more of his fellow soldiers, with curious dress, their long guns, their cartridge belts across their breasts and their queer language."[93]

The Luka fairy tale was followed the next day with the story of Alfred Weber shooting Herman Manthy in the left breast during a brawl in a saloon. Both men belonged to Buffalo Bill's show. Manthy's wounds were dressed, as the injury was not serious. The daily life with Buffalo Bill's men continued.

Saturday, October 24, Buffalo Bill's Wild West arrived in Moberly, Missouri, and gave their final, 332nd, performance. They were on the road for 190 days, set up their tents 132 times, and lost only five performances while traveling more than 10,787 miles [17,356 km] going as far west as Nebraska.

The Georgians and all the other European performers boarded special trains, which took them to St. Louis and then on to New York. They departed October 28 for the approximately twenty-five day journey. The Georgian riders found themselves back in the arms of their families.

---

[14] Morganatic - A marriage between a royal and person of inferior rank. The children of the marriage do not succeed to the titles.

1896 EPILOGUE

Returning home, the Georgians discovered the Batumi harbor had been deepened to twenty-six feet by the Russians. The harbor could now be used by the Black Sea fleet.

Tom Oliver's last known connection with Buffalo Bill and the Georgian riders was in 1896.

Another Georgian arrived in America on July 6, 1896, onboard the SS *Obdam*. This young man, Alexis Gogokhia, was escaping a "Wolf's Ticket" imposed by the czar's secret police, the Okhranka. His crime was associating with Georgian social democrats, nationalists and revolutionaries. He was an active participant in the 1893-1894 student strike at the Tbilisi Seminary. The Wolf's Ticket blacklisted him from work and restricted movements to his village. He was forbidden to continue seminary studies or to hold a job. Alexis wrote a letter to the editor of KVALI magazine in October to thank those who helped him leave Georgia.

"Allow me to express my deepest gratitude on the pages of your magazine to the following people who helped me with money and made it possible for me to travel to America. In Batumi N. gogoberidze gave me twenty roubles. I. Porakov and m. Betanov each gave me five roubles. K. Chkheidze, P. Gogichaishvili, T Tsereteli, K Tavartkiladze, Sepe Chkeidze, N Jakeli and P. Glonti contributed three roubles each. M. Sharashidze, Rev. Totibadze, Maro Eliava, Ekvtime Berdzenishvili, Nina Berdzenishvili, Ivane Lonidze and Vaso Berdezenishvili each gave two roubles. A rouble from each of the following: Anna Galdavadze, A. Lortkipanidze, Ekvtime Chkhartshvili, Ioseb Dumbadze and M Chkhikvadez. Fifty Kopeks were contributed by Tsuladze. B. Glonti bought my passage fare to Konstantinopol. In

In Ochamchire Rev. K Khelaia and R Markelia gave ten roubes each. A Kosmava contributed eight roubles. I Zhordania five roubles, Rev. Svanidze four roubles. Rev. Sahobia, and Rev. Pantsulaia each contributed three roubles. T Chachava also gave three roubles. L. Uratadze two roubles. B. Achachava, G. Gvasalia, G Kviraia raised forty roubles. InkSokhumi Rev. B. Khilaia raised thirty five roubles and eithy kopeks. In Zougdidi: Otar Dadeshkeliani gave six rougles, B. Chichua five roubles. Levan Apakidze raised eleven roubles. In Okumi V. Kandelaki and K. Chkhenkeli each gave three roubles. That latter also raised tn rouble. I apologize for expressing my gratidude so late.

The editor included this message. "This young man left for the USA to receive education. He has been in New York for three months, "but because I ran out of money," he writes, "I had to start some kind of manual work. Now, I'm working at a factory and as an inexperienced worked, I'm paid little not even enough for food. Also, I'm getting too tired. I have no time left since I am working ten hours a day and have no time for self-education. I hope that later when I learn the language, it will be easier for me. Otherwise, it's really difficult to get along. Incidentally they have evening schools for the working people. I attend one of them and study the English language. There are many Russians in New York who also have their society there and give lectures. I was admitted a member there. The lectures are on economic issues. Not long ago I listened to B. Levinson's lecture on the "Theory of Money" a very profound and interesting lecture." If anyone wished to help this young man with money we have his addres in the office.

Within six years, he held substantial sway over the Georgian riders who would participate in many future Wild West shows.

Left: Alexis Gogokhia,
Right: Luka Chkhartishvili, ca 1897
Author's Collection
Plate No. 15

Silovan Kartvelishvili
Author's Collection
Plate No. 16

"Speech may be better than silence, but we often spoil things by speaking."

Shota Rustaveli

1897 PROLOGUE

Luka Chkhartishvili during the off season recruited a new rider for his team, Giorgi Chkhaidze. Giorgi was born in the village Atsana in 1868. As a youth, he studied shoe making in Lanchkhuti, which was a seven kilometer (4.35 miles) walk every day. He was a very clever and gifted twenty-nine-year-old shoe maker and soon managed to buy a little fancy goods store in Lanchkhuti. During his stay in America, the store went bankrupt.

There was competition for these riding jobs, and one correspondent reported one rival wounded Jimshet Lomadze in the leg so he could not go to the United States. Before going, Luka and his band of riders attended a church service to pray for a peaceful journey. They left their homes in Guria to start their trek to America in the first week of March, 1897. Meanwhile, Dexter Fellows, Buffalo Bill's Press Agent, started setting the stage for the czar's "Russian Cossack" troupe arrival. The American public needed to view the "Russian Cossacks" as real Czar Warriors, not just shoe makers. *The Brooklyn Daily Eagle,* March 27 printed, before Luka and his troupe landed in New York, the following story.

"Colonel Cody has had considerable trouble in securing his detachment for this season, owing to the fact that they are enrolled as soldiers in the Russian army. The prospect of war over the Cretan situation made it appear for a time as if the Georgians would have to remain at home at Tifis *(sic),* at the southeastern base of the Caucasian mountains. Colonel Cody's emissary, however, prevailed upon the czar's officials to consent to their coming and they started from Tifis *(sic)* last week and will reach here next week."[94]

BUFFALO BILL'S WILD WEST AND CONGRESS OF ROUGH RIDERS OF THE WORLD (1897)

Saturday, March 27, 1897, Southampton, England (in transit)

Jimshet Lomadze and his companions were staying at the American

Shipping Line's London hotel. Jimshet was short in stature with a thin waist; agile, strong, and on his second trip to the United States. He stood at the window, still dressed in his night shirt, looking toward the western skies. The rain and strong gusts rattling the window panes were depressing. The weather reminded him of his young wife and children whom he had left on a rainy day. Jimshet, who lived in Mamati, remembered the church service he organized to pray for a peaceful journey at the Church of Jacob the Apostle. He might have wondered if the big wall candlestick and two smaller table candlesticks he contributed to the Church were lighted today.[95] Despite the weather, the final leg of their trip to New York was before him, and it was time to get started. A quick coffee in the hotel and Luka, Jimshet Lomadze, Dimitri Tsintsadze, Nestor Khukhunaishvili, Alexi Tskvitishvili, Giorgi Chkhaidze, Luka Ebralidze, and Konstantine Chkhartishvili were headed to Waterloo Station to catch the special train for the Empress dock in Southampton.

Luka and the seven Georgians met with the Europeans who would be in the Buffalo Bill Wild West exhibition this year at Waterloo Station. Several were old friends from the previous season, and there was plenty of backslapping, hugs, handshakes, and greetings among the motley group, which did not get much notice from the Londoners.

The weather for southern England was westerly gales, strong winds, squally, showery and temperature of fifty degrees.[96] The *SS Paris* departed Southampton for New York around 11:30 a.m., and passed Hurst Castle at 1:40 p.m., with Capt Watkins commanding.[97]

The *SS Paris* carried 229 passengers on this voyage and undoubtedly many were below decks the first day, seasick. Despite the weather, Giorgi Chkhaidze stood on deck viewing the Hampshire landscape as he began his first Atlantic voyage. Luka, Nestor, Dimitri, and others were either in a game of cards with some of their old friends or unpacking in their cabin.

Saturday, April 3, New York City (arrival)

The *SS Paris* arrived in New York after seven days at sea. Giorgi, bundled in his great coat and fur cap with the temperature in the low

30s, was on deck to view the New York skyline on this, his first, arrival.[98] A magnificent sight before him: the Statue of Liberty on his left, Manhattan on his right, and the Brooklyn Bridge off in the distance. Giorgi had heard stories from Luka about Brooklyn and Ambrose Park.

New York City was just cold concrete to Alexis Gogokhia as he walked from the lower east side to the west side docks. Alexis arrived the previous July, 1896, and he, too, remembered the magnificent sight of New York City from the deck of the *SS Obdam*, but the reality of living in New York had quickly set in. Alexis, who was without funds, unable to speak the language, and unable to find affordable accommodations or work, spent months living in the hallways of Russian apartment buildings. He found work in bars cleaning spittoons, in laundries ironing shirts, and in a sweatshop sewing skirts. Alexis also found New York City's small Georgian community, and through them arranged employment with Luka Chkhartishvili in Buffalo Bill's Wild West exhibition. Today, in spite of the cold weather, he felt warm in the knowledge he would soon be with his countrymen and traveling across the United States.

The ship was met by Major Burke, Buffalo Bill's press agent. The European artists passed through Customs and found themselves on Fulton Street. Alexis met his riding comrades and boarded the transportation, which took them across the Brooklyn Bridge to Ambrose Park.

Luka, Jimshet, Giorgi, Alexis, and the others spent the next nine days in rehearsals. Alexis, the radical student, and Giorgi, the shoe maker, were the rookies. Alexis and Giorgi had to train their horses, learn the riding routines, and experience life in Buffalo Bill's Wild West. It was their First-of-May[15] season.

■ ■ ■

Buffalo Bill's Wild West opened Monday, April 12, with a parade starting around 9:00 a.m. Buffalo Bill rode his prancing steed just behind the contingent of Georgians. Two shows a day for the next two weeks at Ambrose Park occupied Luka and his troupe. The show moved across the East River into Madison Square Garden, New York City, on Sunday, April 25.

---

[15] First-of-May is a circus expression meaning: Any first-season employee in the ranks of troupers, a rookie, freshmen, or newcomer.

New Yorkers had three weeks to watch Luka and his men perform. Buffalo Bill's Wild West packed, loaded into forty rail cars, and made their first jump to Bridgeport, Connecticut, the home of James A. Bailey, fifty-percent owner, on Sunday, May 16.

Jimshet, Alexis, Giorgi, and Luka's troupe traveled through Connecticut and Massachusetts, with a week in Boston. A reporter for the *Boston Journal,* Sunday, May 23, wrote about the fierce Georgians, and gave an interesting description of the Georgians. He wrote:

> "They wear handsome but somber uniforms, ride the lithe, small horses of the steppes and are mounted on small troop saddles, very high front and rear, which are built up with pads fully four inches thick, so that they seem to perch far above their horses. Instead of a broad clinch to hold the saddle they hold three narrow straps tightly drawn, which would seem to be rather severe. Their stirrups are very small, only big enough to get the points of the toes into, and drawn short. A man must be a good rider who can occupy that aerial roost and steady himself by those toy stirrups. But the *Georgian* does not only that but much more. With his horse at a full gallop he swoops down and picks up a handkerchief from the ground."[99]

Alexis and Giorgi, by the first of June, had eighty-six performances under their belts and were now experienced Buffalo Bill riders. They had become familiar with the daily routine and life on the road. In June they would visit more cities in Massachusetts, New Hampshire, Vermont, and then on a Friday, June 18, Buffalo Bill and the Georgians jumped into Canada.

The Canadians were just as impressed with the Georgian skills as the Americans. The *Evening News* in Toronto wrote: "The savage *Georgians* did the greatest riding at last night's exhibition. The most thrilling riding was done by the *Georgians*, standing on their high saddles and riding at breakneck speed, or dashing away with one heel on the saddle and head within an inch of the ground."[100]

They returned to the United States on July 19 after visiting twenty-one Canadian cities. The Wild West and Georgian riders arrived in Syracuse, New York, Thursday, July 22. A reporter for *The Herald* in Syracuse had an opportunity to chat with the Georgians, and he then wrote an incisive article.

"One of the most interesting contingents of 'Buffalo Bill's' troupe of riders and marksmen who entertained Syracuse yesterday are the *Georgians*....

"Though since their arrival in this country to participate in the Chicago exposition in 1893, the number of the little band of aliens has decreased somewhat, they are still in number large enough for companionship. The party now numbers nine, with Prince Luka Chkhartishvili at their head....

"Passing the small private tent of the colonel, one of the cavalrymen, who acted as a guide, led the way into the large tent occupied by the 'Congress of Rough Riders.' Here, sprawled about in the straw, lay the representatives of the nations gathered, many of them from the most removed quarters of the world, by the agents of the Colonel for the entertainment of the American people. Each little party of strangers occupied a division of the large tent. Between the Bedouins and the South American Gauchos were the Georgians. While the Gauchos were taking their after supper siesta and the Arabs were engaged in preparing their elaborate toilets, our friends from Caucasia enjoyed their leisure in what a Yankee would call loafing. George Tchaidze [Giorgi Chkhaidze] was mending an old pair of boots. Alexis Evanovich [Alexis Estatetovich Gogokhia] was doing stunts with Peyotra Stephanovitch on the ropes outside for a wondering, gaping crowd of small boys. The Prince [Luka] was smoking a real American cigarette.

"'Yes,' said the Prince, 'the Colonel is very popular with our party. He has the respect of the *Georgians* as well as of all the rest of the performers. I have a family in Caucasia, and each year look forward anxiously to the return trip. Some of the parties have wives in the mother country, and some of them have not. We are very much interested in American institutions. Some of the party has decided to stay in this country.'

"It was learned from other sources that several of the *Georgians* were known to have socialistic tendencies in their native land. In speaking with one of the younger members, [Alexis Gogokhia] an attempt was made to have him talk upon this subject. He said. 'There are many of our people who have advanced ideas of liberty and are not in sympathy with the Russian government. I know of the socialistic labor party in this country. They have, however, somewhat different aims than the socialists of Russia. Many of our people are confident of a better government in time.' Such was his reticence and reluctance to speak definitively of the subject."[101]

Alexis, Jimshet, and Giorgi took in the architecture, agriculture, and living conditions of many small towns and cities of New York, Pennsylvania, and Ohio during July and August. Buffalo Bill himself was watching out for men like Detective Bauknecht from Reading, Pennsylvania, who had a warrant for his arrest for non-payment of a $1,000 license.[102] Once Buffalo Bill crossed into Indianapolis, Indiana, on August 27, he was safe from the Pennsylvania warrant. The company's jump into Indianapolis had its own problems, as Luka sustained a second fall.

"The *Georgians* rode with their usual abandon, and their chief escaped a serious accident by a hair's breadth. He was riding at full speed, with one leg thrown across his horse and his body dragging on the ground. His horse stumbled on one of the turns and went to his knees. Quick as a flash, while still in the same position, the chief hit his horse under the chin with the flat of his sword and raised him to its feet."[103]

With horse and rider unhurt in Indianapolis, the show jumped to Lafayette, Indiana, and then another 119-mile jump to Chicago, on August 29. Luka, Jimshet, the other Georgians, and the entire outfit looked forward to the two-week stand in Chicago. Old friendships were re-established, and Alexis and Giorgi saw the windy city for the first time. Alexis Gogokhia was unaware that in seven years he would be living in Chicago. The Chicago press covered Buffalo Bill's Wild West with the usual stories about the parade, the performance, and with an occasional human interest piece such as the one below.

"Their leader, Prince Luka, distinguished from his band by a costume of snowy fur, rode with all the abandon of a madman, hanging to his fiery steed by the point of his small boot, as the mettlesome little beast tore around the arena at breakneck speed.

Then swinging into his lofty saddle he stood erect and swung his heavy, gleaming sword as easily as if it were a diminutive pen knife.

"After the show, Luka turned out to be a mild-mannered and charmingly pleasant gentleman, who spoke in softest tones of his 'papa,' and 'mamma,' his 'sweet little sister' and his 'happy home' in far away Russia as tenderly as one could imagine, and then flashed fire from his great dark eyes when questioned as to his opinion of other riders in the show, making answer: 'If Luka thought that any other men—cowboy, soldier or Indian—could ride so well as he, Luka would leave Buffalo Bill and go back to Russia.'"[104]

The character of Luka and his riders can only be assembled through these small tid-bits of information gleaned from the press. The afternoon of Friday, October 1, turned a little hotter than normal for St. Louis. There were two fires started under the reserve seating by a cigar stump and a careless smoker. These fires were put out quickly by the watchful ushers using the buckets of water which were always placed around the arena. The grounds under the seats were generously sprinkled for the evening show.

Buffalo Bill's Wild West left St. Louis on October 2, and jumped to Memphis, Tennessee, where they might be observed: "lying flat on their backs, stroking their beards, singing softly, perhaps of a sweetheart in far away Russia, with one or two smoking, puffing ring after ring of light blue smoke from their thin lips."[105] The final two weeks were spent traveling back east through Tennessee and Virginia. The season ended in Richmond, Virginia, on Saturday, October 16, after traveling 8,041 miles. Luka, Giorgi, Jimshet, Alexis, and the others were on the road for 189 days, stopping in 104 different cities, and giving 320 performances. Buffalo Bill paid out about $25,000 on the last final Saturday payday, which covered everyone in the outfit. Two special trains were loaded with the performers. One headed to New York City with the Europeans, and the other went out West.

Luka and his band of Georgians said goodbye to Alexis Gogokhia, who stayed the winter in New York City, and they left New York for England on Tuesday, October 19, on board the *SS Paris*.[106] Thursday morning, after nine days at sea, a large contingent of the passengers was on deck to catch the first sighting of land. They anticipated seeing the Needles and Hurst Castle. Luka and his troupe, who passed these shores many times, saw a huge cross on the Isle of Wight, High Down, which was a new monument built in memory of Alfred Lord Tennyson. The *SS Paris* arrived in Southampton later that day, October 28, and from there, Luka and his men returned to Georgia.

1897 EPILOGUE

Jimshet Lomadze presented the Church of Jacob the Apostle a charitable contribution for his safe return to Manati. Giorgi Chkhaidze stayed home for the next two years, and would return in 1900 to ride again with Alexis Gogokhia.

Markoz Jgenti, ca 1898-1899
Author's Collection
Plate No. 17

Data Kadjaia ca, 1899
Author's Collection
Plate No. 18

"How can a physician cure him who tells not what hurts or afflicts him?"

Shota Rustaveli

1898 PROLOGUE

Luka Chkhartishvili gathered a new group of riders for the 1898 season and they left home in late February, traveling from Odessa to New York. Death on the high seas and a funeral in Brooklyn tainted their journey. The Georgians again found themselves involved in arena accidents and terrible weather with thick mud. They also witnessed an ugly side of American life; their first red lighting incident. Red lighting was the name given to throwing people off a train while it steamed down the track, since the last thing the victim saw was the caboose's red lights.

The United States was at war with Spain. The government, needing funds to finance the war, taxed circuses one-hundred dollars and each side show thirty dollars. Buffalo Bill's Wild West continued to be profitable for James A. Bailey and his corporation.

MYSTERIOUS LETTER

An undated letter from Niko to Kato provides conflicting information for the voyage of the Georgian riders in 1898. Here is the famous mysterious letter.

My dear and always remembered Kato,

I am asking God peace and well being for you to be well with your children....had a very good trip. I was sick neither on the land nor on the sea. Only thing that bothered me as terrible cold, it was hard to struggle with snow and frost. One inch snow came in New York. To be away from you bothers me a lot... We arrived in New York on March 8. We had very fast trip. Kato, we have experienced one sad thing. Melitona Tsintsadze got sick in Odessa and our host did the best. He was surrounded by doctors and nurses. He was asked to stay there and after recover they would send him to us. He was completely against it. He asked not to leave him in the sea. We got in the ship. Doctors and Nurses were attending us. Nothing could be done as he passed away in the middle of the ocean. We took his body to New York with the hope to send it to Georgia later on, but we had to pay 2000 roubles for that and we decided to bury his body there. He had very exemplary and exceptional burial ceremony. Please go to Zurabi's, Data's families inform Lukaia Ebralidze and have wake on his name. Please do not get afraid. I am very well. I am sending thousand kisses to Ladiko and Tsitsino. Please give my heartly regards to mother and brother Serapion and Roskanai, as well as Iagot Chkonia with his family and everyone who asks about me. All the friends Zurabai, Datai and others are sending regards to you...Please Kato write about yourself as soon as you receive this letter. Please also let me know if someone died.

Always yours Niko.

BUFFALO BILL'S WILD WEST AND CONGRESS OF ROUGH RIDERS OF THE WORLD (1898)

Saturday, March 12, 1898, Liverpool, England (in transit)

Jule Keen, Cody's Treasurer, and Salsbury were in London during the winter, securing the European acts for the 1898 season. The Georgians were secured by Buffalo Bill after an outlay of much money. It cost $320 per man to get them from the Russian government and have them carried to London, not including their transportation to America."[107] Keen accompanied the German Cavalrymen, Irish Lancers, and the Georgians to Euston Station, London, for the trip to Liverpool. They arrived at the Lime Street station in Liverpool and were met by the Cunard Line horse-drawn buses to take them the 3/4 of a mile to the pier head. There they found the *SS Campania* moored at the world's largest floating landing stage, about a half mile long. To reach the ship, Jule and his company of riders crossed from the pier to the landing stage via a covered bridge.

Captain Henry Walker, familiar with the River Mersey's thirty-foot tidal shift, was eager to get underway Saturday. Firemen and stokers, eighty feet below decks, stood ready to feed one-hundred furnaces the twenty tons of coal an hour necessary to maintain their twenty-two-knots top speed. Porters and stewards were busy settling passengers into their cabins.

Alexander Tsintsadze, who first traveled to America in 1893 with Dimitri Mgaloblishvili in the Adam Forepaugh show, and was billed as *"the man known throughout Russia as the Courier to the Czar and the Demon Cavalier,"* was now forty years old. Alexander became sick in Odessa and his attending doctor advised him to stay behind. They would send for him after he recovered, but he was completely against it. He boarded the *Campania* with doctors and nurses attending. Alexander went straight to his second-class cabin and crawled into a bunk. Nestor squeezed among the other passengers along the starboard rail, waving and cheering at no one in particular. Luka, Alexi Tskvitishvili, Giorgi Chkhaidze, Luka Ebralidze, Jimshet Lomadze, Nestor, Konstantine Chkhartishvili, and Dimitri Tsintsadze, who had made the trip many times, were either in the saloon smoking, or starting a card game, or wandering the decks watching the hustle of leaving port. Alexander would normally lean on the port railing watching the sailing barges, cutter-rigged yachts or the paddle tugs that were just getting into position to help pull the *SS Campania* from the landing stage, but not today.

Those Georgians who remained on deck watched as the spires, domes, and towers of smoky, bustling Liverpool passed from view. Alexander, alone in his cabin, sweating and shaking with chills, coughed up thick rust-colored and greenish phlegm. The *SS Campania* steamed through the murky grey Mersey River. Nestor strolled the decks and leaned on the port railing, watching the Perch Rock Fort (a squat, rounded, sandstone fort), and the lighthouse at New Brighton marking the end of the Mersey River. The ship steamed into Liverpool Bay to cross the Irish Sea.

The *Campania* arrived in Queenstown, Ireland, early Sunday morning. The passage from Liverpool to Queenstown was rough for all the Georgians, because Alexander kept them awake most of the night. They tried rubbing his body with vinegar and vodka to reduce his fever; they discussed where they could get mustard leaves or honey to wrap around his sides. In the morning, Alexander was brought on deck for the fresh sea air. He felt more comfortable sitting in the deck chair shrouded in blankets while he surveyed the landscape and listened to the church bells toll the people to services. He observed the people moving about the pier in Queenstown, aware there would be nothing else to see for another five days. The *SS Campania* sailed out of Cork Harbor that same day. Alexander would not know the shores of Ireland would be his last sight of landfall.

Two days out at sea, Alexander's health took a serious turn for the worse. He could barely breathe, did not eat, and only had occasional cups of broth. He asked his companions not to bury him at sea. His comrades keeping a sick watch did not notice when he broke out in a heavy sweat with vice gripping chest pains, which shot into his jaw and down his left arm. To Alexander, the ship seemed to suddenly lurch violently to port.

The ship's surgeon, Edward M. Finucane, recorded in his medical log the death of a second-class cabin passenger from heart failure as a consequence of acute pneumonia. The records stated a forty-year old Russian named Alexander Tsintsadze from Ozurgeti died Tuesday afternoon, March 15, at Latitude 47.13 N, Longitude 36.27 W.[108]

The surgeon and medical staff prepared the body for burial at sea, as was the custom. Luka Chkhartishvili pleaded with the ship's officers and Jule Keen to allow his men to take the body on to New York. Jule at first agreed with the ship's officers. A burial at sea would accrue no costs, while taking Alexander to New York and then returning him to Georgia for burial was expensive (approximately 2000 rubles). Luka, using his limited English, tried to explain that his relatives back home would think they had murdered or abandoned Alexander. Luka tried to explain their custom for in-ground burials. He told them that next year they would bring some soil from his home to New York and place it in his grave, thus making the place the same as his homeland. Jule advised Luka that the Georgians would have to bear the costs for Alexander's burial in New York. Luka and his troupe hesitantly agreed, even though they had no idea what the costs might be.

The next day, Jule thought about the problems his Georgian riders would encounter and decided they should all help raise funds. Jule organized a small concert and wake as a fund-raiser for Alexander's family and burial expenses. Jule Keen's son played a violin solo, Jule performed a comedy skit that was heartily appreciated, and a Mademoiselle Titenia, a dancer, made an appearance. The little concert had good financial results.

Friday, March 18, New York City (arrival)

The arrival in New York at Pier forty, on the foot of Clarkson Street, was a somber occasion with the offloading of Alexander's body for interment. Sunday March 20, Alexander (Tzintzadze is the spelling of his last name) was buried at Green-Wood Cemetery, 500 25th St. Brooklyn,

New York in section 134, Lot 29725, grave site 340. On Tuesday, March 29, Buffalo Bill and his Wild West went on parade around New York City to launch their season. Wednesday they gave their opening performance in Madison Square Garden. The Thursday newspapers enlighten our understanding of who the Georgian riders either were or weren't. "The riding of the *Georgians* was not quite so interesting as usual last night, on account of two of the riders having been injured in the parade on Tuesday, and most of the others being new men in the show."[109] Reports said there were nine riders with Buffalo Bill in 1898.

■ ■ ■

Buffalo Bill's Wild West stayed in Madison Square Garden four weeks, living in the building built on the site of an abandoned railroad shed at 26th Street and Madison Avenue. *Harper's Weekly*[110] described a large, crowded room with cowboys, soldiers, and eight or ten Georgians partitioned off in a boxlike corner, where they passed most of the day singing their national hymns.

After four weeks, Buffalo Bill's Wild West moved across the East River Bridge to Brooklyn. They remained in Brooklyn for one week, and then took their first train jump to Philadelphia on Sunday, May 1, where the Georgians were observed: "*Georgians* busied themselves with looking after their horses and equipment, their favorite pastime."[111] An accident to a Georgian on Wednesday, May 4, marred their stay in Philadelphia. There were three similar newspaper accounts of this accident.[112] [113]

"One of the rough riders, in the display of *Georgian* horsemanship, found a horse that was too rough for him, last night at least, and he was put in a position very advantageous for biting the dust. Happily, his injuries were not serious; the spirited horse, rid of his rider, followed the evolutions of the troop on his own account."[114]

Buffalo Bill was invited to various dinners and speaking engagements. He often took the leaders of different groups of performers to these events. One such meeting occurred in Newark, New Jersey. Buffalo Bill and troupe leaders were the guests at a Mystic Shriners' dinner in the Continental Hotel. Luka and another Georgian were among the guests.[115] Luka would comport himself at such events as a Russian prince, to the delight of America's middle classes.

Luka found it harder to play the part of a Russian prince when knee deep in mud. Since leaving New York in April, Luka and his Georgians had fought rain and mud. Luka was fond of telling tales to his children when he got home for the winter. One such possible story was the wet weather woes the Wild West show encountered.

"The great wagons were thoroughly embalmed up to the body in the mud and it looked like an impossible task to free them. After six and eight horses had been hitched on and made an inglorious failure, after the number had been doubled and tripled without success, the show looked more deeply foundered than was at first sensed. The horses floundered and went down, their own weight burying them well nigh out of sight. In helping them out, the old process of holding a horse's head down was abandoned and his head was raised instead. All night the work went on in the rain, and word was finally taken to Col Cody that the show was anchored for twenty-four hours probably. The mud seemed to get more and more without bottom and in the midst of it all one of the biggest wagons went over on its side and landed in a position that offered a wonderful field for work. Every rope in the show was brought into use and every man among us, irrespective of nationality, lined up for the tug of war. After much labor, victory crowned the efforts and the vehicle was raised. At daybreak, no change was instituted in the proceedings, and one by one the heavy wagons were raised and drawn to the road. As many as thirty-four horses had to be used in some cases and then the work was accomplished only with great difficulty. The only clean place was the top of the rail cars, where representatives of a dozen different nations sat. The Indians strutted around in full war paint, more or less streaked with the rain and fire water, and punched the Cuban insurgents in the ribs. My comrades and I smoked cigarettes and chewed peanuts, while the young Arabs spent the day trying to hit the telegraph wires with stones."[116]

Luka was not the only one who liked to tell tales. Dexter Fellows, the press agent, had a favorite story line put out in many newspapers across America.

"The particular company of *Georgians* who are traveling with Col.

Cody belong to the most warlike branch of their curiously composite race—the Zaporogian tribe. They come from the Caucasus, a mountainous region where Russia has shed rivers of blood—Cossack blood—in the grim process of planting the Russian standard permanently in that country....

"In the ceaseless wars between Cossack and Circassian, a race of warriors has been produced who are a realization of the centaurs of mythology—in that they are all but born on horseback, live on horseback to great old age, and finally die on horseback....

"It is said, by the way, that the Russian government was only too glad to let Col. Cody have a company of its very finest body of troops. They are perhaps the best advertisement for the might of Holy Russia that the czar's press agent could possibly have devised, and the czar's advertising bureau is almost as good in its way as is that of Col. Cody and the Wild West show."[117]

These "Cossack" stories were based on the truth of the Czar's Don Cossacks; unfortunately, the American public never did learn the whole truth. Georgians in Buffalo Bill's Wild West were never a part of the czar's army, or any army. Luka and his comrades were just men trying to make a living.

Buffalo Bill reached Wheeling, West Virginia, on the fourth of July, which was a milestone each year. The chef marked the half-way point in the season with a special dinner, and there were fireworks after the performance. Near the Colonel's tent was the large pavilion used as a dressing room for the motley crowd of riders with the show. The dressing tent was one of the most cosmopolitan spots a person could get into. Georgians from the Caucasus sat cheek by jowl with Bedouin Arabs, though neither understood the other's jargon.[118] In the dressing tent, the little trunks carrying the performers' costumes were put down, side by side, so close together the riders, tumblers, and clowns could touch hands as they stood in front of them. A local boy, who got picked to work for the day, brought buckets of water to the tent for the performers. Their daily ablutions were fulfilled from this bucket; brushing of teeth, washing face and hands, sponge bathing the torso, arms and legs, and the final act of washing one's feet before dumping the water. Everyone in the show was looking forward to the day's performance since they could count on a full house. Even these grown men, who risked their lives in the arena day after day, were kids again when the fireworks displays were set off. The day seemed perfect to everyone, with one exception: "The only mishap was the upsetting of a *Georgian* rider, whose injuries, however, were not serious."[119] They jumped from Wheeling, West Virginia, back into Pennsylvania and then headed out west during July, ending in Chicago, July 24, for a one-week stay. Outside of New York City, Chicago was the friendliest place for the Georgian riders to relax. A Chicago newspaper reported some Georgians had become "citizens of the United States and promise to infuse democratic principles in their native land should they ever return." Regrettably, the Georgians were not identified. Chicago was like a second home to the Georgians and surely it saddened them to head north into Wisconsin on July 30.

They arrived in Charleston, West Virginia, on Saturday, October 15, where the season closed.

Luka and his comrades traveled over 10,253 miles. They were on the road for 200 days. They visited 133 different cities and towns and gave 347 performances. Buffalo Bill's organization provided their return transportation to New York and tickets for their trip home to Guria and another winter with families, just as they had in the previous years.

1898 EPILOGUE

A Georgian wrote on the back of a photograph "Cody, He is our Master." The Georgian riders were fond of Buffalo Bill and thought more highly of him than their master in Russia, The Czar.

Theodore Roosevelt was running for Governor of New York and using his Rough Rider San Juan Hill charge in his campaign. An editorial writer asked the question, "Does Theodore Roosevelt expect to carry this state on his merits as a Rough Rider? If so, why did the Republican Party not nominate a Russian Cossack as their candidate? I am sure a Cossack is much rougher in his riding than Theodore Roosevelt."[120] Thus the Georgian riders unwittingly got entangled in American politics.

At least one of the Georgians remained in New York, Alexis

Gogokhia. There is a report that a Russian Cossack brought to this country by Buffalo Bill entered a Walking Match held in New York on December 26.

JIMSHET LOMADZE BIOGRAPHICAL SKETCH

Jimshet Lomadze was born about 1867 in the village of Mamati just outside of Lanchkhuti. His parents passed away while he was a young man, and at age seventeen or eighteen he moved to Ozurgeti and lived at what today is 85 Merab Kostava Street. Jimshet had two wives and eight children. His riding speciality was moving around under the belly of his galloping horse. He was known to have made two trips to America. After his return from the Wild West show he was a shoemaker in Ozurgeti. He passed away in 1951. After his death, his family was sent to Kazakhstan. The known surviving relatives are Grigol Lomadze, a professor who lives in France; two grandchildren: Shotiko and Gela; and a daughter-in-law, Magnolia Cheishvili-Lomadze.[121]

OTHER SHOW BUSINESS

Edwin H. Low's steamship ticket agency and Low's Exchange, who for five years arranged the passage of Georgian riders between New York and Batumi, closed their London office in August, 1898. The Supreme Court of the State of New York on November 7 gave notice to all creditors having claims against Edwin H. Low, Low's Exchange, and the West Virginia corporation that the creditors were required to present their claims.[122]

Albert Edward Sheible was born in Baltimore, Maryland on November 1, 1856. He had been a member of Nate Salsbury's Troubadours. He became a business manager on the show and helped in the transportation of Georgians on several occasions. His permanent residence was Morton House, New York City. He died in 1898 and Nate Salsbury was the executor of his will.

"The vow of friendship and love should not be forgotten or broken."

Shota Rustaveli

1899 PROLOGUE

An unexplained change occurred among the Georgian riders over the winter of 1898 and spring of 1899. The Georgians who left their homes in late February 1899 were under the leadership of Data (David) Kadjaia, not Luka Chkhartishvili, who had led the Georgians from 1894 through 1898. Although David Kadjaia, an ethnic Mingrelian from the village Kulashi, had no previous experience in the Wild West shows, he suddenly became Chief of the Georgians.

David Kadjaia was not the only new rider to join with Luka and Dimitri Mgaloblishvili in 1899. Ivane and Bathlome (Toma) Baramidze, brothers born in Lanchkhuti, came from a wealthy farming family. Ivane Bathlome would eventually marry Luka's sister Zekha. Ermile and Mikheil Antadze, Vladimer Jakhutashvili and Miron Chkonia also joined with Luka and David.

SS Cephalonia, ca 1899
Left to right: David Kadjaia, Ermile Antadze, Unknown, Dimitri Mgaloblishvili, Bathlome Baramidze, Ivane Baramidze, Miron Chkonia. Unknown is either: Mikheil Antadze or Vladimer Jakhutashvili.
Author's Collection.
Plate No. 19

BUFFALO BILL'S WILD WEST AND CONGRESS OF
ROUGH RIDERS OF THE WORLD (1899)

David Kadjaia, a tall, slender man with mustache and goatee, cursed the boiling sea pounding the shores of Batumi. His mood was as bleak as the sky and sea. The Black Sea crashed upon the Batumi beaches and hissed in retreat, announcing the storm's ferocity delaying their departure for Constantinople.[123] This was not how he imagined the beginning of his first trip to America. David sensed this was a bad omen. He kept looking over the travel schedule, certain they would not make the connection with the *SS Campania* in Liverpool on Saturday, March 11, 1899.

David, Luka, Dimitri, and the others missed their sailing date and did not arrive in Liverpool until Tuesday, March 14. They were met by Morris Kern, a representative of Buffalo Bill, who waited for them; they boarded the *SS Cephalonia*, bound for Boston. David felt relieved to be onboard and only three days behind the *Campania*. David thought the three-day delay could be made up in New York by working harder during the rehearsals. Luka and Dimitri, who had traveled these waters since 1893, roamed about the *Cephalonia's* decks, observing she had only a single-screw, three masts, and one funnel. She was an iron-hulled ship, which took twelve days rather than the *Campania's* seven days. Luka knew they would not have much time for rehearsals in New York.

The *Cephalonia* anchored off Boston Light at eleven o'clock Friday night, ten days out of Liverpool. She came to her berth at the Cunard Line wharf in East Boston at seven o'clock Saturday morning, March 25. Captain H.W. Pierce informed the harbor master there was favorable weather during the crossing except for the last few days when they ran into snow squalls and rain.[124]

By clearing Customs and dashing into Boston to catch the first train to New York, David Kadjaia and his troupe of riders entered America. None of this was how David envisioned his arrival. David's original schedule gave them ten days for training the horses and learning the routine, but they now had no more than three days. Their arrival in New York coincided with the entire company moving to Madison Square Garden on Sunday, March 26. The next two days were dress rehearsals and final preparations for the kickoff parade set for Tuesday. It seemed the Georgians received their first break; the parade was postponed until Wednesday due to heavy rain and wind.

David and his comrades gained one extra day of rehearsals.

James Bailey, who owned Madison Square Garden, allowed only his tent shows to open there (Buffalo Bill's Wild West, Adam Forepaugh & Sells circus, and Barnum and Bailey's Greatest Show on Earth). On Wednesday, March 29, Buffalo Bill cherished his turn to open at Madison Square Garden. The day began with the parade in a disagreeable, cold, half-gale wind, along Fourth and Fifth Avenue between Fifty-Eighth Street and Astor Place. The evening performance was to a packed house with Major General Miles as the guest of honor. The spectacular feature this year was a re-creation of the San Juan Hill charge.

The press notices concerning the Georgians during the season were very limited, because much of the press covered the Rough Riders' San Juan Hill charge in Cuba. A few bits of information about the Georgian riders were recorded.

> "The *Georgians* are not a heterogeneous lot of bewhiskered horsemen gotten together indiscriminately, but learned to ride in their peculiarly daring fashion in the South of Russia, their native land. Their names on the salary roll give unmistakable evidence of their foreign origin. One is Dimitri Mgaloblishvili, another Luka Chkhartishvili. Their chief does not even attempt to pronounce these names. He designates each of his troupe by a number."[125]

David, Luka and the other Georgians enjoyed the next two weeks living at Madison Square Garden. They gave two performances a day, 2:00 p.m., and 8:00 p.m., with plenty of time to wander the streets of New York City. David and the other new riders learned their first traveling tent show lessons on Saturday evening, April 15, when the show packed up and jumped to Baltimore, Maryland.

The citizens of Baltimore and the new Georgian riders gawked while Buffalo Bill's roustabouts raised their tent city on Sunday, April 16. Guests and press were given facility tours while along York Road, onlookers climbed trees for glimpses of the American Indians, Cubans, Germans, and Russians. By show time on Monday, the trees across from the arena were filled with spectators. David Kadjaia may have witnessed a peculiar American prejudice while observing a group of colored youth and men perched in trees to see the show. White boys took to throwing stones at the colored men, who scampered from their trees and threw bricks back at the youths. Pistols were fired and police arrested a half-dozen colored youth and two colored women, while the white youths were allowed to escape.[126] The Georgian riders were reminded of ethnic Russians being excused for personal attacks on Gurians and other ethnic Georgians.

David and his troupe traveled to Washington, DC, down through Virginia, and by the end of April arrived in Chattanooga, which sits astride the Tennessee River with Lookout Mountain guarding the river's great curve and large railroad yard. It was the scene of a renowned Civil War battle. Unknown to David Kadjaia, he was not the first Georgian to see this part of America. He would have not known that a Georgian, Alexander Eristavi, had been attached to Colonel J.B. Turchaninov's 19th Illinois Infantry, a Russian Chicago company of Union soldiers who fought at the battle of Chickamauga in September, 1863.

Chattanooga was the farthest south Buffalo Bill's exhibition traveled. By May, David and the other new Georgian riders knew their entrance cues. They dashed on after Johnny Baker's shooting, which followed the Arab horsemen. David assembled his men for entrance once the Arabs left the staging area behind the curtain. While waiting for their entrance cue on Monday, May 8, in Cumminsville, Ohio, just outside of Cincinnati, they heard a thunderous crack of splitting wood—the creaking of a building's wooden frame collapsing—combined with screams of men, women, and children. Two enterprising Negroes with an eye toward a profit took possession of the roof of a large vacant building with a view of the Wild West, and sold seating for a nickel. At 8:50 p.m., without the slightest warning, forty feet of the roof imploded with a crash and sixty people instantly were hurled about thirty feet below.[127] The show went on without missing a beat while police and show roustabouts assisted the victims. There were no deaths, only sprained ankles, cuts, bruises, and back injuries.

A fierce storm enveloped the show in Tyrone, Pennsylvania, forcing Cody to cancel the evening performance. The daily routine of overnight jumps, parades, and two shows a day was again interrupted in Reading on Friday, May 26, when a rail car with canvas and wagons onboard caught fire. They arrived in Philadelphia two days later for a one-week engagement. Dimitri Mgaloblishvili, who in 1893 and 1894 spent time in Philadelphia, was the unofficial guide for the other Georgians.

Without a daily parade or nightly jumps to the next lot, the entire outfit relaxed during the week. On Sunday, June 5, Buffalo Bill's Wild West headed north again into New York, Connecticut, and then Boston for another six-day stand. They had to enjoy their stint in Boston since they would not get another break until Chicago in late August.

The Bill Show arrived at 5:00 a.m. Friday, July 21, in Buffalo, New York, via the New York Central railroad. Major Burke and Dexter Fellows, the press agent, talked with David Kadjaia in their press car after arriving in Buffalo, the home of The Courier Lithograph Company. They arranged for this company to take a series of photographs of David Kadjaia and his troupe of Georgians. These photographs were taken before the afternoon performance on Friday.[16] Another memorable event in Buffalo was the wind, rain, and mud during the Friday afternoon performance.

The Bill show's performers looked forward to a week's stand in Chicago during the latter part of August. Along the way to Chicago, David Kadjaia witnessed the daily hazards where rough riders were thrown by their horses, trampled, and taken from the arena. The men and women who worked for Buffalo Bill were a tough bunch—like Edward Sullivan, a porter, who became a victim of a distressing accident on Friday, July 29, in Beaver Falls, Pennsylvania. Ed had just received a five-gallon can of gasoline for a stove in sleeping car No. 56 when the gasoline suddenly exploded. Ed and a canvas man who was sleeping in the car were enveloped in flames. They were hospitalized. The destroyed car had a value of three-thousand-dollars, and the men who lived there lost their possessions.[128] The Director of Public Works in Cleveland, Ohio, who was in the middle of a transportation strike, reportedly said about Buffalo Bill's men: "Those fellows look like fighters. I think they would have a good effect on strikers."

David and his Georgian riders experienced a few more adventures during the heat of August. They visited the State Prison at Jackson, Michigan. In Detroit, Michigan, the performers dealt with a muddy arena causing some horses to slip, and one woman rider was badly hurt; "accidents like these are bound to happen, we get 'em almost daily," as quoted in the *Detroit Free Press*. Another reporter observed some young

---

[16] The photographs are now housed in the Denver Public Library, Colorado, and can be viewed on the Internet [http://gowest.coalliance.org], search under Buffalo Bill or Russian Cossacks.

girls watching a Georgian cleaning himself: "A handsome *Georgian* stopped as he wrung the water from his close cropped pointed beard and waved a graceful salute, his gleaming teeth showing through his fascinating smile. The girls giggled, turned their heads, then looked back again and, hesitating a second, wiggled their flirtatious fingers. The gallant *Georgian* bowed low."[129] Luka and Dimitri felt like they were returning to their home away from home when they arrived in Chicago. September's payday was held in Austin, Minnesota, on Sunday, September 25. The weather turned cold and many show people, including the Georgian riders, hastened to buy warm clothing. The saloons took in all kinds of money, and the *Austin Weekly Herald* reported the "*Georgians* and Armenians were pledging each other with beer."

The first week of October found the Bill Show in St. Louis, Missouri, for a one-week stand. After St. Louis, there remained only one more week of one-day stands before the season ended. Their last performance was in Urbana, Ohio, on Saturday, October 14. Buffalo Bill, the Georgians, and the other Europeans boarded a special train and headed for New York City. During the season, Buffalo Bill told the press he planned to take the show to Paris in 1900. But James Bailey had other ideas, and Cody had to announce in New York that their show would remain in the United States during the next season. In New York, Edwin H. Low, the shipping agent who handled Buffalo Bill's overseas arrangements, was finishing the ticketing for the Georgians, Irish Lancers, and the German Cavalrymen. They left New York on Wednesday, October 18, at 10:00 a.m. onboard the American Line *SS St. Paul*, which docked in Southampton on October 25. A representative of Mr. Low's met them in Southampton and gave them their final payments, tickets, and instructions.[130]

1899 EPILOGUE

David Kadjaia and his band of riders traveled more than 11,111 miles (17,877 km) in America. The tenting season lasted 200 days with stops in 132 American cities or towns. They gave 341 performances and lost only seven performances, which meant they lost seven days' pay.

On May 29, 1899, a student who one day would rule the Soviet Union, was expelled from the Tbilisi Seminary. He would set a policy: "Anyone who has been to the United States is an enemy of the State." The student Isoeb (Soso) Dzhugashvili (Joseph Stalin), along with his childhood friend and his roommate Dorimendon Gogokhia, left Tbilisi and traveled the 53 miles (86 km) to Gori, where Stalin stayed at the home of Dorimendon's uncle, Besarion Gogokhia. Alexis Gogokhia, Dorimendon's older brother, left Georgia in 1896, and during the 1897 to 1899 seasons, rode with Luka Chkhartishvili, David Kadjaia, and the other Georgians in Buffalo Bill's Wild West.

CHAPTER THREE
REVOLUTION AT HOME: 1900 TO 1905

People around the world celebrated as the nineteenth century came to a close and the twentieth century brought a promise of new times and hope for an end to a worldwide economic depression. The Georgian nationalist, socialist, and communist movements lost their innocence and became militant opponents of the czar's Russification program in Georgia.

In 1900, Buffalo Bill's monopoly on Georgian riders came to a halt. Georgians were "on the show" with various outfits during the next five years.

The Georgian riders prospered in 1900, while the burdens of Georgia's economic hardship were borne by the industrial and agricultural peasantry. In Guria, the revolutionary movement was particularly strong, where the peasants' meager land allotments gave rise to an often quoted saying: "If I tie up a cow on my bit of land, her tail will be in someone else's!" The peasants, who were the main agricultural producers, paid high rents to noblemen, gentry, or clergy, for the privilege of raising crops to pay their rents. Those who could not pay were subject to repression by the czar's "punitive expedition," which consisted of Russian Cossack troops. The accommodations, food, and luggage bearers for these troops were forcibly conscripted from the local peasantry. To feed themselves and their families, eighty percent of the peasantry was forced to look for permanent or seasonal jobs in the towns. This search for work took some as far as the United States and the American tent show business. The cycle of taxation and repression spurred the Gurians to moral outrage and open revolution by 1905.

"Evil is vanquished by good for the essence of good is enduring."

Shota Rustaveli

1900 PROLOGUE

In 1900, one-hundred forty-four tent shows took to the road. The Georgians were in only two of them: Buffalo Bill's and Pawnee Bill's Wild West. Luka spent January and February training several new men who would accompany him to Buffalo Bill's Wild West. Luka's riders left their homes around March 23, 1900, arriving in England by April 6.

Alexis Gogokhia went home to Georgia under an assumed name, visited his family and returned to New York. Alexis upon returning changed his last name to Georgian.

Meanwhile, Buffalo and Pawnee Bill's staffs were working on their equipment repairs, programs, and routing for the season.

Russian officials in Odessa boasted that a new oil pipeline being completed between Michaeloff and Batumi would improve the economy of Guria. The pipeline was more than one hundred miles long and eight inches in diameter. The peasants of Guria, like the farmers of America, would not see the benefits of this industrial activity for many years to come. The industrial activities in Batumi became a magnet for starving farmers. As Gurians came to America to earn a living, other family members left the countryside to work in the industrial plants, this further increased the labor of the remaining family members trying to maintain the family home.

BUFFALO BILL'S WILD WEST AND CONGRESS OF ROUGH RIDERS OF THE WORLD (1900)

The steamship *Campania* rolled and pitched with the Mersey River's tidal currents alongside Prince's landing stage in Liverpool, England, on Saturday afternoon, April 7. The special train left London at noon. It arrived at the Lime Street station, and the peaceful morning was shattered by the people and noise the locals had come to expect just before the 4:30 p.m. sailing. Luka's troupe of twelve riders and the British soldiers who would perform in Buffalo Bill's Wild West embarked aboard the Cunard liner *SS Campania*, escorted by Jule Keen. The passage was rough for a great part of the way, encountering head seas and variable gales. Two large icebergs were sighted en route on April 12 at 2:37 in the morning. The *SS Campania's* 264 cabin passengers disembarked onto the pier while the 816 steerage passengers were shuffled into barges for the trip to Ellis Island, Saturday afternoon April 14.[131]

The Georgians: Luka, Dimitri Mgaloblishvili, Vladimer Jakhutashvili, Ivane and Bathlome Baramidze, Konstantine Kvitashvili, Zurabi Pataraia, Markoz Jgenti, and Nikoloz Antadze, spent the week after their arrival at Ambrose Park, Brooklyn, in rehearsals and retraining of their horses. The Georgians and other riding performers rode their horses across the Brooklyn Bridge and down the streets of New York to Madison Square Garden on Sunday morning, April 22, before most people awoke. The remainder of Sunday was spent settling in, with workmen setting up the scenery, and the Georgians and cowboys riding their horses to test the tanbark[17] surface. The show opened Monday, April 23, with the usual 9:00 a.m. parade along Madison Avenue to Twenty-Fourth Street, across to Lexington Avenue, up Fifty-Eighth Street, across to Fifth Avenue, and then back to Waverley Place, to Astor Place, to Fourth Avenue and back to the Garden.

It was often remarked that the Wild West exhibition differed from the circus by the fact, among others, that performers in a circus do tricks learned for the special purpose of exhibition only. Those in the Wild West performed feats that were learned as a trade or craft for an actual purpose outside the show. The distinction was worth noting, especially when dealing with local politicians and taxes. Newspapers often questioned what the Georgian warrior thought he gained by standing on his head in the saddle. The management replied with suggestions that it was a form of psychological warfare; however, every Georgian knew the real reason was to impress the girls back home during riding games.

The season's first jump was Saturday, May 5, after the evening performance. By midnight, the streets of New York were strewn with the paraphernalia of Buffalo Bill's Wild West traveling back across the East River to their Brooklyn encampment on a lot between Ridgewood and Putnam Avenue.

Reporters swooped into the lot on Sunday, May 6, and were escorted about by the press agent, Dexter Fellows. A *Brooklyn Daily Eagle* reporter wrote:

---

17 Tanbark - A tree bark rich in tannin cut in small pieces and used for tanning and then re-used to cover a tent show floor.

"Just outside the arena Mr. Fellows hailed three of the *Georgian* riders who were approaching, and the men came up smiling and bowing. Mr. Fellows produced a clipping from a newspaper and handed it to one of the men, who is known as Prince Luka, and is a sort of chieftain among his people.

"'See,' said Mr. Fellows, pointing to one of the pictures, 'Lucca, Prince Luka, good.' A seraphic smile lighted up the bronze face, and the prince exclaimed: 'Oh! Ah! Luka, me, Prince Luka.'

"His companions were less interested and the three jabbered enthusiastically about the pictures. Prince Luka is the Cossack who does the wonderful riding standing upright in the stirrups and juggling a big sword as his horse goes on a dead run about the arena."

After eight years with Buffalo Bill, the Georgian riders still had top billing. Status in the exhibition could be measured by train section assignment, the last section being the most preferred. The first section would normally arrive between 4:00 a.m. and 5:00 a.m. with the last section arriving one or two hours later. "In the last section were the thoroughbred race horses, the Germans, and the *Georgians*, known as the 'Life of the Czar,' each of which is an 'honor man.'"[132]

The exhibition was in Ypsilanti, Michigan, on Saturday, July 28, and at midnight they left for Pontiac, traveling over the Michigan Central railroad in a two-section train. Sunday about 3:25 a.m. the night air in the Detroit switching yards was interrupted by the blasts of whistles, screeching train brakes, and the crunch of a yard freight pushing the caboose of Buffalo Bill's first section train into and over its last sleeper, car #56. Seventy-eight canvas men were in the bunks crushed by the caboose. The men were pinned under the debris of three tiers of bunks; shards of glass sliced open blood vessels, splinters of wood pierced their bodies, and beams pressed the very life out of their chests. Without waiting to dress, their fellow workers in the other cars scrambled all over the wreckage to extract their companions. Edward Sullivan, the sleeper's porter, was the only death, while ten others were sent to the hospital. The uninjured found bunk space on the flat cars and continued to Pontiac.[133] Nikoloz Antadze, Markoz, and Konstantine—new riders with Luka— witnessed a hard lesson about the dangers of rail travel.

The canvas crew thought their August 12 arrival in Minneapolis would be the same as on other Sundays; it did not turn out that way. They were busy putting up the arena on a Sunday morning. The Reverend William Wilkinson of the Calvary Baptist Church arranged to preach to an audience of about 15,000 in the Wild West arena, and among those in attendance were the Georgian riders.[134] Dexter Fellows conducted his usual lot tour with reporters after the religious service, and in the tower of Babel, as the dressing tent was dubbed, they found Luka Chkhartishvili. The *Minneapolis Tribune* reporter recorded this conversation with Luka:

> "The *Georgians* are some peculiar people. Dressed in their peculiar garb they present an unusual appearance. However, they are all expert horsemen. They hail from the Caucasian mountains, from the town of Batumi, three days' travel from Odessa, Russia. Their tongue is Georgian, although several of them are conversant with the Russian and Turkish languages. The only one who speaks English is their leader, Prince Luka Chkhartishvili. With a pleasant smile and many gestures, he received a party of visitors, headed by Dexter Fellows, the press agent, yesterday. Asked what he would do the coming winter when he returned home, he said with many gesticulations:
>
> "'Plenty friends, plenty wine, good time.'
>
> "Prince Chkhartishvili had just received a letter from his wife at Batumi in which she explained the Chinese imbroglio. She had told him that if he returned home he might be pressed into the service. However, Luka had no fears for the army. He seemed to delight in the thought of fighting the Chinese.
>
> "'Nobody no like Chinese,' he said. 'Russian have good time shoot Chinese. In letter 100 Chinese kill four or five Russians. I like fight. I no care die.'
>
> "'How do you like America, prince?' he was asked.
>
> "'America like everybody, and I like too,' and this seemed to be the general opinion of the *Georgians* regarding the land of the free."[135]

Luka Chkhartishvili was interviewed again in Louisiana, Missouri, and they wrote:

"'America is good country,' he said yesterday. 'Too much money in America, I like it. But not good for me. I got father, mother, wife, and children, all in Russia. I go to see them in winter and take money, I not die here, unless broken neck.'

"He recently had a narrow escape from death when a horse which he was riding fell and broke its neck. He has two brothers now in the Russian army in China, and he himself saw service in the Russo-Turkish war twelve years ago, when the Turks captured his native town."[136]

The Sunday following their stay in Minneapolis, they were in Prairie du Chien, Wisconsin, a tough river town with thirty saloons. Prairie du Chien, like many towns in anticipation of Buffalo Bill's coming, closed the saloons Sunday and appointed extra special police. The citizens came out to watch the exhibition set up Sunday and all was quiet and orderly. The business community convinced the authorities to open the saloons on Monday, and the afternoon performance ran true to form. Business was booming in town from all the visitors and show people. Around 7:00 p.m. the towers of Prairie du Chien found themselves part of a different type of Wild West rendition. Members of the Tenth U.S. (Colored) Cavalry, German Cuirassiers, and other foreign nationals (which probably included Georgians) went into town after the 2:00 p.m. performance to find a drink and relax before the 8:00 p.m. show. Stabin's saloon was the chosen watering hole. A dispute broke out between the proprietor and the colored cavalry, who insisted that Stabin was not taking in all the business offered to him. In the parlance of the day, "coloreds aren't served in my saloon." Stabin displayed a revolver to enforce his rules, but he was disarmed by the show crowd. Thomas Vavra, a cigar manufacturer and one of the extra police officers, responded to a request for help. The showmen insisted that Stabin be arrested, but an altercation ensued and Vavra fired one shot into the crowd, wounding Charles Triangle, an artillery man. Vavra beat a hasty retreat down Bluff Street. The "Hey, Rube!"[18] call went out and now seventy or eighty showmen were in the fray. Thomas Varva continued his flight but was caught near the entrance to Artesian Park Alley. He turned on his

---

[18] Hey, Rube! The rallying cry of tent shows, the call to arms in the event of a fight.

assailants and fired. A showman fell face down at the Alley crossing. Vavra ducked into Kalina & Quilligan's bar and slipped out the rear door. The mob thought he took refuge in Mrs. O'dea's saloon at the corner of Bluff and Church streets. Mrs. O'dea had closed, but the mob smashed its way inside and wrecked the interior. The city marshall, Mr. Lindner, confronted the showmen but was stoned, disarmed, and beaten senseless. The mayor, Mr. Patzlaff, requested militia support from the capital, Madison, and then sought help from Colonel Cody, who rode into town on his big bay horse. He blew his whistle constantly, rounding up his showmen. Twenty minutes later it was all over; the mayor called off the militia, and Buffalo Bill pulled stakes and left town without giving an evening performance. Buffalo Bill's Wild West never again tried to play in Prairie Du Chien, Wisconsin.

As the weather grew colder in October, Buffalo Bill's exhibition headed south. The exhibition entered Texas on October 9, at Gainesville, their first excursion into this state. Houston was the scene of their last train incident of the season on October 22. Arriving from San Antonio, the first section engine derailed, taking many of the fifty-one cars along with it. No property or personnel were hurt and the show went on as usual. The Season closed in Memphis, Tennessee, on Saturday, November 3.

"Home! Sweet Home!" was played as the final act was brought to a close. During the season, they gave 335 performances in 135 different cities and traveled over 11,640 miles. The foreign contingent—Georgians, Arabs, Germans, and Englishmen—left for New York on the midnight special train.

With their tenting season adventures behind them, they were all going home. The Buffalo Bill foreign riders left New York onboard the SS *Friesland*, bound for Antwerp via Southampton on Wednesday, November 7. The *Friesland* encountered heavy seas during the voyage. By a day or two out of port the men had their sea legs and were accustomed to the ship's roll and pitch. The days passed uneventfully until the afternoon of November 15, about 210 miles west of Bishop Rock, Isles of Scilly, when the *Friesland* encountered heavy seas and the passengers and crew were thrown violently into bulkheads, hatches, and onto the decks. The prepared meals were flung across the galley. Plates, saucers, and cups shattered into thousands of splinters. The ship was floundering in the trough of the sea because of a broken rudder stock. The *Friesland*, with only a single screw, was helpless. To stabilize his ship, Captain Nickels deployed a sea anchor made of spars and canvas, which kept the *Friesland's* bow into the wind and sea. During the next twenty-four hours, the passengers and crew wondered if they would survive to reach port. The steamer *Cluden* found them and took her in tow. The *Cluden* towed the *Friesland* to a few miles off the Needles, where she was taken in tow by two Southampton tugs. The passengers thanked the *Cluden* with a loud cheer as she steamed off. The Red Star line steamer *Friesland* arrived in Southampton November 21. The passengers were forwarded to Antwerp by a steamer of the Great Eastern Company from Harwich.[137] The Georgians traveled back to Constantinople and thence over the Black Sea to their homes in Georgia, with one more tall-tale to tell during the winter nights.

PAWNEE BILL'S HISTORIC WILD WEST (1900)

Gordon William Lillie (1860-1942), was born in Bloomington, Illinois, on February 14, 1860, and grew-up in the 500 block of West Moulton Street.[138] Gordon W. Lillie was better known in the tent show business, between April and October, as Pawnee Bill.

Lillie became a distinguished private citizen of Pawnee, Oklahoma. He was president of the Arkansas Valley National Bank, Chairman of the Board of Trade, and a member of the local school board. Lillie contracted for Georgian riders in 1900 and always had a contingent with his shows until he went out of the business.

■ ■ ■

The Pawnee Bill Historic Wild West 1900 season opened on a sunny Saturday, May 5, in Chester, Pennsylvania, the show's winter quarters. Chester was a quiet town on the Delaware River south of Philadelphia and witnessed the arrival of many foreigners, including a band of Georgians. Alexis Gogokhia, Giorgi Chkhaidze, Nestor Khukhunaishvili, Teophane Kavtaradze, and Irakli Tsintsadze came from New York City, where they lived at 234 East Broadway during the off season. Alexis Georgian was billed as the chief of the Cossacks. He also managed an Arab acrobatic troupe led by Salam Hadj Ali.

Alexis' troupe of Georgians were all Buffalo Bill's Wild West veterans, and were accustomed to the usual first week incidents. Pawnee Bill's Wild West was no exception. On the jump from Chester to Phoenixville they experienced their first trouble. "Some good Christian folk of Phoenixville tried to stop the unloading of the train, saying that it was unlawful to work on Sunday in Pennsylvania, and tried to compel them to remain cooped up until Monday."[139] Pawnee Bill's lawyer reminded the objectors that the State ruled it cruelty to animals to keep them confined, and that it should apply to people also. The unloading went on, but to the Christians' delight, the cook wagon slid off the run, toppled over, and two of the heavy ranges were smashed.

The first accident in the arena happened during the ladies race on May 7. The next day, the high diver broke a rib by striking the net wrong. Two days later, "Old Eagle," a bronco, broke his leg and was put down, and then a gasoline stove in the privilege car[19] exploded and was destroyed. During the last performance of the week, a bucking horse charged directly into the center of a densely packed crowd, causing a great scattering and screaming, but no damage. The first week ended Saturday night with a jump to Elizabeth, New Jersey, and Sunday was the show's first payday.

Payday on Sunday normally kept trouble to a minimum since most stores and saloons were closed. However, the Italian saloons adjacent to the show grounds opened and the season's first "Hey Rube" occurred, as reported in *The Philadelphia Inquirer*:

> "Pawnee Bill's Wild West show arrived here yesterday morning and the day being payday the Indians, cowboys, Arabs and Turks began to get gay in some of the Italian saloons adjacent to the show ground. One of the cowboys became entangled in a dispute at Vinzenso Minnetti's saloon on John Street over payment for a pint of whiskey. He went to the camp and came back with a score of Indians, Turks, and Arabs who forced their way into the saloon with axes and crowbars, and smashed the windows, doors, bottles, mirrors and furniture.
>
> "An Italian who attempted to interfere was taken to the General Hospital with his head badly cut with a brick. The police made a charge

---

[19] Privilege car - A club or dining car on a tent show train with food, drink, and recreation facilities.

and the show men beat a hasty retreat. No arrests were made."[140]

Alexis and his men were often identified as Turks in the press. It cannot be ascertained which Georgians or Arabs were involved in this fracas, but it is known that they were men who enjoyed their wine and liquor. There was another fight the same day at Nicola Capola's saloon, earlier in the morning.[141]

The third week of May brought rainy weather, and by week's end, the lots were the season's worst, with mud up to the wagons' hubs. It dried out for the last two weeks of May as Pawnee Bill's show traversed New Jersey and Pennsylvania.

Alexis and his troupe were familiar with the boom towns of Pennsylvania that they visited during June. Tent show life went on—a rain storm now and then, someone fell off a horse here and there or a fight between show employees resulting in a stabbing.

The famous "Duquesne Turkish Baths" in McKeesport, Pennsylvania, were visited by the Georgian riders on Saturday night, June 23.

President McKinley was at his home in Canton, Ohio, as the Pawnee Bill Wild West passed through on its way to Michigan. Pawnee Bill, Oscar Krause, Lloyd Nicodemus, Stanley Lewis and the four principal chiefs, including Alexis Georgian, called on the President and were warmly received with handshakes on Sunday, July 8.

Alexis' home on the road was car 115, where his "yellow-coated *Georgians* came yawning out of their sleepers, vaulted into their saddles and cantered away to the show grounds."[142] This was the daily pace of early rising and late departures. The routine was slightly altered when the show conducted three performances on July 4, starting at 9:30 a.m., which was very unusual.

The show operated under the concept of business as usual except when the occasional thunderstorm blew down tents. People and equipment became stuck in mud. A deputy sheriff from Owosso, Michigan, followed Pawnee Bill's show into Lansing to arrest a ticket taker for short changing.[143] Short changing is the art of convincing a local towner that he only passed a one dollar bill when it was five dollars. Another sheriff in Mount Clems, Michigan, raided the train before it left and retrieved horse blankets and lap robes stolen from farmers' rigs during the day.[144]

July ended with an attempt by a gang of youths trying to cut tent guy ropes, and an ensuing confrontation with the showmen in Clare, Michigan. A young man named McDonald from Vernon was spotted by some cowboys, who lassoed him and gave him a severe beating and dragged him some distance. The city marshall arrested two of the managers, under the mayor's orders, and placed them in Duncan's saloon. The showmen rallied to the saloon and demanded the release of Lewis and Wilson, and when refused, made a raid on the place, throwing bricks.[145] Pawnee Bill retrieved his cowboys and hurried his show out of town. Lewis and Wilson were released the next morning when no one made a complaint against them.

Payday was Sunday, August 5, in Holland, Michigan, and Monday the local postmaster recorded the largest money-order business in its history. August's torridness was palpable, and to beat the heat many Americans spent August along the beaches of Lake Michigan. Pawnee Bill capitalized on this vacation business by finishing the last two weeks of August in Michigan along the lake's east coastline. The transportation master, Al Miller, absconded with $125 in Frankfort, Indiana. The second payday of August was in Peoria, Illinois, on August 19, after the canvas was raised for the Monday show. Peoria did not close its saloons on Sunday; therefore, many showmen spent the afternoon drinking and several fights broke out. The local newspaper item said a Cheyenne Indian was murdered but later discovered he was alive and in the hospital. Pawnee Bill's showmen also needed a diversion from the August heat. For self-amusement they held the first of two sessions of "Kangaroo Court" in Winterset, Iowa.

The second "Kangaroo Court"[20] session was held on September 6 in Audubon, Iowa, with the honorable Thomas Barry, Judge, and Erle Fuller as Clerk of Court.

KANGAROO COURT SESSIONS

Case 1: Prisoner, Willie Ridgeway, of Wyoming. Occupation, sheep herder. Charges (1) not properly saddling his horse. (2) Drawing weapons on law; complainant, the police. Pleads guilty, Sentence, 15 raps: Sentence served.

Case 2: The Butcher of Germany. Charges, general principles, Pleads guilty. Fined 25 cents. Fine Paid.

---

[20] Kangaroo Court - A mock court in which the principles of law and justice are disregarded or perverted.

Case 3: Assistant headwaiter. Discharged; no charges.

Case 4: Boss property-man of Indiana. Charges, wearing other people's clothing and being late in putting up dressing tent. Complainant, C. Humberstone. Placed on $1,000 bonds to appear at 4:30 p.m.

Case 5: Cossack Nestor, of Russia. Charge, eating 20 eggs for breakfast. Complainant, Chief Cossack. Found guilty. Sentenced, 10 slaps. Served.

Case 6: Manger Midway, Chicago. Charge, not eating breakfast. Fine, 10 slaps, Sentence served.

Case 7: "Rube," late of Buckskin Bill show. Fighting. Fine 5 slaps.

Case 8: Cossack Lackery [Irakli]. Charges (1) shaving head and eating 13 eggs. Found guilty. Sentence 10 slaps. Served.

Case 9: Chief Cossack [Alexis]. Eating 12 eggs. Fine 25 cents. Gave orders for Sunday.

Case 10: H. Stanley Lewis. Charge. Not bringing goods ordered by court and getting paint on trunks and bringing stale clothing. Complainant, Tony. Witness Rube. Pleads Guilty. Fine 50 cents. Paid.

Case 11: Rube (Jas. Martin). Charge, taking other people's property without permission. Complainant Chief Cossack, Alex Georgian. Pleads not guilty. Court finds verdict and fines 10 slaps. Paid.

Case 12: Judge Barry. Charges, child's frock found in his trunk. Prisoner discharged. Frock belongs to a boy.

Court closed for season. All cases carried over for next term.

The remainder of September was spent crisscrossing Iowa in opposition with Buffalo Bill's Wild West. Both outfits were trying to capture the farmers' harvest dollars. Many farmers brought in hogs to offer at market to defray the cost of pleasure, and the local banks ran low on coins as towners changed bills into correct change, to avoid the short change artists who worked the box office. In Waterloo, Iowa, a thief broke into one of the cars and snatched a saddle and bridle worth forty dollars, proving that not all the crooks were attached to the shows.[146]

The tail end of a tornado called "Texas Hurricane," struck on the morning of September 11 in Marshalltown, Iowa, shredding the horse tent and spectator covered canvas. Incessant rain in Hampton, Iowa, on September 18 was the cause for the season's first show loss. The next day the cookhouse wagon was stuck in the mud and they raised the dining tent halfway between the train and the lot. Each day brought some unique problem to overcome. The season was drawing to a close and paydays were now counted. The men needed to save money to hold them over until their next job, so the drinking and fighting began to decline.

The town of Lamar was expecting trouble on Sunday after Pawnee Bill paid his men on the first of October. However, there was only a fake gun fight, using blank cartridges. The final announcement for each show came from Pawnee Bill: "This, ladies and gentlemen, concludes our entertainment. We thank you for your kind attention."

Gordon Lillie closed the season in Blackwell, Oklahoma, on Saturday, October 27, and shipped the outfit to its new winter quarters in Litchfield, Illinois, about fifty-four miles north of St. Louis, Missouri. Alexis and his troupe returned to New York City.

1900 EPILOGUE

Alexis Georgian, Nestor, Dimitri Tsintsadze, and Giorgi returned to their apartment at 234 East Broadway, New York City, during the first week of November. Luka and his men arrived later in the week and prepared for their trip home. The New York apartment scene was one of men swapping stories over a good bottle of wine and home-style cooking, telling of accidents, bar fights, women chased, and the bruises earned. Those remaining in New York hastily wrote letters to loved ones, to be carried home by those returning. It is unknown who stayed over in New York during the winter season other than Alexis, but Prince Luka and many others went home.

Dimitri Mgaloblishvili and the other Georgian riders found their homeland caught in the backwash of a world-wide economic depression. Many factories were closed, the export of oil from Batumi was drastically curtailed, and workers were sent back to their villages. Dimitri Mgaloblishvili, who first rode with Ivane Makharadze in 1892, completed his last documented year—1900—as a member of Buffalo Bill's exhibitions.

DIMITRI MGALOBLISHVILI BIOGRAPHICAL SKETCH

Dimitri was very handsome, tall and liked to feast, dance and sing. He married Aneta Akhvlediani from Imereti and they had six children. The sons were Mamia, Misha and Leo; the daughters were Marusia, Sotona, and Tsutsuna. Dimitri became a railway station manager in Navtlugi, a suburb of Tbilisi. He and the family were transferred to Tsagveri in eastern Georgia as the railway station manager. Dimitri was Giorgi Mgaloblishvili's only son and when Giorgi died, Dimitri returned to the family home in Onchiketi and brought with him new roofing tiles. Dimitri was not fond of hard physical labor so he convinced neighbors and relatives to help cover the family's home roof. He was known in the community for stories about his travels around the world and riding in the Wild West shows. Dimitri became the supplier for the school in Erketi, which was two kilometers from Onchiketi over steep mountains. The supplier was responsible for school inventories, manuals, repairs and maintenance. Dimitri quit work in 1954 after he found it too difficult to make the trip from Onchiketi to Erketi. He died in 1961 and was buried in Onchiketi.[147]

Alexis Georgian's troupe, Pawnee Bill 1900-1901
Standing left to right: Nestor Khukhunaishvili, Giorgi Chkhaidze.
Seated left to right: Teophane Kavtaradze, Alexis Georgian (Gogokhia), Irakli Tsintsadze.
Route Book, Pawnee Bill's Wild West Show, 1900. Courtesy of Circus World Museum

Plate No. 17

"When a man is in trouble, then does he need a friend and a brother?"

Shota Rustaveli

1901 PROLOGUE

Luka Chkhartishvili and his troupe of riders left home early in March, arriving in Cherbourg, France, before March 16 for the departure of the *SS Vaderland*. A *New York Tribune* article listed nine Georgians aboard, but the ship's passenger list did not list any Buffalo Bill artists. The United States Immigration Service changed procedures, allowing artists separate entry policies; therefore, their names no longer appeared on some of the passenger lists.

Colonel William F. Cody, in an interview with the *Collier's Weekly*, April 13, 1901, described his difficulties in obtaining Georgians for his exhibition.

"Hardest of all to secure are the *Georgians*. Pulling an elephant's tooth is simple work compared to the diplomatic dentistry necessary in pulling a *Georgian* out of the jaw of Russia. Nine years ago I got my first batch of *Georgians* through the aid of General John C. New of Indianapolis, then United States Consul at London. He succeeded in unwinding the miles of red-tape in which the process was swathed. With the exception of Prince Luka—prince in this instance meaning one of thousands of hetmen, or chief of band—all the *Georgians* are new each year. Even Luka, caught in the meshes of the red-tape, was one season unable to join us. He slapped a Russian's face or something like that, and the slapped gentleman prevented Luka from getting his passport. And unless you have a passport out of Russia you can't get in again. When the show was over last year, Luka as usual took his *Georgians* back to Batumi—distant several days from Odessa—and in the spring brought a new lot of the Czar's Rough Riders to Odessa, where our agent inspected and selected this season's contingent."

Social turbulence and economic collapse in Georgia were more likely the reason the Georgians had trouble getting their visas to America. Officials required additional bribery to get visas, and political activism increased the ruling elite's oppressions. A mass demonstration was planned in Tbilisi for April 22, 1901 *(Old Style)*, to vent the Georgian's social unrest. At midday, the noon cannon shot sounded from the Tbilisi arsenal, which gave the signal for action. The red flag was unfurled on the Russian bazaar or soldier's bazaar square near the Alexander Garden. The fiery words of revolutionary orators were acclaimed by some two-thousand workers with cries of "Down with Autocracy! Up with Republic! Long live Liberty!" Before the demonstrators could march on the main boulevards, they were set upon by police and Cossacks. A savage battle ensued. In the end, fourteen workers lay dead on the square and fifty arrests were made. The Czar's Cossacks, never popular in Georgia, would from that day forth become a scourge upon the Georgian people. On July 25, thirty buildings were wrecked in the vicinity of an exploded magazine in Batumi, and many civilians were killed or injured. The disaster occurred in the center of town,

Alexis Georgian, who rose against the czar's Russification in 1893, and who still preached against Russian domination of his homeland, was in New York City in the spring of 1901. He and his band of Georgian riders were contracted to work for Pawnee Bill again in 1901. The season brought major injuries to almost every Georgian rider and a report of one death.

BUFFALO BILL'S WILD WEST AND CONGRESS OF ROUGH RIDERS OF THE WORLD (1901)

Luka Chkhartishvili and his troupe of eight Georgian riders boarded the *SS Vaderland* in Southampton on March 17 with Jule Keen, his wife and daughter, plus sixteen Boer fighters of South Africa, and fourteen British soldiers. During the last two days of the voyage, they experienced heavy gales and unusually high seas with a small rail on the upper deck being blown away as the only damage. The *Vaderland* arrived at the bar March 26 at 10:10 a.m., but due to heavy fog could not reach Pier No. 14 until 10:45 that night. Luka, Jule and all the Buffalo Bill riders did not leave the ship until the next morning. Debarking, they went to Ambrose Park, Brooklyn, for rehearsals.

The rehearsals were conducted in bad weather and on muddy grounds. On Sunday, March 31, everyone was awakened at the early hour of 4:30 a.m. to trek across Manhattan to move into Madison Square Garden. Monday morning, Luka and his men were seen after breakfast walking about the city in their new Chokhas.[148] They made a unique advertisement for Buffalo Bill's Wild West, and they returned in time for the traditional opening day parade. Two weeks later, a moving picture of Buffalo Bill's parade was shown at the Eden Musée.

The changes in this year's program were the addition of a life-saving drill and the relief by allied power forces of the ministers and Christians from the Boxers in Peking, China, called the Battle of Tien-Tsin. The other features were standard fare, and number twelve on the program were the: "Cossacks, from the Caucasus of Russia, in Feats of Horsemanship, native dance."

New York City was their home for three weeks, until April 20; a two-train special with forty-seven cars carried the outfit out of New York. Their first stop was Baltimore, where the wet weather provided an omen of the hardship to come.

James Bailey's men, who routed Buffalo Bill's Wild West, sent them across Ohio, Kentucky, and Indiana for two weeks. They arrived in St. Louis, Missouri, on Sunday, May 12, for a one-week stand. Luka and his men used the leisure of Sunday afternoon to clean their equipment, rest, or see some of St. Louis. The outfit returned to business Monday morning for the parade at 10:00 a.m., but since they were spending the week there, it was the only parade that week.

Georgians on Parade, ca 1901
Leader, David Kadjaia
Courtesy, Denver Public Library, Western History Collection, NS-790
Plate No. 21

The 2:00 p.m. performance proceeded as normal until Luka was thrown from his horse. Luka was injured during the act where he rode all the way around the arena hanging by one foot with his body hanging far back with one leg and both arms waving in the air while his horse galloped madly. Suddenly, he fell. Fortunately, he landed clear of his steed's hooves, but he alighted on the back and side of his head, and the sound could be heard throughout the arena. He lay motionless while his horse kept on its furious charge. Attendants ran quickly to Luka and carried him, still unconscious, out to the dressing room. An examination showed that he had a severe cut on the side of his head and that the blow on his skull rendered him unconscious. He was soon revived, but he was unable to participate that evening nor at Tuesday's performances.[149] It was reported that when he regained consciousness, they had to restrain him by force for several minutes until he was certain that he was still alive. Luka returned to the arena for the Wednesday evening performance and executed his difficult feats with as much daring as ever. Saturday evening's performance concluded their stay in St. Louis. By midnight, the lot occupied for the week was empty, and they headed east toward Terre Haute, Indiana.

The first train section of Buffalo Bill's exhibition, composed of six stock cars, ten flat cars, four coaches, and one caboose left Altoona, Pennsylvania, at 1:00 a.m. Saturday, June 1. The second section, composed of nine stock cars, seven flat cars, one box car, and four coaches, left shortly afterward. Luka and his men had berths in one of the four coaches on the second train. A dense fog enveloped the tracks, making it almost impossible to see ten feet, and the two sections were running at moderate speed. About forty-five minutes out of Altoona, near Bellwood, at a place called "the tower," the second section ran down the first and struck the caboose, crushing it like an egg shell. The coaches ahead of the caboose were wrecked (telescoped) and pandemonium reigned. Men were rudely jolted from the berths, and from every side came shouts, the noise of cracking timbers, and the rush of steam. On the second train, all the car's platforms were broken. The engine tender crashed into the first stock car behind it, injuring a number of horses. A special train with physicians departed Altoona at 2:45 a.m. for the scene. The Altoona *Morning Tribune* wrote: "no one was killed but many people were seen walking around with their heads bandaged." The damaged coaches were replaced by day coaches, and the first section left at 4:05 for Lewistown; the second section left two hours later.[150] Luka and his men were spared injuries. After each accident or incident, the employees put aside arguments, squabbles, and other petty differences while the escape from destruction was still fresh in their memories.

"It is an interesting sight to see Colonel Cody's riders at mess. The Mexican Vaqueros are seated at one table in their silvery embroidered jackets and wide brim high conical hats. Then the *Georgians* in fur caps, the Boers in brown corduroys and big gray hats, and the Baden-Powell men, the Canadian scouts, the Cowboys, the Life Saving Crew and the Indians."[151] Heat and dust were now the main daily problems. The entire outfit looked forward to a long stand July 14-20 in Chicago. Tempers flared in the July heat, and after their arrival in Chicago, a bloody war between the Boers and British soldiers was imminent. The incident started when an Afrikaner exhibited some photographs showing a view of the battle scene at "Kopje," where the Afrikaners routed the British. The reporter wrote: "In the long grass could be seen the up-turned faces of the heroes who died for 'Merrie England' in that famous battle. Bold troopers' bodies, distorted by the agonies of death, lay strewn about, and as the proud Boers showed them yesterday to the curious onlookers they boasted and gloated over that famous victory." A delegation of British soldiers went over to the South African corner of the dressing tent and demanded a cessation of the offensive display. Buffalo Bill's Indian police, Georgians, and Mexicans took a hand in preserving order.[152]

The Georgians usually received a line or paragraph in the daily newspaper accounts:

> "The *Georgians* were commented on freely, for it is generally understood by the public that their milk of human kindness has turned sour, and their high saddles seem a never-ending source of interest, though, as one man remarked in the crowd: 'If they want camels, why don't they get them, and not try to make a camel out of a horse?'"

The comment about turning a horse into a camel was a reference to the high saddles of the Georgian riders. These saddles prompted a lot of press reporting:

> "The bearded *Georgians*, mounted in little high saddles that looked like two leather pillows fastened together, looked like toys stuck on top the wiry horses."

Or:

"Sitting comfortably on their high saddles, the *Georgians* looked wonderingly around. They were slight fellows for the most part. Ugly looking sabers hung at their sides and all of them had half-burned cigarettes."

By the end of August, they were in Buffalo, New York, for a two-week stand. Their first evening performance resulted in a Georgian taking a fall. The *Buffalo Courier* reported:

"The riding of the *Gerogians* is wonderful, but by reason of the heavy, unwieldy saddle is not as clean cut as the exhibitions of the Americans. Last night a horse ridden by one of the Russians fell while going at full speed and slid for some distance. When it regained its feet and dashed on, the rider kept his saddle."

The two-week stand in Buffalo ended on September 7. The remainder of the season consisted of one-day stands until they were to close in Danville, Virginia, on October 29.

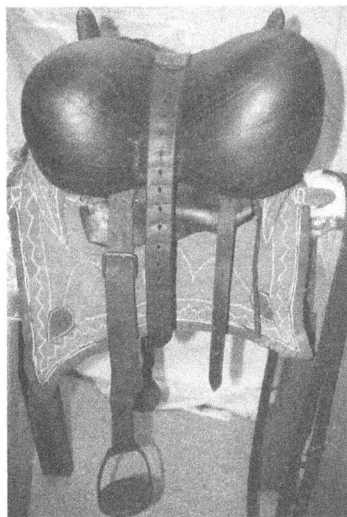

Georgian Saddle
Courtesy of Tom Mix Museum
Plate No. 22

The week of October 14 found them in Alabama and the following week in Georgia and South Carolina. The season's last two scheduled stands were Charlotte, North Carolina, and Danville, Virginia. Buffalo Bill's Wild West arrived in Charlotte on Sunday, October 28, about 7:00 a.m. The usual Sunday afternoon crowds wandered about the tent city, poking their noses into the lives of Luka and his men as they did a little equipment mending. Most men were preparing for the trip home, some shopping to buy new clothes or gifts. The streets of Charlotte were crowded since early dawn on Monday for the parade at 9:30 a.m., and the two shows at 2:00 and 8:00 p.m. that were given as usual. Everyone was glad to be back onboard the train and heading to Danville, Virginia, for the final performance and then to disband for the season and scatter to the far corners of the earth. In the very early hours of Tuesday, October 29, everything changed in seconds.

Leaving Charlotte, Mr. H. A. Williams, the trainmaster, divided Buffalo Bill's exhibition into three sections, since they were using freight engines. Mr. Williams was riding with the engineer, Bud Rollins, and the fireman on the northbound second section consisting of twenty-one cars carrying ring stock, coaches, and Colonel Cody's private car. The trains were running about twenty minutes apart, with the first section due in Danville about 4:00 a.m. The first section engineer, Robert L. Pierce, pulled into Lexington and reportedly signaled Frank Lynch, the engineer on a freight train that was waiting for the passage of the show train. The first section arrived in Danville on schedule.[153]

Engineer T. J. Lynch, onboard a southbound freight, Number 75, understood that his orders called for him to wait for the Buffalo Bill Northbound number 72 to pass him at Linwood, North Carolina. His conductor, Mr. J. M. Graves, who had identical orders, did not read them. Their orders were to wait for the three trains to pass them at Lexington. They misread the orders.

After the first section passed, engineer Lynch headed south running at about forty-five miles per hour on a downgrade and straight-track for about a mile when he spied a headlight— the Buffalo Bill number 72. It was just emerging from a deep cut on a curve when both engineers applied their brakes about four and a half miles south of Lexington, close to the small town of Linwood.[154] Oscar Sisk, of Salisbury, a retired railroad man, was sent by Southern Railway Co. to help clear the wreckage. Sisk said, "The two engines seemed to have tried to devour each other." One ran halfway inside the other and the two reared up on the tracks like two giant beasts in deadly combat—in railroad terms, a butting accident. They collided near the railroad crossing known as the Old Red Mill, along Swearing Creek on the south side, and a swamp on the north side of the tracks.[155]

Both freight engines derailed. The first five cars of Buffalo Bill's second section were smashed. These wooden cars contained the ring stock and most of the best show horses. Upon impact, the horses, buffalo, and other stock were jettisoned onto the crushed tenders and engines. The performers were tossed from their berths like rag dolls. Annie Oakley was thrown from her berth onto her steamer travel trunk and injured her hand and back. The freight coal tender and one boxcar loaded with fertilizer were demolished. It was a horrible scene, with twenty-three of those fine horses mangled in every conceivable way. Timbers were thrust through different body parts, and one, otherwise uninjured it seemed, had his head and neck severed from the body, but the head was not found. On all sides and up and down the track lay the dead horses; some were thrown there by the collision, some were taken out before they died, and some were shot to put them out of their misery. For more than an hour after the wreck, the faint groans of the dying animals could be heard beneath the pile of debris. Willie Cox, a boy of twelve, disclosed that saddles, bridles, costumes, and other show equipment washed down the creek and were scavenged by area residents.

Fearing for their lives, the southbound engineer, fireman, and conductor ran from the scene and hiked back to Spencer, North Carolina. The Georgians, cowboys, Indians, and Buffalo Bill cried over the loss of their horses that had been their riding partners since April first. The third section train waited about a mile down the track from the wreck and was used as a hospital. Many men were shaken up, and Annie Oakley was reportedly carried by her husband, Frank Butler, to the third section. The small farms around Linwood opened their homes and fed the showmen, and Colonel Cody bought all the food stuffs from the small store in Linwood. Late that afternoon, the third section arrived in Danville, Virginia, and the Buffalo Bill Wild West disbanded.

Luka and the other Georgians arrived in New York in the first week of November and departed for home.

PAWNEE BILL'S HISTORIC WILD WEST (1901)

Alexis Georgian, Giorgi Chkhaidze, Nestor Khukhunaishvili, Teophane Kavtaradze, and Irakli Tsintsadze spent the winter on the lower east side of Manhattan, 234 East Broadway, New York City. When Luka and his riders arrived on March 27, Alexis and his group welcomed them with a party. They gathered to collect the news from home, swap stories, drink wine, and discuss the business at hand, the tenting season with Pawnee Bill and Buffalo Bill. Luka and the Buffalo Bill troupe left New York on April 20, and soon after, Alexis and his troupe left for Litchfield, Illinois.

Pawnee Bill's rehearsals started the last week of April in preparation for opening day, Saturday, May 4. May made for a tough start with rain, mud, wagons overturned, missed performances, and late parades, but they slogged on. They crisscrossed western Illinois in twenty-two cars—six Pullman sleepers for the showmen, six stock cars, and ten flat cars for wagons. The show with 228 stock animals and 352 people progressed slowly north.[156] The Pawnee Bill show visited smaller towns, not the big cities. After two weeks, they were in Oak Park, just outside of Chicago. The show grounds were deserted on Sunday because most of the showmen had gone into Chicago. The weather did not improve, and by the third week of May, life on the road fell into the usual grind. Fair weather in Janesville, Wisconsin, on May 28, allowed the public schools to close, permitting the students to see the parade.

On June 1, the first ever Sunday performance by Pawnee Bill's show was held in Milwaukee. A train mishap in Sheboygan replaced the usual rain and mud problems, and later that day the dining tent was blown down in Sheboygan. A few days later the side show front was blown down. The show continued to Green Bay, and then moved away from the lakes and their damaging winds.

On Saturday, June 15, Pawnee Bill's show was in Merrill, Wisconsin. While hanging from his galloping horse's side, Alexis struck a fire plug in the center of the arena. Because of his position on his horse, Alexis did not see the signal warning light stationed near the fire plug.[157] Alexis was taken to the local hospital, where he stayed for several days nursing a fractured collar bone and three ribs.

Friday afternoon, June 28, started as every other day with lunch and the wait for the 2:00 p.m. performance. There were about 5,000 customers for the first Minneapolis show. The clouds boiled and grumbled ominously, but the storm held off during the first hour of the performance. A few large drops of water fell gently during the Mexican Contra dance on horseback, led by Pawnee Bill and Miss May Lillie. A few spectators started to leave, but a large patch of blue sky was visible in the southeast, and most stayed. Alexis Georgian's daring equestrian riders took to the arena and the heavens wept. Astride their spirited steeds, the Georgians, were giving the most entertaining. exhibition when the clouds opened their pores wide and it really began to rain.[158] The huge arena roofing canvas inflated from beneath, and it billowed upward like the dome of a cathedral, lifting the pegs from the ground and bringing the whole mass of canvas, poles, cordage and seating down in a disordered pile. The dining, dressing, and horse tents were blown down, and the kitchen utensils were scattered all over the grounds. John Howard, 10 years old, suffered the only injury when struck by a falling pole.[159] The afternoon performance stopped in the middle of the Georgian's performance. The evening show went on after many repairs.

Sunday, June 30, the show took a 228-mile jump to Ashland, Wisconsin. More disasters awaited Alexis and his troupe the next morning in Ashland when around 7:00 a.m. the entire show canvas blew down. The lot's poor condition caused a Georgian rider to fall and become injured during the evening performance. This fall was not taken seriously after the performance. The injured rider left Ashland with the show, and they went to Iron River, Wisconsin, July 2. The *Ashland Daily Press,* Wednesday, July 3, reported the death of the Georgian who fell in Ashland. "He would be remembered by those who attended the show, as the one who stood upon the horse's back, swinging his saber." The death of one of Alexis' troupe in Iron River has not been confirmed through public records, and Pawnee Bill's 1901 route book does not mention a death, which is rather peculiar. Here are known facts of the five riders comprising Alexis's troupe: Alexis died in 1940, Nestor was injured later in the year, Teophane lived to be over 70, Giorgi died at home in Georgia and Irakli Tsintsadze died in 1912 while riding in the Young Buffalo Wild West. It appears another newspaper had wrong information.

In Chaska, just outside Minneapolis, July 12, another Georgian had a severe fall in the arena, but no bones were broken. Three of the five riders had now been in accidents and the season was not over.

Eager to get out of Fairmont, Minnesota, the workmen began taking down the tent before the show was over, and removing supports for the seats caused the seat to come crashing down. Four ladies sued the show for a total of $50,000 for damage done to them.

Sandwich, Illinois, a small coal town of foreign residents sixty miles southwest of Chicago, was where Georgians and Turks made many friends among their countrymen.

Alexis and his troupe were injury-free during August.

In Norfolk, Nebraska, on September 7 everyone learned that President William McKinley had been shot the previous day at the Pan-American exposition in Buffalo, New York. The following week, in Kearney, Nebraska, the news arrived that McKinley had died. They were in Abilene, Kansas, on September 19, and helped the city pay homage to the President, then gave 4:15 p.m. and 8:00 p.m. performances.

October found Alexis and his troupe in Missouri and on October 5, they were in Clinton, Missouri. Alexis and his men were the fifteenth act, followed by a Grand Military Tournament. During the evening performance, in the military tournament, Nestor was thrown from his horse and broke his collar-bone. J. Dunlap, the show's physician, accompanied Nestor to the Sedalia hospital.

Monday, October 21, after payday in Little Rock, Arkansas, found Alexis and his men in Muller's saloon early, and what happened next was recorded in *The Arkansas Democrat*.

"One of the 'marvelous Imperial Russian Cossacks from the steppes of Russia' of Pawnee Bill's Wild West filled up on red liquor this morning and created consternation in Muller's saloon at 8:30 a.m. He resented the efforts of three of his kinsmen to remove him to the show grounds, and drawing his murderous double-edged sword, 'their principal weapon, which they wield with an expertness that is marvelous,' he proceeded to drive them out of the saloon, other patrons scattering by common instinct before his terrific onslaught. The bartender, Carle King, ran to the sidewalk and called an officer. Deputy Constable R.R. King responded and grabbed the malcontent from the steppes, who essayed to draw his sword upon the officer. Then Constable Jones and Detective Spight reinforced him and the three marched to jail the boozy member of 'the first genuine contingent of Russia's noted Light Horse Cavalry,' in all the regalia of 'handsome but somber uniforms.' There he will be permitted to sober up sufficiently to answer to the charge of disturbing the peace. His name is another matter. No one could distinguish it from his drunken guttural, and 'Theford' (Teophane Kavtaradze) was the nearest the linguists of the constabulary could get to it."[160]

The Pawnee Bill show disbanded Saturday, November 2, in Jackson, Missouri. Pawnee Bill's organization arranged transportation for Alexis and his troupe to St. Louis and then to New York. Alexis and his men arrived in New York about the same time as Luka and his troupe were leaving New York for home.

1901 EPILOGUE

At the season's end, the Georgians recounted their broken bones and lost friends, then thought of home and family. They had left their homes in spring with instructions to their wives, children and relatives as to the planting of crops and husbandry of livestock. They returned to a land where crops had failed and discovered that starving relatives had fled the land and invaded the towns and cities looking for industrial work. They were greeted at the port of Batumi with a notice that all passengers must be closely inspected because plague had occurred in the town. There was still evidence of a naval storehouse explosion that wrecked thirty buildings in the center of Batumi that July, strewing the street with body parts. The seeds of civil discontent were sown and would be harvested in 1902.

Several newspapers during the season commented on the unique saddles used by the Georgians. The type of Georgian saddle ridden in Buffalo Bill's Wild West and all the other Wild West shows or circuses can be seen today at the Tom Mix Museum in Dewey, Oklahoma, and the Cowboy Hall of Fame in Oklahoma City.

GIORGI CHKHAIDZE BIOGRAPHY

Giorgi Chkhaidze first rode with Luka in 1897. He came from a family of peasants and had two brothers and a sister. He married the daughter of Sikharulidze and they had five daughters. The following are edited memories of Ekaterine Chkhaidze.

"They started for America from Batumi, and it took them twenty-one days to reach Chicago. They lived in the countryside of Chicago surrounded by vast fields where they used to train hard all day long. According to my father, he was good at all kinds of tricks. He also visited France, England, Argentina, Mexico, and Italy. My father liked all foreign countries and people but not Englishmen. He used to say that they are very ambitious and arrogant people: 'they liked our skills and were fascinated by our tricks but never expressed their admiration; it was different with other foreigners. In France we were always surrounded by people taking our photos. They called us Cossacks and we tried to explain that we were Georgians, but unfortunately they had no idea about Georgia. Our riders used to not sit but stand on the horses and showed eccentric and unique tricks, thus making the audience enraptured.'

"The President of America, Theodore Roosevelt, was so delighted by the Gurian show, and especially my father, that he gifted him his own ring. The ring was presented to my father on a tray. This tray is still in Lanchkhuti, but the ring was sold. The reason for that was the fact that on my father's arrival to Georgia he talked much about the life style and brilliance of foreign countries, especially America, and that was prohibited in those times. Thus the information reached the village governor who ordered him to be imprisoned. The family was forced to sell the ring and pay for my father's freedom.

"During his first visit to Chicago, streets were lighted with electricity, but a lot of birds were killed by the wires they used to sit on. 'One day walking along an apple orchard, we picked the apples and ate them. At that time the gardener noticed us and secretly took photos describing our bad behavior. Then the photos were distributed to all his friends.'

"In 1903 or 1904 they returned to Georgia, having brought a lot of presents for our families and relatives. My father brought a zinc framed box that was kept in our family for a long time. According to my father, there was a handsome guy among the Georgian riders that had wasted all his money on women and entertainment, and on his way home he had not a single dollar in his pocket. At that time a group of rich people were aboard our ship and this guy decided to give a performance to them.

The Georgians started singing and he began dancing. This attracted a lot of people. The foreigners paid a lot to this guy and actually he made more money than his friends managed to save during their stay in America. The Georgians had planned to return to America but due to turbulence in their motherland they did not dare to travel. Giorgi was reported jailed for some unknown reason."

Giorgi Chkhaidze settled in Lanchkhuti, bought a mansion and everything necessary for the family. Giorgi was calm by nature, but his wife had a hot temper. He bought expensive things in order to use them for a long time. He said, "The things you buy in your youth have to be useful for you even in your late years."

OTHER SHOW BUSINESS

Annie Oakley, following the October train accident, went to Buffalo, New York, to seek medical attention at a sanitarium and the spas. She did not recover at the spas and went home to Nutley, New Jersey, where she underwent five surgical procedures. She stated that her hair went white within seventeen hours after the train wreck on the morning of October 29, 1901. Annie Oakley, who had worked for W. F. Cody since 1885 with only a handshake and no contract, quit the exhibition. She never again worked in a Buffalo Bill exhibition, but she did perform with Georgian riders in another Wild West show in 1911. It may be a coincidence, but Luka Chkhartishvili, who had ridden with Buffalo Bill since 1892, also never again worked for Buffalo Bill after the 1901 season. William Cody settled with the Southern Railway for $65,000 and relieved the company of any and all claims he had against it.

Buffalo Bill's dead horses were sold at fifty cents apiece to Mr. H. T. Hatton of Salisbury, North Carolina, who shipped them to Baltimore for the value of their hides and bones.[161] The remaining seventy-four horses were loaded on cattle cars and taken to the railroad stock yards at Spencer, North Carolina. Dr. R. H. Manogue, veterinary surgeon of Salisbury, and Silas M. Compton, assistant chief cowboy, tended to the remaining horses.[162] A few horses were left with farmers at the wreck site in Linwood. Old timers in the Linwood area say that on rainy nights, the ghosts of Buffalo Bill's dead horses roam the countryside—

whinnying, frantically looking for their masters.

Luella Forepaugh, widow of John Forepaugh, who was the nephew of Adam Forepaugh, married George F. Fish. He worked for the *Philadelphia Inquirer* newspaper for eighteen years as advertising manager. Luella Forepaugh retained ownership of the Forepaugh Theater in Philadelphia, but she sold her interest in the Philadelphia Theater during the 1901 season and in December incorporated "The Luella Forepaugh-Fish Wild West" in Camden, New Jersey.[163] This event impacted the Georgian riders in 1903.

Georgian Rider
Author's Collection

Plate 23

"Better than riches is strength of mind and of soul."

Shota Rustaveli

1902 PROLOGUE

The Georgian riders who were preparing to leave Georgia in March via the port of Batumi were witnesses to the beginnings of revolution in Georgia. Industrial workers lived in poverty and squalor, received starvation wages, and worked fourteen-to sixteen-hour days. The Batumi Rothschild Petroleum Refining plant fired more than 400 workers, and on March 9 over 6,000 people demonstrated along with the workers on strike. Reprisals were swift and harsh, with over fifteen killed, fifty-four wounded, and hundreds arrested. The Gurian peasantry threw down a direct challenge to the czarist authorities and to their own landlords. The Gurian movement began with a series of demands for rent reduction and with protests against the usurpation of peasant land by the state. The peasants refused to pay taxes to the government or tithes to the priests. They boycotted unpopular squires, as well as various organs and representatives of the Russian administration. The village headmen were powerless to keep order and were, in any case, overwhelmingly sympathetic with their stubborn compatriots. The Russians reacted at first with mass arrests and repressions, then sent Cossack troops to round up the ringleaders, who included a majority of the local village schoolmasters and a number of socialist agitators.[164] The papers reported over 300 strikers went to the police station and demanded the release of the ringleaders. Shots were exchanged, and thirty strikers were killed and one solider wounded.[165]

BUCKSKIN BILL'S CONSOLIDATED WILD WEST SHOWS (1902)

A Chicago saloon keeper, Henry E. Allott, and beer brewer, Valentine J. Hofmann, purchased The Buckskin Bill Wild West show on February 14, 1902, from the Terrell Brothers at Paducah, Kentucky. Henry Allott was a circus man at heart; however, he was also known as a member of a gambling syndicate and a theatrical promoter. At fourteen he ran away to join a circus and worked a candy and lemonade concession. Fate intervened in his life the day he accidentally brushed cinnamon red candies off his box into a tub of lemonade, changing the yellow color to a glowing pink.[166] Pink lemonade was invented and became Henry Allott's sole claim to fame. He was best known in Chicago as the proprietor of a west-side, tenderloin district saloon called "Bucket of Blood."

The Buckskin Bill show reorganized in Paducah, Kentucky, with Allott (known as Bunk Allen) as the manager and Colonel John C. O'Brien of Chicago (known as Pogey) as the director. Valentine Hofmann, who invested $200,000 in the company, was treasurer. Harry W. Semon was the general agent and James Leahy, the press agent. They hired William Cahoon, a picturesque man from Arizona, with long sideburns and shooting skills, to play the part of Buckskin Bill. Press reports indicate the show had twenty-two cars consisting of ten flats, six stocks, two baggage cars, three sleepers and one private hotel car.[167] The show's management advertised they had 205 head of stock and 450 people working on the show, but several newspapers challenged those numbers during the season. They also carried a saloon car fitted with a large icebox, beer, and three bartenders who were eager to serve the towners. The empty beer bottles were re-packed into barrels and shipped back to Chicago. In Emporia, Kansas, at least twenty-two barrels of empty bottles were shipped.[168]

The show was a mediocre imitation of the Buffalo Bill and Pawnee Bill Wild West entertainments, using a similar open arena. They advertised as purely educational, genuinely historical, and delightfully amusing. There were approximately 240 showmen, with cowboys, Indians, Mexicans, Cossacks, English, German, and French cavalrymen featured as rough riders of the world. Fancy shooting, a battery of artillery, wild bronco riding, stagecoach robbing, and buffalo hunting were all program acts. They had a 60x120-foot side show tent with a twelve-banner front, all double-deckers,[21] and four ticket wagons. The side show had a colored band of ten pieces and twelve platforms (acts). They ran six gambling games where the percentage of winners was very low. The admission was twenty-five cents with reserved seats an additional twenty-five cents. The Buckskin Bill show used sixteen immense torches to light the arena during the evening performances.

Alexis Georgian and three Georgian comrades signed contracts for the season; however, the records do not identify Alexis' comrades. Alexis and his friends moved to Paducah in mid-April, living in the tent city on

---

[21] Double-deckers - two canvas panels one above the other.

West Tennessee Street. A band of twenty-five Indians arrived on April 23, and the local saloon keepers were warned of possible trouble if they sold liquor to them. Several people who would have an effect on the lives of Georgian riders during the coming years were also in the Buckskin Bill show. Verne Tantlinger and his wife Edith, who had a bicycle and trap shooting act, performed in many different shows with the Georgians. Charles Tompkins,(1873-1957) billed as the king of the cowboys, would one day have his own show and employ Georgian riders.

Buckskin Bill's Wild West Show suffered a blow down on April 26, breaking all the quarter poles and one center pole, and the canvas was torn.[169] Before the full dress rehearsal was held on Friday night, May 2, a cowboy was seriously hurt when his horse tripped and fell on him. After paying the license, the show opened on Saturday, May 3, in Paducah. Their first jump was to Sturgis, Kentucky, where a man was shot and killed, interrupting the performance. Sunday was spent at Mount Vernon, Indiana, where Charles Baer, a cook, drowned while bathing in the Ohio River below Mt. Vernon. During the Monday performance, a Sioux Indian named Big Dog broke his collar bone when his horse stumbled and fell on him. A local doctor, George Spencer, came to the stricken Indian's aid. "When the doctor wriggled the fractured bone, Big Dog yelled and two other Indians thought he was being killed and shot at the doctor." The shoulder remained untreated until the show reached Hopkinsville on May 14.[170] Miss Lillie Cody (no relation to Buffalo Bill) was thrown from her horse and dislocated her hip. The opening week was a harbinger of disasters to come.

A press review, "Tame Wild West," described the lackluster performance of many in this show. The Georgians "did some pretty fair riding; the *Georgians* were up to date in their peculiar exhibitions in horsemanship."[171] The press agent, John A. Leahy, was kept busy.

The Buckskin Bill's roustabouts, grafters, and management were not the same quality of personnel that Alexis and the other Georgians had known in Buffalo Bill's and Pawnee Bill's Wild West shows. While in Cynthiana, Kentucky, James Leahy was assaulted by a Negro employee and died from the injuries. A small riot erupted in Maysville, Kentucky, on June 16 when trouble occurred between the Indians and cowboys. One band member had his jaw-bone broken, an Indian suffered a broken leg and another, a broken arm, and several others were badly cut about the head and body. W. A. Brown was red lighted from the train near Augusta and was picked up unconscious and severely bruised about the face and body. Laura Belle Murray accused four Buckskin Bill employees (Hardin, McCarty, Hayes, and Patterson) of enticing her into a rail car. She alleged they assaulted her and put her off the train at Garrison, Kentucky, enraging people from the local countryside. The four men were arrested; there was talk of lynching and the men tried to escape jail. The evidence purported that the fifteen-year-old girl was a half-witted, unsophisticated country girl who had only been in a town once in her life. She was said to be infatuated with Patterson.[172] The four men were acquitted. Such was life on the rails with the Buckskin Bill show.

Alexis, his comrades, and the show arrived in Washington, DC, on Sunday June 29, for a two-day stand. A brass band led the morning parade along the principle streets in a downpour. The afternoon performance was given in the mud, but conditions for the evening performance were a little better. The first evening's excitement occurred when a steer jumped the ropes and mingled among the audience in the grandstands before a cowboy could lasso the beast.

Alexis had his own reason to remember that night in Washington. Alexis and his comrades were charging around the arena during their usual performance of hanging from the sides of their horses, or standing on their heads in the saddles, when Alexis' horse jarred a pole that held a kerosene lamp. The collision knocked the light from the pole, and an explosion followed. Some blazing fluid fell on Alexis' arm and the sleeve of his chokha was burned away about the arm and shoulder, but he did not lose control of his horse, which plunged furiously around the arena. Alexis pluckily held out until the end of his performance before having his injuries attended to. He was in searing pain from his burns.[173]

After three months of performing in small towns, Alexis and his comrades were glad to spend a week in Baltimore, a cosmopolitan city, during the first week of July. Heading out of Wheeling, West Virginia, Friday night on July 11, they experienced a seven-hour delay due to an accident near the Wheeling tunnel and did not leave there until 8:00 a.m. Their late arrival in Newark, Ohio, caused the cancellation of the parade, but the show had a very good afternoon performance.[174] Foul weather followed them to Mansfield, Ohio, where it was raining when they arrived, rained during the parade, rained in the afternoon and evening performance, and they struggled through mud to get out of town. The show saw only 700 customers.

The Ottawa Republic wrote: "It was a poor, flabby, thin exhibition. It was worse than that, it was robbery." The *Topeka State Journal* wrote: "To begin with, the show was a fake of the worst kind. It was a travesty on Buffalo Bill, and an injunction ought to be secured to stop its career on the ground of fraud." Even Alexis and his comrades were skewered by the *Topeka State Journal*, they reported: "As the Show's *Georgian* troop of four came tearing around the arena, hanging by their toes to their folding-bed saddles, and waving their murderous scimitars, a man in the audience said:

'Well, who couldn't do that with a whole harness shop to tie him on with?' And his companion replied:

'They may be the Czar's pride, but I wonder what some of the Seventh cavalry boys would do to them? That's not the show's fault; however, if the Cossacks want to fight standing on their heads, it is not our business, is it?"[175]

The profits were evidently not shared with the crew. Saturday, August 17, four members attached the show (sued them) for three months' back pay, while in Emporia, Kansas. The young millionaire brewer, Hofmann, bought out Colonel J. C. O'Brien's interest in the show and purchased a new spread of canvas from the Murray Tent Makers of Chicago. The new canvas was first used in Great Bend, Kansas, on August 25.

The show moved south into Oklahoma during the first week of September, and in Guthrie, Sheriff George Foster shot and killed James Sidon, who was connected to the show. It was said Sidon attempted to rob a hotel and pulled a gun when the sheriff tried to arrest him. The sheriff shot first.[176]

They travelled about Texas until their arrival in Texarkana, Arkansas, on October 20. The show continued to receive bad press, with the exception of reports on the Georgians riding. *The Arkansas Gazette* reported: "The riding of the *Georgians*, under the command of Chief Alexis, was a marvelous exhibition of skill and daring. The recklessness with which these fearless fellows throw themselves on and off their racing horses was fascinating and held the crowd's attention from start to finish."[177]

The Buckskin Bill show closed on November 8 in De Soto, Missouri. Alexis Georgian went to Chicago, where he established residence. The others returned home or to New York for the winter.

BUFFALO BILL'S WILD WEST AND CONGRESS OF ROUGH RIDERS OF THE WORLD (1902)

After the train wreck at the close of the 1901 season, Colonel Cody reorganized his entire outfit. Wild horses—untamed, unbroken, fresh from the western ranges of Wyoming and Kansas—were corralled and shipped to Coatesville, Pennsylvania, in February and March. They were then shipped to Bridgeport, Connecticut, by the second week of April. The cowboys broke them in the open air of the old Barnum enclosure. The horses caused considerable excitement and the bucking resulted in calling an ambulance for the wounded. The rehearsals continued, and there were heated discussions on how these raw, green horses would react to the crowd noise and the electric lights at night.

The *SS Philadelphia* arrived in New York on Saturday, April 12, and brought English and German cavalry, Arab horsemen, and Georgian rough riders from England. *The New York Times* reported the Georgian were the object of much attention from the rest of the passengers on the way across, especially at the noon hour, when each would kneel on the deck and say his regular noonday prayers."[178] In fact, the Georgians were Russian Orthodox Christians, and it was, instead, the Arab horsemen who conducted daily prayers facing Mecca.

David Kadjaia, Ivane and Bathlome Baramidze, Pavle Makharadze, Nikoloz Antadze, Porfile Kantaria, Khariton Chkonia, Ushangi Kvitaishvili, Ivane Jorbenadze, Alexander Makharadze, Simon Oragvelidze, and Zurab Pataraia had two weeks to get their horses broken and trained before the opening. Observing David and his bearded and clerical appearing men sedately sitting around a dining table, a *Daily Tribune* reporter reflected that these men were also capable of riding the most vicious horses that ever walked. "You can't hurt those fellows," remarked Colonel Cody, as he responded to the polite bow of David. "Ride? They can ride anything, and if they get thrown, they're up again in a flash. You can't tie 'em down."[179]

The season began April 28 with a one-week stand in Madison Square Garden, one week in Brooklyn and another in Philadelphia. The first week was notable for the eight serious accidents due to the poorly trained horses. In Brooklyn, a cowboy endeavored to help himself to some peanuts from an Italian vendor. A fight broke out, pitting an Italian versus a cowboy and a

Georgian. Several vendors' stands were overturned in the mayhem, but the incident ended with no arrests.[180] This episode attests to the close-knit bonds that developed between the showmen in the Wild West shows.

The Philadelphia press printed stories on the magnificent horsemanship, such as: "Perhaps the most exceptional cavalry soldiers are the *Georgians*. They are 'blindly obedient to their officers, indifferent to danger and death, inured to endurance of the greatest physical hardships, and amazingly skillful in management of their horses.'"[181] Bathlome Baramidze may not have agreed that he was indifferent to danger. In New Bedford, Connecticut, he fell and broke his leg during the evening performance on June 12. He was taken to St. Luke's hospital and his leg put in a plaster cast. The hospital staff called him Willie. Willie was discharged on July 9 and rejoined Buffalo Bill's show in Detroit on July 10.[182]

Cody began a fast trip across the continent in Rochester, New York, on July 1, and reached Omaha, Nebraska, July 31. Another incident involving the Georgians occurred in Minneapolis during the morning parade. "A horse ridden by a Georgian rider became frightened and attempted to bolt down the avenue, throwing in a buck or two as he went, by way of good measure. However, the Georgian maintained control although at one time it seemed as though the horse would get in among the crowd who lined the curb; he was brought under control and continued down the street in his proper place in the parade."[183]

California in September was a delight for the Georgians from Guria. While working in the warm valleys, one could see the snow-covered mountains, like at home. They traveled along the coast from San Francisco to San Diego. While in Oakland, Charles Hunt lost his temper and smashed the skull of Edward Kolley; both were canvas men. Charles used a stake measuring four feet long, four inches in diameter and capped with an iron cap. The beauty of California did not change the temperament of men.

In Los Angeles a dust-up between Cody and his sprinkling superintendent provided a rare insight into Cody's character.

"Col. Cody came from his hotel to the grounds before the afternoon show and summoned the sprinkling boss to his private tent, which adjoins the entrance to the main arena. The Colonel began remonstrating with his employee, a short, muscular fellow about half his chief's age, warning him to be more punctual in this dusty country. But the foreman was primed for a fight and before Col. Cody had uttered half a dozen sentences, broke out with a profane din.

"'I've followed you around like a dog for four years,' he shouted, 'and I've got enough of it. I'll show you up, if you monkey with me—I'll publish you in the papers tomorrow morning.'

"Cody arose from his chair and walked over to his angry subordinate. There was a loud exchange of picturesque words, which attracted everybody within hearing. The tent flap was raised, and the spectators stood at a respectful distance, expecting possibly to see shooting. The efforts of the only other man in the tent, an executive staff member, to pacify the enraged foreman were futile, and he kept pouring out a torrent of abuse.

"Suddenly Bill turned on his heel, took a few strides and swung out with his right, straight from the shoulder. The blow caught the belligerent foreman squarely on the point of the jaw and sent him in a heap to the tent wall, five feet away. The third man then leaped between the men to prevent further damage, but it was needless, for Bill was the most composed mortal on the grounds. He saw he had silenced the fellow and then, turning, discovered he had an audience on the outside. A group of performers had instantly gathered, and so he ordered the tent flap down. Then the curtain fell on the interesting little drama on the inside of show life."[184] The foreman did not publish anything the next morning.

Toward the month's end they were heading east, giving one performance in Yuma, Arizona, a place Major Burke described as "only can be loved by the lung less."

Moving across Arizona and New Mexico, they entered Texas at El Paso in the west and exited October 25 in the east at Beaumont. New Orleans was the last stand in October. The New Orleans newspaper *The Daily Picayune,* wrote a description of David, the Georgian troupe leader:

"Prince David Kadjaia… He is a distinguished soldier and wears several medals for bravery on the field of battle. He has the cross of St. George bestowed upon him at the battle of Khartoum, and also wears a medal for bravery at Plevna during the campaign of 1877-78. He is a tall, fine-looking man, wearing a heavy full beard, and is very intelligent and well educated; although he can only speak a few words of English, but appears to understand simple questions asked of him in English, quite well."[185] As usual it was all a fake.

New Orleans to Memphis, Tennessee, took eight days, and on Saturday evening November 8, the last performance of Buffalo Bill's Wild West in America for the next four years came to a close. They had traveled more than 14,039 miles from Madison Square Garden to Portland, Oregon, to Olympic Park Memphis, Tennessee. It took them 201 days to cover the twenty-seven states in which they gave 339 performances. They made 133 stands with only seventeen one-day performances.

James Bailey, the man behind the scene, arranged for Buffalo Bill to tour Europe in 1903 while his Barnum & Bailey circus returned to the United States. The Barnum and Bailey circus closed its European tour in Dunkerque, France, on October 26, and sailed on the *SS Minneapolis* with ring stock, menagerie, and eighty-four baggage horses, arriving November 7 at Houston Street dock, New York. Barnum & Bailey left behind 480 horses at Dunkerque, which his boss hostler, Jake Posey, prepared for the Buffalo Bill exhibition. Posey picked out 142 horses, harness and all the accessories to ship to England along with the rest of the flat cars and coaches. Posey loaded the stock and cars on the *SS Michigan* in Dunkerque, and they made two trips to Tillbury docks in London, where the equipment was loaded for Stoke-on-Trent, their winter quarters.[186]

Nate Salsbury, who, on paper, remained the organization's vice president and major shareholder in the enterprise, had in fact not traveled with the outfit for several years. He became involved with the Wild West again in New York before they departed for England. He assisted Johnnie Baker in reviving "The Battle of San Juan Hill" and "The Guardians of Neptune's Stormy Coast" featuring the U.S. Life-Saving Service.[22] It was clear to everyone that Nate Salsbury was now a frail man.

Wednesday, December 3, Buffalo Bill's outfit with two-hundred members, including the Georgian riders, departed on board the *SS St. Louis* at 10:00 a.m. from pier 14, New York City. *The New York Daily Tribune* reported from London that due to foot and mouth disease, the Wild West buffalo would not be allowed to land in England. *The London Times* announced the arrival of the *SS St. Louis* on Thursday, December 11, as passing Hurst Castle at 12:50 p.m. The second contingent of Buffalo Bill's

---

[22] U.S. Life-Saving Service was established under control of the Treasury Department in June 1878. President Woodrow Wilson signed into law the "Act to Create the Coast Guard" on January 28, 1915, which combined the LSS and Revenue Cutter Service.

exhibition, led by Jule Keen, departed at 9:00 a.m. December 5, on board the SS *Campania* bound for Liverpool. They arrived on December 14.

Nate Salsbury, the business brains behind Cody, was responsible for much of the business success and the Georgian rider's introduction to the Wild West exhibitions. He died Christmas Eve, December 24, with his wife and four children at his bedside, at home in Long Branch, New Jersey. The cause was a stomach malady, which he had suffered since 1894. Buffalo Bill was once quoted as saying of him:

> "When you die it will be said of you, 'Here lies Nate Salsbury, who made a million dollars in show business and kept it.' But when I die people will say, 'Here lies Bill Cody, who made a million dollars in show business and distributed it among friends.'"

Funeral services for Nathan Salsbury were held at his home, 30 West Ninety-Sixth Street, the afternoon of December 28, with interment the next morning at New York's Woodland Cemetery.[187] Meanwhile in West London, Buffalo Bill moved into "Olympia," a vast indoor arena reminiscent of the Greek classical Olympic outdoor stadium that covered four acres. "This was a centrally heated venue beneath a giant iron and glass roof measuring 450 ft by 250 ft."[188] The arena had two levels of bleachers on three sides. Buffalo Bill's Wild West opened in Olympia, West London, on a cold Boxing Day,[23] December 26. As the company gathered before the 2:00 p.m. opening ceremony, Buffalo Bill notified his staff that he received a telegram stating that Nate Salsbury was dead. They lowered the scores of flags fluttering around Olympia to half-staff and draped the Stars and Stripes that were carried around the arena with a streamer of black crepe.

PAWNEE BILL WILD WEST SHOW (1902)

Billboard announced that Pawnee Bill had signed Prince Luka Chkhartishvili and his troupe of riders for the season. Luka, his brothers Mikheil and Kosta, Miron Chkonia, Ioseb, Araon, and Shardashvili, departed Georgia in late March and arrived in Boulogne-sur-Mer, France, in time to board the Holland-America Line steamer *Potsdam*, which departed on April 11. The ship carried ninety-nine cabin

---

[23] Boxing Day: The name given by Great Britain to the first day after Christmas, on which Christmas presents or boxes are given to errand boys, postmen, etc.

passengers and 973 in steerage. Luka's men were among those in the cabins. They arrived in New York on April 20 and immediately left for Chester, Pennsylvania, where Pawnee Bill quartered during the winter. Luka and his men had to learn the new organization's routine; they were number fourteen on the program, and had to break in new horses.

Pawnee Bill (Gordon Lillie) and his nine partners planned an East Coast tour while Buffalo Bill was on the West Coast and Barnum & Bailey, in Europe. Each partner provided capital investment; for example, Joseph De Wolf financed the side show and horse tents. During the season, the partners divided profits averaging $850 a day.[189]

The season opened Saturday, May 3, in Chester, but the evening performance was difficult to perform or to see because only one light worked.[190] The second day in Dover, Delaware, one of the high tiers of seats came crashing down; Mrs. Lewis—a dentist's wife—was cut and bruised. The outfit headed south along the eastern shore of Delaware and Maryland, ending the first week in Cape Charles, Virginia. The Elizabeth City newspaper, *The North Carolinian*, wrote: "The *Georgian* out classing all other competitors in equestrian ship." They also reported the freshly painted seats would increase the sale of turpentine. The newspaper also recorded the death of an Indian child who was kicked by a bucking bronco and was interred on the exhibition grounds.[191]

Leaving Alexandria, Virginia, Pawnee Bill's twenty-five car train met with an accident. A car was damaged and left on the road.[192] The next day during the evening performance in Frederick, Maryland, the local newspaper article said:

> "The daring *Georgian* riders, who hung from their saddles in all possible ways, delighted the audience. During their performance one of the horses fell and the rider was thrown upon the ground almost under several of the horse's feet. By lying close to the fallen horse, the *Georgian* escaped serious injury."[193]

More trouble erupted in Toronto, Ohio, where many employees got drunk after the show; Heap Big Father, one of the Indians, was killed; and Pawnee Bill and four others landed in jail.[194] The season closed Saturday, October 25, in Dresden, Ohio.

At the end of the season, the livestock and equipment went into winter quarters in Chester, Pennsylvania. Luka and his men returned to Georgia and their homes in Guria by way of Batumi. They returned the next season.

1902 EPILOGUE

A new Russian Orthodox Church of St. Nicholas, 15 East Ninety-seventh Street, New York, was consecrated on November 23. In attendance were ten "Buffalo Bill Russian Cossacks," wearing orange and white coats and white and black hats.

Austin & Stone's Museum billed Buffalo Bill's Russian Cossacks for the week of January 3, 1903, as reported in the *New York Clipper*. Buffalo Bill's Georgian riders were in London, but Georgians from Buckskin Bill or Pawnee Bill may have remained in New York area to work at Austin & Stone's in Boston, Massachusetts over the winter.

OTHER SHOW BUSINESS

The Barnum-Bailey Company, Limited, met in Detroit, Michigan, in the middle of July to discuss the division of territory for the Barnum & Bailey circus, Buffalo Bill's Wild West, and the Forepaugh-Sells Circus; George O. Starr represented James Bailey, William Cody represented Buffalo Bill's Wild West, and Peter Sells represented Forepaugh and Sells Brothers' circus. The resulting plan equally divided the United States, England and the rest of Europe among the three great shows for two-year terms.[195]

Mrs. Frank E. Butler (Annie Oakley) was operated on at St. Michael's hospital, Newark, New Jersey, during the month of June, due to injuries sustained in the October 1901 railroad accident.

Edwin H. Low, the travel agent who had arranged the Georgian riders' transportation from Batumi to New York since 1893, bought a Class R sloop named "Pickaninny" in September.[196] This purchase would be his ruin in July of 1903.

"Falsehood and double-dealing are destroyers of body and soul."
Shota Rustaveli

1903 PROLOGUE

In 1903, there were 158 American tent show companies that *Billboard* listed in winter quarters, and eight of these were Wild West shows. Buffalo Bill was starting a four-year tour in Europe, which opened a void in the United States that the proprietors of lesser Wild West shows were eager to fill.

The tent show barons were a close-knit community of owners, who had an impact on the Georgians over the years. The giants, Barnum and Forepaugh, had passed away, but their names survived on posters across America. In 1903, the Bailey organization was still using the Adam Forepaugh name to draw customers. Bailey used the name, but family members were still connected to the tent-show business.

Mrs. Fish was the widow of John Forepaugh, Adam Forepaugh's nephew. Mrs. Fish called herself Luella Forepaugh-Fish and she still owned the Forepaugh Theater on 8th Street. The exclusive circle of circus owners would include Mrs. Fish and her husband in 1903, and they would entangle the lives of Alexis Georgian and his men.

Lazare Maksimovich *(patronymic)* Jorbenadze on March 3, 1903 *(Old Style)*, received his passport, after paying 15 rubles. The passport was signed by the Assistant Kutaisi *(district of western Georgia)* Military Governor and a colonel who was head of the Batumi region. Lazare was given permission to travel to America because of family circumstances. Lazare and nineteen other Georgian riders departed Batumi in March. A letter from Paris by a Georgian correspondent was printed in *Tsnobis Purtseli (Newsletter)* on April 16 *(Old Style)*.

GEORGIANS IN AMERICA

"Our readers are aware of the fact that recently a Chicago entrepreneur had taken our nationals to America, Chicago Fair. These Georgians are the best riders and singers. An American entrepreneur was lucky; the Americans are enchanted by the riding skills and handsome appearance of our compatriots. The Fair has long ago been closed. But Georgians are still there, giving their performance in different cities. The best American riders could do nothing but let Georgians win the first prize in the competition. Encouraged with such success, the American entrepreneur invited twenty other riders from Guria to New York. The group is headed by Dimitri Tsintsadze and Luka Chkhartishvili. They were specially trained and six days ago departed from Batumi to Marseilles. In Marseilles, the Gurians attracted the attention of this city's population by their eccentric clothes, gait and speed of speech. They were considered to be Russian Officers or Caucasian Cossacks. They were much talked about in the press. For instance 'Le Reveil Du Lion' wrote: 'Yesterday we hosted Mr. Dimitri Tsintsadze and Luka Chkhartishvili. They are Caucasian Cossacks (cosaques du Caucase). They are taking twenty riders to America to demonstrate their riding skills with the Pawnee Bill circus. This group arrived on April 12 *(Old Style)* by ship *Ortegal* and on Monday will make their way to America by 'Nord Deutsch Lloyd' liner *(SS Kronprinz Wilhelm)*. They go around the city accompanied by an interpreter, Osias Cohen. At three o'clock they are going to see the museum of antiquities in the Château Borély. No doubt they will fascinate everyone there.

"Gurians had a very warm reception also in Paris. They arrived there on April 17 *(Old Style)*. Parisians thought them to be Russian Cossacks and welcomed them crying, "Viva Cosaques!

"The group of Gurians was surprised to see us *(Georgian Correspondent)* by chance. They told that the entrepreneur greatly appreciated their professionalism and treated them kindly. 'Most of all we charmed American women. One of them *(American)* wished to marry one of us but our stupid friend preferred to marry a Gurian girl. Now he lives in Guria and has only beans for dinner,' they remarked. Unfortunately all riders are uneducated. Two of them speak a little Russian and only one, Luka Chkhartishvili, speaks English. He studied English in America. 'We are well aware that lack of education is a great obstacle for us. In the future during our next visit to this country, we'll certainly study English as our friend did; in the evening free English lessons are given in several places. We are regarded as Cossacks; it's a shame for us that we can't even manage to explain to them that we are from Georgia.'

"These Gurians informed us about the group of their compatriots that were surprising Londoners by their riding and dancing."[197]

...

The twenty Georgian riders in Paris split up, with four of them going to London to join with David Kadjaia and Buffalo Bill. The Georgians who arrived in New York onboard the *SS KronPrinz Wilhem* on April 15 were Luka Chkhartishvili, Nestor Menagarishvili, Nikoloz Surguladze, Mikha Darsalia, Pallon Baramidze, Leach Tsintsadze, Solomon Imnadze, Parnaoz Shakarishvili, Dimitri Tsintsadze, Kirile Khoperia, Lazare Jorbenadze, Sergo Gvarjaladze, Jordon Surdobadze *(sic)* Silovan Kartvelishvili, Kirle Pirtskhalaishvili, and Mikheli Jrateshvili. In New York they separated into different groups. Luka and three companions traveled to Pawnee Bill's show in Pennsylvania. Nine left New York for St. Louis to meet with Alexis Georgian. Alexis and Dimitri joined the Luella Forepaugh-Fish Wild West and the other four went across town to the Adam Forepaugh-Sells Brothers circus. Four Georgians went to the Cole Younger and Frank James Wild West in Chicago.

Georgians, ca 1903
Standing left to right: Mikha Darsalia, Nikoloz Surguladze, Nestor Menagarishvili, Kirile Khoperia, Mikheil Chkartishvili, Silovan Kartvelishvili, Ioram Mshvidoadze. Seated Middle: Bartiome Baramidze, Mr. Cohen & Daughter, Dimitri Tsintsadze, Luka Chkhartishvili, Parnaoz Shakarishvili. Seated front row: Sergo Gvarjaladze, Solomon Imnadze, Leach Tsintsadze, Kirile Pirtskhalaishvili.
Author's Collection.
Plate No. 24

ADAM FOREPAUGH-SELLS BROTHERS CIRCUS (1903)

Alexis Georgian said he managed four riders who were attached to the Adam Forepaugh-Sells Brothers Circus and Roman Hippodrome show. The show's managers were Peter Sells and his sixty-five-year-old father, Louis Sells. Louis was an old-time circus owner and crony of James A. Bailey. The Adam Forepaugh-Sells circus arrived in St. Louis, Missouri, on Tuesday, April 14, from their winter quarters in Columbus, Ohio. The Georgian riders had not worked under a circus big top since 1893. After ten years of working in Wild West open arenas, the Georgians had to rehearse their routine in a new environment, using the hippodrome track of a three-ring circus. Rehearsals began April 15 and they opened on Monday, April 20, in opposition to the Luella Forepaugh-Fish Wild West Show.

The *"Fearless Russian Cossacks,"* as the four Georgian riders were billed in the advertising circular, continued struggling on the rain-soaked lots. Eight thousand spectators in St. Paul, Minnesota, on Friday, July 3, braved the steady rain and discomfort of water dripping from the tent down their backs and onto their heads just as the thousands who proceeded them did in May and June. The next day, Saturday, the Georgian riders, along with the rest of the outfit, crossed the Mississippi river to Minneapolis and, because of rain, again gave only one performance.

The four Georgian riders may not have realized how fortunate they were to be working under a big top rather than in an open arena. The Adam Forepaugh-Sells circus managers were acutely aware of their opposition with the Forepaugh-Fish Wild West show. The Sells brothers spent considerable effort and money to run opposition advertising against the Luella Forepaugh-Fish Wild West show. They ran an opposition newspaper article in the Austin, Minnesota, *Register,* even though they never planned playing in the town during the season. The rainy season gave rise to press releases touting the new process of waterproofing their tent to shelter the patrons and insure comfort and safety. The managers should have worried more about the price of labor in the fields than the possible loss of revenue to another show. An account in Sioux City, Iowa, said: "The harvest fields of South Dakota were too appealing for over 200 of the laborers who deserted the Forepaugh-Sells circus to earn wages in the fields."[198]

The Bailey organization, which ran the Forepaugh-Sells circus, kept them in the Midwest for the entire season. Meanwhile, they kept the Barnum & Bailey circus on the East Coast and Buffalo Bill in England.

Rain was not the only disaster to strike the show. A yellow fever outbreak in San Antonio, Texas, cost additional lost dates because doctors would not allow the show in other towns after it played in San Antonio. The season ended on November 6 at Cape Girardeau, Missouri.

BUFFALO BILL'S WILD WEST AND CONGRESS OF ROUGH RIDERS OF THE WORLD (1903)

David Kadjaia and his thirteen comrades who four months earlier were traveling through California were now wintering at Olympia, London, from January 1 to April 7. A Georgian correspondent interviewed the "Russian Cossack" riders and wrote home about the Georgians at Olympia in Buffalo Bill's Wild West. His account was published in the *Tsnobis Purtseli (Newsletter)*.

LETTERS FROM LONDON

"Three months ago *(January)* my friend told me: 'On behalf of Russian Cossacks, Georgian riders, they gave performances with an American Circus *(Buffalo Bill's Wild West)*. They have enchanted the public. The American circus named after its owner Buffalo Bill is not only a circus, but also a real Ethnographic Fair where the people of different nationalities demonstrate their clothes and arms. Just imagine 200 riders with two cannons riding to and fro in a circus arena accompanied with orchestra music. The audience exceeds 10 to 12 thousand! Everything is eccentric; first American Indians, exactly like those described in James Fennimore Cooper's books, appear in the arena accompanied by their families and demonstrating their family rites. They are dressed in colored clothes; their gait is light and free. They walk with their heads high and have peculiar smiles on their faces.

"After Americans, our nationals, Gurian riders, appear in the arena dressed in Chokhas, different colored clothes. All of them are armed. They start riding at first slowly and go around the arena, then stop in the middle of it and arrange a circle and start dancing. The audience becomes fascinated. Thousands of people applaud. Then they commence riding and thus demonstrate their skills.

"One of the Englishmen told me, 'They are excellent riders! I've seen a lot of riders in the plains of America and Australia but I've never seen such eccentric and extraordinary ones. It seems to me that they are born-riders brought up on the horses and it refers to the fact that there is a good school for riders in their country.'

"I answered. 'You are mistaken; there are no special schools for riders in Georgia. These are ordinary village youth. In their village, they are used to demonstrating their riding skills in front of their girlfriends and brides.' 'It is surprising,' uttered my interlocutor, with admiration.

"After the show I found those Gurians. They were surprised and very happy to see a Georgian in a foreign country. They flooded me with questions. We talked for a long time. I gave them the Georgian newspapers and sent them articles from time to time. One of the riders surprised me very much. Namely, he asked me to get a London program for his brother, who studied at his expenses at the Medical Institute of Georgia. I looked at these Gurians and could hardly stay on foot because of great joy. 'They didn't speak Russian (Except Kadjaia, who is their head and speaks fluent Russian.) They were not educated at all but were eager to help their family members to get education. Due to this, they used to send them money. It points to the wise nature that is the basis of the future development, and also underlines the fact they are off-springs of well educated and noble ancestors.' I also found out that these Gurians went all around the United States and visited almost all big cities. Most of all they liked California. 'The climate, fruits and hospitality of California reminded us of our motherland,' the Gurians remarked."[199]

■ ■ ■

Lady Colin Campbell described one of these performances in an article for *The World,* titled "A Woman's Walks":

"The musical song of the *Georgians* closes Mr. Baker's exhibition, and the curious minor chanter, with its plaintive inflections, calls up visions of the snow-plains and the retreat from Russia, when the forefathers, no doubt, of these horsemen in scarlet and sheepskins caused so many of the French invaders to leave their bones behind in the land which fire and snow had made invulnerable. They gave an exhibition of horsemanship which reminds one of Dickens' description of the acrobatic boy at Mrs. Leo Hunter's party, 'who did everything with a chair except sit on it.'"[200]

David Kadjaia and his comrades gave 172 performances inside the heated pavilion at Olympia. On one occasion, at the King's special request, the program was reversed for a royal performance. King Edward VII, Queen Alexandra, Princess Victoria, Prince and Princess Charles of Denmark and three children of the Prince of Wales all enjoyed Buffalo Bill's entertainment on Saturday, March 14. "A tearoom, hung with old gold velvet and decorated with flowers, was at the back of the special royal box, and there the King and Queen and their party had tea at the performance close. They afterward visited the Indian camp, where Colonel Cody was presented to them. Cody and Burke then escorted the royal party through the settlement, where the Rough Riders were drawn up in a double line."[201]

A boost in box office receipts from the King and Queen's attendance had short coat-tails, and by the end of March and early April the house was showing more empty seats. They closed at Olympia on April 7 and prepared for the spring and summer touring season.

Manchester's Longsight station on Friday, April 10, was the first of many scenes of eager Englishmen, boys and girls crowding around a train station to watch the unloading and transport of Buffalo Bill's entertainment. The Manchester lot was at Brooks' Bar, almost two miles from the train station, where the arena and white tent city were erected for a three-week stand. They were watching a three-section train unload with sleepers painted red and all the other cars painted orange. There were fifty-five cars in the train.

Opening day was Easter Monday, April 13, in cold, drizzling rain that turned to snow. The Grand Review, which opened every show, began with a "call" by Johnnie Baker, the arena director, to the horsemen to mount and prepare. In answer to his call, two columns of riders—Indians, cowboys, Georgians, Cubans, and others—gathered behind the high, wide, painted curtains at the end of the amphitheater and awaited their cues. "Behind the scene all is dust, quivering feet, the clink of bit and spur, and the noise of crowding men and horses. Here a cowboy is striving with all his skill of bridle and spur to keep his nervous mount in proper place; just behind him an Indian, stirrup-less, relying upon the strength of his bare, paint-striped legs to maintain his seat, is fighting a small battle with his fractious pony, which insists upon backing into its fellow creatures and setting them all aquiver with fright, and on the other side a *Georgian* in his high saddle has under him a beast which persists in whirling about on its hind legs."[202]

Buffalo Bill was the last to enter and introduced the Rough Riders of the World to the guests. The opening day Grand Review concluded with all the cast members riding around the arena and exiting. In the course of this ride, an Indian fell from his horse, and the next horse stumbled with its rider, Buffalo Bill. Everybody thought he was killed, and when he half rose and then fell flat... this fear was almost confirmed. However, Cody's ankle was only sprained and he rode in a carriage for the next five weeks.

David Kadjaia and the thirteen Georgian riders endured the cold, drizzling rain of opening day May 4 in Liverpool. Weather conditions were depressing throughout the season. The Bishop of Liverpool, Dr. Chavasse, along with a large choir of men and boys, could not get the heavens to cooperate while he delivered a sermon to the soaked motley assemblage of rough riders on May 10.

Leaving Liverpool, Buffalo Bill's Wild West returned to its usual touring scenario. Along the way, the advance crew plastered the countryside with press releases and advertising. The Georgian riders were more prominently advertised in the British press than they had been for the last few years in the United States. At Bristol on July 23, Isadore Gonzalez, one of the Mexican riders, was thrown from his horse and instantly killed. While in Dudley a robbery valued at $2,000 occurred.

They stole a pin bearing the initials of King Edward and a pair of diamond cuff links belonging to Buffalo Bill.

Jake Posey wrote: "We gave 333 performances, lost one performance during the entire season, at Bradford on October 6 on account of a wind storm, as a matter of safety. The tour consisted of 194 days, as follows: two stands of three weeks each, one of two weeks, two of one week, two of four days, three of three days, six of two days, and seventy-eight of one day. Only seven parades were given the entire season, and those mainly as competitive measures at points where some of the English circuses were showing on the same day. The coldest day was at Manchester, 31 degrees, the hottest, July 2, at Hereford, 86 degrees—quite a difference from American touring."[203]

It was reported that Buffalo Bill's Georgians found professional engagements in America for the winter season. William Cody, Jule Keen, Major Burke, fifty Indians, and half a dozen cowboys and Georgians sailed on the SS Etrucia from Liverpool on October 26 and arrived in New York on October 31.

THE GREAT COLE YOUNGER AND FRANK JAMES HISTORICAL WILD WEST SHOW (1903)

Alexis Georgian, who rode in the Buckskin Bill show the previous season, contracted five Georgian riders to perform in Henry E. Allott and Valentine J. Hofmann's new incarnation of the same show under the name *The Great Cole Younger and Frank James Historical Wild West Show*. Allott was an alleged criminal and the owner of the notorious Bucket of Blood saloon and gambling emporium in Chicago's near west-side, 206 West Adam (the address used on the show's letterhead). Allott's partner was Hofmann, general manager of the Hofmann Bros. Brewing Company located at West Monroe and the Northwest corner of Rockwell. If Alexis thought the Buckskin Bill show was run by gangsters, he only needed to see what happened this year.

Earlier in the year, Hofmann corresponded with Frank James and reportedly met with Cole Younger the day he arrived in Kansas City, Missouri, after his pardon by the State of Minnesota.[204] Cole Younger, who lived in Lee's Summit just outside the city limits of Kansas City, contacted Frank James and told him about an offer to participate in a Wild West show using their most valuable asset, their notoriety. Allott, Hofmann, James, Younger and a Mr. D. Phillip Philips were all in Kansas City over the weekend of February 14 and 15. Mr. Philips, who became the contracting agent, brought a satchel to Kansas City with $75,000 in cash to let Frank and Cole finger it before securing their signature on a contract. A three-year contract between the owners and Frank and Cole was signed on Monday, February 16. Frank James was to receive $300 per week as a salaried employee. Cole Younger was to receive twenty-five percent of the net profit, to act as general manager, and authorized to appoint the treasurer. Cole hired his nephew Harry Younger Hall as treasurer, who was put in charge of a $5,000 reserve fund. Cole also hired F.G. Linenfelder, an old friend, as bookkeeper.

■ ■ ■

Alexander Franklin "Frank" James (January 10, 1843 - February 18, 1915) was Jesse James' brother and member of the notorious Quantrill guerrillas during the Civil War. He had been a train and bank robber.

Thomas Coleman "Cole" Younger (January 15, 1844 - March 21, 1916) was eighteen years old when he joined Quantrill's guerrillas and met Frank James. Younger and his brothers, Jim and Bob, rode with the Jesse James gang, as reported in newspapers and dime novels, until they tried robbing the First National Bank of Northfield, Minnesota, on September 7, 1876. Cole Younger was captured and imprisoned. He was paroled in 1901 and pardoned in 1903.

■ ■ ■

With contracts in hand, Allott and Hofmann returned to Chicago to repaint their Buckskin Bill equipment, The *Great Cole Younger and Frank James Historical Wild West*. While Allott and Hofmann prepared their equipment, the Georgians readied for their journey to America, unaware of their impending association with legendary American bandits. They arrived in New York on April 15 and were dispatched to Chicago to start rehearsals. There are no documents to inform us who the Georgians were, but several had ridden in the Buckskin Bill show the previous season, and most likely a couple of those men wintered in Chicago. They opened on sandy ground by the river in South Chicago on Wednesday, April 29. Their four days in South Chicago were spent on different lots. They were located at 79th and Halstead on Thursday; Friday, at 35th and Wentworth; Saturday, at 14th and State. It is ironic that James and Younger went to the Lake Street police station on May 2 to report that a horse valued at $100 had been stolen from the show.

Their first jump out of Chicago was to Galesburg, Illinois. They were delayed until 4:00 a.m. due to a claim filed for non-payment for harnesses and saddles totaling $1,227.00.

The Georgian riders, after the first week of travel, found themselves in Kansas City, Missouri. Along the way, they discovered that some Missouri towns, such as Carrollton, were not enthusiastic about seeing the famous bandits because of past Jesse James gang raids. The program was the same as the 1902 Buckskin Bill show, a sham of Buffalo Bill's Wild West. The advertising touted the Jesse James and Cole Younger gang's exploits during and after the Civil War. Many who came to see the show were disappointed there were no depictions of the famous Jesse James gang, bank or train robberies.

For a bit of publicity, they visited the federal prison in Fort Leavenworth, Kansas, where 110 men convicted and sentenced to hanging waited, but the President would not sign the execution papers. The Georgian riders had a supper of hard-boiled eggs in Mansfield, Missouri, on May 19, along with the rest of the outfit, when the cookhouse staff went on strike. Mrs. Hofmann settled the dispute, but another argument with a lady rider could not be settled, and she was told to get off the train. Arriving in West Plains, Missouri, everyone hoped for a good meal, but discovered the local minister published a resolution to the town folk not to patronize the show. To everyone's relief, the show "made the nut,"[24] and supper was served.

The only known Cole Younger and Frank James Wild West show photograph is from *The Phening Collection* and depicts the side show cast. Seated in this photograph is a lone Georgian rider who probably danced in the side show, and seated alongside the Georgian are African-

[24] Made the nut - The amount of money that must be taken in to meet the day's expenses. Legend attributes the term to the practice of creditors, in early overland wagon show days, of removing a nut from a wheel of a key wagon as collateral to assure payment before the circus could move.

American band members.

Mrs. Tantlinger, a lady shootist who also rode in the 1902 Buckskin Bill show, kept a diary. On May 24 she wrote: "On the way from Jonesboro to Memphis had orders to red light all niggers *(sic)*. General mix up, everyone drunk *(sic)*. Grafter Scully shot canvas man on the side show in the leg. He hid in the privilege car and the car was unbuckled from others; and cowboys and canvas men were going after him, but the police came and took him."[205] The Memphis press did not report on the African-American's red lighting, but did report on the shooting of Charles Burrow by Eugene Scully.

Grafters,[25] assisted by owners Allott and Hofmann, followed the show. Their actions forced the owners to make hasty exits and drop the evening performance in a few towns. James and Younger were once arrested for running a gambling game in connection with the show, but because they were employees and not the owners, they escaped jail. The press zeroed in on the "Men Only" show and the "fortune wheels" as examples of disreputable exhibitions.

While in Washington, DC, a few Georgian riders from the Luella Forepaugh-Fish Wild West show joined the Younger and James show. They jumped to Baltimore, and then the show crossed the Mason-Dixon Line into Pennsylvania. While in Dubois, Pennsylvania, they witnessed the death of Lee Marshall, a bronco rider killed trying to ride the horse "Jack Rabbit." They crisscrossed Pennsylvania and worked their way south to Wheeling, West Virginia, by the end of July.

By the middle of August, Frank James was disgusted with the Wild West show business. He vented his frustration during the performance in Louisville, Kentucky, to a *Louisville Herald* reporter:

"Why, they are only charging twenty-five cents admission to the show... If I had my way I would not show myself for a quarter, and never for less than fifty cents. If people didn't want to pay that much to see Younger and me, they should stay home." As Frank spoke, a troupe of Georgians were dashing by and raising a big cloud of dust. This disgusted Frank, and he cornered one of the two shows' fat proprietors and started to upbraid him.

"Why didn't you have this thing sprinkled? You are cheating the people

---

[25] Grafters: Crooks, swindlers who went along with a circus to operate dishonest gambling games, pickpockets, and short changers.

in allowing this dust to stay. Why, a dozen small boys with buckets could have sprinkled the ground and made it all right."[206]

Trouble followed the show, and Frank James was informing local authorities of the show's strong graft in advance. This combination reduced the daily income. Managers were not the only ones who understood the economics of show business. Roustabouts and performers kept a close eye on how many paying customers were inside each performance. The Wild West show did a thriving business in East St. Louis, Illinois, on August 19, and some roustabouts took advantage. They filed an attachment against the show for $600 in back pay. While the sheriff held the horses and equipment, Allott and Hofmann settled the claim with their roustabouts.

Frank James and Cole Younger became more disgruntled with the show's management, and on September 16, when they reached Monett, Missouri, Frank decided to quit the show. He continued to travel in advance of the show and informed local officials about the swindles being run. In Nevada, Missouri, James and Younger dissolved their relationship with the show and said their goodbyes. Cole Younger, H. W. Hall (Younger's nephew), and F.G. Linenfelder were arrested in Nevada on September 24, charged by H.E. Allott with embezzlement of $6,000. The arrests are said to be retaliatory for suits initiated against Allott and his financial backer by Younger for $25,000 and by Frank James for $4,800. Younger and James claimed damages for the failure of Allott and Hofmann to equip the show as agreed and to drive away the grafters.[207] The county prosecuting attorney refused to file against James and Younger because there was insufficient information and would be too large an expense for the county.

> "We have severed all connection with the James-Younger Wild West show. The management was duly notified to choose between grafters and us. They refused to eliminate the grafters; hence we refuse to allow our names to be used with a thieving outfit. Signed: Frank James and Cole Younger."[208]

The Georgian riders were not concerned about their reputations, but rather with receiving their salary. Alexis Georgian, the riders' manager, said, "I had problems getting the pay for my rider's in the Cole Younger and Frank James show," and he was not alone. Many show employees struck for their pay in Oklahoma City on September 29. A representative of these strikers told the *Oklahoman* newspaper, "They never pay us in full. When we ask for our wages, they give us a dollar or two, and after a few weeks, when we want to settle, they get rid of us in some way."[209] Allott and Hofmann settled the claims with their showmen and took the show into Texas.

One last incident occurred in Bowie, Texas, that typified the entire season. The *Bowie Blade* reported: "To be sure there was a street fight and some boys followed the motley crew down to the train after the show to 'have fun' with the 'niggers,' and were fired upon by a showman, receiving a charge of bird shot, which scared them, if it did not hurt them, but after all, there was nothing much doing on show day."[210] A week later, the show closed on October 12 in Fort Worth, where they wintered. Whether the Georgian riders returned home to Georgia or wintered in the Chicago area cannot be ascertained.

LUELLA FOREPAUGH-FISH WILD WEST SHOW (1903)

Alexis Georgian at age thirty-two was a six-year veteran of American tenting shows. Alexis, the former young radical student, spoke six languages: Mingrelian, Georgian, Russian, Latin, Greek, and English. Alexis was fluent enough in English to create his own management company. On January 12, he signed a written agreement with the Luella Forepaugh-Fish Wild West show to furnish six Georgians and eight Arab acrobats for the 1903 tenting season. He was to be paid $325 per week, including board and transportation for his troupe.

Alexis had a contract with Dimitri Tsintsadze, who arrived onboard the *SS Kronprinz Wilhem,* to furnish eight Georgian riders to various shows: Adam Forepaugh-Sells Brothers circus, The Great Cole Younger and Frank James Historical Wild West, and Indian Bill's Historic Wild West. Alexis spent $75 on telegrams, cables, advertisements and communications to place Dimitri's friends in these shows. He also paid $25 to Dimitri to house some of his riders in New York until their shows were scheduled to begin.

Alexis, his riders, and the Arab acrobats arrived in St. Louis, Missouri, on Sunday, April 5, around eight o'clock in the morning. He stayed at the Planters Hotel in St. Louis, while his men were quartered on a ranch near Ferguson, Missouri. Alexis was busy in rehearsals and conducting his management affairs with other shows.

The usual parade was on April 16, but there was an unusual event among the cowboys riding ahead of Alexis' group. "A shot from the pistol of a cowboy of the Luella Forepaugh-Fish Wild West show created a panic at the corner of Jefferson and Washington Avenues as the parade was passing. A *(streetcar)* motorman of the Jefferson Avenue line persisted in crossing the parade's line of march and, as a consequence, a cowboy undertook to stop him. The cowboy wheeled out of line and rode in front of the car, brandishing his pistol. The car moved on its way. The Indians were forced into the crowd and the parade came to a standstill. The cowboy leveled the pistol above his head and pulled the trigger. The report alarmed the crowd. Women screamed and men tried to force their way out of danger. A telephone message to the chief of police resulted in a squad being sent from the ninth district station but, as usual, everything was tranquil by the time the officers arrived."[211]

Before the April 18 opening, Alexis received a request from the Luella Forepaugh-Fish show's management to provide six additional riders. He signed on six more Georgian riders on April 18, at a sum of $20 per week for each man, plus board and transportation. Alexis paid $152 for the transportation of Dimitri's group of six riders from New York to St. Louis.[212]

The Luella Forepaugh-Fish Wild West held an illuminated parade on Friday night, April 17, and opened at Handlan Park, Grand and Laclede Avenue, on a rainy Saturday, April 18, in opposition to the Adam Forepaugh-Sells Brothers Circus. The show used Buffalo Bill's Wild West formula, except that they also carried a small circus menagerie. An open-air arena was used, surrounded on three sides with tiers of seating, with a canvas backdrop on the fourth side from which the acts entered. A grandstand was covered and divided into reserve and general seating. The price of general admission was twenty-five cents, with reserved seats twenty-five or fifty cents extra, and arena box seats for $1. As all Wild West shows did, the exhibition opened with a grand review and rough rider introduction.

On Saturday, April 25, the eight days in St. Louis ended. The first jump of 22 cars was to Jefferson City, Missouri. They left behind the Lawrence Trio after they filed an attachment for their pay. The show also left seventy-five canvas men in Lexington, Missouri, which prompted town leaders to consider taking a new census.[213]

April showers brought more than May flowers; they brought mud and no profit. Touring Missouri, Kansas, Nebraska, and Iowa during the month of May, the show lost twenty-three performances due to rain. Management, performers, and workers all understood the requirement to "make the nut." This meant that if their daily costs were $1,000.00, then, at twenty-five cents a seat, they needed to pull in around 4,000 customers. Everyone knew that their pay depended on squeezing as much as possible out of each patron. May's torrential rain cut deeply into those profits and into troupe morale. In Sedalia, Missouri, the wagons were mired up to their hubs in mud, and only one performance was given. This happened in town after town. Two or three days of constant rain made the canvas almost impossible to lift and weighed down the wagons even further into the mud.

The climax to the month of rain came during the last four stands in Iowa. At Council Bluff, where the show pitched its tents in a sea of mud, the working horses were worn out and riding horses were pressed into labor. Roustabout gangs went on strike and refused to pull canvas or drive a stake until they had some sleep. Half of the United States Cavalry soldiers announced they, too, were on strike due to lack of sleep. The show went on, but during the performance one of the finest horses in the company stopped still, staggered, laid over and died. Despite the mud, the heartbroken horse and the strikers, the show managed to pull in 3,000 of the citizens of Council Bluff.[214] The next day, the show was washed out in Atlantic, Iowa. In Des Moines only fifty-seven people attended the afternoon performance, so the evening show was abandoned. Meanwhile, the advance men contracted about $85 of debt in Pocahontas, their last stand in May, but the show failed to stop and those accounts went unsettled.

June started with a ray of hope, sunshine. As the sun continued to shine Alexis, Dimitri, and everyone attached to the show started to relax, and the tickets were sold. The Sunday layover in Washburn, Wisconsin, was eagerly anticipated since it was the second payday in June. On Sunday, June 21, Alexis received only enough to pay his troupe twelve dollars each. He expected forty dollars per man, for the two weeks' work. The *Washburn Times* reported on the showmen's commendable behavior, even on a payday. The showmen did not have sufficient money to get rowdy. "Shortly after the Monday, June 22, evening performance, the oil lamp and general light car caught fire and together with all of its contents was totally destroyed."[215] The evening performances were seriously handicapped by the poor temporary light rigs that were used thereafter.

The Forepaugh-Fish organization was restructured with John A. Barton as manager. In Eau Claire, Wisconsin, on June 25, Alexis and the Forepaugh-Fish management signed a new contract. Alexis agreed to "faithfully and satisfactorily render" service at a salary of $285 per week including transportation and board. The contract was effective on July 1 and did not include Dimitri Tsintsadze and his six riders.

Alexis and his riders arrived in Minneapolis as the show's star attraction. They looked forward to a three-day stand to close out the month of June, and the collection of their back pay. Alexis did not receive pay. Instead, his photograph and a lengthy article about the Georgians were published in the *Minneapolis Sunday Times*. Being suspicious of manager John Barton's motives, Alexis speculated that they were trying to flatter him. This article misrepresented him and his troupe of riders. He suspected the show would break up, so he sought to disperse some of his men. He paid the transportation cost of $100, the railroad fare from Minneapolis, to Washington, DC, to Dimitri Tsintsadze, for four Georgian riders on June 30. These Georgians joined the Cole Younger and Frank James Wild West show. Alexis continued to look for positions for the remaining three riders.

Alexis Georgian, a member of the American Socialist Party in Chicago, knew a Socialist attorney, George Leonard of Minneapolis. Alexis contacted Leonard and arranged for a writ of attachment, seeking $1,153.33 for payment of salaries due since June 7. They obtained the writ from the sheriff of Olmstead County, where the show would stop in Rochester, Minnesota, on July 3. Leonard also contacted the sheriff of Winona County, in case they failed in Rochester. Many years later, Leonard wrote about the story of attaching a Wild West show:

"My plan was to attach posts for the tent. I phoned the sheriff at Rochester in advance. He did not have enough force to attach, but I promised to have the six *Georgians* to help. On the way to Rochester, I met Wirt Wilson and told him of my mission, and he gave me his card of introduction to George Simpson, county attorney in Winona, should I fail in Rochester. The Arab acrobats were number eight on the program.

I was to wait until after their performance and they were taken to the hotel, excepting the *Georgians*, and then attach after the show was over. During the day, I had a phone call from the sheriff that the town was in the hands of the show people and that the mayor was frightened out of his wits that gambling and liquor were in control. But I decided to go ahead. The county attorney called his lawyer friends together and they all decided that there would be bloodshed should the attempt be made. We therefore abandoned the place and decided to serve the writ on Luella after the performance and attach the North West Railway, which was taking the show to Winona. About midnight or after, Alexis Georgian, the sheriff and I proceeded to the railroad yard from which the train carrying Luella was to pull out, but we were pelted with stones and 'bravely' retired, the sheriff waving the writ and Alexis his saber.

"We decided to follow the show to Winona, where the show was on a holiday (July 4). Doubt arose as to whether service [on a writ] on a holiday could be effective, a case or two in Pleading and Practice convinced me that service would stand up because the defendant was about to leave the state with intention of escaping liability. Whether applicable or not, the chief thing was to attach, and if the sheriff was in doubt or refused, to consult his attorney and convince him that it could be done.

"The sheriff, who was 6'3", stood up, went to his phone, called George Simpson, and I had him come down to his office, after telling him about the introduction from Wirt Wilson. I showed him the two cases I relied on, retained him as counsel by giving him $50.00. He rounded up the sheriff's deputies and city police officers so that there would be at least two of them at each cash box just after two o'clock, when the crowd was inside and before the cash was delivered to the manager.

"Upon attaching, the manager showed up, called for Mr. Lees, a very prominent lawyer, who later became an associate Justice of the Supreme Court of Minnesota. George Simpson and I took a position close to one of the entrances and waited for the attorney. Mr. Lees, confident of his position that the attachment would not hold, confronted us with the proposition, it being a holiday and the service was not any good. 'You can't do it, George,'" turning to George Simpson. Simpson promptly countered, 'But we did it.' Even if Lees was right, he could do nothing on that day, as no court was available and no order could be issued dissolving the attachment in time to have the show move onto Austin. We got our dough then and there."[216] They received $500 from the gate receipts in Winona, Minnesota.

Alexis and his riders continued to perform for the show under their new contract; however, it did not cover all the riders. On July 7, Dimitri Tsintsadze and several other riders quit the show in Austin, Minnesota, and were stranded there for two months. Alexis' troubles were not over. On Tuesday, July 14, in Marshalltown, Iowa, Alexis was arrested for not paying his employees and was taken to jail when he refused to pay a bond. The incident was recorded in the local *Evening Times-Republican* newspaper.[217] The case was dropped later that day when Mr. Georgian settled with his employees and paid all costs.

Luella Forepaugh-Fish, who collected the tickets, felt the receipts were light. She uncovered an organized scheme by which people were steered away from the ticket wagons and paid cash directly at the door. She telegraphed her husband, who was working with the advance team, to meet her in Janesville, Wisconsin. Meanwhile, the press agent submitted a letter to the *New York Clipper* that was published on July 25. It said in part: "We are now in our twelfth week…thirty-nine days of rain, and endless other obstacles we have encountered, our business has been exceptionally big…."

The show reached Janesville from Beloit Saturday morning, about 2:00 a.m., July 25. The day began as any other with the unloading and setting up on the lot, a place called Spring Brook, Eastern Avenue. Alexis and all the other show people prepared for another ordinary stand, but early in the day, rumors were spreading that something was liable to happen. George and Luella Fish huddled in attorney W. G. Wheeler's office, where they prepared affidavits. The afternoon performance was given along with an attempt by an Indian to kill Jerry Sullivan for insulting his wife. The fortune teller tried to hold up a farmer named Johnson for eight dollars as fair compensation for her reading. The show's boa constrictor consented to eat his first meal since the previous October, devouring with serpentine gusto two Belgian hares and six hens.[218]

Consequently, Sheriff W. H. Appleby served attachment papers on the Luella Forepaugh-Fish Wild West show at 4:30 p.m. They were sworn out by George Fish to cover a claim for $15,409 and by Luella Fish, who claimed $7,850. Judge Dunwiddle signed the orders and assigned D. W. Watt as receiver.

The dining tables buzzed with talk about the writs. The side show freaks wondered if their con games and shows were on for the evening. The performers debated whether to prepare for an evening performance. The roustabouts, mostly ignorant of what was happening, grumbled about the change of routine and the delay in dismantling the tents. The razorbacks ate in silence and went back to the train to wait and see what happened. The show was now technically under the management of Sheriff Appleby and receiver Watt. The sheriff agreed to allow the receipts from the evening performance to partially pay some employees, but all other work stopped.

Sunday, July 26, brought a state of confusion; disorder prevailed in the dressing tent, actors gathered their traps among the scattered trunks, saddles, blankets, clothing, and prop paraphernalia. A group played poker with their last pennies. At the North-West depot, roughnecks, Mexicans, Turks, and cowboys gathered to wait for the Chicago-bound train. The telegraph operator burned up the wire with messages seeking positions in other circuses. Oscar Thompson, a cowboy, had his saddle stolen Sunday night, but it was found Monday along the road to Beloit. Alexis, his riders, and the Arab acrobats decided to stay in Janesville to see what transpired. The Indians were not in the least worried. When they left the Pine Ridge Reservation they presumed the show had filed a bond for their return. Their translator sent a telegram to the Pine Ridge Indian agent, seeking funds for their transportation home.

Mr. Watt and the sheriff arranged for breakfast Monday morning, and organized those who remained to start dismantling the tents, seats, and other equipment. There was no lunch, and at five o'clock their last supper was served. The city of Janesville was not going to feed the show's remnants. Mr. Watt scheduled a property sale for the following Saturday, August 1.

Oscar Thompson, Johnnie Blocker, and Jake and Frank Gilman were clever cowboys who organized an exhibition on South River Street, Janesville, on Tuesday evening. They collected over $50, enabling them to remain in the city until the sale on Saturday, with the hope of purchasing several horses. Alexis watched the cowboys conduct their street performance and wondered if he could do the same. The Georgian riders and Arab acrobats were fortunate that Alexis, their manager, was working with them. He took care of their needs while he struggled to find new bookings.

The Indians on Wednesday learned the truth about their contract with the Luella Forepaugh-Fish show. They had not been legally hired, and no bond was paid to the government Indian agent. The Indian agent sent a telegram:

> "No record of High Eagle or other Indians being absent. Must have left reservation without permit. Can't do anything for them. Should be prosecuted. BRENNAN, Agent."[219]

Meanwhile, back in Minnesota, Dimitri Tsintsadze and his group of Georgians were still living off the charity of some citizens of Austin. The *Austin Daily Herald* reported that Dimitri and his group did have some "dough." A poker game was observed with the Georgians and they had over $300 in gold on the table. They were a strange sight, walking around town in their heavy coats, called Chokhas, during the August hot spell.

The receiver's sale was held at ten o'clock, Saturday, August 1. The advertised procedure was for the show to first be sold in parcels and later as a whole, and in case no one bid more for it as a whole than was offered for the parcels, the parcel bidders would get it. The parcel bids' aggregate sum was $12,410. Mr. F. J. Walker, president of the Erie Printing and Lithographing company, made a whole bid of $12,510. There were no other offers and the auctioneer gaveled the sale to a close. Mr. Walker leased the show to John Barton and hired Harry Semon as manager. He announced that he wished all the employees to remain. Mr. and Mrs. Fish left Janesville for their home in Philadelphia on Tuesday, August 4.[220]

Chicago, 109 miles to the south, was the gathering place for many who had left the show. The Sioux made it as far as Chicago and were offered a pay raise from $5 to $7, but they refused to return. These Sioux became stuck at the Chicago Northwest railway depot for three days before assistance arrived on August 5.

Once the word spread that the show was to hit the road again, several performers returned from Chicago. Signing a last minute contract, his third try this season, Alexis was sent by John Barton to Chicago to find a lady wing shot.[221]

Their first jump from Janesville to Appleton took place on Tuesday,

August 4. They arrived at four o'clock in the afternoon, and after a hurried scan of the situation, the managers decided to skip Appleton and push to Green Bay, Wisconsin.

The Luella Forepaugh-Fish Wild West was doomed after four days of rain with only two performances out of four scheduled, and they did not make the nut. Arriving in Ishpeming, Michigan, Wednesday, August 12, *The Duluth, South Shore & Atlantic* railway demanded their $500 in transportation costs, refusing to move the outfit without it. The afternoon show in Ishpeming was lightly attended. The cowboys and musicians refused to perform in the evening unless they were paid. Alexis made a loan of $100 to Barton, even though he had not been paid. Barton made a deal with the cowboys and musicians that he would pay them $5 each after the performance. The evening performance was again lightly attended and during the performance the treasurer and four other managers left town. After the show, when the cowboys discovered they would not get their pay, they cleared the park of all the visitors, threatening them by displaying their guns, and a riot was barely avoided.[222] After negotiations with the roustabouts, the show was loaded, but the railway shunted it to a side track near the Moro mine of the Cleveland Cliffs Company. The Luella Forepaugh-Fish Wild West now owned by Walker and leased by Barton, was finished. Walker, on Saturday, August 15, shipped the equipment to Chicago for disposal and sent the horses to Erie, Pennsylvania, where a higher price could be obtained than in the West.

Alexis found himself stranded with seven Georgian riders, Arab acrobats, and the lady wing shot. They proposed to put together their own show. Alexis and his troupe rented some horses and gave a Sunday afternoon performance at Union Park to a large crowd. They charged twenty-five cents and made a neat sum. Alexis suggested his little troupe go on the road for the balance of the season, giving similar shows. A few of the remaining acts fell in with Alexis: Muly Ally, a champion acrobat; Lone Star May, the famous girl horseback shot; Harry Niece, a famous revolver shot; and the Ishpeming City Band. Their first engagement was in Marquette, Michigan, on Thursday, August 20. They gave an afternoon exhibition of riding and shooting at the fair ground to a modest crowd. In the evening, only a handful of people gathered at the opera house to see the performance. It is unclear if they made their nut, or if they continued on the road.

Alexis' friend, Dimitri Tsintsadze, was still stranded in Austin, Minnesota. By the end of August they were out of cash and had lost contact with Alexis. Dimitri and his companions were hired by the county fair in Austin to exhibit their horsemanship each afternoon.

Alexis returned to Janesville in November to settle his claim in court. He had one of the largest claims against the Luella-Forepaugh show, in the vicinity of $1600. He stayed at the Grand Hotel.[223]

PAWNEE BILL'S HISTORIC WILD WEST (1903)

Luka Chkhartishvili arrived in New York with fifteen fellow Georgian riders on April 15. Alexis Georgian, who rode with Luka between 1897 and 1899, was now managing all the Georgian riders. Alexis and Luka contracted with the Pawnee Bill show to provide four riders. Luka and three comrades traveled by train from New York to Pittsburgh, Pennsylvania, and then took the short trip to Carnegie. Luka's troupe had two weeks to prepare for the season opening Saturday, May 2, in Carnegie. During these rehearsals, Luka caught the act of a new performer, Lulu Bell Parr. She performed trick riding and shooting, but she was best known for riding bucking horses. She stayed with Pawnee Bill's show until 1908, the same year Luka left. Her career paralleled that of other Georgian riders from 1903 onward.

Pawnee Bill, trying to keep up with the latest in tent show business, added an electric power plant to help generate gate during the night performance.

Luka, in his eleventh season and his second with Pawnee Bill, knew the program. They rode in the arena five times each show. They first rode in the Grand Entrée, and their second entry was a race between Georgians, Indians, and Mexicans. Their third event was to give a ten-minute performance of native song, dance, and riding. Before the end of the show, they took part in the hippodrome races and the final salute. The total time in the arena was approximately fifteen minutes twice a day and participation in the daily parade. Unfortunately, they were also familiar with railroad accidents. During the first week while en-route to Wheeling, West Virginia, Pawnee Bill's outfit was involved in a small railroad accident that delayed their arrival and caused the cancellation of one performance.

The Pawnee Bill show worked its way around Ohio during May, one day at a time. On Sunday, May 24, the daily monotony of parades and shows was interrupted in Xenia, Ohio. Luka's troupe was ready for its usual Sunday break because the day's work of unloading and setting up camp did not involve the cast. However, as the ammunition wagon was being driven to the lot the jolting caused by crossing a railroad track exploded a loose cartridge, which set off the other ammunition.[224] The wagon contained two kegs of powder, the Georgian saddles, Pawnee Bill souvenirs, and other equipment belonging to Luka's troupe. The wagon crew and other showmen reacted quickly to remove the kegs of powder and salvaged the saddles. Luka's saddles and support equipment were badly damaged but repairable. Luka's men spent the rest of Sunday repairing their gear.

The next morning, a windstorm toppled the horse tent. Xenia, Ohio had one more surprise for the showmen. A local physician called to the lot to check the condition of several deathly sick showmen, determined they used standing water from a hydrant. They all recovered.[225]

Luka could take pride in his men's performance. The local newspapers stated: "the show is a small scale version of Buffalo Bill's but not quite as good," and then they would add "the feature that seemed to make the greatest impression, judging from the applause, was the riding of the *Georgians*."[226]

On August 29, there was a storm to remember in Cambridge Springs, Pennsylvania. Rain began at the start of the evening performance, which was not unusual. The storm rapidly developed into one of the most severe electrical storms ever witnessed in Cambridge Springs. "The lightning was almost incessant, and the terrific peals of thunder seemed determined to jar all the water out of the sky. Still the show went on, out in the open arena, where horses, riders and actors were being drowned by the soaking rain. It was after ten o'clock, with the show a little more than half over, when a gust of wind blew down the east side of the tent."[227] A general stampede ensued, and it was miraculous that no one was seriously hurt. Not many stayed for the concert. Luka and his men spent the next day trying to dry out and clean their clothing.

The show closed in Pana, Illinois, on October 31 with a celebration by a number of the younger braves attached to the show. The Indian braves met some coal miners and procured a quantity of whisky. The local good citizens having read dime novels and the yellow press supposed the

Indians all charged up on fire water would terrorize their town. The good folks sought shelter. But nothing happened; the fifty-five Sioux Indians left on a train headed for St. Louis and then on to the Rosebud and Valentine agencies in South Dakota and Nebraska. The remainder of the show returned to their winter quarters in Carnegie. Luka and the Georgians from other shows, who arrived with him in April, returned to their wives and families in Georgia.

INDIAN BILL'S HISTORIC WILD WEST AND MEXICAN HIPPODROME (1903)

Alexis Georgian reported he managed Georgian riders that rode with Indian Bill's Historic Wild West and Mexican Hippodrome show. The "Cossack Cavalry" was led by a Lieutenant Tobinowsky, who arrived around March 1, 1903. The true identity of Tobinowsky has not been determined; he may have been of Russian heritage, Georgian, or just an American working in the Cossack riding act. However, in later years, other Wild West entertainments owned by John Augustus Jones (1868-1918)—the Jones Railroad show 1906 and Jones Bros. Buffalo Ranch 1910—used Georgians as "Cossack" riders.

J. Augustus Jones and his brother Elmer H. Jones were the proprietors of the 1903 show. Elmer was the manager, H. H. Whittier was General Agent, and H. J. Leonard was the press agent. Captain William Powers was hired to act as Indian Bill, and he secured the Indians from Oklahoma (Indian Territory). Before opening, Augustus purchased horses in Chicago, and his brother Elmer went out to the Dakotas for saddle stock and a new bandwagon and tableaux wagon. The season opened at McKees Rocks, Pennsylvania, on April 22. The show traveled as a twenty-five car outfit with six Pullman sleepers, eleven flats, five stocks, and three advance cars. It was reported in the *New York Clipper* that they carried 470 employees.

The program was a typical Wild West show with an opening presentation by the horsemen of all nations. The Cossack Cavalry in their wild, daring riding were near the end of the program. The finale included hippodrome, Indian, and chariot races and the burning of a trapper's cabin.[228] The whole performance was a run-down-at-the-heels affair. The advertised beautiful western girls consisted of a half dozen females who looked as though they had seen anywhere from forty to sixty years of sawdust. The outfit would pitch its tents (arena, horse department, side show, and dining tent) and start shooting craps. It was a big fake.

The railroad show jumped daily from town to town, and as one would expect, it was involved in an accident. The evening of May 12, the train wrecked between Mt. Jewet, Pennsylvania, and Bradford, Pennsylvania, about two miles north of the famous Kinzue bridge. This did not slow down the outfit. Indian Bill's Historic Wild West arrived as a thirteen-car show on Saturday, August 22, at Hagerstown, Maryland, and then, for unexplained reasons, they arrived as a three-car show the following Monday at Shepherdstown, Virginia. The smaller show spent September in Virginia and West Virginia, closing at Grafton, West Virginia, on October 3, 1903. Their winter quarters were in Clifton Forge, Virginia. Augustus Jones took a small rail show south for the winter, closing on Christmas Day.

1903 EPILOGUE

On December 20, the *New York Clipper* reported Georgians were working at Huber's Museum, at 14th Street, New York City. These were likely the Georgians who returned with Buffalo Bill at the end of their season in England.

Alexis Georgian was in Janesville, Wisconsin, by Monday, November 23, and planned to stay in the city until his claims were settled. The suit was heard in district court by Judge Dunwiddle, Monday, November 30, and Alexis acted as his own lawyer. Additional arguments were heard on Saturday, December 5. On December 28 the attorneys gathered at the court only to learn that the litigation was delayed because of John Barton's absence. It was officially noted that Barton was seriously ill in a hospital in Chicago. The court heard the case on January 21, 1904, and Alexis was present, but Luella, George, and John Barton were absent. The judge again heard arguments on Alexis' case on January 30, 1904. The final judgment was handed down on February 25, and Alexis received a sum of $807.50.

Alexis Georgian's struggles with tent show managers, courts, and disgruntled employees were insignificant compared to the strains the Georgian people were enduring at home. Czar Nicholas II signed a decree on June 25, 1903, confiscating the property of the Armenian (Apostolic) National Church, causing uproar in Tbilisi. The landowners and peasants of Guria were unable to negotiate a solution to their problems; therefore, the peasants created their own solution. They made life unbearable for the local landowners by various boycotts and provocations. The landowners left for the larger cities and started using pressure on the czar's government to intervene. A general strike broke out in July. This spread to the southern provinces, including Guria. The czar sent the Governor-General of the Caucasus a personal telegram demanding "the most energetic action" to put down the disorders. Cossack troops and police took up arms against the peasants in many Georgian towns, and the casualties were heavy. Russia's repressive Interior Minister Von K. Plehve's solution was a mixture of pogroms against the Jews, forced Russification of minorities, floggings and the shooting of unruly peasants and factory workers. To create patriotic zeal and divert attention from the czar's troubles at home, Plehve remarked, "In order to hold back the revolution, we need a small victorious war," and in 1904 he arranged a war with Japan, which ended badly for the czar.

Alexis Georgian resided in Chicago, Illinois, at the season's close. He assisted Dimitri Tsintsadze and four other Georgians by paying their room and board ($250) for their stay in Chicago between December 1903 and April 1904. Alexis may have had a bad business year, but the American tent show business was booming. Alexis, a member of the American Socialist Party, was interested in the Russian and Georgian revolutionary (Social Democrats) movements. During their London convention in July and August, the revolutionary Social-Democrats split into two factions. These factions were the Mensheviks (Men of the Minority), who aimed at the establishment of a constitutional republic as a step toward socialism, and the Bolsheviks (Men of the Majority), who stood for the overthrow of the regime by revolutionary methods and the establishment of the dictatorship of the proletariat (laboring class) of professional agitators and party men. Alexis leaned toward the Bolsheviks.

OTHER SHOW BUSINESS

Edwin Hollis Low, the travel agent for Buffalo Bill and other tent shows, booked more than twenty-one ocean voyages between New York and Batumi for the Georgian riders. Edwin (1859-1903) was born in New Orleans. He married Fannie Tucker and became a tourist and steamship agent with offices in Paris, London, and New York. He was the shipping agent for Barnum & Bailey and all their associated tent shows. Edwin, a non-swimmer, drowned during a yachting race in a squall that overturned his sixteen-foot knock-about yacht Pickaninny on July 18, 1903.[229] Fannie Low continued to run the Edwin H. Low's Steamship Agency.

Pawnee Bill's Georgian riders, ca 1908
Somerville, Massachusetts
Left to right: Konstantine Chkhartishvili, Teimuraz Chkhartishvili,
Kaisar Kvetaishvili, Vaso Tsuladze, Platon Murvanidze
Author's Collection

Plate No. 25

"The traitor and liar deserve to be pierced with a lance."

Shota Rustaveli

1904 PROLOGUE

Russian Interior Minister Plehve's "small victorious war" started the night of February 8- 9, 1904. The Russo-Japanese conflict erupted out of the growing clash between the expansionist ambitions of the two countries. Czar Nicholas II claimed special privileges in Manchuria and exacted lumber concessions from Korea. Japan viewed encroachment into Manchuria as a threat to its security. Not bothering to actually declare war, the Japanese fleet attacked the Russian Far East Squadron, bottling them up in a harbor at Port Arthur with a blockade. Russia's opposition revolutionary Social-Democratic organizations immediately started printing broadsheets condemning the war. The goal of this propaganda was an anti-government demonstration on April 18 *(old style)*, First of May *(new style)*, to show that the workers opposed the czar's unnecessary war with Japan. The slogans that reverberated across Russia and in Ozurgeti were "Down with Autocracy" and "Hurrah for political freedom." The governor-general in Tbilisi issued a secret circular that ordered "persons carrying even old-fashioned weapons and revolvers shall be regarded as persons relating to enforced protection." Students in Tbilisi showed their opposition by refusing to salute the governor-general in the street and insulting his portrait.

David Kadjaia's men, who were returning to England, and Luka Chkhartishvili's, who were returning to the United States, worried about leaving their families. It was a dangerous time, but they had become dependent upon the income and the stature they had achieved. David and Luka were unaware that their tent show masters had new features designed for the "Cossack and Jap" performers.

Alexis Georgian, who was living in Chicago, in an interview, said: "I have a brother in the Russian army, who is among the troops ordered to the front by the czar. I think that the officials will be kept busy watching the people of Russia themselves lest an uprising against the government occurs."[230] On March 22, Alexis arrived in St. Louis, trying to arrange for his troupe of Georgian rough riders to perform at the St. Louis World's Fair. He gave another interview and said: "Russia has a greater foe within her borders and a far more dangerous one than the Japanese. The working people and the students are dissatisfied with Russia's rule... war costs money, and the people will not stand the taxation.... While I admit the majority of the Russian people do not favor the war, we wonder why the United States, or any other outside power, should display any attitude of sympathy in the commercial struggle between two despotic powers. Neither side is fighting for liberty. And both nations are weak, though from different causes. Russia's calamity is yet to come after the Japs are defeated. An opportunity, never offered before, will present itself then to that class of people in Russia who, since 1895, have been trying to disrupt the government."[231] Alexis' politics may have had a bearing on his inability to secure a place for the Georgian riders at the World's Fair. At the same time, the Russian government waffled on even having a pavilion at the World's Fair, and time ran out for Alexis. He had to arrange contracts quickly for his Georgian riders who were arriving in New York. Later in the season, a Russian pavilion opened.

The circus trust, at their winter meeting in Springfield, Ohio, decided to discontinue the street parade. This had been under consideration for some years. "They cost too much in expense and labor and bring no revenue... electric wires, streetcars, congested conditions all impede the progress" were reasons cited for abandoning circus parades. This decision had no impact on circuses and Wild West shows that were not in the circus trust.

BUCKSKIN BILL'S CONSOLIDATED WILD WEST (1904)

At his Fort Worth, Texas, ranch, Henry Allott employed a crew to transfigure the Cole Younger and Frank James Wild West outfit back into Buckskin Bill's Wild West. The preparations included repainting the wagons, advertising cars, and side show banners. The train contained seven flats, five sleepers, and six stock cars all painted orange-red with blue lettering. New billboard posters and advertising flyers were created and ready for a lithograph company just as war between Japan and Russia, called the Russo-Japanese War, captured America's attention on February

9. An amusing note: The officers of the Russian fleet were attending a circus when the Japanese attacked.

Mr. J. Delmar Andrews, from Perry, Iowa, arrived early in April to become the press agent.[232] Allott decided to scrap the art work for the lithographs and gave Andrews the job of generating all new lithographs and newspaper ads. Forty-eight days after the surprise attack on Port Arthur, Andrews' press team had the show's new main attraction, "The Siege of Port Arthur," ready for print. This attraction pitted their Japanese performers against the "Russian Cossack" riders.

The season opened in Fort Worth on Thursday, April 7. The season's first parade was late starting, due to the threatening weather, and an "educated" pig killed by a streetcar. The free exhibition to gather the multitude was a high-dive act requiring a little more nerve than usual because of the wind. It turned into a rainy day with a middling crowd for the afternoon and a good evening crowd. Alexis Georgian, Dimitri Tsintsadze, and their troupe of Georgian riders and Arab Acrobats arrived late Thursday evening.

Texas in April can be bitter cold and windy, as it was in Cleburne and Farmersville. The show required the Indians to perform shirtless. Alexis and his men wore their woolen Chokas and were acclimated from spending the winter in windy Chicago. Attendance was low from the cold weather, and because the cotton planters were busy this time of year.

Alexis and the show arrived in Paris, Texas, around eight o'clock Sunday morning, April 10. The show lot location was undecided when they arrived; therefore, Alexis and the others spent the day around the rail yard. The tents were finally raised on the beautiful hospital grounds. Sunday night, a fire burned three of the nicest buildings in town. The matinee performance on Monday was poorly attended, but there was a fair evening crowd. Three days on the road and the nut still had not been made, so money was tight.

Alexis and Dimitri, having traveled together for the last four years, were familiar with American towns with one-story brick buildings built around a square, like Honey Grove and Sherman, Texas. Wolfe City was an even smaller town and the show set seats on only one side of the arena. Mrs. Tantlinger's diary recounts that Henry Allott found himself in a little trouble in Wolfe City when he hit a boy, and a performer, Tom King, got into some trouble. Everyone was ready to spend Friday and Saturday in Dallas. The Friday evening performance in Dallas was spoiled by rain, and the front that brought it turned the weather cold the next day. Alexis and his troupe were looking forward to the weekend in Gainesville and the first payday, but up to now business had been bad.

Alexis, Dimitri, the other Georgian riders, and Arab acrobats had a few surprises waiting for them during the week of April 18. The terrain changed with their movement north into Paul's Valley in the Indian Territory. It was now hilly with more trees. *The Paul Valley Sentinel* reported that a motley army of grafters arrived in town and that the people of Paul's Valley came out for the afternoon performance, but due to the strong graft, the evening performance was poorly attended. The gambling games with the side show were plentiful, and the show's manager was arrested for shortchanging patrons. Henry Allott and his cronies were conducting the same type show they had for the last couple years.

Oklahoma City was plastered for weeks with lithographs and newspaper articles concerning Buckskin Bill's Wild West. The "Siege of Port Arthur" and the fierce "Russian Cossacks" featured prominently in this advertising.

The show arrived in Oklahoma City on the morning of April 20. Several events took place that morning. Joe Gorman, the master of transportation for the Buckskin Bill show, was shot dead by W.L. Durant, the show's night watchman, at 6:30 in the morning while they were unloading the train. Alexis, meantime, conducted an interview with a reporter from the Oklahoma *Daily Times* in the Compton Hotel lobby. He was unaware that some of his Arab Acrobats also conducted their own interviews with lawyers. Alexis learned about it later that day. His interview was published that afternoon on the front page.

"Captain Alexis Georgian, who has charge of the detachment of *Georgians* with the Buckskin Bill Wild West, is an entertaining conversationalist, speaking English and a number of other languages with but a slight accent. Asked this morning if he was going back to fight for Russia, he said: 'No, we will make the United States our home in the future because we would be conscripted if we went back, and we don't want to war against Japan. I feel sorry for the Japanese as there are too many Russian soldiers for them to beat. Russia has all of Europe afraid of her, and there will be no intervention by the other powers. If England should interfere she would find France and Germany opposed to her, and it would be so if any other country should take up the battle for the Japanese. Russia has a great many more foes within her borders than she has outside of them and the government fully realized this fact, but all they can do is to fight internally and externally to the end. We have millions and millions of acres of land in Russia that are unoccupied and should be cultivated, but the condition of the common people is such that they are not able to obtain title to lands or implements to work the lands with, and this condition is one that will eventually cause the end of the present form of government in Russia. I feel more sorrow when I think of my own people in Russia.'

"Captain Georgian has been in this country several years with different tent exhibitions and he and his compatriots give the untruth to the current idea that Cossacks are savages. His men are strong, intelligent and liberty loving and will all make themselves citizens of this country as soon as possible. The Buckskin Bill show has a number of characters on its rolls and a lot of fine men are connected with it."233

The afternoon and evening performances went on as scheduled, but later that evening Alexis discovered his Arab Acrobats performers were angry that they had not received their two-week pay in Gainesville, Texas. *The Daily Oklahoman* reported the arrest of Alexis Georgian.

"Captain Alexis Georgian, the noted Cossack officer, who has for some time been connected with Buckskin Bill's Wild West show, was last night arrested by the police at the instance of some Turks who have been in his employ.

"While the charge made against Georgian is for vagrancy, it was made in order to detain the Russian and secure the payment of salaries alleged to be due to several Turks who have been with him. The Turks claim that they entered into a contract with Georgian for an engagement of two weeks, but have not received no compensation *(sic)* and that Captain Georgian was paid $500 by the show management yesterday, then quit the company and was arranging to leave the city last night without notifying them of his going or paying them for their services.

"The Russian officer was much put out at his detention and chafed over the fact that a personal bond was denied him. He said it was true that he had quit the show, but he was going to join Campbell Brothers' show and intended to take fifteen people with him, including the complaining Turks, for whom, he claimed, he engaged lodging at the Compton hotel last night. His agent made an offer of settlement last night, but the Turks declined to make terms with him."[234]

Alexis was released Friday, April 22. He took his band of riders and acrobats to Fairbury, Nebraska, to join Campbell Brothers' circus.

The Buckskin Bill Wild West started its downward spiral into bankruptcy on June 11, in Bradford, Pennsylvania, when the band and several other groups of employees and creditors filed attachments against the show. The show closed in Erie, June 14.

BUFFALO BILL'S WILD WEST AND CONGRESS OF ROUGH RIDERS (1904)

From October 1903 to April 1904, Buffalo Bill's Wild West outfit was encamped at the Barnum & Bailey, Ltd. winter quarters on an estate called Etruria at Hanley, about two miles from Stoke-on-Trent, England. The estate had twelve buildings of brick and iron, putting everything under a roof during the winter. There were barns, stables, meadows, and grazing land plus living quarters for the men wintering over. The winter crew made repairs where necessary, repainted all the wagons, canvas and banners, and manufactured new parts as required. The London Office at No. 8 Beaconsfield Terrace, West Kensington, was busy in March gathering the staff from around the world for their arrival at the Barnum & Bailey winter quarters in April.

The *SS Cedric* sailed March 23 from New York and arrived March 31 in Liverpool. Onboard were six Georgians: Nicoloz Surguladze, Silovan Kartvelishvili, Nestor Menagarishvili, Mirian Darsalia, Solomon Imnadze, and Ivane Jorbenadze.

Buffalo Bill and Jule Keen sailed from Philadelphia on the *SS Friesland* with thirty-six Indians and others on March 26. They arrived in Liverpool, April 8, a miserable looking lot of characters. The passage ran into stormy weather causing considerable suffering. Despite some legal challenges, the exhibition continued with rehearsal call Monday, April 18, at Hanley. "Before opening at the Old Racecourse, Bootham Bar, Stoke-on-Trent, Buffalo Bill invited the mayor of Hanley, Councillor H.B. Shirley, to bring his entire council to watch a dress rehearsal at Etruria. It was a way of thanking them for making the cowboys who remained behind so welcome in their community. The civic dignitaries arrived in two electric tramcars chartered for the occasion."[235] Buffalo Bill's Wild West began its final Great Britain tour at Stoke-on-Trent in Staffordshire on a fair Monday, April 25, to a capacity crowd.

Buffalo Bill and his manager Fred Hutchinson liked to keep the show "up-to-date," and they had a surprise for David Kadjaia and his troupe of fifteen Georgian riders. The war between Russia and Japan provided Buffalo Bill an opportunity to pit the "Russian Cossack" riders against a troupe of Japanese riders. The English were afraid of the expansionist policies of Czar Nicholas II and supported the Japanese in this conflict. The Georgians, as was perhaps not surprising, had a rather chilly reception at their appearances. The thunderous applause of years past was absent. Silence, catcalls, and other derogatory gestures were witnessed for the first time by David and his compatriots. David and his men rode hard to win over the audience and they succeeded day after day.

Accidents plagued Buffalo Bill in the first three weeks of touring the midlands and Wales; three sleeping cars were wrecked in transportation mishaps.

James Bailey and those in his circus organization did influence one aspect of the Wild West show. Bailey and his men added a side show annex with their usual "freaks." Charles E. Griffin, the side show manager, included a "Jap and Cossack" in his opening "Ballyhoo." One morning, in a fit of exhilaration, after the "Jap" finished a clever juggling act, Griffin said: "And that's the way they juggle with the Russians," whereupon the Georgian balked and could not be induced to mount the "ballyhoo" stage again.[236]

The Wild West entered Scotland at Hawick on July 26. The show reached Glasgow August 1, and they were doing the biggest business since 1893 in Chicago. The Scottish capital, Edinburgh, was played between August 7 and 13. Alexander Murvanidze, Simon Oragvelidze, and Pavle Makharadze had a group picture taken at a studio in Edinburgh, and Silovan Kartvelishvili also had his picture taken at the same studio on 16 Prince Street. The chandelier wagon, an Edison steam electric power plant, burned at Dundee August 20. The show's mechanics re-built the wagon, and the evening shows continued under lights. Frank Small, the press agent, took several company members from Inverness on September 3 to John O'Groats' for publicity photographs. Dumfries was Buffalo Bill's last stand in Scotland, September 14.

The Charles Urban Trading Company spent a week in September with Buffalo Bill's outfit, filming the show. The biograph film was shown to the staff Sunday, October 2, in Glossop. They slapped themselves on the back and laughed watching the movie; their laughter might have sounded hollow if only they had known that this form of entertainment one day would mean the end of Wild West tent shows.

The season ended back in Hanley with a final performance at the Agricultural Show Field, Birches Head, Friday, October 21. The *Staffordshire Sentinel* reported in headlines: "positively the last two performances of Buffalo Bill's Wild West in England—EVER!!" The *Sentinel* added: "As a mark of affection for Buffalo Bill, it has been suggested that the popular song of affectionate remembrance *'Auld Lang Syne,'* be sung as a wind-up after the performance."[237] After the final performance and Buffalo Bill backed his horse with profound bows to the audience, the entire company heard the audience of 12,500 people singing to them from the arena.

It was rumored that the Georgians returned to their homeland for the winter. The horses, rolling stock and paraphernalia went into winter quarters at the Barnum & Bailey estate. The rebuilt equipment was to be shipped to the Continent in early spring for the 1905 season in France.

Georgians in Edinburgh, Scotland, ca 1904

Left to right: Alexander Murvanidze, Simon Oragvelidze, Pavle Makharadze
Author's Collection
Plate No. 26

CAMPBELL BROTHERS GREAT CONSOLIDATED SHOWS (1904)

Alexis Georgian on February 8 signed a contract with the Campbell Brothers Great Consolidated Shows to provide four Georgians and seven Arab Acrobats to perform with the show from May 1, to on or about the last part of October. Alexis, Dimitri Tsintsadze and their men worked for two weeks in April with the Buckskin Bill show before moving onto the Campbell Brothers. Alexis, Dimitri, and the others were joining a true family circus that had its beginnings in 1889.

■ ■ ■

Charles Campbell, Alexis Georgian, Dimitri Tsintsadze, along with their fellow Georgians and Arab Acrobats, arrived in Fairbury with one week to prepare for the opening of the Campbell Brothers circus. Alexis engaged additional Georgians and Arab acrobats for which the Campbell Brothers agreed to pay $35.00 per week. A hard week of rehearsals and getting to know the new show routine ended with their first performance in Fairbury on Saturday, April 30. Sunday about 2:00 p.m. the show packed and took a short jump to Pawnee City, Nebraska. The day of rest was a blessing, and yet disaster befell the show Sunday night.

A fire occurred on the show train about 11:00 p.m. Sunday night. The elephant keeper, Nadge, returned to the animal car to feed and bed the stock. Seven men were in the car when Nadge entered carrying a gasoline torch. A portion of the burner broke, letting oil escape freely. The escaping oil caused a blaze to flash and burn Nadge's hand. He turned the torch to keep the blaze from burning himself seriously, and somehow the oil-can came unjointed and fell into the straw. In a moment the interior of the entire car was a mass of flame. The men escaped without serious injury, but three elephants, four camels, two sacred cattle and one black bear burned to death. The loss was estimated at $20,000 with no insurance, which was an inauspicious start to the season.

Alexis, Dimitri, and the other Georgians gave their performances in Nebraska towns in spite of the rainy and wintery conditions that prevailed during the first two weeks of May. Fortunately, Alexis and his men were performing under a circus tent, not in the open as they had in the Wild West shows. Meanwhile, Al Campbell traveled to New York and purchased replacement animals from the Hagenbeck's show. Their troubles were not over. A large flat car carrying one of the largest canvas wagons was wrecked at Schuyler, Nebraska, on May 10.

Performing under a tent provided some relief from foul weather, but there were other hazards in riding at full speed inside a tent. In Sioux City, Iowa, a race between an American and Georgian furnished some excitement for the crowd. The Georgian struck one of the big tent poles with his shoulder and nearly knocked it over. But that made no difference to him; he rode merrily on. The American won the race.[238]

Alexis found a reporter in Sioux City who was eager to arouse Russian and Japanese tensions between himself and the leader of a Japanese acrobatic troupe. The reporter wrote:

"'The Japs will win, sure thing.' So says George Mizuno, of Tokyo, who does all kinds of hair raising stunts in Campbell Brothers' circus, which was in Sioux City yesterday. 'If they can't win with the soldiers they now have over there,' he went on, 'they can send over to this country for us fellows, and we will go over and help give the czar a black eye.' The Jap stood just outside the door of the dressing room. Alexis Georgian, a subject of the czar, came up to the group and heard the statement of the little Jap. Georgian is a finely built, handsome fellow. A belt full of cartridges added a little to the ferociousness of his appearance. Did the Russian take exception in the remarks of the little Jap? Not a bit of it. He put his right arm around the little Jap's neck and said: 'We're good friends, George and I. And the Japs aren't any more anxious to see the Russians get the worst of it than we are.'"[239] Chances for an argument which the interviewer hoped to bring about by getting the two men together immediately vanished. Instead, a love feast followed.

A newspaper headline read: "Cossacks are cruel. They maltreated their horses and are held in contempt." This was in an opposition newspaper to the one that Alexis had given the previous interview and provides another viewpoint. The story read:

"'They incite the contempt of every performer in the circus,' said Charles Campbell yesterday in speaking of the *Georgians*. 'They have absolutely no feeling for their horses, using fine wisps of wire for whips, which cut the hides, and will drive a pointed spur into a horse's side until the blood spurts out. They kill more horses than any troupe of performers on the road, and there is no such a thing as stopping their cruelties, if you desire to keep them with the circus."[240] It should be noted that the Campbell Brothers kept Georgians in their show until it went bankrupt in 1912.

Alexis, Dimitri, their riders, and all the show people battled the weather, the daily grind of putting the show on, and in Le Sueur, Minnesota, a case of smallpox. The board of health in Le Sueur quarantined one showman in a pasture outside of town; the health officials also vaccinated all members of the Campbell Brothers after a great deal of trouble.

"Doc" Campbell took reporters around to the dressing tent between performances and, on one occasion in Neola, Iowa, in July, he introduced a reporter to Alexis Georgian. The article read:

"We were introduced to Alexis Georgian, Russian manager of the *Georgian* riders, whom we found to be a highly educated gentleman and who spoke English fluently. Mr. Georgian is very favorably impressed with the commercial outlook of the United States. The railroads, the post office department and the large commercial enterprises he thinks excel the whole world.

"Mr. Georgian showed us his saddle. It was very unique. The ivory mountings cost $175.00. The padding, about six inches thick, is stuffed with deer hair. The ordinary *Georgian* saddle is worth about $75, Mr. Georgian's, about $275.00. For out-and-out daredevil riding, we give these *Georgians* the cake."[241]

Dimitri Tsintsadze, who spent three months in Austin, Minnesota, last season, looked forward to his return to Austin on July 14. However, there was a railroad accident in Renova, Minnesota, between Spring Valley and Austin that forced the cancellation of their performance in Austin.

Blue Earth, Minnesota, was the scene of the next Georgian rider accident, on July 21. "The *Georgian* rough riders were exceptionally good. The careless and reckless manner in which they performed on the backs of the horses was such that it very nearly frightened a person.

One of the horses fell in the evening, throwing its rider and nearly stepping on him."[242] A month later there was another accident, this time involving the train. In Galt, Missouri, the show had a late night derailment, causing them to arrive in Trenton, Missouri, about 9:00 a.m., August 19.

The Campbell Brothers normally spent the entire season on the northern plains, but this year they ventured southwest through Colorado, New Mexico, Texas, Oklahoma, and Arkansas. After a season-opening disaster, it wound down on a lighter note with a problem gorilla, on September 21. The gorilla, named "Bob," escaped from its den while in route from El Paso, Texas, to Alamogorde, New Mexico. "The agile beast made his way over seven horse cars to the engine, and the first intimation that the engine crew had of his presence was a huge chunk of coal which the hairy brute hurled with crashing force against the boiler head. Fireman Harry Nelson was in the gangway firing up, when he was attacked by the huge animal and hurled to the floor of the cab. The engineer set his air to 'emergency' and sustained a broken arm. The sudden stopping of the train brought out a swarm of animal keepers, who promptly surrounded the engine where 'Bob' was in full possession. Bob burned his hands quite severely on the furnace door, but succeeded in grasping the whistle cord and seemed delighted with the terrific noise he was making."[243]

Early in October, one of Alexis' performers left the troupe for an unknown reason. The season closed in Hennessey, Oklahoma, on November 5. Alexis and his troupe had an engagement beginning the following week, in St. Louis, and requested travel expenses from Hennessey, Oklahoma, to St. Louis.

PAWNEE BILL'S WILD WEST AND GREAT FAR EAST EXHIBITION (1904)

Luka, who traveled between Batumi and New York for eleven years, could see trouble brewing before he left home. The dock workers in Batumi were hostile; the officials, stern and impolite. Tension was in the air. It was a mixed blessing to leave; on one hand they feared for their families, and on the other they were glad to leave the trouble behind them.

Gordon Lillie (Pawnee Bill) saw an opportunity in the Russian/Japanese war since he had signed contracts with both Russian and Japanese performers. He had a surprise for Luka's troupe at the first rehearsal. The new feature was a battle scene between the Georgians and the Japanese. As the announcer set the stage, Luka and his men marched across the arena singing. The Japanese fired a volley at close range from an ambush and then opened up with a Maxim gun.[26] The fierce warriors from Russia fled in disorder. Luka and his men were not accustomed to being the bad guys. The fact that the czar's Cossack troops were harassing villagers back home only added to their thoughts of betrayal to their countrymen.

Luka Chkhartishvili and his troupe of riders visited the Barnum & Bailey show in New York on April 20.[244] Pawnee Bill opened on Saturday, April 23, in Carnegie, Pennsylvania. As Pawnee Bill's show traveled across Pennsylvania in April and May the crowds booed and hissed the Georgian riders. "When this show of feeling first asserted itself," said Pawnee Bill, "the *Georgians* demanded to know what it meant. I explained to Prince Luka that the jeers were from boys, and that their efforts were being appreciated. They have grown to be very sensitive about it, because they met with the same reception in Pittsburg, Reading, and other cities where we have appeared."[245] In newspaper after newspaper came the same statements: "When the Japanese cavalry made their appearance they were loudly cheered, but there was not one to cheer for the czar's *Georgians* when they dashed into the arena."[246]

Pawnee Bill's show instituted what is believed to be the first telephone used in a ticket wagon while they played in Philadelphia. The telephonic connection was made direct with the ticket wagon, and the show announced that seats could be ordered by telephone from any part of the city. The public took kindly to this radical novelty, resulting in exceptional sales of reserved seats. The telephone was also extensively used for carriage calls after the show.[247]

The political audience in Washington, DC, gave Luka and his rough riders

---

[26] Maxim Gun - The world's first automatic portable machine-gun. The Maxim used the energy of each bullet's recoil force to eject the spent cartridge and insert the next bullet. The Maxim Machine-Gun would therefore fire until the entire belt of bullets was used up. Trials showed that the machine-gun could fire 500 rounds per minute and therefore had the firepower of about 100 rifles.

a different reception. In the opening procession "the Japanese riders received a large share of cheering while the *Georgian* riders, though as skillful as any there, got nothing but silence… Cheers re-echoed when the little dark-skinned fellows drove their big adversaries back and off the field."[248] Another newspaper wrote: "It was noticeable that the *Georgian* were roundly hissed when they appeared, even as the small boy hoots the villain from the gallery. While the Japs were loudly cheered, the *Georgian*, however, were the best riders, and did some splendid work in their own peculiar style."[249]

Luka and his comrades traveled the rails of the northeast territory of the United States between June and October with the usual—and some unusual—occurrences. They encountered cases of smallpox when two Negro laborers with the show were stricken in Washington, DC, sending everyone into a panic, but health officials found no additional cases.

The season closed in Circleville, Ohio. The show returned to Carnegie, Pennsylvania, on October 16 and it was said they wintered in Beaver Falls.

1904 EPILOGUE

Alexis Georgian during the off-season lost his contracts with his fellow Gurian riders. Alexis did not perform in tent shows after the 1904 season. In 1905, Alexis only managed his troupe of Arab Acrobats "Eight Wild Bedouins," which he took on the Orpheum Theatre circuit, and he tried his hand at operating a moving picture side show.

Alexis Georgian's tent show career mirrored that of Harry W. Semon, a well-known tent show manager. Alexis and Harry worked together in Pawnee Bill's 1900 and 1901 season, Buckskin Bill's 1902 season, Luella Forepaugh-Fish's 1903 season, and the Campbell Brothers in 1904. Harry W. Semon died July 16, 1904. Personal relationships in the tent show business accounted for most of the contacts and contracts between show management and performers. Alexis Georgian and Harry Semon's relationship over the years was a possible reason Alexis Georgian ended his active riding after the 1904 season. Harry Semon was not there to grease the wheels to get Alexis the engagements.

OTHER SHOW BUSINESS

A report in early January stated that Cody purchased the Nate Salsbury interest in his Wild West show from the Salsbury estate.

Colonel F. Cummins, who in the future would operate several Wild West shows that Georgian riders rode in, opened the Cummins' Wild West Indian Congress and Rough Riders of the World at the St. Louis exposition.

Georgian Riders, ca 1902
Madison Square Garden
Author's Collection
Plate No. 27

"But like a rock stands firm amidst all misfortunes and troubles."

Shota Rustaveli

1905 PROLOGUE

In Guria, Ozurgeti District, Kutaisi Province—the homeland of most Georgian riders—armed peasant detachments began to appear in late 1904. The Gurian committee of rural workers, with links to the Batumi and Caucasian union committees of the Russian Social Democratic Labor Party, RSDLP, seized power locally and took over the fief holder's lands and equipment. The Russian-appointed village leaders were removed from their positions by the second half of January 1905. The most odious of these were exiled from their villages. The peasants killed one leader, wounded one, two of them escaped, and four resigned their positions. The local police lost control, and the peasant committees held authority. The czarist authorities entered into negotiations with the insurgents, whose demands included the confiscation of the fief holders' land and its transfer to the peasants without compensation; the return to the peasants of redemption payments; freedom of speech, the press, and association; the right to strike; amnesty for political prisoners; the election of judges who were to be responsible to the people; the separation of church and state and the exclusion of the church from the schools; and free universal and compulsory education in native language, with compulsory teaching of Russian as the state language. In March Russia declared martial law in the Ozurgeti and Senakh districts, in the governments of Kutais and Batumi. In November Cossacks who were escorting M. Lazarenko, a county official and M. Perkarski, a justice of the peace, were ambushed in Ozurgeti district by the revolutionaries who were fighting the troops sent to restore order. It was reported two entire companies were entirely wiped out.

The 1905 Russian Revolution led to the establishment of a limited constitutional monarchy, the State Duma of the Russian Empire, a multi-party system, and the Russian Constitution of 1906.

Ernest Poole begged the editors of the magazine *The Outlook* for a contract to tour Russia, and to write a series of articles about the Russian riots and strikes in January 1905. The imperial city of St. Petersburg was his first point of entry. Here he met one Tarasov (pseudonym), who became his traveling companion and revolutionary guide. Between January and May 1905, Poole and Tarasov traveled around Russia. His trips took him to Batumi, Tbilisi, Kutaisi, in the South Caucasus, now the Republic of Georgia. Ernest Poole chronicled his Georgian travels in his book *The Bridge*. The following is an excerpt from his meeting with one of the Wild West riders in a small village in the mountains of Georgia.

"First we saw only poverty. The children all were weak and thin; no jolly shouts, only dreary silence. The bare cabins looked bleak in fast-thickening rain.

"'Well,' I said to Tarasov, 'I hope the governor learns of this and has us fired out of here. For all of the cold wet holes on earth.'

"'Right, stranger,' said a sad-eyed peasant on crutches, who stood close by. 'It's a damned dead place for sure.

"'Where in hell did you learn English?'

"'Four years with Buffalo Bill,' he replied. 'He make me a Cossack in rough rider troop and we have one hell of a good time. But I broke my leg bad. So here I am home.' He spat sadly into the mud. But when I told him why I had come, he brightened up. 'Good. Write in all your most big papers how we are poor and why we strike! I will show!' And he took us to peasant huts where all morning we heard their stories of woes.

"Poorer and poorer every year!' one stooping white-headed old peasant declared. 'Ever since I was a boy we have been slaves to the landowners here! Always they kept raising the rents; and besides, the judges and priests and police made us pay and pay in bribes, or they would beat us or curse our souls! And as we could do nothing, for we were unarmed! But so at last we decided to strike. We stopped work in their fields and the owners grew angry. They took our cattle! We took them back! And the police and judges shouted: 'This is revolution!'

"'We cannot revolt without any guns,' the little village doctor said, so we outlaw our oppressors instead. We say to the landowners: 'Keep your fields.' And to the governor: 'Stay in your town. We will pay you all your taxes; we will pay for your judges, priests and police. But let the judge sit alone in his court, the priest in his church and the policeman in his jail. We ourselves will settle our disputes, punish our criminals, marry our lovers and bury our dead.' And so we have done. But now this outlawed government in fury has brought the Cossacks here to drive us on to violence, and God only knows how soon it will be till our young hotheads rise with only knives and clubs! For as a doctor, night after night, I am called to young girls bleeding from rape. Twenty Cossacks had a girl one afternoon a week ago! I could do little! She died last night! They are not men but devils.'"[250]

The Buffalo Bill rider was Bathlome Baramidze, who had broken his leg in 1902.

The revolution of 1905 awakened the hopes of the Georgian nation for better treatment, and the entire nation unanimously demanded Home Rule. But this movement was drowned in oceans of blood, and thousands of the best Georgians were banished to Siberia, never to return. We do, however, discover some of these revolutionaries or bandits in the American Wild West shows.

Alexis Georgian, who managed many of the Georgian riders in 1903 and 1904, planned to take a troupe of riders to the Byron N. Hulburd *(sic)* Helberd Wild West. However, the Hulburd show did not materialize and Alexis' troupe of riders went instead with J.T. McCaddon to France. Nine Georgians arrived in New York on April 30, onboard the SS *La Lorraine* that sailed from La Havre on April 22. Three of these Georgians were going to Chicago: Casse Alegrelidze, or Oragvelidze, or Arobelidze *(sic)*, Noe Tsilosani, and Higo *(Mose)* Gigineishvili. They were most likely joining Dimitri Tsintsadze in Chicago to ride with the Campbell Brothers. The remaining six were going to New York: Kirile Khoperia, Ilarion Ebralidze, Mikheil Chkhartishvili, Bartlome Mshvidobadze, Serapion Imnadze, and Giorgi Chkonia. They were most likely joining a group of five Georgians living in New York to ride with the Pawnee Bill Wild West. The five in

---

[27] "At Liberty" indicated a performer was available for hire.

New York had published an "At Liberty"[27] advertisement in the *New York Clipper* April 22. The ad said "5 Russian Cossacks Rough Riders, The most remarkable and sensational, Trick Horse Performers in the World NOW AT LIBERTY, address Chikito, 49 West 28th Street, Room 17, New York."

James A. Bailey announced "that the street parade will be omitted this year....The circus parade is no longer popular, on account of late arrivals of the show, inclement weather, unavoidable long waits and the consequent delay of the afternoon performance."

BUFFALO BILL'S WILD WEST AND CONGRESS OF ROUGH RIDERS (1905)

On March 3 the *SS Michigan* brought the first load of paraphernalia of Buffalo Bill's show, 150 draught horses and thirty 60-foot railroad cars, to Dunkerque, and then returned to London.[251] Cody, after he concluded his deposition at Omaha in his petition for divorce, left New York on March 11, on the *SS St. Paul,* for Cherbourg.[252] Frank A. Small, by March 15, had left the beautiful and commodious Paris office, located at 45 Avenue Rapp, which was just across the street from the lot, for Hungary to bring back the Georgians.

Buffalo Bill's lot in Paris was laid out on the Champs-de-Mars (Military Fields), between the École Militaire and the La Tour Eiffel *(the French Military Academy and the Eiffel Tower).* Paris used these grounds as the capital's fairground. The lot was situated close to the Galerie de Machines from the 1889 universal exhibition and the la grand roue (Big Wheel – Ferris Wheel) one hundred meters high, built in 1900. The lot was surrounded by a high fence. Buffalo Bill's white tent city was artistically arranged in national groups, on grassy lawns, with graveled walks strewn with shingles so the frequent showers would not interfere with the comfort of the sightseers. Regulation army field tents were used and contained camp-beds and

28 Saratoga Trunks - They got their name from the wealthy people visiting the spas and racetrack at Saratoga Springs, New York. The Saratoga Trunk was a very large, domed-top style with fancy trim, covered in either leather or metal. Early trunk catalogs and ads describe Saratoga trunks as a "large round top of the highest class." Round top trunks (also called humpback, camelback, monitor top, and barrel top) were made in a wide range of sizes and coverings. It is believed that the round tops were made for those who wanted to try to have their trunk packed on the top of baggage cars, so they would not be damaged.

Saratoga trunks.[28] There were ten ticket booths at the entrance and a large restaurant leased to a prominent caterer that could accommodate several hundred customers. There were two side show tents. The gates opened at 10:00 a.m. and the admission ticket was good for strolling around the park and the matinee or night performance. The main arena was the largest ever used in France for a similar exhibition, with a seating capacity of 17,000.

David Kadjaia, Solomon Imnadze, Silovan Kartvelishvili, Pavle Chkhartishvili, Simon Oragvelidze, Nicoloz Tsintsadze, Porpile Kantaria, Lazare and Ivane Jorbenadze, Khariton and Miron Chkonia, Ivane Baramidze, Nicoloz Surguladze, Ushangi Kvitashvili, and Alexandre Murvanidze departed Georgia in the fog of revolutionary fervor. The three most important navigation companies calling at Batumi—namely the Messageries Maritimes, the Austrian Lloyd, and the Paquet Company—suspended their services to this port.[253] David and his men traveled to Paris via train through the Ukraine, Hungary, Austria, and Germany. On Friday, March 24, they arrived in Paris at la Gare du Nord (The North train station). Their arrival did not go unnoticed, thanks to Mr. Georges Clemenceau.[29] *La Republique (The French Republic)* in their Monday edition, March 27, wrote:

"Mr. Clemenceau, yet not a gullible fool, comes to let himself be carried off by political passion, to one of these errors, quite comical, which remain legendary. In his article yesterday morning, the leader of *L'Aurore (The Dawn)* instituted legal proceedings against Russia and accumulated the arguments intending to demonstrate the permanent confusion which reigns in the Army 'Friends and Allies.' And, in a beautiful piece he wrote:

"It's not too significant that one did see arrive, yesterday, at the North train station, twelve Cossacks in uniform who deserted and crossed all of Germany in order to come to enter into our foreign legion rather than to let themselves be led to useless slaughter."

Unfortunately, one could read several hours later in the evening paper this note:

---

[29] George Benjamin Clemenceau (1841-1929): A French stateman, physician, and journalist. He served as Prime Minister of France 1906-1909 and 1917-1920.

"Someone said that several Cossacks, deserters of the Russian Army, after having crossed Germany in order to come into France to enter into an enlistment in the foreign legion, had left Friday from the North train station. To be more precise: It's about the foreign legion of Buffalo Bill riders, whose exploits have remained peaceful until now.

"The error of Mr. Clemenceau is evidently excusable...."

Buffalo Bill and his press staff arranged a dinner party at the Elysée Palace Hotel, on avenue des Champs-Elysées, the evening of March 27 to introduce Cody to the Parisian social community. The dinner gossip included Mr. Clemenceau's Cossack faux pas, and Cody's divorce proceedings.

It may possibly have been the longest parade ever given. The Wild West saddled up at 12:30 p.m. on March 31, and the men were in the saddle until 9:00 p.m. The immense crowds were very demonstrative and noisy and made the progress slow. They were constantly bombarded with confetti.

Cody held an inaugural gala performance by invitation only, on Saturday, April 1. The house held every first nighter in Paris including the presidents of the senate and chamber, and all the cabinet ministers, and ambassadors. The official season opened on April 2, to an immense crowd. A reliable report said 10,000 persons could not be accommodated and were turned away. The 2:30 and 8:30 shows featured the attack on the Deadwood Coach, Custer's Last Stand, unruly broncos, samples of Indians on the warpath, and a jostling between Japanese and Cossacks.

The weather during the first week was grey, wet and miserable, but the crowds still came out. Chief Iron Tail made good medicine under the "tree house," what he called the Eiffel Tower, to conjure away the rain and wind. The next day the sun shone and the Indians took the credit.

David Kadjaia and Cody discovered on Tuesday, May 9, that fourteen Georgian riders no longer responded to the summons of the roll call in camp. These men demanded a raise in salary, considering the extra expenses of living in Paris. Cody and Johnny Baker refused, and the riders struck, left the show, and moved into the Hotel Champs-de-Mars, near to their white tent encampment. Mr. Harry Schwartz (a close friend of Alexis Georgian), Colonel Cody's lawyer, instituted legal proceedings before the Fifth Tribunal Chamber of the Seine. The Georgian riders left the tribunal without saying anything, and the tribunal deferred the case until the following Saturday. Cody asked for 500f ($100) damages from each. He also begged the court to decide at once, owing to the urgency of the case. After three days, the riders asked if they could come back, but the show's management wanted to take them to court. The *New York Times* reported on Buffalo Bill's Georgian strike, but as might be expected, the story took a different twist. They wrote:

"The strike leaders threatened those of their comrades who hesitated to join them, declaring that their homes would be burned and their families massacred after their return to Russia."[254]

The strike was born out of the czar's repression in Guria, where Cossack troops were burning villages, raping women, and where local communities fought against the fief holders, and went on strike themselves. Buffalo Bill's Gurian riders received distressing letters from home and their relatives sought financial assistance. The Gurian riders needed more money to send home. Newspaper accounts inform us that the Georgians were riding in the show by May 20, but how the affair was settled was not stated.

Another facet of their tour in France was the continuous showing without Sunday's rest to break the monotony. Their farewell performance in Paris was Sunday night, June 4. Buffalo Bill's exhibition was loaded on a three-section train. David Kadjaia and his troupe of riders left their field tent and went to bed in their own sleeping cars, to awake eighty-eight kilometers southwest of Paris in Chartres. The next two weeks they traveled the western provincial district along the English Channel coast. They arrived in Le Havre, on Saturday, June 17, for a two-day stand with four performances; they left Sunday night unaware that difficult times were ahead. The first inconvenience was a soft lot forcing them to abandon their afternoon performance and the last evening performance on Sunday. The disaster was a case of glanders[30] breaking out among the broncos used as bucking horses. "At Roubaix four horses had to be slaughtered, at Lille the number increased to ten, and at Cambrai the

---

[31] Glanders - (also known as Farcy or Equinia) is a usually fatal disease of equines caused by the bacteria Pseudomonas mallei (Actinobacellus or Malleomyces mallei). Humans can be infected and die. The acute form is characterized by a high fever, septicemia, respiratory signs and a thick nasal discharge, with death in a few days. Chronic disease can occur in surviving horses with ulcerating nodules on the skin and nasal cavity, and nodules in the lungs. These animals are carriers and spread the organism.

authorities took action. An official from the Ministry of Agriculture, assisted by civil military veterinary surgeons, examined all the horses. This examination, which occupied two days, resulted in forty-two animals being slaughtered."[255] Throughout the season the broncos were quarantined from the show horses.

The well fortified towns along the frontiers of Belgium, Germany, and Switzerland were the route Buffalo Bill's Wild West took in July. These towns were mostly military and, as was the custom, soldiers were accorded a reduced rate for admission. The exhibition struggled to make the daily nut. The superstition that accidents came in threes seemed to bear out in August. A huge stock car derailed by a misplaced switch while in route from Rion to MontluÇon on August 22. Buffalo Bill's razor-backs replaced the car on the tracks. A severe storm struck at Orleans, August 25, completely demolishing the big tent and injuring scores of people. A partial eclipse of the sun at Thouars on August 30 was followed by a terrific electric storm. Lightning hit one of the horse tents and instantly killed four valuable white Arabians which Cody used with his private carriage. The weather turned cold, wet and just plain nasty in September and October. In southern France, the hooligan element was a menace. Their favorite pastime was throwing stones at the drivers, out of the darkness.

Buffalo Bill's outfit arrived at Marseilles on Wednesday, November 1, for their last stand. It was a tough year, and the weather in Marseilles did not cooperate. A tempest raged Saturday and Sunday, and no performance could be given on Sunday, November 5, a big disappointment since this was their big box-office day. The season closed on November 12 in Marseilles, France, after opening seven-and-a-half months earlier. The season lasted 225 days, 443 performances, with 114 different stands and only seven lost performance dates. They traveled over 6,219 miles in France.

David Kadjaia and his men remained in Marseilles for a period, undecided about returning to their own troubled homeland.[256] Colonel Cody and James Bailey, after consultation, decided to kill all the remaining 200 horses on December 7. They burned all the saddles, bridles, and other equipment, as well as the clothing of the stablemen, and disinfected the railroad cars.[257] They knew this was the only way of stamping out the plague before importing new horses and trappings from America for the next season, and to relieve the local farmers' fears.

CAMPBELL BROTHERS GREAT CONSOLIDATED SHOWS (1905)

Dimitri Tsintsadze spent the winter at 322 Wood Street, Chicago. Three of Dimitri's new riders—(Casse Alegrelidze, Oragvelidze, or Arobelidze), Noe Tsilosani, and Mose Gigineishvili—arrived on the *SS La Lorraine* on April 30. A thirty-hour train trip brought them to Chicago at a cost of approximately $42.

Dimitri and his troupe missed the Fairbury, Nebraska, opening on Saturday, April 29. Opening day was a nice spring day and people came from the surrounding country. The next morning, around 11:00 a.m., the circus pulled out for Grand Island for a three-week tour in the local vicinity. Dimitri might have wondered if the Campbell Brothers were jinxed. Bad luck struck again when their trick elephant died of indigestion the first day, and Monday evening a bad storm with high wind tore one of the tents and forced them to cancel the evening performance. The weather was miserable all week. They lost a show date in Osceola, Nebraska, and the bad weather caused their late arrival in Lincoln, Nebraska.

The weather in Lincoln the next morning was the kind that makes people rejoice and be glad. A bright, warm sun glistened from the chariots and animal cages. There was a good house at the afternoon performance and a little excitement generated by a Georgian rider. A local reporter had a little fun writing the story: "One of the famed Georgians' let his horse get the better of him and ran away. The horse appeared to dive through the canvas and into Antelope creek, but in fact it ran west on O Street and when last seen was going toward the viaduct with the saddle on the underside. The famed and unrivaled rider was simply knocked out in the first round, much to the horror of the people who had paid their money to see him ride. He was able to get up before time was called. The fight would have been awarded the horse if he had been there to receive the trophy."[258]

Dimitri, a seasoned rider who first rode with Buffalo Bill's Wild West in 1896, was familiar with many towns that he visited repeatedly over the years. Austin, Minnesota, was one of those towns. "Some of the

Georgians who are with the Campbell show have familiar faces. They were residents of the city for several months two years ago. It was interesting to watch one of them as he came up the street. The first familiar face he met was Ed Sutherland, and the meeting was almost as pathetic as that of a prodigal son and his father. The *Georgians* hung upon 'Pipe's' neck in a most affectionate manner. Salvation Army soldiers, circus performers, Negro minstrels and all drum players coming to town all know Ed, for in his time he has played many parts."[259]

Dimitri may have received a warm welcome from Ed Sutherland of Austin, but the *Austin Daily Herald* ran this editorial. "Austin has no use for the *Georgians*. The statement of the ring master, that the management paid '$500 weekly,' to five men to abuse horses in a five-minute exhibition, produced a smile. We all remember seeing some of these fellows around Austin for weeks at a time living practically on the charity of the people. The Cossack, in the war with Japan, has shown himself a great fighter when it came to attacking a Japanese field hospital o60murdering an unarmed populace in a city."[260]

Dimitri Tsintsadze and his wife were entertained in Waterloo, Iowa, by old acquaintances and friends, Mr. and Mrs. A. D. Wood. The Woods were residents of Chicago in 1903, and were next door neighbors to Mrs. Tsintsadze, an Irish lady, who at that time was not married.

A bonus to any circus management and the performers occurs when a community requests the presence of their show on a given date. It assures ticket sales, low taxes, and extra business opportunities. The business men of Marengo, Iowa, wrote to the Campbell Brothers requesting they book their circus in town as part of their annual celebration on July 4, 1905. Dimitri and his troupe occasionally enjoyed the benefit of a showmen's banquet. Marshall "Butch" Nellis celebrated his birthday in Groton, South Dakota, by serving an elaborate dinner. These festive affairs broke the daily grind of, rain, mud, and the expectation of the next accident.

Dimitri and the rest of the Campbell Brothers circus were involved in a train accident Tuesday night November 7, two miles west of Temple, Texas, en route to Goldthwaite. "…a large number of animals were either killed or escaped. The accident occurred on a down grade. The train broke in two, and the sections ran together. Cages were broken, and many animals escaped into the woods, and several were killed, including an elephant.

Posses of men were organized for their recapture, and something like a panic struck the rural district."[261] The *Galveston Daily News* reported: "The wreck was caused by a drawhead[31] pulling out of a flat car, letting a circus wagon which spanned the space between the cars to fall on the track. The cars following were promptly ditched as a result, five cars being involved. No one was injured and none of the animals were in the wreck.[262] The engagement at Goldthwaithe was cancelled.

The season closed December 2, 1905, in Duncan, Oklahoma, that was then called the Indian Territory. Dimitri and his men returned to Chicago for the winter.

MACCADDON'S GREAT INTERNATIONAL SHOWS (1905)

McCaddon, as the manager of the Adam Forepaugh circus, brought the first Georgian riders to the United States in 1893. McCaddon managed many of Bailey's operations between 1888 and 1903. He had experience working for Cooper and Bailey, the Adam Forepaugh shows, Buffalo Bill's Wild West, and Bailey's Greatest Show on Earth. His last manager experience for Bailey was as director of the Greatest Show on Earth during its four-year tour of Europe, 1897 to 1901, and their United States tour in 1902/1903.

McCaddon applied his vast tent show knowledge and contacts to organize a Wild West show. He traveled to Chicago, New York, London, and Paris, collecting stockholders for his project including.

He assembled some of the finest managers in the business and gathered equipment from the defunct Buckskin Bill show and cars from Sig Sautelle. He outfitted his show in Clifton, New Jersey. He contracted Panteleimon Tsintsadze and three other Gurians to perform as Georgians in his Wild West. He even changed the spelling of his name to "MacCaddon," thinking it appeared more European.

---

[31] Drawhead – The flanged outer end of a drawbar; an open mouthed bar at the end of a car, which receives a coupling link & pin by which the car is drawn.

McCaddon's Great International Shows, ca 1905
Second from left: Panteleimon Tsintsadze.
Princeton University Libraray, Plate No. 28

The MacCaddon show left the United States in three waves for a two-year tour of France, Belgium, Holland, Switzerland and Germany. McCaddon anticipated it would prove so prosperous he could repay his stockholders their principal and a very generous bonus, and leave himself so enriched that he could retire. He had a company of 427, with high-class performers, two bands, menagerie, museum, hippodrome, a small Wild West of cowboys, Sioux Indians, a troupe of Georgians, Arabs, and Streator Illinois Zouaves, with canvas men, and other employees. The advance force left New York on March 4, 1905; the performers sailed on March 25, from New York on a specially chartered steamer to Antwerp, Belgium, as a sixty-seven-car circus. The circus menagerie stock departed on April 5, on board the *St. Andrews* of the Phoenix line, from the docks at Hoboken, New Jersey, headed for Dunkerque, France.[263] The steamship *St. Andrews* arrived in Dunkerque, the same port where Buffalo Bill's Wild West landed the week before, and took three hours to clear Customs. The baggage and ring stock, some 350 horses, took three days to get through the same Customs agents Buffalo Bill slipped through. MacCaddon's show was held by French officials at the docks. It was widely believed customs agents were bribed to hold the show.

"Mistakes were made in opening the show in the middle of April in towns along the English Channel, such as Lille, Dieppe, Dunkirk, and Calais, for the weather was raw and stormy. McCaddon failed to have his tent waterproofed before sailing, and in one place we showed it rained pitchforks. The water came through the tent in bucketfuls, and those excitable French raised an awful row."[264] "It seemed like every snowstorm, hailstorm, windstorm and just plain ornery storm that was cruising around Europe headed for Joe McCaddon's show. It rained so hard that the canvas rotted, and then the wind blew so hard that it ripped the rotten canvas."[265] McCaddon said that it rained thirty-five days out of forty-nine.

McCaddon's press agents busily submitted glowing reports to the *New York Clipper* and *Billboard* magazine stating the tremendous success the show was meeting in France. These reports were countered with personal witness accounts later in the season. Gracie, the Bearded Lady, said:

"Joe is a religious sort of guy. Mrs. McCaddon never would stand for a Sunday show. Long before Joe started out for himself and was working for old man Bailey, his brother-in-law, Mrs. McCaddon wouldn't let him work on Sunday."

"Now Sunday in France is the gayest ever. That's the one day in the week when the Frenchmen turn loose and want to spend their coin. When Joe took the Great Internationals over there—and it was a corker to start with, a sixty-four-car show—he wouldn't give Sunday performances. The Messrs. and Mademoiselles used to gather around the tents by the million and shout 'Veeve Mistaire McCaddong! Veeve Mistaire McCaddong!' To get Joe to open up; but he wouldn't. He stuck by the Missus and his principles and it put the bunch on the droop. There was thousands lost by that play, thousands."

James Bailey's people in France were keeping a very keen eye on McCaddon's show. Only fifteen days after McCaddon opened, Hutchinson and Dean sent a telegram to Bailey outlining McCaddon's problems and positions on May 4, 1905.

"McCaddon doing very bad business, feels our newspaper notices in opposition. Cody has sent Burke to talk with him and has evidently made proposition to stop our opposition if McCaddon drops name Wild West from billing and programme and keeps out of our way. McCaddon wants an assurance from us that we will not interfere with him under these conditions. We believe McCaddon is desperate and will run if left alone.

Burke not a shrewd negotiator and McCaddon has scared him by threats of personal attack on Cody and talk of his big money backing. Advise not to make any compromise or agreement with McCaddon, reply to Cody. Hutchinson, Dean."

Bailey's reply from Somerville, New Jersey on May 4, 1905:

"To Col. Cody, Wild West Paris.

I most earnestly request you will not make any sort of compromise or other promises to or with McCaddon. If you should, he will annoy or interfere elsewhere; besides he may circulate reports or publish that he compelled us to compromise. Please allow Dean without interference from anyone to handle all this McCaddon affair. McCaddon backers amount to little. He will be compelled soon to skip our route entirely or possibly bust and disband. Please consult with Dean. I have cabled Dean to consult and explain in detail all matters. Bailey."[266]

Buffalo Bill and McCaddon did a little horse trading. McCaddon had a problem with his Indians that he could not pay, and Buffalo Bill's Georgians were out on strike. Buffalo Bill used the threat of replacing his Georgians with McCaddon's to bring that problem to conclusion, and Buffalo Bill sent the unpaid Indians back to McCaddon in Soissons. The route taken by McCaddon in northern France is sketchy; however, when Buffalo Bill departed Paris, June 4, McCaddon moved into the suburbs for a short run. McCaddon followed Buffalo Bill into central and southern France, just barely hanging on. In Blois, a woman spectator was shot in the eye and the show paid five thousand francs, and the railroad journey from Vésoul to Dijon cost another five thousand francs.[267] He needed more financial help, but his backers were too far removed and were not forthcoming. The performers looked forward to July 4th. They anticipated evening fireworks, a special dinner, extra enthusiasm from the towners, and more important the ghost was walking, which in tent show lingo meant it was payday. July 4, 1905, in Montluços, central France, was a disaster.

"We had a terrible fight in Montluços, where they stoned the men and cut our American flag into bits."[268] "The lot was ideal one for a clem (fight). It was covered with hard rocks, which were about the right size and shape for long distance throwing. Apparently, trouble was brewing all day and about eight o'clock in the evening the crowd cut down the kid show paintings and set fire to the light wagon. They then turned their attention to the big top where they cut ropes and pulled down sections of the sidewall. They drove the Italian windjammers from the bandstand, and cut enough ropes that the back end of the big top swung into the quarter poles. The workers were in the process of loading two blue plank wagons when the bombardment really began, and they were forced to take cover. During lulls in the shower of rocks, the workers charged the crowd, but they were too strong to scatter. The working men then sent for reinforcements from the train, and the performers arrived on the scene. It was not until the early hours of the morning that the tired crowd went home, allowing the lot to be cleared and the train loaded. The show blew the next day's stand, but it was almost the end." It was also the last day the ghost walked.

McCaddon, in a post script to a letter to his wife on July 11, 1905, wrote: "I have received a telegram that owing to a disease among their horses the Wild West *(Buffalo Bill)* have had fifty killed and had not exhibited since last Wednesday; if it is true it is a just retribution. I hope for the sake of the Governor that it is untrue, for it would be a very serious matter for him as I don't believe Cody has any money."[269] They traveled southern France, showing in Rodez on July 17. McCaddon's circus arrived in the outskirts of Grenoble, France, on the bank of the river Isère, August 2, 1905. The show went on the rocks on August 7, and was abandoned by the management August 10 in Grenoble. Wyoming Jack said: "You can figure what the show was up against, when I tell you that for a month the receipts ran about $3,800 a week, while the daily expenses were $1,000 at least."[270] McCaddon reportedly said before he left: "everyone would be paid dollar for dollar." McCaddon escaped to England to avoid the French courts. The show equipment was impounded by the Grenoble authorities, who sought to sell the property to care for the destitute showmen. French Customs officials declined to permit the sale due to a bond that was provided for the return of the property to the United States. The artists learned a lesson in French politics when they discovered that the unskilled laborers would have first claim on any funds.

The days turned into weeks and the food supplies ended on August 23. Management offered the artists fare to London and $4.00; twenty members of the company accepted. The company slowly dwindled as artists found other work or found passage on a ship, shoveling coal. Panteleimon Tsintsadze and his men were caught in a terrible bind. While the American Consulate and the American Express company collected contributions to assist the Americans, Tsintsadze and his men had to fend for themselves. "It is related that the *Georgians* of the show secured from police headquarters an 'order for grub' on a local charity institution. But that the manager of the latter repelled them so coldly that they wanted to break the Franco-Russian alliance. The *Georgians* were afraid to appeal to the Russian Government because they did not want to risk being sent back to Russia."[271] They were able to sign a contract, along with some other artists, to perform at a Grenoble fair for ten days. They received five francs a day for the exhibitions.

The Georgian riders eventually left France along with the other stranded performers, who left Grenoble by the end of September. The sad story of McCaddon's European adventure concludes with the death of his wife. Mamie McCaddon - nee Gray, J.T. McCaddon's wife died in Worthing, Sussex, England, on their seventeenth wedding anniversary at six o'clock in the morning. Mamie McCaddon's coffin, J. T. McCaddon and his children embarked on the American Liner *St. Louis* bound for New York, but before sailing McCaddon ventured onto the dock just before the vessel sailed. He no sooner stepped from the steamer's gangway when he was arrested on a warrant charging him with fraudulent bankruptcy. He, his children, and Whiting Allen disembarked. McCaddon could not retrieve his wife's body, and it was taken to America. His arraignment was brought up in the extradition court at Bow Street, London, on October 2. He paid his $80,000 bail and later, when the case came up for a hearing, the court refused to grant the French Government's extradition request.

Meanwhile, McCaddon received a letter of condolence and support from his old friend C. M. Ercolè, the man who brought the Georgian riders and McCaddon together in 1893. Ercolè had escorted McCaddon's two sons, Joseph and Stanley, to America. "It was a rough journey and Joseph was sick two or three days, but Stanley was as chipper as a sand piper, and the boys delighted everyone on board."

He finally left from the port of Liverpool onboard the *SS Baltic* and arrived back home on December 8, when he reportedly said: "my arrest was simply an attempt to blackmail me through official channels. I have rich connections in England and America, and my enemies tried to make me pay the company's debts, as though they were personal ones."[272]

PAWNEE BILL'S WILD WEST AND GREAT FAR EAST SHOW (1905)

Luka, Konstantine (Kosta), Mikheil Chkhartishvili, and Jordan Schividadze are the known members of the Georgian troupe of riders that worked for Pawnee Bill in 1905. A feature of the show this year was a passenger air ship that made two demonstration flights a day. The air ship required two specially built wagons of 120 feet and a team of thirty-two horses to carry it from the train to the lot. The cast and crew, including the Georgians and Japanese, started rehearsals for opening day on April 29.

Pawnee Bill's thirty-nine car exhibition left its winter quarters in Carnegie, Pennsylvania, and began its season in the Pittsburgh area. The show used the old Wild West standbys: cowboys, Indians, lariat throwing, attacks on a settler's cabin, the Deadwood stagecoach rescue, and expert shooting. The Great Far East portion of the show capitalized on public interest in the Russian and Japanese war. The bill included Chinese horsemen, soldiers, dancers, Japanese juggling and balancing feats, a camel race for the laughs, Arabs, Malayans, and "a troupe of Georgians doing difficult feats unequaled by any other race." The weather in late April and early May was cold and wet, and the afternoon performance had just concluded in Homestead, Pennsylvania, on May 16 when a wind storm blew down the main arena tent, stampeding towners about the show grounds.

Press accounts of local human interest were probably unknown to Luka and his brothers or other members of the show. There was an incident in Kalamazoo, Michigan, where a groom broke from his marriage ceremony to rush to the window to see the parade, while leaving an embarrassed bride at the altar. Or, in Kankakee, Illinois, where a music teacher injured herself when her opera chair collapsed during the evening performance and by 11:00 pm had a lawyer and had begun a $5,000 damage suit against Pawnee Bill. On the other hand, press accounts of an Indian rain dance performance on a Sabbath, or a washed out railroad outside of

Lincoln, Nebraska, everyone on the show would know about.

The last known heavy damage to the show occurred on September 21 in Tulsa, Oklahoma, (called the Indian Territory in 1905). "Shortly after the night performance began a cloudburst demolished the big tent, doing considerable damage and injuring several women and children, who were panic-stricken because the heavy canvas fell on them."[273]

The season closed on November 4 in Malden, Missouri. Luka and his men once more headed east to New York and then returned home for the winter. The show left Missouri for winter headquarters at Canton, Ohio.

1905 EPILOGUE

The General of the Caucasian provinces sent the following telegram to the Minister of Interior at St. Petersburg: "The situation in the Ozurgeti district and the surrounding areas is assuming the character of a rebellion, finding expression in open defiance of authority, the murder of government officials, squires, priests and persons not in sympathy with the revolutionary movement. The population is repudiating the oath of allegiance to the crown and pledging fidelity to the revolutionary committee. Officers of the government are fleeing. All measures hitherto taken, including the cooperation of the army, have failed to produce any results."[274]

The men of Guria, who played the role of "Russian Cossack," learned upon their return home of the atrocities of the czar's Cossacks upon the people of Georgia. "On August 29, in Tbilisi, a public meeting was organized in the Town Hall. The acting governor, General Yatskevich, hastened to the scene with several hundred Cossacks and infantry. The Cossacks opened fire on the assembly through the windows, while others invaded the hall and shot down the audience from the platform. One shot killed the orator at his tribune *(Dias)*. The mob fled from the building and were shot down indiscriminately or felled with rifle butts and sabers. A woman doctor who happened to be present was wounded but, in spite of her injuries, was bandaging other casualties with strips of her own clothing; a Cossack came and brained her with his rifle butt. Some victims were cornered in the narrow corridors and hacked to death; others were pursued into the streets and shot or cut down on the public highways. About sixty persons were killed and several hundred wounded. The relatives of the dead were refused permission to remove the bodies, which were flung into a common grave."

Throughout the winter of 1905, Batumi and Tbilisi were battle grounds between Czarists, Georgians, Armenians, Tartars, peasants, social democrats, and the bourgeois. The dispatches to the *London Times* poured in during September, October, and December, reporting on the attacks upon and reprisals of the Cossacks.

ALEXIS GEORGIAN BIOGRAPHY

Alexis Georgian, who for several years managed the Georgian riders, by 1907 had moved to Minneapolis, Minnesota. He married Stella W. Campbell (not associated with Campbell Brothers circus) in 1910. They had two sons, John C. Georgian and Carl C. Georgian. In 1911, Alexis and Stella became the owners, writers, and publishers of an English Language Socialist newspaper *The New Times*. Alexis opposed the 1914 war and the U.S. government drove him out of the newspaper business by 1919 because of this opposition. Alexis was a founding member of the American Communist Party in September 1919. He was persecuted by the U.S. government for his political views, sent to Ellis Island for deportation on the *SS Buford* in 1920, but a writ of habeas corpus from the Supreme Court removed him from this ship. He owned a bookstore, then a gas station and restaurant, and finally he returned to his roots and was a truck farmer. Alexis died in November 1940, still under a court order for deportation.

CHAPTER FOUR
TROUPERS TO CONCERT ACTS: 1906 TO 1911

The Georgian riders, after fourteen years in the tent show business, were old time troupers. Their riding act was becoming stale and they were no longer the headlining act; instead, in the parlance of tent show performers, they were *behind the parade*. They were still a required act for any Wild West show. Luka Chkhartishvili reintroduced women riders into his act hoping to increase interest. These years were not kind, and slowly the Georgian riders were shifted to concert acts. Concert acts were held after the big show, when the patrons would pay an additional ten cents to hear a concert from the band and view a few stunts, such as the "Russian Cossack's" riding act. These performances were held while crews dismantled the remaining lot structures. Concert acts did not receive billing and were very seldom mentioned in advertising or newspaper stories.

The Georgian riders were spread over eleven different shows between 1906 and 1911. As their spot in the limelight faded, less information appeared in newspapers and other documents.

The end of season trek to "home sweet home" became more difficult as revolution, poverty, and threats of violence increased. Luka and many of his riders decided to winter over in America. They found work in other venues, such as the New York Hippodrome, performing in the *Battle of Port Arthur*. They traveled to South America and Australia during the winter season. They traded seeing their wives and children for earning more dollars to send home, a decision still made to this day by many immigrant laborers.

225

"Opening one's heart to a friend is comfort and balm to the soul"

Shota Rustaveli

1906 PROLOGUE

The Russian General Alikhanoff, who during this period was dispatched to western Georgia in 1905 with plenary powers, suppressed the Georgians through use of the Cossacks. The czar received an upbeat telegram from the Viceroy of the Caucasus: "Order has been restored in the province of Kutais. General Alikhanoff informs me that he has everywhere been received with the customary presentation of bread and salt and that the taxes are being paid in full. Confidence has been restored among the majority of the landowners. Cartloads of arms are being brought in and the agitators and deserters are being delivered to the authorities. The levying of recruits will be carried on with some difficulty, as all the official administrative lists in the province have been destroyed. The people are now convinced that they made a mistake in lending credence to the words of evildoers, and they have frankly promised to combat the agitators and hand them over to the officials. Calm has also been restored in Tbilisi and the taxes are being paid."[275] The American vice-consul in Batumi, William H. Stuart, was murdered in his villa,[276] an act which belied the calm claimed by General Alikhanoff. An open letter to women of the world was published in the London Times.[277]

"A disaster, terrible and unprecedented in our history, has befallen our country. By the order of the Russian government the central and western provinces of Georgia have been invaded by Cossacks and soldiers. Four towns and two-hundred villages have been destroyed and burned.... The fate of the women has been especially terrible. Even girls of eleven and twelve were not spared violation and outrage.... Our complaints are stifled by our oppressors."

BUFFALO BILL'S WILD WEST AND CONGRESS OF ROUGH RIDERS (1906)

Buffalo Bill's troupes wintered over in Marseilles, France, from November, 1905 to March, 1906, except for the Indians. During the winter season, Jake Posey had the task of taking twelve horses to an incinerator, ten miles out of town, each day. New horses and six mules, for the stage coach, and all their equipment were brought over. The arriving horses were the worst looking Jake Posey had ever seen, and some were so weak they had to be hauled to the lot, but by show time looked fairly well.[278] The showmen wintered under canvas, meaning they used their traveling tents to house the animals and men. The cookhouse and horse tents were up all winter, and repair and painting was done under the side show tent. The Georgian riders, with David Kadjaia, probably went home for the winter and returned in late February to prepare for the March 4 opening. The season opened on the same ground in Marseilles where the show had wintered.

Buffalo Bill's touring began immediately after the Marseilles opening, using three trains. The cars were painted yellow with Buffalo Bill Wild West inscribed on each of them. Of the fifty cars, thirteen were sleeping cars equipped with all the conveniences. The one-and-one-half hour performance was composed of twenty-two acts with the Indian and Georgian horsemanship receiving the loudest rounds of applause. Buffalo Bill included a troupe of Japanese warriors after their victory in the Russian-Japanese war of 1904/05. The Georgian riders were again portrayed as the bad guys and one reporter contemptuously described the vulgarity of a Georgian using his finger for cleaning his nose.

After over a year on French soil, Buffalo Bill's exhibition traveled along the Riviera (Nice to Genoa) with the Mediterranean on one side and snow-covered mountains on the other. Cody stood on his railcar observation platform and received ovations from throngs of people at every station. They arrived in Genoa, Italy, on March 13. The city of Genoa Board of Health prohibited Buffalo Bill's Wild West from camping in Genoa due to an alleged infectious disease among the horses.[279] The conflict was settled after the Genoa Chamber of Deputies threatened to bring the question before Parliament. Cody was also not permitted to pitch tents in Pisa for fear of an epidemic among the show horses.[280] The daily grind of parades, two shows a day, and packing for the jump to the next town was broken by the occasional incident, as written in C. E. Griffin's book.[281] In Livorno on the evening of March 19 a strong wind began at about six o'clock, and the night show had to be abandoned. This allowed the Georgians and other company members an opportunity to witness a magnificent display of fireworks in celebration of the city government's 300th anniversary. In Rome the performers put on an additional private performance on March 26, for the King, Victor Emanuel, the Queen, and their children. Word of the death of James A. Bailey reached Buffalo Bill on April 12, while they were in Ravenna, Italy.

The last year Buffalo Bill was in Europe was artistically successful, but a financial disaster, as they reportedly lost close to $250,000. Their final afternoon performance, given in the old-fashioned town of Ghent, Flanders, on September 21, closed the 1906 season. Buffalo Bill's Georgian riders headed home to Guria for another winter.

CAMPBELL BROTHERS CONSOLIDATED SHOWS (1906)

The Campbell Brothers' season opened in Fairbury, Nebraska, on April 28, with Dimitri Tsintsadze's riders in their third season with the Campbell Brothers. The Fairbury newspaper said that Captain Dimitri was "a favorite of Fairbury audiences for several seasons."[282]

The Campbell Brothers show was enlarged to thirty-five cars, with two carloads of draft horses and a car of fine racing stock, and traveled in two trains. They used a big top with two rings, a stage, and a hippodrome track. Captain Dimitri performed while racing around the hippodrome track. *The Wakefield Republican* in Dixon County, Nebraska wrote: "The fast riding by the *Georgians* was alone worth the price of admission."[283]

Dimitri and his troupers in the Campbell Brothers circus witnessed some of the seamier sides of life in America. One incident started in Lemars, Iowa, on June 7, around 10:00 p.m., when a Negro named Ebenezer (Will) Davis assaulted a young white woman, Josephine Wilmes. The town folks gathered as if by magic and the sheriff intended to quickly round up the approximately twenty-five Negroes with the show. The first batch of nine Negroes were arrested and taken to the Union passenger station. Miss Wilmes declared one of these men her attacker. Sheriff Arendt took all these Negroes to the jail for questioning. An angry crowd talked about storming the jail and lynching the suspect. Sheriff Arendt discovered Miss Wilmes' description of what the suspect was wearing did not match the man she had pointed out, Walter White. Sheriff Arendt followed the show to Luverne, Minnesota, and found the proper man who fit the description. Will Davis confessed that he planned on robbing the woman, but when she fell down, he became afraid and ran away. Justice was served and in this incident an innocent Negro, Walter White, escaped being lynched.[284] A Presbyterian minister once said: "The circus is not a place for ladies and gentlemen; therefore it is not a place for ladies' and gentlemen's children." This attitude prevailed in much of the Midwest, and newspaper editors tried to placate both the secular and religious readers. One newspaper compromised and wrote: "It is better to have some fun and frolic than to have all dull care. Yet it must not be forgotten that after circus day the mind and soul as well as the body need a bath."[285] These attitudes toward the circus and their performers were not universal.

The Campbell Brothers' tenting season records for 1906 are incomplete; therefore, one cannot determine when or where they closed. Dimitri and his men in all likelihood returned home to Georgia or wintered in Chicago.

PAWNEE BILL'S WILD WEST AND FAR EAST EXHIBITION (1906)

Pawnee Bill's Wild West opened April 28th on a warm and pleasant circus day with a cool breeze blowing, in Canton, Ohio. Luka Chkhartishvili, his brother Mikheil, and the other Georgians arrived in Canton before the season opened to re-train their horses. Luka and his men attracted much attention riding in their high, curiously shaped saddles during the morning parade. Many persons remarked that the horses in the parade seemed very thin, but a reporter remarked that the towners must remember that they are ridden by Cossacks and must keep up a great speed and they have no chance to accumulate flesh.

Well-filled benches greeted the performers at their opening performance. Luka's band of men thrilled the audience and, in the course of their performance one of them took a bad fall caused by the uneven ground. Thus began Luka's fourth season riding with the Pawnee Bill show.[286] Luka and his men were number twenty-two on the program. They demonstrated their expert horsemanship and were followed by a series of races. The show closed with the burning of a trapper's cabin.

In Brighton Beach, New York, from June 13 to 30 there were accidents reported. On June 19, in an endeavor to jump over some property rocks, the horse crashed through them and threw its *Georgian* rider, who was carried from the area suffering from minor injuries. "While the *Georgians* were giving their riding exhibition… (Thursday afternoon June 21)… one of the horses, while going at full gallop with the rider standing on his head in the saddle, stumbled and fell, throwing the man heavily to the ground. The horse and rider following also fell, but both men remounted almost immediately. After the performance it was learned that both of the *Georgians* had sustained injuries. One had three teeth missing and a split lip, and the other had a badly wrenched shoulder. They were attended to by Pawnee Bill's physician."[287]

Pawnee Bill's Wild West witnessed two memorable storms. The first occurred in Bayonne, New Jersey, at 2:30 p.m., in the middle of the afternoon performance, on July 17. The sky had been threatening during the day, but the severity of the winds surprised everyone. Although the main tent did not completely collapse, just about all the smaller tents did. The lightning and thunder frightened the horses in the horse tent. They dashed madly about and knocked down the poles, bringing the tent down and engulfing them in the heavy folds of the canvas. Those who escaped raced madly about the lot. The 2,500 spectators panicked; the buffalo, camels, and the elephants ran helter-skelter around the lot, causing more damage. The only person hurt in this storm was Pawnee Bill himself when he wrenched his shoulder trying to hold one of the tent poles in place.[288] The cowboys, Georgians, and attendants did valiant work in rescuing the women and children from the wreckage of the main tent and in getting the frightened animals under subjection.

Twenty-one days later in Harrisburg, Pennsylvania, the Georgians experienced a repeat performance of a blow down. A terrific electrical storm struck just as the afternoon performance was starting on August 6. Chic Befrandi, a Filipino in the Japanese acrobat act, was sitting on his trunk by the large center pole in the dressing tent waiting for his entrance cue. Suddenly there was a crash above and the tent filled with smoke. Later the cowboys, Georgians, and others found Befrandi's body. He was burned in various places; and in the middle of the chest, right below the neck, there was a huge raw scar which showed where the shock had taken effect. Across the chest the skin peeled off like bark from a tree, and his clothing was torn in strips almost to his knees. Several lightning bolts were felt around the lot. May Lillie was in her special tent and the shock threw her to the ground, where she was found in a semi-conscious condition. Charles Robeson, chief property man, was stunned by the flash and his right arm was affected to such an extent that he was unable to move it temporarily. Benny Weiss, custodian of the ammunition wagon, was thrown to the ground and unable to use his right arm. Many of the spectators were shocked and for some minutes stood paralyzed, unable to move their legs or arms. The spectators stampeded and rushed for the exits or the center of the arena. The people who headed for the exit were stopped by show attendants because to get into the open it was necessary to pass through the horse tent, which was in danger of being blown down. The vast throng made a dash for the arena. In the rush, many became entangled in the ropes and were thrown to the ground in large pools of water and mud. The performance was started again after about ten minutes, but then after only two acts had been completed, a blinding flash of lightning occurred and another heavy blast of wind and driving rain swept over the lot. The horse tent blew down and one bronco was killed. A spectator clutched one of the tent poles, but a burst of wind hurled the pole and man about ten feet in the air and he fell into a puddle of water and mud. The afternoon performance was in shambles.[289] Weather was always a factor in daily tent show life.

Luka, Mikheil, and the other Georgians also had to keep their act fresh and interesting. Cowboys over the years had learned the Georgian riding styles. Cowboys were emulating the distinctive Georgian trick of standing on their heads on a running horse. Luka devised a new twist: while riding he would discard his saddle and give his daring exhibition of saber tricks while riding bareback. He performed this trick as well as if he were standing on the ground. Whether Luka was using a saddle or riding bareback, he and his men would bring the spectators cheering to their feet, until the battle between the Georgians and Japanese cavalry. Two years after the start of that "small war," Luka and his men were still the bad guys.

Luka and his men were not the only "bad guys" in the Wild West shows. Pawnee Bill included an act of lynching the horse thief. When the show moved into the southern states tension between colored and white spectators was especially obvious. The act which heightened this friction was the lynching of a Negro horse thief. The Negro was dragged around the ring and then strung up to a pole, making a realistic picture. The colored section in Richmond, Virginia, sat stony quiet.

Pawnee Bill's Wild West skipped show dates in Shelbyville and

Murfreesboro, Tennessee, and headed to Nashville, to close the season on November 15. The final performance in Nashville was cancelled due to a snowstorm. Claims were filed against the show for hold-back pay as the troupers disbanded. Luka and his men traveled back to New York, some returning to Georgia for the winter and others remaining in the United States. Pawnee Bill's show wintered over in Nashville.

1906 EPILOGUE

Pavle Makharadze's passport was issued in 1906 and he has written on it that he returned with spoons, towels, a cap, bread, 5 candles, 20 cartridges, food and cheese.

OTHER SHOW BUSINESS

Jule Keen, sixty, Buffalo Bill's treasurer for many years, died October 31 ten days after returning from the European tour in his room at the Ashland House, while his wife's funeral was taking place at St. James Baptist Church. His wife died on Monday, and that same day he learned that it was believed that Col. Cody had been lost on a hunting trip in the valley of the Big Horn. double shock was too great for him, and the illness with which he had been suffering took a fatal turn for the worse.[290]

Nicolas Surguladze, July 11-12, 1904
Author's Collection
Plate No. 29

232

"It is said that even in hell a bribe settles matters."

Shota Rustaveli

1907 PROLOGUE

General Alikhanoff, the former Governor-General of Tbilisi, and one of the most hated military governors of Georgia, was blown to pieces in a coach by Alikhanashvili in Giumri, Armenia, on July 16. Prince Ilia Chavchavadze, a great man of letters in Georgia, was waylaid and murdered by a gang of assassins close to his country home on August 28. His wife was wounded in the same attack. His funeral was a national event. Alexis Georgian, who had ridden for Buffalo Bill, Pawnee Bill, Buckskin Bill and Campbell Brothers, had known Prince Chavchavadze while he was a student in Tbilisi.

BUFFALO BILL'S WILD WEST AND CONGRESS OF ROUGH RIDERS (1907)

Buffalo Bill's outfit returned from Europe and wintered in Bridgeport, Connecticut, at the Barnum & Bailey winter quarters. Cy Compton, a man with a soft voice, pleasant smile and calm blue eyes was head cowboy. Mr. Compton, who had seen his horses killed in the train wreck of 1901 and slaughtered in Europe due to disease, gathered a new herd of over 400 horses for the 1907 season. David Kadjaia, his men, and the other performers and staff were reassembled in Bridgeport by April 14 to begin a week of rehearsing. The week was filled with hard riding, games of poker, and catching up on gossip and news. Panteleimon Tsintsadze, who in 1905 rode with the McCaddon show in France, was riding with Kadjaia and Buffalo Bill this year. The buzz around camp was the announcement that Buffalo Bill's exhibition was not going to give parades any more. Management's published rationale for this decision was the fact that the horses and men gave an improved performance when they were not compelled to parade in the hot sun or disagreeable rain for a couple hours. The press agents further advanced that by eliminating the street cavalcade the riding stock and performers are fresh for their important duty of giving a high-class exhibition, enlisting the best of their abilities and returning to the public the full benefit of their talents to which they are entitled. Another factor propounded by management was the inconvenience to the merchants and municipal governments.

Without the usual parade, the exhibition opened at Madison Square Garden, on Tuesday, April 23. The production was the same except for three new scenic features: "The Battle of Summit Springs," fought July 11, 1869, and in which Cody was said to have killed Tall Bull; "The Great Train Holdup;" and "A Holiday at T-E Ranch." David Kadjaia and his Georgian riders were moved to the next to last scene, giving their usual reckless and daring horseback riding routine to great applause.

The first jump was to Brooklyn, but the week before, on May 6, three large sight-seeing automobiles were used to carry the Indians, Georgians and cowboys on a tour through New York City and Brooklyn. This stunt was covered by the press and was an attempt to generate interest in the show. The press agent was remiss in not informing the drivers of these vehicles that they would need to pay the toll over the Williamsburg Bridge. "The drivers went past the ticket-takers, and as a result the entire caravan of machines was chased by a mounted patrolman, who demanded fares."[291]

Bus Tour, New York City, ca 1907
Author's Collection
Plate No. 30

Buffalo Bill and his rough riders had not toured for several years in the United States, and the crowds were large; many towns accounted for sell-out performances. Except for the McCaddon French opposition in 1905, Buffalo Bill's outfit had enjoyed clear venues since 1903. They encountered opposition from Pawnee Bill's Wild West, and responded by covering Chicago with heavy Buffalo Bill paper announcing their coming in July. Pawnee Bill's general manager, Eddie Arlington, pulled his show out of Chicago a week early. Buffalo Bill's traveling Wild West exhibition was back to the usual routine.

Buffalo Bill's press clippings do not cover Cody's financial problems; however, the lives of the Georgians in Buffalo Bill's exhibition were covered by newspaper reporters several times during the season. Reporters were always looking for story angles, and they would transcribe any observation, such as: "It is said that the Japs and the *Georgians* get along together as peacefully as though there had never been a Japanese-Russian war." On a hot muggy Sunday afternoon in Indianapolis, Indiana, a reporter witnessed one of the favorite pastimes of men in the show, a game of poker.

"The card game in the big tent started. Pedro, his dusky face with its good nature masked in indifference, played silently. Next to him was a *Georgian*, whose dark eyes and bristled mustache waxed fiercer and fiercer as he played. Next to him were the mobile features of an oriental, a Japanese juggler, and then an American cowboy, who 'anted in' with a roar of protest. It was a small congress of nations, ever the great American game, poker."[292]

The spelling and pronunciation of Georgian names baffled the American newspaper reporters and general public. The Georgians took on American names and, unfortunately, to this day, many of their names cannot be attributed to the real Georgian. One such report occurred on Monday, August 26: "Hundreds of horses raced round and round the big arena at breakneck speed, with shouting riders in all sorts of positions, yet only one accident occurred to put an extra thrill to the afternoon performance. Nymi Christus, a Georgian, was thrown to the ground and underneath his horse when the animal, at top speed, stumbled and fell. Christus was carried away to the dressing tent—lifeless, many spectators thought—but he was only stunned."[293] In the evening another Georgian fell from his horse, but he jumped up and ran off himself.

Buffalo Bill's Georgian riders could not read newspapers, which was probably fortunate because if they did, their blood may have boiled even hotter. These men received letters from home telling of the czar's Cossack troops enforcing the czar's law while the newspapers printed stories linking these Georgian riders to these same Cossacks. One article read: "Here you have the Cossacks who were called upon as the strongest part of the great army of the czar of all the Russians to try to stop the undefeatable, unconquerable little Japs, and are even now throughout Russia trying to quell the ever growing spirit of the revolution. You may see with this show how they ride, for the *Georgians* are among the famous riders of the world. Side by side with the *Georgians* are the little brown sons of Nippon, the Yankees of the East, who are all the time becoming of greater concern for us Americans."[294]

As the season came to a close, there was a series of rail accidents. On September 27, due to a wreck on the C & O, Buffalo Bill's exhibition did not reach Lexington, Kentucky, until 3:00 p.m. and the afternoon show was abandoned. Then while leaving Jacksonville on Sunday, October 13, early in the morning, in the rail yards of North Springfield, Florida, several of the cars jumped the track and two flat cars were turned completely over while an engine was switching. Several men were injured.

On a nippy Saturday, October 19th evening in Richmond, Virginia, the season came to a close.

CAMPBELL BROTHERS GREAT CONSOLIDATED SHOWS (1907)

The Campbell Brothers' season opened on Saturday, April 27, in Fairbury, Nebraska. Captain Dimitri Tsintsadze, Sergia Gvarjaladze, and two other Georgians arrived the same day. They hurriedly acquainted themselves with their horses and the show routine and made the evening performance. Then everyone boarded the twenty-seven car train to start the season's run.

The Campbell Brothers' opening weeks encountered several difficulties. They arrived in Alliance, Nebraska, on Sunday, May 12, with the weather cold and cloudy, and a slight snow at times. Charles Campbell, who had been sick, became demented and was taken to a sanatorium in Council Bluffs, Iowa. The next day, Monday, during the afternoon performance, Sergia Gvarjaladze broke the small bone just above his ankle when his horse fell. Sergia might have been glad to be out of commission for some weeks, as the evening performance was given in bitterly cold weather.[295]

The Campbell Brothers' adventures, mishaps, accidents, or other events of the 1907 season are as obscure as their 1907 routing. The Campbell Brothers was a hold-out circus and they protected themselves from the "Circus Trust" by not publishing their routing. The re-creation of their route, therefore, has depended on finding contemporary newspaper articles about the season, an extremely difficult task. A small notice in the *Bismarck Daily Tribune,* on August 20, informs us that the Campbell Brothers paid a one-day $40 license fee.[296] *The Chillicothe Constitution* in Missouri on Monday, September 30, published a notice: "William P. Hall, the famous horse buyer, has purchased the Campbell Brothers circus and menagerie, now traveling in Nebraska, and will take possession at the close of the season."[297]

PAWNEE BILL'S HISTORIC WILD WEST AND GREAT FAR EAST (1907)

Pawnee Bill's Wild West stock and equipment wintered in Cumberland Park, Nashville, Tennessee, while the executive staff and headquarters were located in the Knickerbocker Theatre Building, in New York City. Edward Arlington, for many years a confidential advisor of the late James A. Bailey and who routed the Barnum and Bailey Circus, purchased a half interest in the Pawnee Bill's Wild West and Far East Show. Arlington was to take an active part in the management.[298]

The SS *St. Louis,* a twelve-year-old steamship of the American Line, arrived at the port of New York on Monday, April 15, 1907, with five Georgian riders on the passenger list: Konstantine Chkartishvili, Mikheil Chkhartishvili, Tomas Chkhartishvili, Jordan Schividadze, and Sergia Jorbenadze. All these men would perform in Pawnee Bill's show. Luka Chkhartishvili, their leader, had spent the winter in America and in March was working at the Austin's and Stone's Museum in Boston. The Georgians who arrived on the SS *St. Louis* only had three days to travel to Nashville, and start rehearsals. Toma Chkhartishvili, who was on his first trip to the United States, would need to train his horse, learn the performance routine and adjust to life on the road in a tent show.

Pawnee Bill's Great Wild West and Far East Show pitched their tents in Nashville, on Sunday, April 14, and started rehearsals Monday morning. Gordon Lillie, aware that the "Circus Trust" had abandoned parades, planned a spectacular cavalcade the night before opening, using Roman candles, skyrockets and other fireworks to light the journey. The weather did not cooperate and the parade was held in the rain without the fireworks. The first performances of the season occurred Wednesday afternoon and evening, April 17. The season had opened and now the hundreds of men and horses daily gathered in rail yards, boarded the two-section fifty-car train, and proceeded to crisscross the American Midwest.

Early in Pawnee Bill's season, the weather was cold and rainy, and it was noted by the press that few Indians or cowboys who were shot in the arena died. It seemed none of the performers wanted to fall into the muddy arena, but would just ride off into the exit.

The men and women in Pawnee Bill's shows divided themselves into clubs or social groups. One could find chess clubs, fishing clubs, baseball teams, knitting circles, and probably the most curious was "The Lillie Paws," an eight member golf club. In 1907 the President of the club was Luka Chkhartishvili, or as the press wrote "Prince Luka, the colonel of the Cossacks. He is a veteran of the late Japanese-Russian war, and as such is honored by his associates."[299] The best player was Mulok Karsh, a South Sea Islander. The press exploits and adventures of the Georgian riders in Pawnee Bill's show—or any of the shows—must be read with a jaundiced eye; a story printed in the *St. Louis Star*, on May 7, is an excellent example of a fabricated story.

> "A full blooded native of the plains of Tartary, with an ancestry that can be traced in direct line to the kings who ruled most of Central Asia… Luka, son of Lon, is the first prince to visit St. Louis.… Luka held a commission from the czar in the recent Russian-Japanese war… having come up from the forbidden land of Tibet… he has been in the service of the Grand Lama.… He is a soldier of fortune.… Pawnee Bill's agents met him in Port Arthur.… He enlisted a score of Cossacks from his former troop.…"

Pawnee Bill ran into significant opposition from the "Circus Trust." Luka and his brothers Mikheil and Kosta, and other riders who had been working for years in the tent shows, were familiar with the problem of tent shows' opposition campaigns. This year was particularly vicious; the *Minneapolis Tribune* told the story. "Probably never before in the annals of the circus has a tented organization been subjected to the opposition tactics which have been directed against the Pawnee Bill show since it opened its season in Nashville, Tennessee, last April. The so-called circus 'trust' has followed it from city to city, using every artifice known to the cunning circus men to detract patronage. So bitter and determined is the warfare against this independent amusement institution that, in some cities, the newspapers, billboards and store windows have been employed to advertise the coming of one of the 'trust' circuses three months distant. In Chicago and in St. Louis, where the war waged most vigorously, the newspapers published news stories that the 'trust' shows were fighting among themselves in the matter, and that the Ringlings were on the point of breaking with Barnum & Bailey, and allying themselves with Pawnee Bill's show."[300]

Opposition from the "trust" was not the only problem that Luka, his men, and the other performers observed during the season. Pawnee Bill carried around 450 laborers (canvas men, drivers) to put up and take down the show in each town. They left Chicago with a full complement of men, but by the time they reached Minneapolis they were down to 175 men. "Ever since the show started into the Northwest, the men have been leaving in swarms. Sunday, June 16, they were paid off and forty quit."[301] It did not help the morale of the laborers when one of them fell under the train while trying to jump from a flat car to the dining car, crushing both his lower limbs below the knees and fracturing his skull.

Luka's men were not able to read the newspaper headlines: "Pawnee Bill Didn't Make Good," "Pawnee Bill's Show Disappointing," "A Bunch of the Pawnee Bill People Quit the Show," or "Pawnee Bill Fails to Create a Furor." Luka did know how to interpret the applause of the audience. The headlines were disappointing, but in the newspaper columns you read accounts such as: "The only thing that had any merit at all was the riding of the *Georgians*," "*Georgians* with Wild West show worth price of admission," "The *Georgians* elicited the most applause," or "The *Georgian* horsemen give a first class exhibit of daredevil and skilled riding." Pawnee Bill's press agents used the audience reaction in their future advertising. As the season wore on, more often advertising pieces were printed titled, "Wild Riding Cossacks from

Russia," with accompanying photographs and story.

Pawnee Bill and Luka left behind one of the Georgians in Amarillo, Texas, on October 5, because of an accident during the show. Luka and his men did not find out what happened to their companion until they reached Houston, Texas, on October 28. "Prince Luka's band of *Georgians* gave an exhibition of acrobatic and daring horsemanship that was grand and spectacular. Since the little Japs made the fierce Cossacks look so cheap during the late hostilities the populace don't warm up to them as they once did. One of the most skillful of the Russian riders died yesterday (October 28, 1907) in Amarillo and this cast a gloom over the entire Russian colony."[302] There is no record of who this Georgian rider was, but through deduction one can safely say it was Jordon Schividadze, as he does not appear again in any Wild West show.

The season ended in Denison, Texas, on November 9. Luka and his men returned to New York City. Most of his men stayed in New York to perform in the "Battle of Port Arthur" at the New York Hippodrome.

1907 EPILOGUE

The manifest of the SS *St. Louis* from Cherbourg, France, lists five artists going to Philadelphia to work on the Pawnee Bill show. The information included they were all Russian and left from Batumi, had $10 in their pocket, and were going to 605 Sansom Street Philadelphia. The individual information:

Kosta Chkhartishvili, age 38, married, he can read and write, he had been in the U.S. in 1905 and 1906.

Mikheil Chkhartishvili, age 32, married, he cannot read and write, had been in the U.S. in 1905 and 1906.

Toma Chkhartishvili, age 25, single, he can read and write, he had not been in the U.S. before.

Jordan Schividadze, age 35, married, he cannot read and write, he had been in the U.S. in 1905 and 1906. (Presumed died in Amarillo, Texas)

Sergi Jorbenadze, age 33, married, he can read and write, and had not been to the U.S. before.

OTHER SHOW BUSINESS

The New York Times informed their readers a new Wild West show portraying the everyday life on a Western ranch opened in Chicago on May 2, 1907. The Miller Brothers 101 Ranch Wild West show went on to the Jamestown Exposition.[303] This was the opening of a new tent show that would survive into the 1920s, and which from 1908 until its demise featured Georgian riders.

Mikhako Kobaladze
Author's Collection
Plate No. 31

Sergo Gvarjaladze, Chicago ca 1914
Author's Collection
Plate No. 32

"It is better to have no man by your side than an ungrateful one."
Shota Rustaveli

1908 PROLOGUE

The Russian army during early 1908 was building up forces at Batumi in anticipation of conflict with Turkey. Hostilities were expected in March.

January 6, 1908, the New York Hippodrome opened a new show, *The Battle of Port Arthur,* a combat extravaganza with a guaranteed appeal. The Russo-Japanese war was still a momentous topic in late 1907/1908. This production was put together by Messrs. Shubert and Anderson as managers. It was billed as "The Colossal Japanese-Russian War Spectacle." In Scene I, Luka Chkhartishvili and his troupe of Georgian riders again acted as Russian Cossacks.

SCENE I

The scene opens on a public square in Port Arthur. The ground is covered with snow, which is still falling. On one side is the enormous city gate, the only opening in the high wall which surrounds the beleaguered city. At the back is an old warehouse now used as a military prison. Beyond are the streets of the city. The prison and gate are guarded by Cossacks. In the yard of the prison, a crowd of Japanese prisoners press their forms to the iron bars. Crowds of half-starved women and children beg of the passers-by.

There is a clatter of horses' hoofs outside the gate. The guards unbar the way and a troupe of Cossacks ride in. They are led by Captain Garbedioff, Luka Chkhartishvili, who dismounts to meet Barnsky of the prison guard. At the sight of the soldiers, the people clamor for food. The Cossacks drive them back and are interrupted by an aide who precedes Colonel Ostag. The commander enters in his sleigh and announces that he has brought food. The people rush about the sleigh, fighting for food. Riuka, a Japanese girl, asks for food. As she speaks, Cossacks enter with Captain Tonkoka, who was captured as a spy. He asserts his innocence and tells his captors that he is searching for the daughter of Colonel Ochigi, who was lost riding while with her groom. Riuka recognizes him.

Tonkoka breaks from the guards and takes her hands. They are separated and Riuka is driven away in Colonel Ostag's sleigh. Soldiers come on laughing and talking. There are dances with peasants, Cossacks give an exhibition of fancy riding and there is a drill by the soldiers.

BUFFALO BILL'S WILD WEST AND CONGRESS OF ROUGH RIDERS (1908)

Buffalo Bill's cowboys, ranch girls, Mexicans, staff and laborers all headed east toward Bridgeport, Connecticut, in the first weeks of April. The troupe of Georgian riders, Germans, British and other European performers crossed the Atlantic and were in Bridgeport, Connecticut, for rehearsals by Thursday, April 16, 1908. The whole outfit bundled their belongings in forty-seven railcars, divided into three train sections, and headed to New York City on Saturday, April 18. Dress rehearsal was on Monday. Tuesday, April 21, the Buffalo Bill 1908 season opened in Madison Square Garden.

Buffalo Bill's Wild West still omitted the parade on occasions while the Ringling Brothers, who now owned the Barnum and Bailey show, re-instituted the circus parade at the Greatest Show on Earth. This year's new feature was a football game played on horseback by five cowboys and five Indians, a timid game compared to those played by Georgians in Guria. It was not unknown for the cowboys, Indians, Georgians and other performers to bet on the outcome of these games. The Georgians were again the closing act, dashing around the arena at breakneck speed, holding to their horses by only one foot in the stirrup. In an interview, Colonel Cody said: "The *Georgians* are marvelous horsemen, and do more fancy acrobatic feats than any other class of riders, but show me the *Georgian* who can ride a bucking bronco."[304] After the Georgians finished their feats of horsemanship, they turned around and rode in the final salute.

Buffalo Bill's Wild West traveled from coast to coast and from the Great Lakes to the Gulf of Mexico. They traveled over 15,000 miles. The Georgian riders were in the arena for the grand review, the ethnic races, and their ten minutes in the spot light just before the final salute. The rest of the day was spent waiting and on one occasion a reporter wrote: "A tall *Georgian* with a brush-heap beard had swathed his forehead in a wet cloth and lay down to sleep. It was hot under the tent but everyone seemed inured to this feature."[305] Another feature that the Georgians endured was the occasional blow down, thunderstorms which blew the canvas down, as occurred in Pittsburgh in June.

Sweeney's Cowboy band played, *"Home Sweet Home,"* Thursday evening November 19, in Memphis, Tennessee, bringing the twenty-fifth Buffalo Bill season to a close, and the sixteenth season with the Georgian riders. Major Burke said: "There are about fourteen different points to which our people are to be sent, in all directions, and Memphis has the facilities, on account of the connections, par excellence of any place in the country." The Georgians headed for New York and then either home to Guria or stayed behind and worked the winter in various venues.

CAMPBELL BROTHERS GREAT CONSOLIDATED SHOWS (1908)

The Campbell Brothers owned winter quarter circus barns on the Little Blue River, about one and one half miles from Fairbury, Nebraska, a town that Dimitri Tsintsadze and his three companions had been visiting for the last four years. "Their farm had a mammoth horse barn, wherein during the winter months were stabled their 250 head of horses. Next to the horse barn stood a large building made of concrete blocks known as the cat building, which was the home for lions, tigers, leopards, cougars, hyenas, monkeys, and birds. A large frame building known as the elephant house was home for the herd of performing elephants. There was a camel barn, Shetland pony barn, and ring barn. The ring barn was where the dancing elephants, Shetland ponies, and cakewalk horses were taught their tricks during the winter months."[306] The Campbells' homes were across the street from the circus barns, and the rest of Fairbury was a typical small American town: a courthouse in the center of the town square, the hotels, the saloons, and the town bank, all facing the courthouse. Fairbury was a railroad junction town.

Dimitri and his men were familiar with Fairbury in April and wore their great coats against the cold weather while strolling around town before opening day. The opening day parade left the Campbell's circus lot, at 10:00 a.m., with Pete Campbell in a buggy leading the way and the calliope bringing up the rear. A raw wind and afternoon sprinkles greeted the audience for the Saturday, April 25, opening performance.

Dimitri and many of the old timers with Campbell Brothers must have wondered what tragedy might befall them this year, as in each of the previous few years the season opened with some kind of accident. They did not have long to wait. The show did not leave Fairbury until five o'clock Sunday morning April 26, because of an accident to one of the rail cars. They arrived late in Red Cloud, and gave two performances despite the cold weather, and did not miss a performance date during the rest of the week. After the first week, Dimitri and others might have thought the string of opening bad luck had been broken. By the end of May, everyone connected with the circus knew their run of bad luck was not over.

Captain Dimitri and his Georgian riders were the last act in the Campbell Brothers' performance. The Campbell Brothers were in Muscatine, Iowa, on Wednesday, September 16, and the usual events took place. The train arrived and the town kids gathered to watch the unloading and transport of the circus wagons to the show lot on East Hill. The children watched the erection of the immense tents and then scurried home to plead with their fathers and mothers for the price of a ticket. The parade in the afternoon helped convince some doubting parents and by 2:00 p.m. a large crowd was gathered inside the circus big top. The last act was introduced, as Dimitri and his Georgians charged onto the hippodrome track. Dimitri Tsintsadze probably does not completely remember the end of their performance or even leaving town.

"With the left foot looped in the saddle, hanging to the right side of his horse in a sort of sitting posture, Dimitri… was violently hurled to the ground by striking one of the large tent poles as the horse attempted to round the turn at a rapid gallop. Dimitri lay quite still for a moment, while the crowd near the accident sat breathless, but soon he raised himself on one elbow and looked around dazed but perfectly conscious. He was carried outside the arena, laid upon the grass for a few minutes, and later got up and with the aid of one of the attendants walked to the dressing room, and shortly after was removed to the sleeping car, where medical aid was summoned. Dimitri was painfully bruised about the hips and back, and the surprising part of it is that he was not seriously hurt."[307]

The Campbell Brothers' season, which included a month of traveling through Canada, closed on October 31 in Clyde, Kansas. The show returned to Fairbury and their winter quarters, while Dimitri and his men headed for Chicago. Dimitri and his men were going to spend the winter in America, and his intentions were published in *Billboard*. Captain Dimitri, as Dimitri Tsintsadze was known, "closed a very satisfactory season of twenty-seven weeks with the Campbell Brothers' Great Consolidated Shows and is now engaged in booking a strong attraction known as Capt. Dimitri's Troupe of Genuine Russian Singers and Dancers, composed of four men and four women, with an elaborate wardrobe. The act will be presented for the first time at the National Theatre, Chicago on November 16."[308]

MILLER BROTHERS 101 RANCH WILD WEST SHOW (1908)

The Georgian riders contracted in 1908 with a new tent show: the Miller Brothers 101 Ranch. Three Brothers: Joseph Carson Miller (1868-1927), Zachary Taylor Miller (1878-1952), and George Lee Miller (1881-1929) were the sons of George Washington Miller (1841-1903). These brothers became known in tent show business as Joe, Zack, and George, the owners of The Miller Brothers 101 Ranch Wild West Show.

Edward Arlington a partner of the Miller Brothers contracted Luka Chkhartishvili and his Georgian riders to perform in the 101 Ranch. Prince Luka and his Georgian equestrians was the only feature of the program not distinctly typical of the American western range. The show's management concocted a story line in the press for the audience to compare the exhibition of the Georgians and Cowboys. A typical press release read:

"Equestrianism in all its reckless and skillful forms is displayed in the arena of the 101 Ranch Wild West show. Every performer, cowboy, cowgirl and Indian is a product of the prairie, except the contingent of *Georgians*, under the leadership of Prince Lucca. These members of Russia's noted light cavalry were brought to this country by the Miller Brothers as a comparative exhibition with our native horsemen.

246

"The *Georgians* do not attempt the bronco busting feats of the cowboys, but they perform acrobatic exploits that for sheer daredevil achievements are a sensational revelation. The cowboys of the 101 Ranch, learning last winter of the coming of the czar's riders, selected George Elser, one of their number, to represent them before the public in opposition to *Georgians'* claim of all-around equestrian superiority. Elser is known for his horsemanship on every western ranch, and has never left the 101 Ranch to compete in frontier celebrations that he did not return with a trophy of his prowess. Whose riding—Elser's or the *Georgians'*—is the more daring and difficult, the audience may decide. Both fill the mind and eye with incredulous amazement. The Georgians do not once touch the ground as they circle the enclosure upright in saddle with swinging sword; sitting face backward in saddle; dangling head downward between the mount's flying hoofs; prostrate and unsupported on his back; or perpendicularly upside down. Their horses, accompanying them from the steppes of the Siberian border, are lithe and fiery animals of great speed and endurance.

"It is needless to relate that relations between the Cowboys and *Georgians* are formal, even strained."

■ ■ ■

To reach the Miller Brothers 101 Ranch, Luka and his men arrived in Bliss, Oklahoma, in early April, along with other performers who rode across the five miles of gently undulating prairie out to the ranch. Luka's men in the days and weeks before opening had to break in new horses and learn their parts in the performance. The first show was held in Ponca City, eight miles from the ranch, on April 15, 1908.

The Miller Brothers 101 Ranch worked their way to Chicago and played in the coliseum, then headed back to St. Louis, with half a dozen towns declaring a holiday so the people could see it. The Miller Brothers on June 15 were in Saint Paul, Minnesota, where Sergia Jorbenadze took a fall.

"Dashing around the ring at the 101 Wild West show yesterday afternoon, performing his most difficult feat, one which none of the others dare do, Sergia Jorbenadze, the best of the Georgian riders, leaned a little too far out in his stirrups, causing his horse to miss its footing and fall, carrying him underneath. Several men and women in the grandstand fainted.

"When the rider crawled from beneath his horse he limped to the animal's side and then collapsed. He was carried out on a stretcher, his leg being broken. The horse, prancing and pawing on three legs, one of its forelegs helplessly dangling, was led from the ground behind the big curtain and shot. Its foreleg was broken.

"All the riding at the Wild West show was daring and rough riding of the true variety, but the feat Jorbenadze was performing when the accident occurred was the most dangerous of all. The horse was one of the finest carried by the Miller Shows."[309] Sergia Jorbenadze was left behind at St. Mary's Hospital in Minneapolis.

Bill Pickett, an African-American cowboy, was billed as "Man and bovine in terrific struggles for mastery." Pickett was credited with inventing bull-dogging or steer wrestling, and he became another famous American western cowboy from the Miller Brothers 101 Ranch. His trademark was using his teeth to hold down a steer, bulldog style. Bill Pickett, Tom Mix, and other riders in the 101 Ranch became famous in the years that followed. The Miller Brothers 101 Ranch show had more than 550 people with the show and over 250 horses and mules. The six Georgian riders were famous and infamous in 1908, and were highlighted in press releases and stories from the 101 Ranch Wild West show. *The Hutchinson Leader* reported: "The *Georgians* were the real thing, right from the czar's army. Splendid horsemen and brave fighters, they are also fierce and cruel. They were members of the same regiment that charged upon a throng of men, women, and children in the streets of St. Petersburg two years ago, and shot, sabered, and murdered a thousand."[310]

Despite being vilified in the press, Luka and his men continued to receive applause and appreciation for their trick riding. *The Bay City Times* reported: "The *Georgians* do not once touch ground... dangling head downward between the mount's flying hoofs; prostrate and unsupported on his back...."[311] It was from these positions that occasionally one reads about an accident in the arena. "One *Georgian* rider and his horse overbalanced during a furious stunt and went hurtling to the ground. The *Georgian* got a badly skinned arm but otherwise was uninjured."[312]

The Miller Brothers season ended in Brownsville, Texas, on December 3. Eddie Arlington took the 101 Ranch Show into Mexico to close out the season. The Georgian riders found themselves a long way from home.

PAWNEE BILL'S HISTORIC WILD WEST AND FAR EAST
(1908)

Wonderland, "fairyland by the sea," was an amusement park on Massachusetts Bay to rival Coney Island in New York. A detachment of Luka Chkhartishvili's men found themselves at Revere Beach around May 19. They were attached to Pawnee Bill's Wild West show that was the main attraction at an amusement park called Wonderland. Revere Beach is five miles north of Boston along a large crescent of sandy shore on Massachusetts Bay. Wonderland was built on 25.9 acres of land with a beautiful lagoon as its centerpiece, and opened on Memorial Day, May 30. The lagoon was surrounded by a canal and boardwalk promenade with access to restaurants, arcade amusements, and a Wild West arena and theater productions. The arena was occupied by Pawnee Bill in 1908. The Georgian men who rode in the Pawnee Bill Show that year were not going to have the usual season of one-day stands and overnight train jumps. The Pawnee Bill riders soon discovered many of the unique features of their home for the summer. The entrance building, called the administration building, contained a telephone exchange and a nursery and playroom where parents could drop off their children. There were two buildings dedicated to theatrical performances. The Darlings' circus, with horses, dogs, monkeys, and the famous kicking stallion, was a free exhibition. A thrill ride called "Shoot the Chute" was an exciting ride. Passengers were lifted in a gondola to the top of a steep grade, and once at the top, the gondola was dropped down a water slide back into the huge lagoon. The management each season would vary the character of the shows.

On a typical day the gates opened at 1:00 p.m. and closed at 11:00 p.m., and on holidays and special occasions they opened early at 11:00 a.m. The entrance fee for the Pawnee Bill show was ten cents. Each day there was a 2:00 p.m. and 7:00 p.m. parade around the boardwalk with participants from each of the various productions at Wonderland. Pawnee Bill's Indians, Cowboys, Cowgirls and Georgians strolled the promenade to attract attention to their show. Pawnee Bill had an afternoon and evening performance just like those given for years on the road. The show was given with painted cycloramic effects and with music, sharpshooting, boomerang-throwing, Georgian riding and picturesque illustrations of Indian ways of travel, dances, cremation of the dead and methods of warfare. The Indian village was considered a side show attraction where patrons could wander around their tepees; "where the ways of the aborigines could be studied." There were around fifty Indians in Pawnee Bill's troupe, among them nine squaws and several papooses. At sunset the park took on a completely new character when over 150,000 lights were turned on. A whistle announced the closing of the park every night. Wonderland was open seven days a week under a new Sunday law.

The season at Wonderland closed on Sunday, September 20, after the 11:00 p.m. whistle that signaled the gates' closure. Pawnee Bill took his show on the road and headed south. The road show featured the dismantling and destruction of Port Arthur, a great thirty-minute pyrotechnic show, the whoops and war cries of Indians, and portrayal of life on the plains by Indians and cowboys. The Georgians, each night, were overrun by Japanese who worked like Trojans, and the Russians fought with the courage of despair at the battle for Port Arthur. The Pawnee Bill season closed on October 27, after a two-week stay in Atlanta.

Bud Atkinson Wild West, Australia, ca 1913
Captain George Georgian
Author's Collection
Plate No. 33

"Horns cannot beautify an ass nor roses the crow."

Shota Rustaveli

1909 PROLOGUE

Luka Chkhartishvili and Dimitri Tsintsadze apparently took part in the realignment of Wild West amusements in 1909. The consolidation of Buffalo Bill and Pawnee Bill meant that there was an excess of Georgian riders, and helps explain some changes as to where these men performed during the 1909 tenting season. Luka rode with the Miller 101 Ranch, and he also had a troupe of riders for the first and only time with the Norris & Rowe circus. Buffalo Bill & Pawnee Bill continued to have Georgian riders, but the record of where Dimitri Tsintsadze spent the season is unclear, since no record of them with the Campbell Brothers in 1909 has been uncovered. *Variety*, in the January 16, 1909, issue reported that The Rhoda Royal Circus had a Capt. Dereske and his Cossack riders performing with them during the season. Panteleimon Tsintsadze arrived in New York on April 17 onboard the *SS Prinz Friedrich Wilhem*.

The interest of the Bailey estate in Buffalo Bill's Wild West and Pawnee Bill's Far East shows was bought at Philadelphia by Cody and Lillie in May of 1909. The Two Bills' show, as it became known, was managed solely by Major Lillie, while Colonel Cody took a prominent part in the performance.

BUFFALO BILL'S WILD WEST AND PAWNEE BILL'S FAR EAST COMBINED (1909)

The troupe of Georgian riders in the newly formed Buffalo Bill and Pawnee Bill show arrived in Bridgeport, Connecticut, around April 20. The combined show had moved from their winter quarters near the railroad station to the Bridgeport show grounds on the edge of the city. The Bridgeport show grounds by Sunday, April 25, was a muddy field, where it was reported the Georgians ran about for warmth and watched the Japanese tossing each other into somersaults, while the cowboy band practiced with collars turned up and hats on.[313] The next day the outfit moved down to New York City. The season opened on Tuesday night, April 27, in Madison Square Garden, at 8:20 p.m. Although the whole show had gone before and the roughest kind of rough riding had been viewed, the Georgians were turned into the arena just before the close. The wonders of the steppes seemed, however, to hold their popularity, for the audience still had enthusiasm to spare for their remarkable feats. The evening closed at 10:40 p.m.

Buffalo Bill's and Pawnee Bill's Combined shows had a contract with the Chicago & North Western Railway System, dated June 17, which illustrates the equipment moved on a special train of two sections. The train consisted of twenty-one flat cars, fifteen stock cars, one box car, and ten passenger cars, being in all forty-seven cars. The contract was for the period July 13 to July 21, to include hauling three advance cars, at a cost of $2,800 for these movements. These trains were hauling around 800 people and 600 animals from lot-to-lot. Reporters were always asking about how the diverse nationalities communicated. Buffalo Bill was quoted as saying: "Perhaps one of their number, I mean, say, one *Georgian* for instance, can talk a little English, and that is all. If he wants to talk to one of our Arabs he has to let out those few words of English that he knows and the Arab does the same."[314]

A visitor who was walking behind the scenes on a Sunday afternoon in Kansas City was reported to remark about a Georgian rider getting ready to go into town. He was quoted as saying:

"And that *Georgian*, what's he putting on his pink frock coat for and curling his mustache before the mirror for, as if he was going on to do the Merry Widow act, when there isn't a show for twenty-four hours? Where's a fellow to get the delightful disillusionment of 'behind?'"[32]

A showman responded: "Well," said the unruffled showman, "it happens that that *Georgian* is human and thinks his own costume the correct one like everybody else does. He's probably on his way down town to catch the eyes of the Kansas City maidens and whisper in their ears if he can get close enough, that all real gentlemen wear pink frock coats."[315]

In Chattanooga, Tennessee, a reporter observed: "All the male performers of the show, about 300 in number, were found in a single large tent. In one corner was a *Georgian*, his head bandaged from a horse's kick, writing a letter to his kindred in Europe, with a dozen of his race seated around him, all dressed in Dolmans *(Chokas)*."[316]

[32] Behind - The newspaper's euphemism for "going out to find a lady for the night."

Buffalo and Pawnee Bill's season ended in Richmond, Virginia, on Saturday, November 6. The show wintered in New Jersey.

THE GREATER NORRIS AND ROWE MUSEUM, MENAGERIE, HIPPODROME CIRCUS (1909)

The Greater Norris and Rowe Museum, Menagerie, Hippodrome circus winter quarters were in Sacramento, California, and Luka's troupe of Georgian riders had to arrive in California before the Thursday, March 11, opening date in Santa Cruz. The sole owner, H.S. Rowe, had the twenty-two train cars repainted in orange and purple while in winter quarters. The Norris & Rowe circus started as a trained animal show, but over the years it had added more traditional circus acts. The Luka troupe of seven Georgian riders had fallen in with a bunch of tough circus people. Local newspapers reported the police closing gambling games, "hootchy kootchy" dancers, pickpockets, and many cases of short changing. The employees had problems collecting their pay, and in Sacramento thirty men filed an attachment against the circus for back pay.[317]

The Norris and Rowe advance men had another scheme to swindle local charitable organizations. They pitched their circus as a great money maker to local organizations by over- stating how many seats could be sold. In Stockton, California, on April 10, the local paper *The Mail* reported: "Of course, the advance man led the local Woodmen of the World to suppose that they would make a barrel of money. All the order had to do was to assist in paying the local advertising bills and then take all the circus made over $2,500 to $3,000, and fifty per cent of all above that figure; it looked very good, when the circus man finished telling about it. The Woodmen local lost between $200 and $300." This story of "share the benefits" was repeated over and over, and more than one ladies group, club, or association was taken for a circus ride.

The circus was due in River Falls, Wisconsin, around 5:00 a.m. on Saturday morning, July 3, but did not arrive until ten o'clock. On the jump from Le Sueur to River Falls, at Hudson, one of the long flat cars loaded with wagons and tent poles careened and spilled its cargo, killing one man instantly and wounding three others, two of whom died later in hospital.[318] July 4th was on the worst possible day of the week for a circus,

Sunday, a day the circus was forbidden to operate. The performers and crew on July 4 were treated to a lavish holiday dinner. The dining tent was gaily festooned with bunting. H.S. Rowe's picture was prominently displayed, garlanded with laurel; the tables were decorated with ferns, carnations and roses in lavish profusion, and an elaborate menu was served to every person.[319] Luka and his men sat at table No. 4 with Ed Nathan, Merritt Belew, F.J. Griffin, and Roy Miller.

Princeton, Indiana, Friday, October 21: "During the night show, a high wind began to blow. The circus managers started cutting the acts short so as to complete the performance before the storm struck. They had miscalculated a few minutes, for just as the last act was finished and spectators were leaving their seats at shortly after 9:00 p.m., there was a sudden roar; the tent lifted, swayed like a great wave, and came crashing down. Some 1,500 people were trapped beneath the fold of canvas. The lights were out; fire started in the menagerie straw; husbands, wives, and children were separated; roars of animals and trumpeting of elephants added to the confusion. Suddenly, someone yelled "cut the tent," and immediately knives began to slash at the canvas. All persons were removed to safety and physicians on the grounds began treating the wounded. A score of the spectators had been injured when struck by falling poles or were trampled on in the dark and confusion. None were seriously hurt."[320]

The Norris and Rowe season closed after thirty-three weeks on the road in Evansville, Indiana. The show was to winter in Evansville, but folded after a local feed dealer took possession of several head of horses for his feed bill.

MILLER BROTHERS 101 RANCH REAL WILD WEST (1909)

Luka and his six men arrived at the Miller Brothers 101 Ranch in early April to rehearse for the opening on April 17, in Ponca City, Oklahoma. It took a two-section train to carry the twenty-two rail cars, nine flats, seven horse cars, and six sleepers from lot-to-lot. The newspaper *Variety* reported: "There are about 40 Indians, 30 cowboys and girls, 7 Georgians, with some steers included in the many numbers."[321]

Luka's brother, Mikheil Chkhartishvili, in Davenport, Iowa, on August

29 was badly injured in a fall. *The Daily Times* of Davenport reported: "Mikheil Chkhartishvili, a member of the *Georgian* troupe with the 101 Ranch which showed here Saturday, met with a very serious accident while putting on their act in the afternoon. Chkhartishvili was in the act of vaulting over his horse when he missed his hold upon the horse and pitched headlong to the ground on the opposite side of the horse.

"It was seen that the man was badly injured and the city ambulance was called to take him to the city. He was taken to St. Anthony's hospital, where he was attended by Dr. Weber, the company's physician.

"Upon examination, it was found that he had fractured his leg badly and he will not be able to continue with the troupe for some time. If possible, Chkhartishvili will be attended to in such a manner that he will be enabled to be taken from the city and allowed to rest until he is able to take his place with the troupe."[322]

Leaving Wichita Falls, Texas, for Fort Worth, one of the stock cars was wrecked, crippling several fine mules, who were shipped back to the 101 Ranch. In Fort Worth, Texas, on September 27, the arena was very slippery and several horses fell during the night performance. Prince Luka, chief of the Georgians, suffered a fractured shoulder.[323]

The Miller Brothers' season closed in East St. Louis, Illinois, on November 1, and the 101 Ranch wintered over in East St. Louis.

1909 EPILOGUE

Whether or not Dimitri Tsintsadze rode with the Campbell Brothers during 1909 could not be determined. Both Norris & Rowe and Miller Bros. advertise and report Prince Luka as the leader of the band of Cossack riders. Edward Arlington took members of the 101 Ranch to Argentina at the end of the season and we have records that Luka was a member of this troupe. The conclusion is that Dimitri Tsintsadze was the leader of the troupe with Norris & Rowe, and Luka led the troupe with Miller Brothers.

I.X.L. RANCH WILD WEST SHOW (WINTER 1909/1910)

The steamship *Vasari*, of the Lamport & Holt Line, sailed from New York on Saturday, November 21, for Buenos Aires, Argentina, with a complete American Wild West show for an extensive engagement. The Wild West show, called I.X.L. Ranch Wild West Show, was composed of 101 Ranch members and headed by Eddie Arlington. The show had about sixty riders, men and women, and twenty Indians. Luka Chkhartishvili and three other Georgians were among the riders. The show reportedly carried brand new seats and canvas, and there was a $30,000 guarantee from a group of Buenos Aires business men.[324]

The Buenos Aires Herald, in the Sunday, December 5, issue ran an advertising piece that reported: "In reckless and daredevil intrepidity, it is announced probably none of the hundreds of horsemen with the big amusement organization from the Oklahoma prairie surpass the Cossacks, who joined the I.X.L. forces straight from the military services for the czar on the Siberian border. They are the only members of the show not original with the I.X.L. Ranch, and were selected as the only equestrians in the world able to compare with the native cowboy product. Prince Lucca (Luka) is their chief. He has done duty as a member of the Royal Guard of Russia, picked for the post for bravery in war and riots. He and his score of comrades perform exploits which kindle the blood of every beholder. Limb and even life are at stake every time they circle the arena. Not a week passes that one or more is not carried to the emergency hospital the showmen maintain." The fable of the Georgians as Cossack warriors is now spread to another country. Regrettably, there was truth in the number of injuries.

"Straight poised on the saddle, prostrate on their mount's haunches, dangling by one stirrup or from the pommel, head up or down or astride the neck with inverted face, they sweep in the broad circles, in apparent enjoyment of the feats. American horsemen look on aghast."[325]

The I.X.L. Wild West set up camp in Palermo Chico, Buenos Aires, and opened Sunday, December 19, at 4:30 p.m., and again at 9:15 p.m.. The encampment was composed of Indian tepees, fifteen sleeping tents, ammunition tent, dining tent, cook tent, dressing rooms, and arena with an 8000 seating capacity. The performance was the same as given during the 101 Ranch season. The show's management pitted the Georgian riders against the American cowboy George Elser. The audience was encouraged to vote who was the better horsemen with their applause. The last opportunities to see the I.X.L. Ranch in Buenos Aires was at the afternoon and evening performances on Monday, January 24, 1910. The I.X.L. Ranch special train departed Retiro between 1:30 and 2:00 a.m. to arrive in Rosario around 8:00 a.m.[326] The train was composed of one luggage car, three first-class cars, one big box car, three cattle cars, and two sleeping cars.

The I.X.L. Ranch Wild West performers were homeward bound on Wednesday, February 17, onboard the *SS Verdi*, leaving from Buenos Aires. The *SS Verdi* arrived at Pier twelve on the East River on Monday afternoon April 4 at 5:00 p.m. "Everyone looked fine; the only thing that seemed to bother the crowd was the twenty-seven day trip on the water each way."[327]

Panteleimon Tsintsadze
Author's Collection
Plate No. 34

Alexi Tskvitishvili
Author's Collection
Plate No. 35

"None shall attain the pearl who shrink from the arduous effort to get it."

Shota Rustaveli

1910 PROLOGUE

Foreign artists arriving or departing the United States had to have their "theatrical effects" inspected and appraised by the Customs Service. Luka and the Georgian riders who had come to America earlier remembered when the Customs Service inspected their trappings on the steamship wharves. The Customs Service in late 1909 issued an order that all inspections shall be held at the Public Stores and passed upon by inspectors and assayers. Luka found that they had to complete an invoice, and if it was not properly filled out their possessions were more thoroughly inspected. The regulation read: "The invoice filed must describe them in such manner as to insure their identification at the time of export and the values thereof must be duly set forth. That is, all packages must be marked and numbered, and each article contained therein must be described, either by material or character, and a separate value given for same. Not more than one item should be placed on a line."[328] These procedures were instituted to account for items brought into the United States and to identify those same items when the baggage left the country. "If anything is missing then, it is the duty of this office to collect the tariff upon it."

The SS *Rhein* departed March 26 from Bremen and arrived in New York on April 7 with fourteen Georgian riders onboard. The passenger list included: Veliko Kvitaishvili, his wife Maro Kvitaishvili, Joseph and Karaman Imnadze, Luka, Konstantine and Teimuraz Chkhartishvili, Joseph Swidoradze *(sic)*, Bartlome Baramidze, Khalampri Pataraia, Sergia Jorbenadze, Kristine Tsintsadze, Ilarion Ebralidze, and Ilarion Zinzadi *(sic)*.

Luka Chkhartishvili's passport was issued in February 1910 with a returned date stamped 26 August 1914. He also wrote that he bought fish and gare and had 55 roubles and 50 kopeks upon his return.

Another Georgian rider, Jean Baramidze, age thirty-six, arrived on the SS *President Lincoln* on April 14.

The motion picture industry in 1910 was coming of age. In late 1909, a film titled *The 101 Ranch* had been produced by a company controlled by the organization of motion picture makers known as the "Patents Company." The patents company controlled the distribution of such manufacturers as the Biograph, the Vitagraph, Pathé Freres, Edison, and other big firms by allowing their films to be shown using only their projecting machines. Vaudeville theatre owners were the main source for distribution of these films. The owners of American Tent Shows had not yet seen the potential loss of patrons to the motion picture industry.

BUFFALO BILL'S WILD WEST COMBINED WITH PAWNEE BILL'S GREAT FAR EAST (1910)

Buffalo Bill's Wild West and Pawnee Bill's Far East Combined Shows (the Two Bill Show) wintered in Trenton, New Jersey, and by April 15, rehearsals for the combined shows had begun. The 1910 Census was enumerated on April 15 and nine Georgians were listed as homeless but associated with the Wild West Show at Madison Square Garden. Those listed: Mirian Chkonia, age 40, single; William Baramidze, age 32, single; Noe Tsilosani, age 40, married; Alexander Murvanidze, age 38, married; Islam Urushadze, age 44, single; David Dambour, age 26, single; Vaso Tsuladze, age 25, single; Khariton Chkonia, age 30, single; Pavle Covaleshvili, age 29, single. Not on the list but known to be in the show were Nikiphore Ebralidze, Onophre Tsuladze, and Sergo Givardgladze, as recorded in the Buffalo Bill roster. The pay rate for the Georgians was $10.00 per week.

During the weekend of April 23 and 24, the show moved into New York City. They opened Tuesday evening, April 26, in Madison Square Garden, for a three-week stand. Cody declared that this would be his last appearance in New York, and "the old scout" bade farewell to two generations of amusement seekers. Thus began Buffalo Bill's farewell tour, which was to last two years, but actually ended at the close of the 1916 season under circumstances Cody would never have expected.

The Georgians were part of the seventy-eight car, two-train Two Bill show that when erected covered the more than eight acres of ground necessary to handle the arena and twenty-two tents. The only available payroll records from this period document that their first week's pay was held back, as was the custom, and that on the first payday, April 30, the

Georgians received $7.50 per rider. The next week, on May 7, each rider received $10.00, and this was the normal pay per week, which was paid out every two weeks. This averages out to $1.43 per day plus food and board (living onboard the train and in tents). George Utz, a baker with the show, claimed that the show people had a scheme whereby they held back two dollars a week on each employee so that they could have a savings fund at the end of the season.[329]

Buffalo Bill and Pawnee Bill's season closed on November 19, in Little Rock, Arkansas.

CAMPBELL BROTHERS GREAT CONSOLIDATED SHOWS (1910)

The Campbell Brothers might have read the *Billboard* magazine report that Captain Dimitri Tsintsadze and his troupe of riders arrived in New York from Georgia around March 1. *Billboard* also reported that Dimitri would "take a few months' rest before going to the Campbell Brothers' winter quarters, at Fairbury, Nebraska."[330]

The Campbell Brothers pulled out of Fairbury on April 6, with their twenty-six car circus train and two additional advance cars, headed to El Reno, Oklahoma. Rehearsals were held April 7 and 8 with the opening on Saturday, April 9. Dimitri and his troupe, who had ridden with the Campbell Brothers since 1904, were in for a new experience. The Campbell Brothers took their circus out west to California at the season's beginning. Dimitri and his troupe were the nineteenth display, in the two-and-one-half-hour performance.

The Campbell Brothers' showmen, including Dimitri and his Georgian riders, boarded their train in Grand Rapids, Wisconsin, and settled into bed expecting to wake in Sparta, Wisconsin. Everyone received a rude awakening around 3:30 a.m., Tuesday, August 16, when their train was struck amidships by passenger train number fifteen northbound from New Lisbon to Star Lake. The circus train was pulling out of Babcock and crossing the "Y" where the New Lisbon and Tomah lines come together. The Campbells' train was traveling about six MPH and the passenger train was moving about twenty-five MPH. The result of the collision was the wrecking of the passenger engine and about six cars of the circus train. John McKay, a circus employee from Texas, was killed and six more were seriously injured with eighteen other employees suffering cuts and bruises. Dr. Crosby, the Campbells' physician, was given credit for his care of the injured. Fortunately, the train struck the animal cars and not the sleepers. Seven or eight cars were in a heap mixed with dead animals and debris and were partially consumed by fire. Two elephants were so badly injured that they had to be killed; a half dozen camels were killed; a llama, the sacred cow and a number of Shetland ponies and horses were killed. A big box of fancy imported snakes was broken open and some of the reptiles escaped to the woods. The damage to the two trains was estimated at $50,000.[331] Campbell Brothers missed their Sparta, Wisconsin, date but did show in Portage on Wednesday.

Billboard reported: "Captain Dimitri and troupe of Cossack rough riders left the Campbell Brothers circus at Ackerman, Mississippi, October 8."[332] The circus stayed out until December 19 and closed in New Orleans.

JOHN ROBINSON BIG TEN SHOW (1910)

The John Robinson Big Ten Show was the oldest in the country, having given their first performance at Columbia, South Carolina, on May 7, 1824. They added a Wild West exhibition as the final spectacle in 1910. The Wild West exhibition consisted of Indians, cowboys, U.S. cavalry riders, and Georgians. Prince Luka's troupe of riders included: Maro and Veliko Kvitaishvili, Kristine Tsintsadze, Teimuras Chkhartishvili, Khalampre Pataraia, and led by Konstantine Chkhartishvili. They performed circling the hippodrome track in the sixteenth and final spectacle.

■ ■ ■

The John Robinson Big Ten season opened in Circleville, Ohio, with the 10:00 a.m. bugle call to announce the opening parade. The parade circled the town for about thirty minutes and returned to the lot. The first performance started at 2:00 p.m., "One of the *Georgian's* was thrown from his horse during the matinee performance, but was not seriously injured."[333] The John Robinson circus fixer, a legal adjuster who was assigned the duty of smoothing over legal issues with local officials, was kept busy during the season. A little difficulty with a city over the license fee was solved in the simplest way possible. The circus license fee was usually calculated by the number of curb rings under the big top. The fixer would point out they had just one curb ring, while they, in fact, marked out two others in the dirt, and would let it go at that. City officials who would not compromise on a $30 license fee might be told the circus would not unload and bypass the town. This tactic did not always work, since the circus managers could see the influx of people in the town, meaning good ticket sales. The fixer, besides fixing license fees, had to adjudicate accidents such as the one that occurred after a soaking rain in Richmond, Kentucky, on July 28. The softened earth caused the seating support timbers to give way. The seats collapsed, piling over 300 people in a jumbled mass of arms, legs and timbers. Eight damage suits were filed by those most seriously injured and the fixer left a $12,000 bond behind.[334] The season was not complete without an assortment of attachments against the show for non-payment of wages or bills.

The John Robinson Big Ten season closed in Booneville, Mississippi, on November 10.

JONES BROTHERS BUFFALO RANCH WILD WEST SHOW (1910)

The Jones Brothers Buffalo Ranch Wild West was assembled from parts of the Cole Bros.' property that were sold at auction: ticket wagon, calliope, bandwagons, chariots, cages, three tableaux, railroad cars, and baggage stock. The advance car was purchased from the Gentry Bros., and flats and other cars from Pawnee Bill.[335] The show opened in Corry, Pennsylvania, on Saturday, April 23; despite several days of rain and no rehearsals, everyone did very well. The train consisted of four coaches, six flats and three stock cars, and one advance car. The only early incident occurred in Wellsboro, Pennsylvania, when Thomas O'Donnell, a cowboy, was shot in the left leg by wadding from a revolver while repelling an attack on the Santa Fe Coach by Indians.[336]

The Jones Brothers Buffalo Ranch had four additional Georgians join the show and included a female rider "Babilina," (reported as Babinina Zascetely in American documents) as reported in the July 16 issue of *Billboard*.[337] Shortly after Babilina arrived there were several incidents reported in the press. While parading in Coshocton, Ohio, a freight train thundered down the track and caught the six-hitch horse-drawn steam calliope on the track when the gate fell. An attendant leaped to the ground and caught the horses and pulled them back from under the gate. The horses pranced and made for the crowded sidewalk, but the men held them. It was a close call.[338] A seventeen-year-old girl who asserts that she eloped with R. C. Dillon, who was with the show, was left penniless at the Barrett Hotel in Canal Dover, Ohio, not an uncommon occurrence.[339] The show was involved in a train wreck going into Bessemer, Alabama; however, no additional information was reported. J. Augustus Jones was arrested in Pulaski, Tennessee, on a warrant as a fugitive from justice in New Albany, Mississippi. He put up a $1,000 bail for his appearance on November 26.

The Jones Brothers show failed and was sold in parcels by the Peru Trust Company. Thomas F. Wiedemann purchased most of the touring equipment and in 1911 went out as Kit Carson's Buffalo Ranch.

MILLER BROTHERS 101 RANCH REAL WILD WEST (1910)

The Miller Brothers' winter quarters were in East St. Louis, Illinois. Luka Chkhartishvili and Teophane Kavtaradze assembled a troupe of five additional riders before the season opening on Saturday, April 16, in St. Louis. On opening day, Joe Miller stated: "On my arrival at the lot I found a beautiful city of new white tents, all of the latest improved workmanship, and with every accessory entirely new." The arena was rain soaked, with mud reported to be a foot deep, and the temperature was 40 degrees (4 degrees C.). The arena was three-quarters filled, and even though the towners were chilled to the bone by the cold wind, not one of them left the tent until the last number of the nineteen displays was given. The performers were applauded as they went though their acts, a little slow in spots, due to the weather.[340]

The Miller Brothers, after a week in St. Louis, loaded the two trains, of twenty cars each, and rolled east into town after town. Unlike the Buffalo Bill Wild West, which had deleted the daily parade, the Miller Brothers used the bugle call "Boots and Saddles" to announce the parade formation, and the line of march began within a half hour.

Framed photographs from Luka Chkhartishvili's home
Notice bullet holes in top left and bottom right photograph
Top left: Luka performing "Russian drag over the neck."
Top right: Luka sitting next to Pawnee Bill (1906 Rambler).
Bottom left: Luka performing "Suicide drag." Bottom right: Luka performing "Hipporome stand."
Author's Collection
Plate No. 36

In Yonkers, New York, the cook wagon broke down before it could be loaded onto the train, causing a delay in departure. This event threw off the train schedule. The train was sidetracked a couple of times and did not arrive in Hudson until 11:00 a.m. It was a late breakfast for everyone. Another kind of hazard caused the death of a young laborer, Roy Prindle, aged seventeen. He was killed while riding on top of the circus train where he was struck by an overhead bridge.

On Sunday, July 23, the Miller Brothers were in Long Branch, New Jersey. Luka and his men would spend a normal day. Luka was unaware of a tragic scene taking place at his home in Lanchkhuti. Erasti Jorbenadze and three others, who the czar's police considered terrorists, were at Luka's home after escaping from Metekhi prison. An informer notified the police. Seven police squad officers, including its chief, pinned down the terrorists, demanding their surrender. The shootout lasted two hours. Police officer Shapatava was killed. There was one wounded woman in the house as well as one dead horse and one wounded horse. The roof of the house was badly pockmarked with bullet holes. Erasti Jorbenadze was hiding behind a fence when a local merchant, Kolia Reshetnikov, noticed him. Jorbenadze killed him, and the police, in turn, killed Jorbenadze. Bullet holes in the wall and photos can still be seen today.[341]

The Lincoln, Nebraska, newspaper, *State Journal,* reported September 18 on feeding the 101 Ranch showmen and wrote: "The *Georgians* go it strong for a goulash and prefer meat stews to roasts or even poultry. They are great coffee drinkers and will get away with half a dozen cups at a meal. Not one of the *Georgians* with the show used either milk or sugar in coffee."[342]

On October 7, ten days before the Miller Brothers' arrival in Greenville, Mississippi, the local Bijou Theater featured the silent movie "101 Ranch." The theater was packed, the music was reported as "splendid," and a lecture by Mr. Fred Bouvier was described as "well delivered and greatly enjoyed."[343]

The Miller Brothers 101 Ranch closed in West Point, Mississippi, on November 19.

YOUNG BUFFALO WILD WEST AND FRONTIER DAYS 1910

The Young Buffalo Wild West and Frontier Days situated their winter quarters in Peoria, Illinois, while general offices were at 108 East Madison Street, Chicago. The show was incorporated under the laws of Illinois and Vernon C. Seaver was president; other partners were C.F. Gerdes, and Charles F. Rhoads. Seaver hired William A. Lavalle to play the part of Young Buffalo. The train consisted of thirty cars painted yellow and red. A group of Georgian riders, led by Dimitri Tsintsadze it is believed, attached themselves to the Young Buffalo Wild West.

The Georgians, Mexicans, Indians, cowboys, cowgirls, and the entire usual tent show employees assembled in Peoria, Illinois, for the May 7 opening of Young Buffalo Wild West and Frontier Days. Opening day was marred by a deluge of rain. The rain fell continuously during the parade and both performances. The arena was a sea of mud and the entrance was also a bottomless sea of mud. But in spite of this, the seats were half full in the afternoon and two-thirds full in the evening. It was reported that it rained twenty-three out of the next thirty days, and the show was losing money.

The Young Buffalo Wild West owner's son, Vernon C. Seaver Jr., who was billed as Young Buffalo Jr., joined the show on the road during his summer vacation in June. Excerpts from a proposed book by *Vernon Jr.* were published in the circus magazine *The White Tops* in 1967. *Vernon Jr.* reported that one of the troubles the show ran into was Tom Mix. "Tom was chief-of-cowboys and a trouble maker. One day before a matinee he led a bunch of cowboys up to the marquee to demand more money and other things. Father met them before they got there. He was a little fellow, but wasn't afraid of those cowboys. He had had enough trouble with bad weather and he wasn't going to be bothered with a strike. He raised hell with them and ordered them back to the pad room where they belonged." *Vernon Jr.* also reported on the character of Tom Mix; in 1910 he wrote: "Tom used to get his pay Saturday night and get drunk. With no show on Sunday he could sleep it off and be ready for the Monday matinee, but one time he got a little too drunk, shot up the town (with blanks) and was thrown in jail. Father just left him there. Needless to say, Tom was with us only that one short season."[344]

The Young Buffalo Wild West obtained a license from the mayor of Kenosha, Wisconsin, to put on a show on Sunday, June 19, and the afternoon performance was held. However, the district attorney and sheriff objected to Sunday performances and put pressure on management to not hold the evening performance.[345] Another sheriff, in Rockford, Illinois, tabooed the Salome dance given in the side show, on the grounds that the dance was of the spiciest sort, and was conducted on immoral lines. Despite these kinds of setbacks, former President Teddy Roosevelt arrived on the Illinois Central train at Freeport, Illinois, on September 7 and was escorted to the show grounds by the cast of cowboys, Indians and Georgian riders. This event was the season's highlight.

The Young Buffalo season closed earlier than planned, on October 3 in Du Quoin, Illinois, because of dissension in the ranks which made continuing very difficult. The show returned to Peoria, Illinois, to winter over. The Georgian riders returned to Chicago, where most of them now lived during the off season.

1910 EPILOGUE

The Georgian style of riding was spreading into American culture, evidenced by the New York National Guard, Troop D's exhibition of Cossack riding. It was reported: "The Cossack riding was an innovation for the local organization and is in fact practiced by but very few National Guard companies. It was introduced into Syracuse, New York, by John Slack, a former member of the 101 Ranch Wild West show."[346]

The manifest of the *SS Rhein* from Bremen, Germany, lists fourteen artists going to New York under the care of agent Edward Arlington at 83rd Street at corner of 3rd, Brooklyn, New York. The information states they were all Russians from Lanchkhuti, all married, and each paid their own way. It also lists the years they were in the U.S. before. The individual information:

Veliko Kvitaishvili, age 36, can read and write

Maro Kvitaishvili, wife of Veliko, age 22, can read/write

Joseph Imnadze, age 36, cannot read or write

Teimuraz Chkhartishvili *(sic)*, age 37, can read/write

Joseph Swidoradze *(sic)*, age 36, can read/write, 1903/1905, height 5.7, hair grey, eyes brown

Bartlome Baramidze, age 33, can read/write, 1904/1909, height 5.9, hair black, eyes brown

Karaman Imnadze, age 35, cannot read or write, 1900/1903

Konstantine Chkhartishvili, age 40, can read/write, 1905/1908, height 5.7, hair black, eyes brown

Khalampri Pataraia, age 34, can read/write, 1906/1908, height 5.8, hair black, eyes blue

Sergia Jorbenadze, age 35, can read/write, 1905/1908, height 5.6, hair black, eyes brown

Kristine Tsintsadze, female, age 36, can read/write, height 5.0, hair black, eyes brown

Luka Chkhartishvili, age 42, can read/write, 1904/1909, height 5.2, hair black, eyes brown

Ilarion Ebralidze, age 31, can read/write, 1904/1907, height 5.8, hair blond, eyes blue

Ilarion Zinzadi *(sic)*, age 40, cannot read or write, 1901/1904, blind left eye, hair grey

Miller Brothers 101 Ranch
Courtesy, John and Mabel Ringling Museum of Art
Plate No. 37

"Grief proves the strength of the heart; joy needs no courage to bear it."

Shota Rustaveli

1911 PROLOGUE

The Georgian riders who lived in New York, Chicago, or came from Georgia, appeared in seven different tent shows in 1911. Onophre Tsuladze and Nikiphore Ebralidze arrived March 27 onboard the *SS Amerika* sailing from Hamburg on March 19.

BUFFALO BILL'S WILD WEST AND PAWNEE BILL'S GREAT FAR EAST (1911)

Buffalo and Pawnee Bill's Georgian riders—Islam Urushadze, Noe Tsilosani, Khariton Chkonia, Alexander Murvanidze, Vaso and Onophre Tsuladze, Nikiphore Ebralidze, and Sergo Givardgladze —assembled at the winter quarters in Trenton, New Jersey, in early April. A lady "Cossack" rider was a featured performer. She was a sixteen-year-old named Arlene Palmer, not a Georgian, with her companion David Dunn. Activities for the week before leaving the winter quarters included the usual rehearsals and the arrival of 175 Indians. Saturday, April 15, the show left Trenton for Washington, DC. The eighty-seven car, three-section train arrived early in Washington, DC, greeted by rain and a small army of spectators. A baseball park at Fifteenth and H Street was the intended arena, but the ballpark could not accommodate the show and they set up their tents on a lot next to the ballpark. The season started with a new tent, 750 feet long and 385 feet wide, over 200 feet longer than last season's tent. The season's first accident occurred when "Iron Tail," the famous Sioux Indian, who was nearly one-hundred, slipped in the mud and broke his leg during Saturday's setup. He was taken to the hospital car, which was now a part of the exhibition's equipment.[347] New tents and equipment, a hospital car, and opening in Washington seemed like a well planned political strategy to counter the "Educate the Indians" movement. Buffalo and Pawnee Bill even hosted President and Mrs. Taft and a party of fifteen from the White House on Tuesday night. The Two Bills, having greased the political wheels as best they could to ensure their Indians would be returned for another season, headed into rainy Baltimore and then Philadelphia. This season the exhibition was divided into nineteen episodes, and was billed in all the newspapers as Buffalo Bill's farewell tour. The Georgian riders rode in the opening "grand review" followed by the "rough rider show." Their solo act came in episode eighteen, where they presented their daredevil horsemanship.

Cody and Lillie were now transporting trucks along with their other equipment over the railroads. In the early morning, 3:00 a.m., eight miles outside of Lowell, Massachusetts, near Brookside station, the second section consisting of twenty-eight cars was involved in an accident. As the train passed over a switch, a truck on one of the cars was ripped off by a "split" switch. The wrecked car contained elephants, horses, burros and buffalo. The men in charge of the animals had to be rescued by smashing a hole in the overturned car. Two burros were crushed by the elephants.

In Muncie, Indiana, on July 10, the exhibition was marred by a severe storm and followed that night with an accident. Harry Powers, a member of the train crew, was run over and killed.[348] On July 15, in Chicago, the most severe weather disturbance of the season struck just as the horsemen were assembling to enter the arena for their grand entrance. An estimated 5,000 patrons were thrown into a panic when a blinding flash of lightning was followed by a wind flurry that lifted the roof of the tent, tore the canvas walls free from their anchorage and sent seats and poles flying. Enveloped in thousands of yards of wet, flapping canvas, terrified men and women struggled to escape. Fortunately, there were no serious injuries and everyone managed to extricate themselves with the help of the canvas men and employees of the show.[349]

The Two Bills' thirty-week season ranged from Maine to Colorado with a dip to the South and then back homeward to winter quarters in Trenton, New Jersey. The last exhibition of the season was in Richmond, Virginia, on November 1. The Georgian riders and a troupe of Russian singers and dancers were booked passage back to Russia. The Indians returned to the Pine Ridge reservation in South Dakota, while Buffalo Bill and Pawnee Bill headed back out West.

CALIFORNIA FRANK'S ALL STAR WILD WEST (1911)

California Frank's All Star Wild West winter quarters were in Augusta, Georgia, and a contingent of Georgian riders arrived there in late April.

Among these Georgians was a lady rider called Princess Babinina Zascetely. Edward Arlington, manager of the 101 Ranch show, provided financial support to California Frank. The season opened May 4, in Clifton, New Jersey, and operated as an eleven-car outfit. In Dover, New Jersey, a young girl alleged to have had a narrow escape from one of the show's cowboys. The police warned that hard characters followed this show.[350]

California Frank's show carried about 317 personnel, and had two side shows. The Pittston, Pennsylvania, newspaper reported, May 20, that the show's rolling stock and equipment were brand new. The show performed in an uncovered arena with seats arranged under a waterproof canopy, just like Buffalo Bill's show. It was reported they had about 200 head of stock, including an especially fine showing of horses.

Babinia Zascetely, the Lady Georgian rider, took a serious fall on Monday, May 22, in Carbondale, Pennsylvania. *The New York Clipper* reported: "The lady *Georgian* rider had her left collarbone disconnected at the shoulder after leaving the arena in the evening. Her horse tripped while making a leap, and she was thrown against a stake. The bone did not break but was forced through the ligaments one-and-one-half inches. The lady left hospital on Friday and with her husband joined the show at Hancock, New York." The California Frank press agent wrote to *The Billboard* magazine: "She had the misfortune to have her horse fall with her during the evening performance at Carbondale, Pennsylvania. Before the cowboys could release her the horse kicked her several times, breaking both collar bones and right shoulder-blade. At present the Princess is resting easily, but it will be several weeks before the public will have the pleasure of witnessing her daredevil riding act again."[351]

The next incident the Georgian riders experienced was a blow down by a "cyclone" in Bangor, Maine, on July 6. No one was seriously injured and the night show was given in front of the fairground band stand.[352] *Billboard* on July 22 reported: "Princess Zascetely has returned to California Frank's Wild West show after a six-week confinement at the hospital. All hands of the show extended her a hearty welcome."

KIT CARSON'S BUFFALO RANCH WILD WEST (1911)

The Kit Carson Buffalo Ranch Wild West was owned by Thomas F.

Wiedemann. Wiedemann purchased J. Augustus Jones' touring equipment in November of 1910, after the Jones Bros. Buffalo Ranch failed. Apparently, the Georgian riders contracted with Tom Wiedemann for the 1911 season.

■ ■ ■

The Kit Carson Buffalo Ranch Wild West wintered in Harrisburg, Illinois, and opened in early April as a twelve-car show. The program was a combined Wild West and circus under a big top with the Georgians performing around the hippodrome track. The outfit started with a couple tragedies. In Dixon, Missouri, on April 29, the elephant trainer James Hildebrad, forty-five, while endeavoring to put Monte, the show's smallest elephant, into a car, was killed by the animal. The elephant wrapped its trunk around the trainer's body, raised him in the air, crushed him and threw him to the ground, pierced his breast with its tusks and dragged him thirty feet along the railroad tracks. The elephant was killed by the management.[353] Two weeks later a valuable chimpanzee was killed in a fierce battle with a South American lynx on Wednesday, May 17, in Colorado Springs.[354]

Only a few details for the Kit Carson 1911 season could be located. A bronco rider named Milton David Hinkle wrote an article published in *The Bandwagon*[355] and *Frontier Times*[356] describing his season in the show. This article provides a few details on the show's routing and one story involving the Georgians. Milton wrote about the show's thieves and describes in detail how one of these tricks worked. The trick that Milton describes concluded when the man who had been robbed received help from the Georgians who worked in the show. He wrote: "The show had ten to twelve Georgians working, doing Russian riding in the show, and when the Jew started rattling off in Russian, telling the Georgians all that had happened, they sided in with him. After a lot of Russian conversation, the Jew left the lot and we did not see him anymore that night. However, upon our arrival in the next town, the first person I saw was the Jew and he was with the Georgians. We were ready to leave the lot for parade when I saw the Jew and the Georgians once more, and this time they were talking and I heard 'Unless you give him back his money, eight hundred dollars, we will tell the cops all about what the legal adjusted.' I rode up just in time to hear the leader of the *Georgians* say, 'We refuse to work unless you give him back his money, eight hundred dollars, or we will tell the cops all about what is going on.' The legal adjuster took a piece of paper from his pocket and had the Jew sign his name to it. He then handed the Jew five one-hundred-dollar bills, and the Jew was satisfied. He admitted later that he had lost only four hundred dollars and said the experience was worth it."

The closing date and location for Kit Carson's Buffalo Ranch has not been determined; however it is known they returned to their winter quarters in Harrisburg, Illinois. The show closed with a train inventory of one advance car, three stocks, six flats, and four coaches.

JOHN ROBINSON BIG TEN COMBINATION (1911)

The John Robinson winter quarters were in Terrace Park, Ohio. Luka Chkhartishvili and five other Georgians arrived in Terrace Park to prepare for the 1911 season. Show managers were always on the lookout for preseason publicity, and their press agent released such a story on April 9, a week before opening. Two brothers, Robert and Herbert Simons, were reunited after a separation of eighteen years when, unknown to each other, both men were hired for the season and met in Cincinnati.[357] The season opened in an Armory at Cincinnati, Ohio, on April 18 for a one-week stand. The first jump was to Wilmington, Ohio, where the canvas was first spread for the season. The John Robinson show was a circus, but it carried a complete Wild West show including fifty cowboys, thirty cowgirls, Indians, Georgians, Japanese scouts, Mexican horsemen, Vaqueros, and Arabs. Prince Luka and his six Georgians, in daring and breakneck riding displays, closed each performance. The show traveled in a train consisting of fifty-two cars with around 500 horses and 710 people.

The John Robinson circus was held inside a six center-pole Big Top with three rings, and the Georgian riders had to change their style of riding to conform to the hippodrome track inside the circus tent. John Manigal, a Georgian rider, fell from his horse and was injured on Saturday, May 27, in Canton, Ohio, during the afternoon performance. He fell directly under the horse of another Georgian who was riding close behind him and was badly trampled under the horse's hoofs. The performer, who was said to be the best rider with the circus, was carried from the arena, but on Saturday night was able to resume his part of the act.[358]

On July 4, Luka and his men, who preferred the open arena of the Wild West shows, had the chance to perform in the open during the matinee and night show. In the afternoon just about two o'clock, when perhaps a thousand people had passed into the large tent ready to see the performance, a heavy rain, wind and electrical storm struck the town. In less time than it takes to tell it, the top of the big tent fell in, lightning having struck one of the main center poles and loosened the ropes so that the wind caught the big cover and soon had it down. Fortunately, it came down so slowly that no one was injured. Mr. Robinson ordered the canvas removed and the sidewalls put up and at four o'clock the show was started and carried out in its every act.[359] Wind and heat were big top hazards; however, the big top did protect the performers from rain downpours and the resulting sloppy conditions that occurred in the open Wild West arenas. A tornado in Bellefontaine, Ohio, July 11, resulted in the big top being blown over, the center pole snapped. The canvas was riddled by hail, and several crew members were hurt. The menagerie tent blew over and the cries of the wild beasts added to the excitement. There was water knee deep on the lot after the matinee performance, and no evening performance was attempted.[360]

The John Robinson season closed on November 16 in New Albany, Mississippi. The Georgians returned to New York, Chicago, or home to Georgia. This was the last season that the John Robinson circus was under the ownership and management of the Robinson family.

MILLER BROTHERS & ARLINGTON
101 RANCH WILD WEST (1911)

The Miller Brothers 101 Ranch wintered in Bliss, Oklahoma. The show's twenty-six car train left Bliss on April 5, for Boston. Bartlome Mshvidobadze, whose moniker in the American press was Chief Bothlome, and his fellow Georgian riders Miron Chkonia, Ilarion Ebralidze, Karaman and Joseph Imnadze, and Teophane Kavtaradze assembled in Boston before the season opening on Saturday, April 8. Twenty of the cars with the outdoor arena parts were sent on to Philadelphia, since they would not be needed in Boston for the indoor opening.

The show had twenty-two displays with the Georgians performing in the grand review and trick riding two displays before the end of the program.

The Miller Brothers 101 Ranch toured for thirty-three weeks after opening in Boston and closed in Pomona, California. The coast-to-coast season was reported as financially successful. The show's winter quarters were in Venice, California. The Georgians would have felt very much at home in Venice, since the landscape was very much like the shores of the Black Sea along the Gurian coast. *Billboard* magazine reported that the 101 Ranch would give two shows a week during the winter months, one each Saturday and Sunday.

Serapion Imnadze, ca 1914, Miller Brothers & Arlington 101 Ranch Wild West
Author's Collection

Plate No. 38

PRAIRIE JOE'S WILD WEST AND SKERBECK'S RAILROAD SHOWS (1911)

Prairie Joe's Wild West wintered in Dorchester, Wisconsin, and a troupe of Georgian riders led by Chief Gerom arrived prior to opening day on May 15. Whether or not Gerom and his troupe were Georgian riders has not been determined. The Monday opening day was held in the rain and reported a capacity crowd at both afternoon and evening performances. The 1911 outfit consisted of two railroad coaches and about thirty-five people.

Prairie Joe's Wild West and Skerbeck's Railroad shows advertised: "The principal feature was the troupe of 'Russian Cossacks,' who had appeared with all the largest circuses in America."[361] The other attractions were the great Skerbeck family of acrobats, aerial artists and gymnasts. The Skerbecks gave a free street parade daily, which was led by Professor Kroonschable's Silver Comet Band.

Prairie Joe's was scheduled to tour Wisconsin, Minnesota, North and South Dakota, Eastern Canada, and British Columbia. Skerbeck's showed in Henning, Minnesota, on Saturday, July 8, but had to cut out the afternoon performance owing to its inability to raise the tent in the prevailing strong wind. It was reported the show returned to Dorchester, Wisconsin, early in the season to avoid bankruptcy.

W. H. COULTER'S FAMOUS RAILROAD SHOWS AND INDIAN PETE'S REAL WILD WEST COMBINED (1911)

W. H. Coulter's show in Lancaster, Missouri, had arranged for a troupe of Georgian riders for the 1911 season. Captain G. Dimitri, believed to be Dimitri Tsintsadze, was the manager of two troupes of Georgian riders, and it was reported in the February issue of *Billboard* that his No. two troupe was going with Coulter's Railroad shows. Captain Dimitri awaited the arrival of the Georgian riders in Chicago, Illinois. His troupe that joined the Coulter show would have arrived prior to opening day, which was Saturday, April 29. Wade Coulter had a fourteen-car circus with a reported 100 fine horses, and elephants and camels. Mr. Coulter would make a nice little speech to the tented audience before the concert act, in which he would say his sole ambition was "to become the greatest showman in the world."[362] Mr. Coulter, in an interview, reported that his daily expenses were over $1,200.00.[363]

W. H. Coulter combined his show with Indian Pete's Real Wild West in Grand Rapids, Wisconsin, on July 26. Indian Pete was Pete Culbertson, who said he received the name since he was taken by Indians when a very small boy and brought up by them. Ann Fleming wrote: "He wore his hair long and wore pearl handled pistols. Above the door to his house, he rigged an apparatus that held a pistol aimed at the head of anyone who knocked at his door. He may have been an outlaw. Alex Chasing Hawk remembers that he slept with his holster above his bed. Culbertson was thought to have come from Montana." It was reported that Indian Pete's had 110 personnel, which included nine full-blooded Sioux and twenty cowboys.[364] The combined shows counted around 260 employees. W. H. Coulter's last performance was in St. Joseph, Missouri, on September 9, after which they went into winter quarters at Lancaster, Missouri. There were no known incidents involving Georgian riders in any newspaper reports, and it cannot be assured that Georgian riders performed during the complete W.H. Coulter season.

YOUNG BUFFALO WILD WEST SHOW (1911)

The Young Buffalo Wild West wintered in Peoria, Illinois. The Tsintsadze brothers, Dimitri and Irakli, assembled their riders in Chicago before traveling down to Peoria. Col. Vernon C. Seaver opened the Young Buffalo Wild West season on Friday, April 28, at Lakeview Park, Peoria. Rain on Thursday caused the parade's cancellation; despite the threatening weather Friday, the people of Peoria came out to see the show. The twenty-three car show, with two advance cars, first jumped to Rockville, Indiana. The show advertising reported carrying 200 performers, 400 horses and 700 on the payroll, with five big spectacles listed: "The Siege of the Alamo," "Shooting up the Town," "The Cheyenne Frontier Day Celebration," "Night Attack on the T.B. Ranch," and a "Horse Thief being Lynched." There were four bands including one cowgirl band known as "Salome Jane's Brass Band." The stars were Annie Oakley, Ambrose Means (the man who lassoed a lion), and Capt. A.H. Bogardus. The Georgian riders who were working the Young Buffalo show had years of experience in the day-to-day routine and hazards of tent-show life. The usual thunderstorms, riding accidents, and poker losses were all routine to the Georgians and other show people. The Georgians were reported to all be riding black cavalry horses.

The Young Buffalo Wild West season closed in Hopkinsville, Kentucky, on Wednesday, November 1.

1911 EPILOGUE

The manifest of the *SS Amerika* from Hamburg, Germany, lists two circus riders. The information states they were Russians from Lanchkhuti, and married. The individual information:

Onophre Tsuladze, age 27, can read/write

Nikiphore Ebralidze, age 38, can read/write

Campbell Bros., Georgian riders, ca 1910
Author's Collection
Plate No. 39

CHAPTER FIVE
HOME SWEET HOME: 1912 TO 1916

how people have many superstitions and a couple of them concern the circus band. The band cannot play Franz Von Suppé's *Light Cavalry March*—ever, and the only time you can play *Home Sweet Home* by John H. Payne, composed in 1822, was the very last song during the very last performance of the season. Otherwise it could mean the immediate closing of the show. Our Georgian riders at the end of each season, at the last performance, would hear a rendition of Home sweet Home as the last piece of music. *Home Sweet Home*, however, did not mean the same thing for many of our Georgian riders. Joseph Stalin years hence—in 1930—decreed "anyone who has been to the United States" as an enemy of the state. This decree would have an immense impact on the lives of many of the Georgian riders.

This chapter deals with the effects of World War I, the Russian revolution, and film, and how all conspired to end the era of the Georgian riders.

"Every like gives birth to its like is the saying of the Sages."

Shota Rustaveli

1912 PROLOGUE

Billboard reported on March 2 that Buck Texas and his Western Rangers carried a troupe of Russians. It has not been established if these were Georgian riders or a Cossack-type riding act, which was becoming more popular. These Cossack riding acts were American cowboys who rode in the Cossack style.

The Georgian riders in their second year with the Young Buffalo Wild West became associated with the Colonel Fred Cummins' Far East. Frederick T. Cummins was not a newcomer to the tent show business. Frederick Cummins and his Far East and Indian Congress spent the previous six years touring Europe. The Cummins' famous Indian Congress was featured in the 1898 Trans-Mississippi Exposition, Omaha, Nebraska; the 1899 Greater-American Exposition, Omaha; the 1901 Pan-American exhibition, Buffalo, New York. Cummins exhibited in 1903 in Madison Square Garden, New York, and at the St. Louis World's Fair in 1904. Cummins was known as an Indian fighter, scout, a friend of Buffalo Bill, and a member of a posse in the hunt for the notorious Jesse James. In 1906, Cummins was associated with Walter L. Main, a well known showman.

In 1912 the Miller Brothers 101 Ranch produced a two-reel moving picture, sometimes called a photoplay that toured the United States. The admission for this film was five to ten cents. The program included a forty-Indian buffalo hunt, the uprising of the savages and the attack on the whites, the massacre of isolated settlers with a spectacular conflagration as the cabins are burned, and the saving of an infant from the maelstrom of death.

BUFFALO BILL'S WILD WEST AND PAWNEE BILL'S GREAT FAR EAST (1912)

Cody, Lillie, hundreds of show people, and eight Georgian riders adjusted their schedules to arrive in Harrisburg, Pennsylvania, before the season opening on Tuesday, April 20. The Two Bills' season started under wet conditions for the first few weeks. There were many reported accidents, and the horses and men were sore and tired by their arrival in New Haven, Connecticut. As the season progressed there were additional periods of rain; for example, six weeks from the middle of July to August there were almost continuous cloudbursts.

The Two Bills' three-train, fifty-car exhibition included an elephant act, lions, and other beasts that were unusual for Cody's Wild West.

It was unusual for the bill posting cars for the Two Bills' and Young Buffalo's Wild West to arrive in Connellsville, Pennsylvania, on the same day, May 9. Not so unusual were the pickpockets who followed the tent shows and who reportedly got away with a good sum in Connellsville. The other side of the human experience could be seen after an afternoon performance when cowgirls hurriedly changed clothes to go into town to watch a movie. The Indians—still in war paint from the performance— would go to the baseball grounds, throwing curves, practicing pitches, hitting, with apparent knowledge and details of the game.

Women knew by the empty store shelves that Buffalo Bill was coming at least a week before the scheduled event, even if they did not see the posters plastered all over the county. A local newspaper reported the housewives' dilemma: "Yesterday it was scarcely possible to obtain eggs or country butter at any store in town; today both are plentiful. It is said the presence of the circus is the solution to the problem. The farmers did not come to town yesterday or the day before, but waited until circus day to bring in their produce and at the same time take advantage of the show."[365] Col. Cody, having observed the workings of "votes for women" in Wyoming, had a few words to tell the folks in Lima, Ohio. He said: "Woman's suffrage is an unqualified success in Wyoming and the votes of the women of the state constitute the more intelligent half of the total vote there. Equal suffrage has also improved the moral tone of the state generally. Before the women obtained the right to vote, some forty years ago, there were all kinds of rowdyism at the polls, but there has been none since. Today, politics are clean in Wyoming."[366]

Buffalo Bill's Georgian riders, after twenty years in the show, continued to receive exceptional audience reaction and press coverage. The Georgians were still described as fierce of eye and mustache; they rode like the devil was on their tail, and a troupe of Russian folk dancers performed at show's end.

The Buffalo Bill season closed October 30, in Columbus, South Carolina.

CAMPBELL BROTHERS GREAT CONSOLIDATED SHOWS (1912)

The Campbell Brothers, for the second year, wintered in the Deep South at Beaumont, Texas, an unusual event in their twenty-three year career. Texas was in the doubtful column regarding the treatment of shows. In February, C. W. Howth filed a suit against Campbell Brothers for $1,105.45. The petition alleged claims of laborers against the defendant. It was a harbinger of things to come.

The Georgians were required to be there before opening day, Saturday, March 30. The first jump, in twenty-two cars, was to Houston, Texas, where the ground was very soft. The Georgians were scheduled to perform in the following displays:

Display No. 1	The grand entrance
Display No. 18	Capt. Jerom and his eight Russian Cossacks in feats of reckless daring and rough riding
Display No. 20	Races, No. 8 Cowboys, Cossacks, and Indians.

The Georgians who rode in the grand entrance did not return for their trick riding due to the soft ground. The Campbell Brothers' motto, "Honorably Conducted, Truthfully Advertised," did not guarantee a profit. The history of the financial difficulties of the Campbells dated back two years; before that for several years the show was prosperous and grew rapidly. On January 22, arrangements were made with creditors holding seventeen notes of the Campbell Brothers to take a chattel mortgage[33] on the circus property. The notes were in the following amounts: one for $10,000, two for $5,000 each, four for $4,000 each, four for $2,000 each, and six for $1,000 each, all notes being payable on demand. John Heasty was made a trustee for these creditors and was given a mortgage on the entire circus property for $50,000. The First National Bank of Fairbury was a creditor to the extent of $6,000, secured by chattel mortgage. Plato Turner was put in charge of the ticket wagon to protect the interests of all

---

[33] Chattel Mortgage - A lien on assets (tangible personal assets) other than real estate backing a loan.

parties concerned, as an agent for all of them, and the Campbell brothers themselves were put on salaries.

The Campbell Brothers went on the road with this arrangement but found business bad nearly all the time. A few days before reaching Fairbury, the outlook was brighter, but Mr. Turner resolved to bring the show to Fairbury and make some different arrangements. Saturday morning, August 10, difficulties arose and the parade was postponed until noon and was finally pulled off about twelve-thirty. The employees were prevailed upon to remain with the show upon the promise that they would get all the receipts taken in Fairbury. There was about $7,900 due the employees when the show reached Fairbury; of this, $2,300 was paid. This scanty pay did not satisfy many of the employees, and they were very restless Sunday and Monday and gave the police plenty of trouble.

On Monday morning, Sheriff Ed. Hughes took possession of the show under writ of replevin issued from the district court upon the petition of Mr. Heasty, holding the chattel mortgage. With the assistance of W. Shoeothem and C. W. Smith, acting as appraisers, the circus was appraised at $19,283.28. This included four elephants, several camels, some lions, tigers and other animals; plus a lot of railroad cars, circus tents, horses, etc. It also included some property held under a lease. On Wednesday, the outfit was removed to the Campbell Brothers' farm south of the river. J. L. Hutchison was selected to look after the property and, in order to give him authority to protect it, he was sworn in as a deputy sheriff.[367] The horses were sold in October to a dealer in St. Joseph, Missouri, and in early 1913 William P. Hall purchased most of the equipment.

KIT CARSON BUFFALO RANCH WILD WEST AND TRAINED ANIMAL EXHIBITION (1912)

Thomas Wiedemann wintered the Kit Carson's Buffalo Ranch Wild West and Trained Animal Exhibition in Harrisburg, Illinois, and the show toured in seventeen cars, one advance car, five stocks, five coaches, and six flats.[368] The show had a nice parade, with plenty of flash for a show of this kind—circus and Wild West, mostly Wild West. The show played the West Coast for twenty-six days.

The advertising early in the season listed "Prince Luigi's Troupe of Royal Imperial Russian Cossacks," and later "Prince Botloine's Troupe of Russian Cossacks." A photograph of the Kit Carson Buffalo Ranch Wild West shows six Georgian riders; however, they are not identified. Four of the Georgians were taking English lessons from a Mrs. Powell, who was also home-schooling her three children. Classes were held in the dressing tent.

The show carried a genuine Curtis Farnum Biplane, furnished by the Chicago Aeroplane Manufacturing Company, and it made flights daily, rain or shine, from the show grounds, circling the city. It was a real money maker, carrying passengers.

It was known as a rough outfit, a real fast mover, and in Vallejo, California, William Holmes, a Negro employee, was shot just above the heart after a row with another employee. Holmes identified his shooter as Hugh McCarthy, who was arrested in St. Helena. Another incident occurred during an afternoon performance in Woodland, California. A cowboy and cowgirl "engaged in a dispute which culminated in a rough and tumble fight during which wicked blows were struck and the cowgirl apparently held her own."

When and where the show closed for the season is unknown, but it did return to Harrisburg, Illinois, for the winter.

MILLER BROTHERS & EDWARD ARLINGTON'S 101 RANCH REAL WILD WEST (1912)

The Miller Brothers & Edward Arlington's 101 Ranch wintered in Venice, California, and opened at Anaheim on Monday, April 1. They traveled in a three-section train touring western states, Canada, and the Midwest. A souvenir route book lists the Georgians who rode in the show: Bartlome Mshvidobadze, Miron Chkonia, Ilarion Ebralidze, Karaman Imnadze, Joseph Imnadze, Teophane Kavtaradze, Solomon Pataraia, and Mikheil Chkhartishvili. *Billboard* reported: "The same old bunches of *Georgians* are with the show this season and they give a very good trick riding act."[369] As became the custom, several of the Georgians took on Americanized names: Teophane was Prince Tephon, Ioseb Imnadze was Joseph Garnia, Karaman Imnadze was Aramon, one called himself Buffalo, and Miron took the name Miron de Chronia. The arena director and chief cowboy was Vernon Tantlinger, who performed a boomerang act. He first rode with Georgian riders in 1902 in the Buckskin Bill show.

The season closed on November 19 at Ponca City, Oklahoma. "Prince Tephon (Teophane Kavtaradze), chief of the Cossacks, who has been with the show for the past five seasons, will return again with more riders next season. He expects to winter in Los Angeles."[370] The Miller Brothers 101 Ranch wintered at a park two miles from Hot Springs, Arkansas. More than fifty cowboys, horses, and others returned to Venice, California, to work in the 101 Bison pictures.

RINGLING BROTHERS WORLD'S GREATEST SHOWS (1912)

The Ringling show opened at the Coliseum, Chicago, on April 6. The show had three advance cars painted in bright red with blazing letters in gold. The show was carried on eighty-five cars in three or four sections. The first advance car carried twenty-seven men consisting of twenty billposters, six lithographers, and a manager. A large steam paste-making machine in the car was used every night by the car porter to make twelve barrels of paste to use the following day. At six sharp every morning, the men were up and by seven at the local livery to start billing the town and local area. This routine continued three weeks in advance of the show's arrival in the town. In Iowa City tacks from the billposters were scattered over the street and Ringling was fined $10.

A troupe of Georgian riders joined Ringling Brothers circus in the middle of May and would continue riding with them through the 1920s. They included sisters, Maro and Barbale Zakareishvili, Veliko Kvitaishvili (who married Maro), Christofore Imnadze (who married Barbale), Victor Kvitaishvili, Baudi and Gabiel (last names unknown).

Ringling Brothers on Parade, ca August 15, 1912
Leading: Veliko Kvitaishvili. Mary and Barbara Zakareishvili.
Other riders: Christofore Imnadze, Victor Kvitaishvili, Baudi and Gabiel.
Courtesy, Jo Anne Steinberg, Cline Studio
Plate No. 40

The Zakareishvili sisters, Mary and Barbara, began riding in their native Surebi (Chokhatauri district) at an early age. In a letter, dated 1964, to academician, Amiran Tsamtsishvili, Barbara gave a brief account of her life. "I'm from a poor family from Sajavakho. My father's name is Spiridon. My mother's name is Phedosi. When I turned eight I moved to Lanchkhuti with my elder sister. I went to the States when I turned sixteen, thanks to my sister and brother-in-law. They had gone three years earlier and invited me to join them. I arrived in America in 1912. They found me a job so that we were all performing at Ringling Brothers circus. There were seven men and two ladies all in all. But then, due to the war, the show was closed down. In 1918 I went to Chicago with Veliko Kvitaishvili and several other Georgians. All of them are dead. Only two men are alive, Kaisar Kvitaishvili, he is 88 and Vaso Tsuladze, he is 80. In 1920, my brother-in-law returned to Georgia. I decided to settle in Chicago, married Christopher Imnadze and had four daughters."

The Ringling big top provided some relief from rain that the Georgians did not enjoy in the open arenas of the Wild West show. The big top did not provide enough protection from a deluge in Allentown, Pennsylvania, May 29. The rain resounded ominously on the taut canvas and the peals of thunder scared timid folk. The water found its way through the tent lacing, puddled around the big top and seeped onto the hippodrome track where Maro and Barbara had to perform. There were no accidents, but the homeward bound throng floundered helplessly through masses of soft clay that clung to the shoes. The rain soaked canvas and wagon wheels clogged with the sticky morass made for a tough departure.

YOUNG BUFFALO WILD WEST AND COL. FRED CUMMINS FAR EAST (1912)

The Young Buffalo Wild West owned by Vernon Seaver, and Colonel Cummins Far East and Indian Congress owned by Frederick T. Cummins were combined for the 1912 season.

Billboard reported: "Captain George Georgian has signed contracts with the Young Buffalo Wild West for the coming season with his troupe of six Royal Cossacks: Vaso Tsuladze, Sam Sergia, Kaisar Kvitaishvili (born in 1876), Platon Murvanidze, Irakli Tsintsadze."[371] Annie Oakley, after an eleven-year absence, returned to the Wild West business in The Young Buffalo Wild West and Col. Cummins Far East. The show opened at Peoria, Illinois, Saturday, April 27. The advance agents contracted for show grounds, feed, water, bread, meat, teams and wagon used by the reported 225 horses and 482 people in the show. A usual complaint was "the circus takes all the money out of town," Sam Feidler, the contracting agent would reply, "Stand around the ticket wagon at three o'clock on the day of the show and watch the money go out the side door in payment of the bills that I have contracted today and you will change your opinion."[372]

The season's first rail accident occurred outside Bay City, Michigan, on May 11 at five o'clock in the morning. The twenty-car circus train was crossing a new switch when the wreck occurred. The engine's forward truck took the track leading to a spur and the hind truck kept on the main track, and there was a parting. The engineer and fireman, realizing that the engine was going to take to the ditch, jumped and escaped injury. The engine and four box cars of horses went over on their side, killing two horses and injuring others.[373] Four days later, a bucking bronco created some excitement of his own. The horse, in a desperate leap, cleared the canvas barrier and landed in the reserved seat section. The panic-stricken crowd of 200 arose as one and made a mad dash for safety. Three women were trampled and fainted, and a man was slightly injured in the crush.

Cumberland, Maryland, May 24 began as any other day with arrival in the city early in the morning and then the parade. The afternoon performance was given without incident, but by the end of the day everything had gone wrong for the Georgian riders. It all began when a Georgian rider, who the newspaper called "George Heeney," took a hard fall. Heeney was riding with one leg thrown over the saddle, the other in the stirrup, and his body straight out from the body of the horse and parallel to the ground. In rounding the turn in the front of the reserve seat stand, the horse slipped and horse and rider went to the ground. Heeney lay still until a cowboy came up, and companions threw him across the back of the cowboy's horse and he was trotted from the arena. So coolly was it done that nearly everyone in the audience thought it was part of the performance.

On the very next lap, Irakli Tsintsadze, whose name for American use was Steve Graceley, attempted the same feat on his horse, which also slipped while rounding the corner. Irakli's head was nearly touching the ground during the maneuver. Hanging as he was, he had no chance to escape and his head was thrown violently against the ground. Irakli's senseless body was thrown across the horse's back and he was cantered from the arena. Heeney's injuries were found to be severe but not serious, but Irakli was at once rushed to the Western Maryland Hospital by automobile. Following the accident, the other Georgians continued their exhibition of the daredevil riding, and there were more spills.[374]

Irakli Tsintsadze, age fifty two, died at Western Maryland Hospital the next afternoon at 2:30. His skull was fractured and he suffered a concussion of the brain and other injuries. He never regained consciousness. The body was taken to Stein's funeral parlor to await disposition. Mr. Stein, when he asked management about the care of the body, was advised, "The management has no further interest in the man."[375] Captain Georgian collected $84 from his friends in the show and buried him, which cost $40, and the balance was sent to his widow and six children.[376] Irakli had worked in Wild West shows for twelve years, the last three with Young Buffalo's show.

Management might not have had interest in the death of one of their own, but when it came to money that was another issue. Walter L. Main, one of the financial backers, on August 6 filed action to attach the show on three notes of $1,000 each, dated January 27, 1906. The sheriff in Ashtabula, Ohio, seized $1,200 from the ticket wagon and then visited the horse tent where he levied upon seventeen draft horses. This was the second time that Main had attached property.[377]

The season closed in Boonville, Missouri, on October 5. The Georgian riders went home to Chicago, where they signed up for Bud Atkinson's show.

BUD ATKINSON'S AMERICAN CIRCUS AND WILD WEST SHOW (1912-1913)

Bud Atkinson grew up in a family of Irish farmers who moved west from Minneapolis, Minnesota, and in 1898 he joined the U.S. Army in San Francisco. Bud spent a few years working as a cowboy, riding bucking horses in shows. He was reported to be an early pioneer of moving pictures in Canada. He played an engagement in Australia and stayed. The thirty-three-year-old native Minnesotan joined with Mr. J. D. Williams, an Australian entrepreneur who owned "The Greater J. D. Williams Amusement Company" in Sydney. Atkinson became the managing director of the "Crystal Palace" in Sydney. Bud arrived in Chicago, where most circus contracts were developed, as an unheralded, unsung, un-press-agented upstart Australian. He spread articles in the *Clipper* and *Billboard* that he was one of Australia's best known amusement promoters. Atkinson and Williams negotiated the establishment of Bud Atkinson Enterprises, Ltd. with a capital of £15,000 in shares of £1 each to carry on the business of theatre and circus. Bud, on October 12, signed an agreement with George Georgian to provide five Georgians for a one-year engagement in Australia: Vaso Tsuladze, Sam Sergia, Kaisar Kvitaishvili, Platon Murvanidze and George Georgian.

When selecting paper from the Donaldson Lithographing Company, Newport, Kentucky, Bud was put in touch with H.S. Rowe, who was suggested as a capable agent. Rowe worked the advance as contracting agent.

The show assembled in San Francisco for the November 10 departure on the *SS Ventura*, via Honolulu, Pago Pago, and Suva Fiji. They arrived in Sydney on December 9, and the first performance was Monday, December 16, at Moore Park, Sydney. A big orange-colored motor car with a huge pair of bullock's horns attached to the front was an advertising vehicle used in Sydney and Melbourne.

The show was the usual Wild West affair with a grand review, pony express riding, stage hold-up, Indians, Georgians, and horse-thief hanging. The circus portion included juggling, acrobatics, and clowns. They included some Australian bushmen, cowboys, and buck jumping.

On the third day, a wind storm kicked-up, canvas billowed, rain poured, and the performance was discontinued. The management generously passed out tickets for another performance. The Christmas show was a sell-out and they turned away business.

1912 EPILOGUE

The *SS Niagara's* manifest provides interesting details of the five Georgians.

George Georgian, age forty, paid for his own passage, cash on hand $500, spent eight years in the U.S.; he lived at 190 South Morgan St. Chicago, was 5ft 6 in tall, had blue eyes and was born in Tbilisi.

Vaso Tsuladze, age twenty eight, passage was paid by George, cash on hand $200, spent five years in the U.S., he lived at 119 South Morgan St. Chicago, was 5 ft 10 in tall, and was born in Lanchkhuti.

Sam Sergia, age twenty-eight, passage was paid by Georgian, cash on hand $20, spent eight years in the U.S., he lived at 119 South Morgan St. Chicago, was 5 ft 7 in tall, was born in Lanchkhuti, and his wife's name was Christina.

Platon Murvanidze, age forty, passage was paid by Georgian, cash on hand $215, spent six years in the U.S., he lived at 119 South Morgan St. Chicago, was 5 ft 9 in tall, was born in Lanchkhuti, and his wife's name was Ephrasina Murvanidze.

Kaisar Kvitaishvili, age thirty, passage was paid by Georgian, cash on hand $25, spent nine years in the U.S., he lived at 119 South Morgan St. Chicago, was 5 ft 6 in tall, was born in Lanchkhuti, and his father's name was Peter Kvitaishvil.

301Miller Brothers Georgian riders
Grant's Tomb, New York City
Author's Collection
Plate No. 41

"Man does more harm to himself than the cruelest of foes to his foe."

Shota Rustaveli

1913 PROLOGUE

Cody was in Denver, Colorado, in late January, 1913. He negotiated a $20,000 loan payable in six months at six percent interest with Frederick Bonfils and Harry Tammen, the owners of the Sells-Floto circus, the *Denver Post*, and *Kansas City Post* newspapers. The Pawnee Bill interests now associated with Colonel Cody's Wild West Show were not included in this agreement. The *Denver Post* reported: "When Colonel W. F. Cody put his name to a contract with the proprietors of the Sells-Floto Circus, the gist is that these two big shows consolidate for the season of 1914 and thereafter."[378]

Bonfils and Tammen bought the *Denver Post* in 1895 and *Kansas City Post* in 1909. In 1899 both were shot several times by an attorney, W.W. Anderson, after the *Denver Post* had accused him of taking a client's savings as a retainer. Anderson was tried three times but never convicted while Tammen and Bonfils were convicted for jury tampering. In 1900 another lawyer horsewhipped both Bonfils and Tammen for their yellow journalism. These were the type of characters Cody was dealing with. Cody's financial deal led to the demise of Buffalo Bill's Wild West and Congress of Rough Riders.

The *SS George Washington* sailing from Bremen arrived in New York on March 17, 1913. Eight Georgian riders were passengers:

Teimuraz Chkhartishvili, married, age 28;
Solomon Pataraia, married, age 34;
Khalampri Pataraia, married, age 35;
Markoz Lomadze, married, age 30;
Noe Lomadze, married, age 35;
Giorgi Gvarjaladze, single, age 25;
Irakli Tsilosani, married, age 34;
Mose Mshvidobadze, married, age 35.

They told the Customs inspectors they had paid their own fare and the local New York residence listed was in care of Mr. Schiffers, 236 and 4th Street, New York.

Chief Tephon (Teophane Kavtaradze) used the *New York Clipper* Post Office for his mail from 1913 to 1916.

Upon arrival March 18, 1913, Giorgi Gvarjaladze wrote home:

"My unforgettable mother... I was tired out during the fifteen days of being in the Ocean. Thanks God we went to New York City safely. Truly amazing city, you will never see anything better in your life....

"My dearest Mishiko, I am asking the Almighty to have a chance to see you again. You are my soul my dearest boy. Pelo (his wife) I am asking you to be wise and to take care of my child.... I was stupid to leave my dear boy, but now it is too late to talk about it....We rest for ten days and then we will start to work. The guys were very much happy when I joined them. Islan did his best to help me.... Mamanti (his brother) take care of fire wood, do not lose or sell the trees. Do not sell Lomai (an ox), do your best to buy another two cows.... P.S. Dear mother please do your best to change a piece of roof of our house...."

P.S. Dear mother please do your best to change a piece of roof of our house. Tell Shaliko if he has got some Lanchkhuti wine left, ask him to drink one glass of it per month instead of me.

ARLINGTON & BECKMANN'S OKLAHOMA RANCH WILD WEST (1913)

Edward Arlington and Fred J. Beckmann, who both worked together in various shows for many years, joined forces to stage the Oklahoma Ranch Wild West Show. Their winter quarters were in Clifton, New Jersey. On April 5, in the *New York Clipper,* they called for clowns, Mexican ropers, musicians, candy butchers, canvas men, drivers, cook house workers, trainmen and others. Rehearsals were to start on Monday, April 21. The show carried two advance cars, four stock, seven flats, four passenger coaches, and a privilege car.

Fred Beckmann's first job was as an errand boy in a theater, and at age nineteen he left his Iowa home to join the W. W. Cole circus in 1883. He later worked the advance for Barnum and Bailey, moved to the Adam Forepaugh circus and went with it to England in 1887. When Bailey assumed interest in the Buffalo Bill show, Beckmann joined that show with McCaddon as an advance agent and filled other positions. By 1913 he was a well-rounded tent show operator and theater manager during the winter season.

Luka Chkhartishvili and five companions were the "Wild-riding Cossacks" in Arlington & Beckmann's Oklahoma Ranch Wild West. The show opened on April 23, in Passaic, New Jersey. The story line that the Cossacks were the czar's finest fighters continued in the show's advertising "Prince Lucca, whose cleverness as a horseman is in keeping with his reputation as one of the most intrepid of the czar's Cossacks fighters…"

Arlington & Beckmann continued the tradition of the circus parade, and since several competitors had discontinued parading, they pitched their parade in the local press. The show toured upper New York and Canada in May. By May 21, they were back in Fort Plain, New York, and that evening, on their way to Weedsport, the first reported rail accident occurred. This delayed their arrival and postponed the parade, which had been heavily advertised. There was also heavy rain in Weedsport and the attendance suffered. Heading west through Indiana, Illinois, Wisconsin, and Minnesota, they went back into Canada for six weeks. The two-trains of double-length circus cars arrived late in Winnipeg, Canada, due to the extensive Customs and Immigration examination of the hundreds of men and animals at the Emerson, Manitoba, crossing. The horse doctor declared: "…these horses were the finest specimen which any circus had ever brought into Canada." At Winnipeg, thousands were clamoring for admittance at the evening performance, and management decided to give two evening performances, an unusual event. In Canora, Saskatchewan, the stage coach overturned in the arena, but no one was hurt.

On August 18, in Oakland, California, the *Tribune* reported Luka had a dozen Georgians. Several of the Georgian riders from the defunct Buffalo Bill Wild West may have joined Luka.

The Wednesday, August 27, arrival in Reno was delayed by a washout along the Southern Pacific line and the show lost the afternoon performance. The evening show lacked some of the customary thrills because of the heavy rainstorms.

The September 13 issue of the *New York Clipper* displayed a half-page ad to sell a quarter or half interest in Arlington & Beckmann's Oklahoma Ranch. The reason for the equity sale was stated as: "My *(Arlington)* reason for selling due to recent developments which require my undivided attention to big show and foreign contracts." Edward was the manager of the 101 Ranch and was working to arrange for the Arlington-Chandler Wild West show that was sailing for South America November 1. Gordon Lillie that next week visited the show at their stop in Pawnee, Oklahoma. The day before, in Stillwater, just as everyone was sitting down to supper, a heavy gust of wind blew down the dining tent. No one was hurt, but supper was served in the open.

The last known performance was on October 18 in Texarkana, Texas. The show was quartered at Lake View, New Jersey, and just what was to become of the show was problematical. The November 29 issue of the *New York Clipper* ran the following announcement: *"To Whom This May Concern: Notice is hereby given that the co-partnership heretofore existing between Fred Beckman and the Undersigned, doing business under the name of Oklahoma Ranch Wild West, was dissolved by mutual consent on October 29, 1913. Signed Edward Arlington."*

Luka and his troupe of riders sailed to South America with Edward Arlington under the name of the Arlington-Chandler Wild West.

BUD ATKINSON'S AMERICAN CIRCUS AND WILD WEST SHOW (1912-1913)

(Continuation in Australia from 1912) New Year's Day, 1913, began with an explosion. T. W. Beckman, twenty-one, suffered considerable burning about the face after powder he was working with exploded. On January 15, a wedding took place during the afternoon performance. The bride was a local Australian, Rose Jean Isabella Durack, and the bridegroom, Harry Murphy, had been a gunner in the United States Navy. The couple met during the American Fleet visit to Sydney. The bridegroom returned with the show, and their wedding was celebrated in true western fashion with gunpowder and smoke instead of confetti. The performances in Sydney concluded on Saturday, January 18. Sunday, a crew was shifting the several thousand chairs out, and during a lull in the job a stranger standing by cried out in a loud voice, "Oh, I don't want these chairs. You kids can have them." There was a wild rush, and in a very few minutes 570 seats disappeared. Youngsters in scores raced across the road to their homes, carrying as many folded chairs as their strength would allow. Then Mr. S. Walder, owner of the chairs, appeared on the scene and received quite a shock when he saw his supply was so depleted. The matter was put into the hands of the police, and on the following Tuesday morning 190 of the stolen seats were returned.[379] George Wirth, the Australian circus mogul, kept a weather eye on Bud Atkinson's circus and said they came from the land of Bluff and Blowhards.

The first jump was to Parramatta and then west to Penrith and Cootamundra. On February 18, in Cootamundra, at 6:00 p.m. a dust-storm preceded a thunderstorm, which turned into a gale with hailstones. Atkinson's circus felt the full force, and extensive damage was done to the tents, but the 150 men repaired the damage and the evening performance started on time. Railroads were another problem, since the rail gauges were different between some jumps. This meant transferring the show to other cars in the middle of a long jump.

The four weeks the show was in Melbourne were four weeks of hell. It was deluged with rain. The black mud in the arena was two feet deep, and the cowboys and Georgians floundered about on disgusted steeds. By March 27, the show was "washed out" and disbanded.

Betty Parker told her story: "It is such a pity; there was so much bad luck.... We all like the country.... It was the weather that spoilt the show.... I want to forget about Melbourne. It was not only weather, and the hardship, but the people used to come in and steal everything we had. It was really bad. The place is full of thieves. They carried away our things in broad daylight, sometimes during the show and other times while people were looking at them. They robbed Hoot Gibson of his saddle and bridle and blanket, took them right away. They were worth eighty dollars. My husband lost a beautiful silver-mounted bridle worth fifty dollars. One mean thief broke open my trunk and stole my little purse with my two diamond rings. That hurt.... Hurt bad, because I was saving those as a last resource to get back home. Even the *Georgians* were despoiled—one lost his great tower of a hat. Goodness knows what anyone wanted that for, a curiosity, maybe. Everybody got robbed, but it got to the limit when one guy, not satisfied with getting Hoot Gibson's saddle and blanket, came back next day and stole his boots. Tex McLeod lost a beautiful fancy hair bridle. They caught a couple of vagabonds on the last day of the show. They had pulled an iron bar out of the ground and smashed open the armory chests with it. One of our boys saw them, held them up with his gun, and took from them everything they had stolen. Then they let them go."[380]

Bud Atkinson appeared in district court to say the company was formed in Sydney with a capital of 8,300 £1 shares. He held half of the shares, and had gone to America to bring the members of the show to Sydney. He was managing director of the company, but he did not hold himself personally responsible for the debts it incurred. Meanwhile, the seven Indians were lodged and cared for by the consul in Melbourne, and then repatriated at the expense of the United States Government.

H.S. Howe, the advance agent, did not know telegrams were not reaching him; they were being mailed. One morning, picking up a newspaper, he read of the closing of the Atkinson show with all the people stranded. He attempted to get back to Melbourne, but his transportation credentials were cancelled.

Captain George Georgian and his four comrades had to fend for themselves. They received the first nine weeks' pay, but five-and-a-half weeks' wages were owed. "The leader of the *Georgian* rough riders… obtained final judgment in practice court for wages due to him and his party. The case was brought by George Georgian against the Bud Atkinson Enterprises, Ltd., of Sydney and Bud Atkinson for £120 6s 3d. Defendants did not appear, and an order for final judgment made by Mr. Justice a'Beckett."[381]

The leading theatre managers in Sydney arranged a comprehensive entertainment to aid the stranded Bud Atkinson performers. They raised over $1,800 that paid for the transportation of most members back to America. Those that were left behind worked their passage home as galley boys and dishwashers.

The Georgian riders returned on the *SS Niagara* sailing from Sydney on May 5, and arriving in Vancouver, Canada, on May 28. The group joined the Irwin Bros. Cheyenne Frontier Show on June 14.

BUFFALO BILL'S WILD WEST AND PAWNEE BILL'S GREAT FAR EAST (1913)

On March 27, the performers left their winter quarters in Trenton, New Jersey, crossed the river and started rehearsals in the Philadelphia Convention Hall. To exhibit inside the Hall they removed fourteen rows of seating to expand the stage area to conduct the Wild West in this unique setting. The season opened on April 3. The opening numbers were the Pawnee Bill Far East acts. Then Buffalo Bill appeared, driving two beautiful cream-colored horses attached to a carriage. He addressed the opening-night audience in a strong clear voice, declaring: "...when I retired, two years ago, I meant what I said: that I was out of the saddle as a performer for all time. I have fulfilled a purpose in bringing to the Eastern mind a true appreciation of the West, making the Indian a man respected instead of a man despised...." At the close of Cody's remarks he introduced Major Gordon Lillie (Pawnee Bill) as his successor.

The Georgians immediately followed Cody and Lillie's remarks. Khariton Chkonia, Barbara Imnadze, Giorgi Gvarjaladze, and Tsilosani were four of the known six Georgian riders. Khariton started riding in Buffalo Bill's show in 1902, and by 1913 he was managing his own "Caucasian Troupe and Russian Cossack Rough Riders" with a mailing address of 944 West Madison Street, Chicago. *Billboard* reports on April 12 that the "...second episode brings in the Wild riding *Georgians*, the two girls, both exceedingly pretty, and one, I believe, an American, carry off the honor of this number." The routine Wild West show closed with a new feature, the "Auto-Polo."

The 101 Ranch show felt it was strong enough to operate in opposition to Buffalo Bill's show and travelled in advance of them along the East Coast. Cody and Lillie's show was transported in forty-seven cars: ten coaches, a box car, fifteen stock cars, and twenty-one platform cars.

Sundays continued to be a day of rest and maintenance of equipment. A reporter noted in Norfolk, Virginia: *"Georgian* busied themselves with looking after their horses and equipment, their favorite pastime."[382] A storm struck Buffalo Bill's show with fatal and disastrous results in Henderson, North Carolina. The day started with rain breaking up the parade and then wind, lightning, and thunder blew down the tents during the afternoon show. Flying poles and ropes inflicted injuries, including broken ankles, arms, a crushed jaw, and one death. It rained in torrents, yet a few customers remained to see the show. The evening performance was also broken up. The next day in Raleigh the rain continued to come down in buckets, but the exhibition was given and the newspaper reported: "One of the startling feats of the performance was the horseback riding and high hurdling of the *Georgians* as they traversed the length of the arena at breakneck speed." Then in Durham the show was called a disappointment…"the whole thing was cut pretty short."

Newspapers reported Cody was stricken by illness after the afternoon performance in Knoxville, Tennessee. He was taken to the home of Charles O. Ward, a cousin. Physicians who examined him said that his condition was grave. The reports were that he was suffering from nerve exhaustion, serious stomach trouble, and advanced age. Colonel Cody, when arriving in Atlanta two days later, said: "The fact is I never felt better in my life. It was the work of some over conscientious newspaper men who imagined I was sick, that was all."[383]

Whether or not Cody was ill, a few days later he and Lillie were served attachment papers in Birmingham, Alabama. The allegations were that a little child, Lula Dunn, was burned by coffee when the Wild West show was in Birmingham in 1911, and that she subsequently died. The results are unknown.

On Monday, July 21, 1913, around 1:00 a.m. the first of three trains pulled into Denver, Colorado, from Julesburg. The usual crowd of around 200 was waiting. As the train rumbled to a stop, the voice of Pete Herz bellowed out to his sleeping men "get up and get out of there, and let's get this unloaded," in a not too gentle tone of voice. The kids under foot gazed wide-eyed and expectant. The unloading of the cook outfit, tents, and wagons proceeded as it had for many years. The second train carried Buffalo and Pawnee Bill, who, upon arrival, stuck their heads out a small window and said "Howdy" to the kids. Buffalo Bill showed the arm of his pajamas that looked like bright red in the pale light. Then the third train with the elephants, mules, horses, tigers, and other wild animals of the Far East came steaming in on another track. This sequence of events that for years had played out around the world would not go on.

Meanwhile, in Tacoma, Washington, Major Burke was with advertising car No. 1. The car was seventy feet long and divided into compartments to accommodate a business office, buffet, staterooms, Pullman berths, lockers, closets, and drawers for various kinds of advertising matter. There was a steam boiler for making paste, and a baggage room for cans, brushes, tools of the trade, and sufficient lithographs to advertise for a week. Major Burke was expecting the show to be in Tacoma on August 12. The show must go on, but it did not.

The people of Denver may not have noticed during the Monday evening performance that over twenty deputy sheriffs were stationed about the grounds watching the show's possessions. Frank Tammen, the brother of Harry Tammen, was in the ticket wagon while the sheriff deputies collected the proceeds from the evening performance and turned it over to Alexander Nisbet, the commissioner of safety, as ordered by Judge Perry. The judge had issued an attachment, Monday afternoon, asked for by the United States Lithographing and Printing Company of Chicago, which claimed the show owed the company $66,000.00 for printing done this season. The lithograph company had deposited a bond of $132,000.00 with the court. Cody and Lillie held conferences Monday night and Tuesday with Adolph Marks of Chicago, representative of the lithographing company, and John T. Bottom, attorney for Harry Tammen and Fred Bonfils. Tammen and Bonfils wanted payment of the $20,000.00 Cody had borrowed in January.

The Tuesday shows were held, but again the funds were collected by the sheriff's office. The lithograph company was willing to settle for $25,000.00, and let the show continue, but Cody would not accept the proposal. Lillie was willing to pay his half, but Tammen and Bonfils wanted their $20,000 from Cody. The show's adjuster, C. M. Thompson, said: "There is a good long story behind all this. Bonfils and Tammen want this show." The conferences failed and late Tuesday night, the deputy sheriffs, under the orders of Marks, took formal possession of the tents, animals, and the rest of the paraphernalia. Cody said: "It may be four or five days, maybe longer, before we can settle the matter. We will hold the employees and all but the Indians here until everything is cleared up."[384]

By Wednesday night, Lillie is quoted as saying: "I haven't the slightest idea when we will get on the road again, if we ever do. The matter is very complicated, but there is a story back of it all I am going to tell. Tammen and Bonfils and Buffalo Bill cannot make another attack on me like they made yesterday without me starting something. I am doing my best to settle matters. I mean to stick with my employees, and am doing all I can do to see they do not suffer. But my responsibility is only that of half-owner of the show."[385]

The 114 Indians were sent back to their reservation at Pine Ridge, South Dakota, on Wednesday. The employees were fed at the lot, Union Park, or at restaurants Wednesday. The show freaks were looking to obtain a license to put on their own show in Denver. The laborers sought relief from the mayor's office, but the mayor said he was sorry, he could not help. The concession owners left town to work state fairs or join circuses. The performers started looking for new gigs with other shows.

Gordon Lillie left Denver on Saturday, reportedly to go home to Pawnee, Oklahoma, but on Monday he was in New Jersey to file action in federal court for involuntary bankruptcy. Back in Denver the deputy labor commissioner filed legal action to secure the salaries due the employees, over 500 in number. Citizens who were owed for services filed petitions of involuntary bankruptcy in United States District Court in Denver. The company that leased the railroad cars, wagons, and forty-six horses filed suit in district court to recover their equipment held by Commissioner of Safety Alexander Nisbet.

Khariton Chkonia and Barbara Imnadze and the other four riders were staying in the Windsor Hotel. They first waited to see if the show would get back on the road. When it became clear it would not, Khariton scrambled, along with other cast members looking for work, to fill out the season. By July 31 the show was abandoned and up for sale.

IRWIN BROS. CHEYENNE FRONTIER DAYS WILD WEST SHOW (1913)

The Y-6 Ranch about thirty-six miles outside of Cheyenne, Wyoming, was the home of the Irwin Brothers: Charles B., Floyd, and Frank. They were called cattle kings and with another cattleman, John Cuthbert

Coble, were the owners of the Irwin Bros. show. Charles was the ranch manager and also livestock commissioner for the Union Pacific railroad. Floyd rode in the show, and Frank was the arena director and trouble shooter. Several of their children worked in the show: Pauline, Gladys, and Frances Irwin.

The Interior Department authorized Sioux Indians to perform the "Ghost Dance," for the first time since 1890, at the opening of the Irwin Brothers in Cheyenne, Wyoming, on June 14. George Georgian and his troupe from the Bud Atkinson Australian show arrived in Cheyenne on the same day. The opening was witnessed by Theodore Roosevelt and William Howard Taft. The press agents released these statements. Roosevelt said: "The best show I ever saw," and Taft said: "I have been well repaid for my long journey."

The Frontier Days show was more like twentieth century rodeos where contests between riders were rewarded with prize money. The *Sioux City Daily* on July 3 reported: "Two *Georgians*... engaged in the riding contest, performed original daring feats, their style of riding being very different from that employed by the cowboys."

The show traveled in twenty cars across Nebraska, Iowa, and Minnesota. They spent from July 7 to August 21 in Canada. The police in Manitoba, Canada, closed the annex due to the nature of a lewd Oriental dance. Along the way, ten moving picture concerns applied for the rights to record the Frontier Days on films.

Billboard reports on September 13 that "two of the lady *Georgians* from the Buffalo Bill Wild West joined the Irwin Bros. Wild West."

The season closed on October 4, after ten days in Omaha, Nebraska.

KIT CARSON BUFFALO RANCH WILD WEST (1913)

Billboard reported that "Prince Jimmie has eight *Georgian* riders with him;" however, there are only six in a photograph. The show opened on April 1 in Harrisburg, Illinois. The show had a reputation of being a rough and tumble outfit where gambling, grafting, and skins games of various kinds were openly played.

"*Georgians* are a fine lot of horsemen...." was a typical newspaper account of the Georgian riders. Another newspaper reported that Prince

Jimi, the head of all the *Georgians* in this country, had command of all *Georgians* with shows all over the United States.

The advertising touted a $25,000 herd of buffalo, hundreds of Indians, and a menagerie of trained wild animals. What the show really carried was two scrawny buffalo, a dozen Indians, and the menagerie consisted of two monkeys, an ape, and an educated pig.

On July 18, in Edgerton, Wisconsin, the show ran up against hard luck. They had lost the evening performance the previous day and the show grounds were in a low place. The show was short of helpers and did not get off the parade, but the afternoon performance was well attended. At 7:00 p.m., a big storm drowned out the evening performance. The wet canvas bogged down the wagons, and every horse in the outfit was needed to pull them out. All night long the water-soaked and discouraged men tugged and swore, prying up wagon after wagon as it sank to the axles in the mire. It was not until eight o'clock the next morning when the last wagons were loaded on the train. The local newspaper said: "an outfit made up so largely with rough necks and swindlers deserves little sympathy in their hard luck."[386]

The season ended in Rockmart, Georgia, on November 28; they wintered in Birmingham, Alabama.

MILLER BROTHERS & ARLINGTON 101 RANCH REAL WILD WEST (1913)

Billboard reported on March 3 that "Prince Tephon (Teophane Kavtaradze), Chief of the Russian Cossacks, will return to the 101 Ranch with a troupe of riders shortly." Bartlome Mshvidobadze was known to have joined up with Teophane in Hot Springs, Arkansas, for the opening on April 5. There were four additional Georgians in the troupe of riders, but their names are unknown. The show headed to St. Louis for two weeks and then on to the East Coast.

Teophane, who first came to the United States in 1900, had learned the value of the two entertainment trade magazines, the *New York Clipper* and *Billboard*. He used them to advertise, give notice for mail delivery, and keep in touch with Georgians and friends. During the season, Joe Lewis, an arena clown and the 101 Ranch correspondent to the *New York*

Clipper, wrote about Teophane (Tephon) several times. He wrote that Teophane said: "Russian tobacco is harmless," Lewis' response: "He is dreaming, dreaming Mecca." Teophane also said, "*New York Clipper* good paper." Tephon's friendly call is "Hey Ho I am Prince Tepho!" Lewis wrote a more cryptic note in the Clipper: "Chief Tephon, the *Georgian*, is the idol of the 101 Ranch dressing room."

The Georgians had seen it all: the runaway boys and girls, the equipment catching fire, the storms and blow downs, the accidents where members fell off wagons, the train derailments, and accidents in the arena. It was the same this year on the 101 Ranch show.

Billboard reported July 5 that "Prince Tephon (Kavtaradze) had several Russian visitors while the show was in Boston, and his *Georgians* do excellent stunts in their daredevil riding."

After the collapse of Buffalo Bill's show, one of the Georgian's from Buffalo Bill joined the 101 Ranch in late August. The season closed in Houston, Texas, on October 28.

RINGLING BROTHERS CIRCUS (1913)

On March 27, the Ringling circus started moving from their winter quarters in Baraboo, Wisconsin, to Chicago for their season opener on April 5. Veliko and Victor Kvitaishvili, along with several other Georgians and one woman rider, were in Chicago for rehearsals. The Georgian riders were the sixth event in the last display called the Grand Wild West hippodrome races. Performing in a circus was under a big top tent, unlike the arena of a Wild West show. The Ringling big top was 499 feet long by 232 feet wide, and sat 12,000 people.

Leaving Chicago, the Ringling circus moved to the East Coast using eighty-six cars and sometimes divided into four trains. Upon arrival in the East, it ran into opposition from the 101 Ranch and Arlington-Beckmann's Wild West; both were managed by Edward Arlington.

Every Wild West show or circus had the same type of incidents: a brakeman switching the train in the local yard is badly squeezed between two cars; a local sues Ringling for damage to his automobile when a pole extending out of the rear of a circus truck spears his car; area flooding destroys the route and the advance men have to scramble to re-route the show; crew members come down with smallpox; veteran circus man falls under the wheels of a wagon and is killed; Alphonse Reimuke, an aerialist, plunges to his death in Tacoma, Washington, when the apparatus collapses.

Veliko Kvitaishvili's female rider (Maro Zakareishvili) took a spill in San Francisco on August 30. As part of the concert act, the Georgians were riding around the hippodrome when she "lost her balance and rode half the length of the tent hanging by a toe-nail." The band quit playing, and stage hands ran to her rescue. The lady was unhurt but the horse "took a cut across the midsection from the irate rider's whip."[387]

The rainy season ended in Okmulgee, Oklahoma, on November 1, and then the four-section train returned to winter quarters in Baraboo.

TOMPKINS REAL WILD WEST AND FRONTIER EXHIBITION AND COOPER-WHITBY CIRCUS (1913)

Charles H. Tompkins and Al F. Wheeler organized a new show in January. Six carloads of paraphernalia were shipped from Wheeler's winter quarters at Oxford, Pennsylvania, to New Hope. The Tompkins' Wild West and Cooper-Whitby Circus was an overland road wagon show. This would be the first show Georgians worked on that was not a railroad show. The season opened May 14 in Ridgewood, New Jersey. As a wagon show, it made short jumps from village to village, which might include a feeding stop. They advertised a real old-fashioned Wild West show including a band of genuine Sioux Indians, Georgians, and genuine cowboys from the Ben X Ranch, Oklahoma. There were a number of circus acts, and it was reported as a clean show with no gambling.

A principal feature of the show was Archil Tsereteli's Georgians with lady Georgian rider Princess Babilina Tsereteli.

The show traveled through Pennsylvania, New York, New Jersey, and Maryland. The last known show date was October 25.

YOUNG BUFFALO WILD WEST, VERNON C. SEAVERS HIPPODROME & COL. FRED CUMMINS FAR EAST (1913)

The season opened in Peoria, Illinois, on Thursday, April 24. The advertising posters prominently displayed ten Georgians astride their horses, raised sabers, and the leader standing in his saddle, with a subtitle

"Captain Georgian's Russian Cossacks." *Billboard* reported: "Sergia Georgian's troupe of *Georgians* has signed for the third season with Young Buffalo Wild West." The show had to compete with a local baseball game, which hampered the afternoon sales. The weather was fickle and the Illinois River was in a flood stage. The part of Young Buffalo was played by the imposing figure, Joe Smith.

The exhibition contained between twenty and thirty cars, running in two trains. The performance was conducted in an arena like other Wild West Shows. The star attraction was Annie Oakley. Even though Annie Oakley received star billing the Georgian riders received the usual great press reports.

During every season, on every show, accidents and incidents happened. Young Buffalo's Wild West was no exception. An employee whose job was to light the hundreds of gasoline torches was seriously burned when one of them exploded. An elephant escaped during loading in Mahanoy City, Pennsylvania, and ate four bushels of potatoes before being captured. Another elephant, Muggins, devoured a clothesline of laundered shirts left out to dry. Several employees, including three Indians—John Peabird, George Little Crow, and Harry Eagle Bear—discovered in Waynesboro, Pennsylvania, that it cost $2.79 to swim in a creek that was owned by the trolley company. On October 3 it was discovered that the Texas steers used in the show had Texas fever[34] and were quarantined. The season closed on Saturday, October 4.

1913 EPILOGUE

The archives at the Lanchkhuti museum contain five letters written by Giorgi Gvarjaladze.

"Undated: My unforgettable dear mother…You are writing that you have sold the buffalo. To tell the truth I was upset first, but then… Dear mother do not buy bad buffalo. You will receive money soon. Islan did not allow me to send a little amount of money. He said that when you are sending money it had to be worth it. What are you going to do with the maize field? Giorgi Gvarjaladze is writing to you."

---

[34] Texas fever was also called stampede fever, a cattle contagion, also called Babesia. Babesia is a protozoan parasite of the blood that causes a hemolytic disease known as Babesiosis. There are over 100 species of Babesia identified; however, only a handful have been documented as pathogenic in humans.

"November 14, 1913: My dearest mother I send you my greetings.... This year I have had a loss but what can we do...this time I was making enough money just for my everyday expenses.... It is very difficult to work here. It is especially difficult to work in winter time in America. We are able to work at least two days a week to make a living.... I am very upset that this year was so hard for me, but still I am hopeful... I would be able to make money in the future."

"December 7, 1913: Dearest mother... Mother I was planning to send you some money but unfortunately I cannot do this at this moment, it is becoming more and more difficult to get a job.... I was making very little and I could not send money to you. If not for little Sergi's help I would not be able to survive.... Panteleimon Tsintsadze found a good show and offered me a position.... I would have 12 or even 13 dollars per week. He has got a business for 15 dollars per week... but he has to keep some amount of money for his own benefit from that amount. Originally he wanted to hire somebody from Russia, but as there are so many of us unemployed he has changed his mind.... He offered to Laphier Mshvidobadze positions for three men... and he offered four positions to Kaisar Chkonia. So Laphier Mshvidobadze, Iorama Mshvidobadze, Tsilosani, and me are all going to this place. Kaisar Chkonia, Kvitaishvili, Urushadze, and Nithipo are going to take the four men position.... The show has been performing for seven months this year... working till November... and will be opened from the first of April.... Panteleimon is 500 miles away from us now.... He stays where his show is now... Your son Giorgi is writing to you."

"Undated: Pelo (his wife) I am writing to you to ask you to let me know what is going on in Panteleimon's family.... He said there were some misfortunes in his family and he thinks that he doesn't know everything, he prefers to know all the truth.... Write everything on the separate sheet of paper so that I could pass this letter to him.... Please put in the envelope a small letter written by Mishiko's (his son) hand. Don't forget it, ask him to write at least something."

"December 7: My dearest Pelo I think about you every second and every minute.... I also pray that nobody ever had any reason to sneer at me for you. Do not leave the house in an inappropriate time otherwise you know the people might say something, and if I would hear something wrong about you, you know... For now I receive only good news about you and remember that even if I would not receive letters from home I have other sources of information.

..... Pelo, when somebody will be taking Veliko Kvitashvili's clothes, please send with them my underwear and red pants embroidered with golden thread, also two pairs of shoes.... I trust you stay devoted and honest and take care of your Mishiko...."

"Undated: My dearest mother... the business I put so much hope on, unfortunately failed. The Master (owner) said no and now I have no idea how it will go.... There are many of us unemployed... seventeen of us without having a position and I am doing my best to find some ways of coming back home.... The time is getting hard for us in this damned country.... Panteleimon did his best to do something.... Nitipo and Irakli Tsilosani wants to come back home, but we did not have yet any money for coming back.... I find it difficult to write to Pelo, what should I write to her?"

Markoz Lomadze was born in the village of Chibaki in 1879. He had five children and worked in the timber industry after returning from America. The family history reports once he came back from America without enough money to get from Batumi to Lanchkhuti. He died in 1926 due to Pneumonia.

Teimuraz Chkhartishvili after returning worked as a farmer and during the Second World War was a postman. He had three children: Shota, Aryelina and Tamari. He died in 1958.

OTHER SHOW BUSINESS

Roy Chandler, a South American manager, and Edward Arlington signed an agreement to send a complete Wild West show to South America. Arlington was to provide all the equipment: blue seats, reserved seats, grand stand chairs and boxes to seat 3,500, flags, canopy to cover all seats, sidewall, tents, scenery, properties, wagons, draft horses for wagons, band wagons, steam calliope, and lithographs. Edward was also to furnish ten Indians, eight cowboys, six cowgirls, twenty horses, four bucking horses, ten-piece cowboy band, two Mexicans, two Georgians, gunpowder used in the performance, horse feed, steers, and arms. On October 18, Prince Luka joined the Arlington-Chandler Wild West show that sailed November 1 for Buenos Aires, Argentina. Prince

Tephon (Kvataradze) had also signed on to sail to South America. The contract was for six months with an option for an additional six months.

The Buffalo Bill and Pawnee Bill show was auctioned off on August 21, and brought $16,000. It was reported that Cody openly wept when his white horse, Isham, was placed on the auction block. A Colonel C. J. Bills of Lincoln, Nebraska, bought the horse, determined to return it to Cody.

On Saturday, August 30, Cody and Harry Tammen spent a few hours in Chicago on their way from Denver to Detroit, where they visited the Sells-Floto circus and conferred with Cody's Canadian mining interests. On Tuesday, Cody strode into the center ring of the Sells-Floto circus and announced he was not finished. They returned to Chicago Wednesday, staying at the La Salle Hotel. Cody was on his way to the Big Horn Basin, where a moving picture would be made in which Cody would personally appear.

"Hazard kills equally be it one or a hundred."

Shota Rustaveli

1914 PROLOGUE

By all appearances, 1914 was going to be the usual routine of working off-season either in vaudeville theaters or overseas. Georgians were in South America, Chicago, New York, and a few were with the Rhoda Royal's indoor circus for the winter. During the 1913 season, Rhoda's circus had worked with Sells-Floto as a Horse High School act.

One rider, Ilarion Imnadze, age 32, arrived in New York on the *SS Amerika* on Sunday, March 14. Laphier and Iorama Mshvidobadze, Giorgi Gvarjaladze, and Irakli Tsilosani were known to be riders in 1914. The year ended with Georgians stranded in America and unable to continue their travels to and from Georgia. August 1914, Germany declared war on Russia and then the whole of European nobility. As Alexis Georgian put it: "The War of the Kings for land grabs has started."

October found the Turks preparing for war with Russia. On November 6, the Turkish fleet bombarded the port of Batumi, where decades of travel had begun for the Georgian riders in America. Turkish troops were fighting near Batumi, and on November 24, there was a general revolt against Russian rule in Tbilisi.

The war was the beginning of the end for Georgian riders in America.

ARLINGTON-CHANDLER WILD WEST (1914)

Ed Arlington had taken a second unit of the 101 Ranch to South America. Luka and the rest of the 101 Ranch arrived in Buenos Aires after a twenty-three-day voyage on the *SS Vasari*. The show settled in for a six-week run in the Japanese Gardens, a beautiful park owned by the city. The makeup of the show was a selection of people from the 101 Ranch and Arlington's Oklahoma Ranch, as well as a few of Buffalo Bill's people.

Performances were given at 5:00 p.m. and 10:00 p.m. in deference to South American culture. A twenty-minute intermission was part of each show. They had a six-week stand in Buenos Aires followed by two weeks in Montevideo. There were no stands less than three days while working their way to Rio de Janeiro. They were in Porto Alegre, Brazil, until

February 15, and at Sao Paulo through March 1.

Edward Arlington, returning to the United States, reported: "Upon arrival in Buenos Aires, the animals were put in quarantine for eight days, and one of the horses developed something that was said to be glanders by the Argentine veterinary surgeon. He ordered that all of the horses should be shot. I pleaded with the officials to segregate the horses on a ranch for six months to see if it was really glanders, which I doubted, but they would not do it. Naturally I had to have more horses, and I bought them in Argentina, paying $110 each... plus the export tax of $30 each. The result has been that they have cost me about $200 each to get them to Trinidad, where the show is now playing. They are among the finest horses in the world of the polo pony type. I shall dispose of them in Trinidad."[388]

In late March, the show left Trinidad. Two Georgian circus performers—Luka, age 50, and Marcus, age 28—arrived on the SS *Vauban* from Trinidad on April 11, at the port of New York. The arrival was not without incident. While off Sandy Hook, passengers were aroused by an explosion in steerage. Fire followed the explosion but was quickly extinguished. The investigation showed that a Syrian rifling the baggage of a fellow passenger had opened a box of cartridges and, in so doing, set them off.

On arrival, Mrs. Rose Wentworth, rider and trainer of American Buffalo, discovered her bison were barred from landing in the United States. The Bureau of Animal Industry said: "Buffalo and other ruminants from South America are not permitted." The Buffalo were onboard the SS *Vasari* when it sailed and they were presumed thrown overboard.

IRWIN BROTHERS REAL CHEYENNE FRONTIER DAYS WILD WEST (1914)

On June 15, the season opened in Cheyenne, Wyoming. The general admission was one-dollar, grand stands an additional dollar, bleachers fifty-cents, automobiles a dollar, and valet parking autos another dollar. The Irwins traveled to Nebraska, Colorado, Utah, Nevada, and California.

The Frontier Days Wild West traveled in thirty double-length cars and advertised that they carried 250 head of livestock and over 200 performers. They had a twenty-four piece cowboy band and a calliope. H. Chkonia (khariton) and a troupe of Georgians (possibly, Kvitashvili,

Urushadze and Nithipo) were with the show. A three-reel picture was also in circulation around the country titled: *"The Round-Up at Y-6 Ranch."*

There were some fireworks of another sort on July 4 in Fort Collins, Colorado. Charles Johnson secretly married Pauline Irwin the month before; but her father, Charles Irwin, and Uncle Frank did not find out about it until July 4. Johnson was attacked from behind in view of 10,000 spectators by Frank Irwin. Frank stepped behind Johnson and struck him. Johnson was felled with the first blow, but witnesses say Frank continued the attack. Following the attack, Frank entered his auto and drove to Fort Collins, where he procured new tires and supplies and escaped. Frank pleaded guilty in court on November 18 on a charge of assault and battery and was fined $100. To say the least, the Irwin Brothers were known as rough bosses.

In September they were in Spokane, Washington, for the State Fair, and in Salt Lake, Utah, for that State Fair in October. It is unknown when the season closed, but they returned to winter quarters in Cheyenne, Wyoming.

KIT CARSON BUFFALO RANCH WILD WEST (1914)

This was known as the toughest circus on the road. Hearsay said that when a man came to hire out he was asked to repeat this oath: "I weigh (so many pounds), I will fight for the show and also steal for the show." After wintering in Birmingham, the show erected the four-pole, two-ring big top in Bessemer, Alabama, where rehearsals were conducted. Khalampri Pataraia, Sergia Gvarjaladze and another Georgian rider had signed on for the season. The season opened in Bessemer on March 22. The show was carried on eighteen rail cars.

A method for the show to avoid city license fees based on the cost of tickets was discovered by the chief of police in Connellsville, Pennsylvania. The manager told the mayor that tickets would cost forty cents and paid a $50 fee instead of the $100 fee if tickets sold for fifty cents. The day of the show, the actual cost was fifty cents and the police chief forced the show to hand over an additional fifty dollars for the full fee.

In one town, Homestead, Pennsylvania, the audience saw both tragic and humorous accidents. Albert Wallace, the horse-thief actor, was

311

trampled when six horses rushed upon him. Wallace was being dragged out of the big top when the horse pulling him stopped suddenly and the rider behind could not stop in time. Shortly, a Japanese acrobat standing ringside ready to go through his exhibition encountered a skittish horse, which kicked him in the posterior. The acrobat turned three somersaults and alighted on his feet.

A pickpocket working the crowd in Cazenovia, New York, was caught in the act. He raised a cry and some 100 circus workers with iron stakes surrounded the villagers and took him away. In the free-for-all fight, a villager's head was split open. A warrant, in the name of Bayne, was taken out for the manager. The show people a second time surrounded the officials and villagers and rescued the manager. The show left town in a hurry.

At Louisa, Kentucky, on Saturday, October 10, before the beginning of the afternoon performance, Khalampri Pataraia was murdered. From the newspaper account here is what happened:

"Mrs. Alien Kirk, sister of attorney W. T. Cain, had a reserved seat. On the opposite side of the tent there was another section of reserved seats. A steady rain was falling, and the tent was leaking, causing many people to raise umbrellas. Mrs. Kirk said she would go across to the other seats where her brother was and get an umbrella. She proceeded to do so but failed to ask the woman at the reserved seat entrance for a return check or ticket. When she attempted to enter the reserved seat section on the opposite side the two men on duty there demanded a ticket or a quarter. One was an American and the other was *Khalampri Pataraia*. Mrs. Kirk stated that she had a seat on the other side and only wanted to get an umbrella from her brother. *Khalampri Pataraia* could speak no English except perhaps a few words, "ticket" "quarter" etc. Mr. Cain saw that Mrs. Kirk was trying to get in and went to her, leading her into the seats. A controversy resulted and Cain struck an American showman. *Khalampri Pataraia* had followed several steps when Cain turned and struck him with an umbrella. He drew a small whip from his belt… and struck Mr. Cain. There was much confusion and people stood up on the seats. It seems that Khalampri went back to the entrance ans was short distance outside when the shot was fired by Nathan C. Day."[389]

The examining trial a week later provided these details: "…after the trouble between Mr. Cain and the showman subsided, *Khalampri Pataraia* made his way back to the reserved seat entrance and then turned toward the side wall of the tent near the end of the reserved seat section and was within about two feet of the tent when the shot. Witnesses saw no knife on Khalampri or in his hands. He carried a small riding whip. Mr. Day had been sitting about halfway up in the tier of the reserves and, during the trouble, came down to about the third row of seats, near the end, and it was while standing there that he is said to have fired the shot. 'Jimmie the Cossack,' (probably Sergia Gvarjaladze) another *Georgian* working in the riding act with the man who was killed, testified as to his dying statement, which was that when the shot struck him he was just in the act of stooping to raise the tent and get out of there. Jimmie swore the man had no knife but wore only a sword and whip. The physicians testified that the ball entered an inch-and-a-half on the left of the spine and was removed at a point near the center in front, about the end of the breast bone, and almost on a level with the wound in the back. There were also three or four cuts and bruises on Khalampri's head and face."[390] Certificate of Death, File No. 26485, stated death occurred at 5:45 a.m., Sunday, October 11.

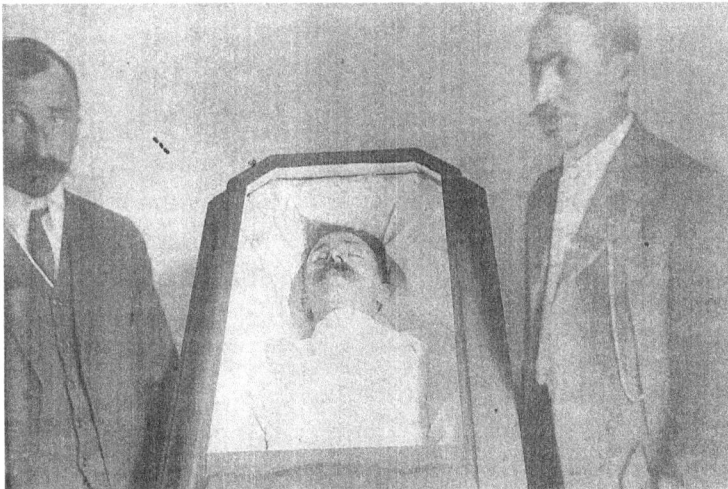

Khalampri Pataria, ca 1914
Author's Collection
Plate No. 42

Khalampri Pataraia's funeral was held Sunday and the body laid to rest in Pinehall cemetery at Louisa, Monday, October 12. Floral offerings were many. Khalampri was thirty-six years old and had a wife and four children. Nathan C. Day, a hotel proprietor, was convicted January 21, 1915, and sentenced to twenty-one years in the penitentiary, on the charge of killing Khalampri.

On Friday, October 23, at Harlan, Kentucky, the show was shot out of town by irate natives, and the next day, October 24, at Barboursville, the show halted. Creditors had stepped into the picture and closed the show and had it shipped to the U.S. Printing and Lithograph Company plant at Cincinnati, Ohio, where it was advertised for auction. The stock was sold in December, and March 20, 1915, was the date set for the sale of other properties at Cincinnati, except for five cars and twelve wagons that were still stored at Harrisburg, which the rail car company later took over. The Kit Carson property sale went for very low prices. Tom Wiedemann received nothing from the sales. He turned up for the 1915 season as manager of a seventeen-car circus called "Barton and Bailey World Celebrated Shows," owned by John Barton and Harry Bailey with leased equipment from William P. Hall of Lancaster, Missouri.

MILLER BROTHERS & ARLINGTON 101 RANCH REAL WILD WEST (1914)

Luka and his men from the South American tour arrived on April 11. The 101 Ranch assembly area was in Lakeview, New Jersey. On April 19, the cowboys, Indians, and Teophane Kavtaradze (Tephon), Luka, Sam Sergia, and three other Georgians came across to New York City for the three-week stand at Madison Square Garden. In a drizzling rain and chilly wind, the citizens of New York City watched a long, illuminated night parade down Broadway, composed of Georgians and members of the 101 Ranch.

During the 1904-1905 Russian-Japanese war, the Georgians were the bad guys in the Wild West Show. This year it was the Mexicans' turn to be the enemy. Joseph Miller issued an order that the Mexicans could not carry their national flag in the grand entrée. The cowboys nailed a placard on the Mexicans' door reading: "Headquarters General Villa, Rebel Army Inside."

The 101 Ranch carried a physician, Dr. Crawford, who had a small tent with two cots, three stretchers, a sanitary wash stand and medicine chest.

"Chief Tephon has a fine bunch of Far East riders." "The *Georgians* ride with reckless abandon." "Capt. Chief Tephon, The Russian Demon, has an act of perfection." These are some of the accounts written in *Billboard* magazine. The press started paying more attention to the *Georgians* after WW I started. "In view of the part Russian Cossacks are playing in the present European war... it is especially interesting... No position on the back of a running horse seems too difficult for these daredevil soldiers of the czar to occupy with apparent ease. They ride as well standing on their heads, or rather shoulders, as sitting in the saddle; and springing on and off the back of a flying horse is accomplished apparently with slight exertion... using the imagination a little, secures a very good idea of what the Austrian and German soldiers are going up against."[391]

Billboard was used by many showmen to send messages to others in different shows. Teophane Kavtaradze (Tephon) wrote: "'Dan Dix' – Tephon wants to know why you don't write." The *Billboard* response, "Dan Dix was in the London show." And later *Billboard* reported: "It has not yet been decided whether Dan Dix will have his trunk next to Tephon or Rocky Mountain Hank (Walker)." To clarify the record: "Dan Dix says his name is Clyde Miller, he is not the Miller Brothers."

The season closed November 21 in Hot Springs, Arkansas, where the show went into winter quarters.

MILLER BROTHERS 101 RANCH IN LONDON (1914)

After the Madison Square Garden engagement, the Miller Brothers divided the show into two units. It sent the U.S. unit on to Philadelphia and the second unit to White City, London, England, to the Anglo-American exposition at the Shepherd's Bush Stadium. On May 1, the *SS Philadelphia* left New York with fifty-three Indians in steerage; forty-two cowboys, cowgirls, and Mexicans; four cavalrymen (for monkey drill), four auto polo drivers; Billy Sweeney, director of the cowboy band; and Prince Luka and three Georgians. The production was called "The Civilization of the West" to commemorate 100 years of peace between Great Britain and the United States. On May 2, the *SS Minneapolis* left New York with Zack Miller, his mother and daughter; Johnny Baker, the adopted son of Buffalo Bill, and his wife and daughter; ten cowboys; and 107 head of stock. The same day the *SS Oceanic* departed New York with Louis E. Cooke, the general Manager of the show. The *Philadelphia* and *Oceanic* arrived in South Hampton and the *Minneapolis* arrived at London's Tilbury Dock.

The Anglo-American exposition officially opened on May 14. There were two performances daily, 2:30 p.m. and 8:30 p.m., except Sunday, with a seating capacity of 12,000 people. The first performance had the usual incidents as reported in *Billboard* June 6. "Jane Fuller's horse fell... gave a severe tramp on the head... bruised considerably.... Mable Klein's horse fell with her, wrenching her ankle.... 'Mex' George Hooker's cinch broke, dropping 'Old Hook' on the ground, skinning him up some.... Florence LaDue, while shaking a jacket, was struck in the eye by one of the buttons... her sight may be impaired."

The Queen of England and Empress Marie of Russia were entertained by the 101 Ranch in early July. The party consisted of four automobiles. The entire royal party reviewed the line-up of the whole company after the performance, just another command performance for Luka Chkhartishvili.

On August 2, Germany declared war on Russia and World War I began. Americans all over Europe started a scramble to get home. Passenger shipping was booked solid. The steamship companies placed the number of Americans in Europe, mostly tourists, at 150,000. Monday, August 2 was a bank holiday and the Anglo-American exposition opened up; the 101 Ranch gave four shows instead of the usual two and did huge business. The show continued through August; however, Miller and Cooke decided to send home some of the Indian families. The *SS New York* left England August 2 with a contingent of fourteen Indians in steerage, and arrived on Sunday, August 9. The remaining members of the company were scrambling to find passage by August 10. Passages that had been booked were cancelled, the result of sudden appropriation of the ocean liners for purposes of war.

On Friday, August 14, newspaper reports started reaching America. "The British government has seized all of the horses of the 101 Ranch Wild West Show for war purposes in England."[392] The British government requisitioned 103 horses and paid Miller Bros. and Arlington thirty-five pounds apiece for them, cash in hand. Zach Miller returned to the U.S.

with a contract to purchase 10,000 horses for the British government, and the money to pay for them was deposited in New York. On September 17, ads "War Horses Wanted" were placed in Texas and Oklahoma newspapers by Miller Bros 101 Ranch, Bliss, Oklahoma.

The show kept going on as usual with the exception of the musical ride and the Georgians, who left by August 14. Luka and his three companions said good-bye to the Miller Bros. cast with tears in their eyes, and Luka told them he would not return to the United States.

Luka Chkhartishvili
Miller Brothers 101 Ranch.
Courtsey, The John and Mable Ringling Museum of Art
Plate No. 43

RINGLING BROTHERS CIRCUS (1914)

The Chicago Coliseum was the venue for the opening of the Ringling circus on April 11.

Veliko Kvitaishvili's troupe of riders included Victor Kvitaishvili, Kaisar Kvitaishvili, Kristine Tsintsadze and Barbara Zakarashvili-Imnadze. The Georgian races and display of horsemanship were the last before the closing.

Ringling Brothers had the largest circus on the road, using eighty-three cars. This did not stop them from running opposition advertising against the smallest of circuses. An example occurred in Charleroi, Pennsylvania, where they told the newspaper that the Jones Bros. and Wilson's show had fourteen cars and that everyone should wait for the Ringling circus. After the Jones Bros. played the town, Ringling cancelled the date in Charleroi. "Railroad trouble" was given as the cause.

Two newspapers can get a story completely different. On May 9, the *Newark Advocate* reported that Granville Gross, thirty, was killed when he was struck by a passenger train moving in the opposite direction. The story tells us he was stretching his legs while the circus train stopped in Pataskaia, Ohio, to take on water. The *Lima Daily News* reported, from Newark, that Gross, twenty-five, was thrown from the Ringling train at Pataskaia. He was ground to pieces beneath the wheels of a limited train No. 14, which followed closely. In either case, Gross met a gruesome death.

In Cleveland, Ohio, on May 25, a big fire destroyed forty-one cars of Ringling's circus train. The show was forced to dismiss its performance and suffered $100,000 in losses. The telegraph wires were red hot with traffic securing new equipment. The show made their next date in Marion, Ohio. Eleven days later, eight employees were injured severely when two sleepers and a flat car of the first section derailed. It was said a brakeman caused the accident by throwing a switch before all the cars had passed.

The show closed on Saturday, October 24, in Cairo, Illinois, and the performers and Cossacks arrived in Chicago on Sunday afternoon.

YOUNG BUFFALO WILD WEST AND CHEYENNE DAYS (1914)

The show opened in Peoria, Illinois, April 25 under the ownership of Vernon Seaver. Annie Oakley had withdrawn from the show. The show was a smaller eighteen-car show, which traveled the upper Midwest. The season opened to poor attendance due to cold and wet weather.

A newspaper photo shows four Georgian riders, Captain Dimitri's Cossacks, and they are probably the riders from the previous year.

Newspapers started printing stories of criminal activity following the show. Some of the standard old tricks were reported: the time-worn magazine subscription soliciting game, changing bills with lead coins, short changing, and the shell game.

Massen came down from Chicago on Wednesday and said the show owed him $35,000, and that six of the cars were his, also horses and wagons valued at $75,000. The showmen milled about the town, Indians found a saloon that would serve them liquor, and none of them were getting fed. More trouble came when a promise to the men that they would get their money was broken. Vernon C. Seaver, the owner, was supposed to pay over the money but instead he took the 10:00 p.m. train to Chicago. The workmen believed that Seaver had sold the show to William Hall of Lancaster, Missouri, and would get his money when the show started moving on the rail, and Hall took possession of the property. The show train was to move out at midnight, but when the crew arrived they found about twenty men with Winchesters bristling defiance. A wagon blocked the track and guards told the train crew to be careful about the wagon. A fusillade of shots filled the air from the men holding the train as the train crew got aboard the engine and heated up to make a getaway.

Deputy Sheriff Fitzgerald spent the night at the scene and reported that the men were not breaking up any property but merely holding the cars and sixty-two head of horses to insure their getting paid. The train stayed put.

Meanwhile in East Alton, twenty-five or more Negroes created wild excitement when a train crew came to hitch on another train with about fifty horses. The Negroes drew guns and fired. The train crew left and the Negroes took the stock down into a thicket of trees where they announced to the manager that they would hold them until they got their money.

Arrangements were made on Thursday to feed the showmen. A delegation of town ladies intervened on behalf of the horses. It seems no one was feeding the horses either.

On Friday, July 31, a final agreement was reached with the showmen, but it was not simple. The proposition made established that a sum of $1,500 would be divided among the men and women to relieve them in their present straits on condition that they would sign an agreement to waive all other claims. The money would not be disbursed until the men had re-loaded the show property sold to W. P. Hall, and the engine attached to the train and made ready to steam away. The showmen debated this and finally realized that as soon as proceedings against the company got into the bankruptcy courts there would be long delays in anybody getting their money. The plan was to put the money in the hands of Sheriff Fitzgerald as evidence of good faith. A final conference was held at the Illini hotel, where M. C. Cookson got all the bosses and men to consent to the division of $1,500 on the basis of one week's salary to each man. The money was deposited in Citizen's National Bank. At five o'clock Friday afternoon the men would be paid off at City Hall.

The Georgian riders went home to Chicago.

1914 EPILOGUE

Luka Chkhartishvili, after twenty-two years of riding for Buffalo Bill, Pawnee Bill, the Miller Brothers and many other outfits, came home for the last time. Luka and his companions arrived in Odessa on September 1. Luka's arrival home coincided with the imminent capture of Batumi by Turkish troops.[393] Another dispatch from London reported: "a general revolt against Russian rule has broken out at Tblisi *(sic)*."[394]

LUKA CHKHARTISHVILI BIOGRAPHY

Luka Chkhartshvili, after twenty-two years riding for Buffalo Bill, Pawnee Bill, the Miller Brothers and many other outfits, came home for the last time. Luka and his companions arrived in Odessa on September 1. Luka's arrival home coninceded witht he imminent capture of Batumi by Turkish troops. Another dispatch from London reported: "A general revolt against Russian rule has broken out at Tbilisi."

Luka Chkhartishvili spent his remaining days in Lanchkhuti with his wife, three daughters Tebrone, Leonina, Marusia, and his two sons Platon and Leonio, who were adopted. He returned to being a jeweler who decorated swords and daggers; he managed his cornfields that his wife had tended the past twenty-two years. Luka was known as the man who sent clothes to Lanchkhuti from America. He would collect them at yard sales and send bundles to Lanchkhuti.

He taught youth riding but did not make any money at it. He was known for sitting under his pear trees at a table and telling stories of these adventures in America. In 1925, a silent film was produced about the riders in America. It is known that Luka taught some of these riders in this film, Ileas Lazishvili being one of them. Luka's riding days were over; he used a cane to walk after his knees gave out. Luka was well known in Lanchkhuti and when the Bolsheviks came to power they left him alone. Luka Chkhartishvili died circa 1934 or 1935 in Lanchkhuti, and was buried in his home town of Gvimbalauri. He told his neighbors: "I have a great name in America, and when I die my name will be remembered in America." Luka was correct; he, Ivane Makharadze, Tephon, and Chief Georgian were the only Georgians who are named in American history books as Wild West show "Russian Cossack" riders.

IVANE BARAMIDZE BIOGRAPHY

Ivane Baramidze, who first joined Luka Chkhartishvili in 1899, also did not return to America after 1914. In 1915 Ivane married Luka's sister Zekha, and their first child, Vaso, was born in 1916. Another son, Levan, was born in 1918. Ivane Baramidze returned to being a farmer.

Ivane Baramidze, who had ridden with Luka as early as 1899, was arrested by the Bolsheviks in 1937 as an "enemy of the state" for having been in America. He was never heard from again. Ivane Baramidze's brother Bathlome died riding in America, and his other brother Samson had a son named Givi who, in the year 2000, was eighty-two and lived in Tbilisi.

OTHER SHOW BUSINESS

William F. Cody was now an employee, not an employer; he worked for the Sells-Floto circus during the year.

The Oklahoma Ranch Wild West opened at Luna Park on Coney Island, New York, in June of 1914. Edward Arlington, manager and producer of the Oklahoma Ranch Wild West show, filed a voluntary petition of bankruptcy on December 17, 1914. His liabilities were given at $42,166.55 and his assets at $17,249.00.[395] The bankruptcy notice, to appear for the assigned May 21, 1915, hearing for all creditors and other persons of interest, was printed in the *Brooklyn Daily Eagle* on Tuesday, April 20, 1915.

"Fate, like the weather, is fickle; sometimes it smiles upon us, sometimes it whirls down like a tempest straight from wrathful heaven."

Shota Rustaveli

1915 PROLOGUE

By January, the Russian forces had forced the Turks to retreat within their own borders. The Russians, in desperate need of war supplies, discovered the Turkish blockade of the Bosporus and Dardanelles. The British and Australians attempted to capture the heights overlooking the straits, but they failed and were forced to withdraw. On April 24, 1915, began the Turkish expulsion and massacre of Armenians, who had supported the Russians. The Germans "…to keep Turkey on our side until the end of the war, no matter whether or not the Armenians go under," played an ignominious role in the affair. All this warmongering caused Georgia to be isolated and the Georgians who had been going to the United States were unable to return.

The European war also affected the availability for purchase of bronco busting horses for the Wild West Shows. Thousands of horses were taken from Colorado, Wyoming, and other western states. The British, French, and Italian agents had invaded the West, combing the country for mounts.

MILLER BROTHERS & ARLINGTON'S 101 RANCH WILD WEST (1915)

On February 12, members of the 101 Ranch left Bliss, Oklahoma, joining members of the 101 Ranch Moving Picture Company in San Francisco for the Panama Exposition. Four carloads of equipment and fifty personnel were taken from the ranch.

The regular show train carried fewer cars then the previous year. One train carried twenty-four cars: ten flats, seven horse cars, and seven sleepers. The flats carried thirty-four wagons and one auto. The flat and stocks were painted yellow; the sleepers were red, green, and yellow. The wagons were painted red and yellow. The general admission ticket wagon was white, while the reserved-seat and grandstand ticket wagon was red. The show had fifteen tents on the lot: the arena, side show, six-in-one, snakes, dressing, ring stock, cookhouse, five Indian camps, Jess Willard's private top, two candy stands, and concessions.

The consequence of a broken axle on a flat car in the second section train delayed the parade in Butler, Pennsylvania. This gave Tephon and his three men time to relax as they were the second to last parade unit, followed by a calliope pulled by six horses.

The tough life on the road ended on November 20 in Ponca City, Oklahoma, the winter quarters for the 101 Ranch.

"The Georgians will winter in Chicago, Illinois."[396] said Chief Tephon.

RINGLING BROTHERS CIRCUS (1915)

The Ringling season opened at Chicago's Coliseum on April 17, despite a strike going on in the city. Veliko Kvitaishvili's troupe of riders— Victor Kvitaishvili, Kaisar Kvitaishvili, Kristine Tsintsadze and Barbara Zakarashvili-Imnadze—were content to open in Chicago, as they considered it their home town. They could sleep in their own beds, a rare comfort in a traveling show.

The show hit the road on May 2, going to St. Louis, using eighty-nine double-length railroad cars divided into four or more sections, depending upon the grades to overcome. There were twenty-three tents in what was called "Ringlingville."

All those tents could be a significant problem during stiff winds. The flapping canvas in a storm could cause the elephants to get nervous and stampede; therefore, they would be taken out of the tents during a storm. The canvas men would struggle to keep the big top from bellowing up by tightening ropes and keeping a watch on the stakes.

Elephants may not be the only ones with long memories. The city of Fort Wayne, Indiana, remembered Ringling showing in their town twenty years before. On that occasion, horses took fright of the elephant herd and stampeded, killing three people. When Ringling arrived in town this year they demanded a $10,000 bond for the privilege to parade elephants and use a steam musical instrument on the streets. In a new twist, during a parade in Akron, Ohio, an elephant leaned against a car and broke Joseph Schaat's arm. Joseph was watching the parade and had his head and arm out the window when the elephant passed.

John Kastle Jr., age fifteen, asserted that he was thrown off the Ringling Brothers' train on August 22 in Minnesota. He claimed his foot was caught in the track in such a way that it was severely and permanently injured.

The show closed November 1 in Memphis, Tennessee. The Ringling returned to winter quarters in Baraboo, Wisconsin, November 10, after a 700-mile trip from Memphis.

1915 EPILOGUE

Maro Kvitaishvili returned to Georgia in 1915, after she gave birth to two children in America, while two older children were waiting for her in Georgia. Maro Kvitaishvili did not return to America.

KRISTINE TSINTSADZE BIOGRAPHY

Kristine (Christine) Tsintsadze was born in the small village of Sujuna. Her maiden name was Nodia. She spent her childhood in Lanchkhuti and, in her relatives' words, she often pretended that she had business in neighboring villages just to be able to ride a horse. Kristine was reported to be very slim, pretty, and not very tall, but very quick and graceful. Luka Chkhartishvili was responsible for bringing Kristine to the United States even though her parents were against the idea. She was determined to go and underwent training with Luka. She first arrived in 1910 and, over the years, had several falls. One incident was when her horse fell and she hit her head on the ground and lost several of her teeth, but nevertheless managed to finish her set, and was awarded fancy clothes, a gold watch and ring. She had three near death experiences during 1910 and 1915. Kristine recalled that nearly all her fans, even the women, tried to kiss her on the mouth after performances. "Probably it was my white teeth in 'perfect' shape that they liked." She joked. Kristine returned at the end of the 1915 season, and continued to perform in Georgia and once won 1,000 rubles in a race. Christine Tsintsadze became a well-known healer, and healed neighbors with folk remedies. Christine collected herbs, making various extracts that facilitated the condition of patients. On her deathbed, Kristine gave away all her dresses and other personal belongings that she had been presented with in America and regretfully burned a huge box full of private correspondence.[397]

"Heart should be given for heart, and love be the bridge of true friendship."
Shota Rustaveli

1916 PROLOGUE

Edward Arlington and Harry Tammen pulled off an amazing switch during the winter. Jess Willard was traded to the Sells-Floto circus for Cody to the 101 Ranch. Cody found himself just another traded commodity.

Onetime bandit and Wild West promoter Cole Younger died in Jackson County, Missouri, March 21, at age seventy-two.

The manganese for making glass was mined along the line of the Trans-Caucasian Railway, between Batumi and Tbilisi, and it was shipped from Batumi on the Black Sea. This justified the advance in price of glass manufacturer's manganese, which was selling at $20 a ton before the war and now brought $420 a ton.

BUFFALO BILL & 101 RANCH WILD WEST SHOW (1916)

Homer Wilson said the following in *Billboard*, April 29: "Chief Tephon requested me to advise you that he and his troupe of *Georgians*, five in number, left Chicago during the week of April 10 for Ponca City, Oklahoma, to join the Buffalo Bill-101 Ranch show." The show opened in Ponca on April 20. The eighteenth event was the wild riding Georgians, presenting reckless feats of horsemanship.

On May 11, in Akron, a storm panicked the audience during the evening performance when a terrific gale rocked the big tent. Ropes were broken, poles swayed, women and children shrieked, and men tried to calm the turmoil. No one was seriously injured, though several were bruised in the mad rush to escape.

A week later in Syracuse, New York, the Indians refused to die. The weather was terrible, the afternoon performance was called off, and the evening performance went on even under the muddy conditions. The Deadwood Stage act called for Sioux Indians to surround the stage and then cowboys armed with '48's rushed to the rescue, killing the Indians. Volley after volley was fired, and the Indians scattered but refused to die and fall into the mud, much to the amusement of the crowd.

On June 27, two cars of the Buffalo Bill train bound for Manchester, New Hampshire, from Portland, Maine, were derailed. One of the cars was filled with Indians, several of whom sustained sprained ankles but no serious injuries. The train proceeded soon afterward without the two cars.

The health officer in Poughkeepsie, New York, advised the mayor to telegraph the 101 Ranch show that they would not be allowed to detrain. The city had an infantile paralysis (polio) epidemic situation. In Stamford, Connecticut, and Mt. Vernon, New York, kids were not allowed to attend the show, which severely reduced the amount collected toward meeting the nut.

On October 9, the 101 Ranch train on the Virginia Railway to Norfolk from Lexington, was wrecked near Victoria, Virginia, at 4:30 a.m., Sunday morning. Thirty-seven horses were reported killed, seven cars were demolished and considerable baggage destroyed, but no persons were injured. A truck (set of wheels) on one of the cars left the track, causing the cars to pile up on the wrecked car.[398]

The show continued into the southern states, closed on November 18, and returned to Norfolk, Virginia, to their winter quarters.

RINGLING BROTHERS CIRCUS (1916)

Ringling was the biggest circus on the road. The marketing department published these factoids:

The average daily expense, $8,000; eighty-nine double-length railroad cars; 1,370 performers; 735 horses; three advance cars employing 115 men and twenty-three advance agents; 4,000 meals served a day using ninety cooks and waiters; sixty ushers; fifty property men; a secret service department; Red Cross department with two physicians, three nurses, three veterinary surgeons, and an elephant doctor; an attorney, postmaster, and a weather forecaster; blacksmith, wagon, paint shops employing thirty-six men; and three men who did nothing but grease wagon wheels.

Ringling opened at the Coliseum in Chicago on April 15. The parade included eight Georgians mounted—seven men and one lady—in native costumes. Barbara Imnadze's act included standing on the shoulders of two men as they balanced atop a pair of galloping horses.

In town after town, the advance crew along with the billing would post notices offering two-and-one-half dollars per day and board for laborers. They were often unable to get the men and would offer free tickets to kids to set seating planks.

Pennsylvania required Ringling to have state insurance against liability for compensation to injured employees. The rate was $5.41. The insurance did not help when the range (cook) wagon, weighing six tons, rolled into a ditch in Reading. It took thirty-four horses to pull the vehicle to the surface. It was the heaviest vehicle in the circus. In Appleton, Minnesota, an elephant hesitated entering the rail car and the keeper goaded him. The elephant roared and scattered the crowd and then wound his trunk around the keeper's leg and shook him while holding him in the air. The keeper was rescued. Maybe he would have preferred it to have happened in Pennsylvania, where he could have claimed compensation for injuries.

On Saturday, October 28, in Huntsville, Alabama, a fire destroyed thirty-four horses and burned about fifty others so badly they probably were put down. The fire, which was believed to have started from a match thrown aside by a driver, was not noticed until it had gained great headway. The work to rescue the horses was difficult because they were chained to their places. All ring and baggage stock was saved and, as the wind was blowing away from the menagerie and big tent, no damage was done there.[399] Two days later, the circus was playing Greenville, Mississippi.

The show closed on November 4 in Baton Rouge, Louisiana.

1916 EPILOGUE

Four shows reported Georgian riders in their shows: The Oklahoma Ranch Real Wild West and Circus, Pawnee Bill's Wild West and Pioneer Days, Texas Bill's Wild West, and Tompkins Wild West. The best evidence is that these were American cowboys acting as Cossacks. George Gresaff led a troupe of Cossacks in the Oklahoma Ranch outfit, Prince Jimmie or Jemi had a troupe of Cossacks in the Tompkins and the Pawnee Bill show, and Prince Joe was the leader in the Texas Bill outfit.

The nickname for the Georgians on the 101 Ranch show was "Coffee-sacks," due to their large consumption of coffee.

"Can light exist and be bright when darkness attends it?"

Shota Rustaveli

CHAPTER SIX
THE CLOSING ACTS:
1917 AND BEYOND

1917 PROLOGUE

The year 1917 is the beginning of the end of several major events in the twentieth century and the slow demise of Georgians in Wild West shows. "The War to end all Wars" was at its height in 1917. Russian troops mutinied March 10 (February 26, Old Style) and Czar Nicholas II en route home by private train March 15 had the train pulled into a siding and abdicated in favor of his brother Michael. Michael abdicated March 16 in favor of a provisional government. The German high command sent V. I. Lenin and other Bolshevik leaders to Petrograd (St. Petersburg) in April by sealed railroad carriage, from Switzerland across Germany, in a calculated move to undermine the pro-Ally provisional government. On April 6 the United States declared war on Germany.

The Bolshevik revolution began at Petrograd the night of November 6 (October 24, Old Style). Civil war erupted between the "Red" (Bolshevik), and "White" (anti-Bolshevik) factions, which continued for several years.

Meanwhile, in Georgia, Bolsheviks and Mensheviks were in a coalition with other parties and formed the Social Democratic Movement. In June 1917, the Bolsheviks, on Lenin's insistence, split from the Georgian Mensheviks.

In the Wild West show business several major players, who had a significant impact on the Georgian riders, perished.

William F. Cody once said: "Out West, you know, we don't die. We just dry up and blow away."[400] It happened, on January 10, 1917, at five minutes past twelve, while Cody was at the home of his sister, May Decker, in Denver, Colorado, 2932 Lafayette Street.

Mrs. Louisa Cody was the sole heir of the estate, estimated to be worth $65,000 to $75,000 and property. The New York Tribune on January 11 announced all the funeral arrangements; Sunday to lie in state, and final burial on Lookout Mountain.

Cody, dressed in a frock coat on which were pinned the badges of the Legion of Honor and of the Grand Army of the Republic, lay in repose in a bronze casket bearing the inscription "Colonel William F. Cody, "Buffalo Bill." Cody was brought to the Colorado State Capitol Rotunda on Sunday, January 14. Viewing was open to the public at 9:50 a.m. and closed at 12:30 p.m. It was estimated 25,000 passed the bier. Cody was taken to the Elks' Home for a funeral service and then to a mortuary vault.

Tammen and Bonfils, who owned the Buffalo Bill franchise, had a major influence on where and how Cody's memorial took place. The Boulder Camera, an opposition newspaper, wrote: "Why not let the Denver Post proprietors determine the kind of shaft to erect over Buffalo Bill? He was their meat. It was they who brought him down after a gallant career, by breaking his proud heart. Why should not the shaft be crowned with a miniature 'Red Room,' bearing 'Abandon hope, all ye who enter here.'?"

Cody's final resting place is on Lookout Mountain, twenty miles west of Denver. A vault was blasted from solid rock. The Masonic Lodge of North Platte Valley requested the Golden, Colorado, Lodge No. 1 confer the Masonic burial rites. On June 3, thousands paid tribute to the memory of Colonel William F. Cody. There were eight Masonic brothers as pallbearers dressed in their Knights Templar uniforms. At the request of Mrs. Cody, the casket was open. One account written in Timber Line summarized the event. "There was a circus atmosphere about the whole thing. A lot of us drank straight rye from bottles while speeches were being made by expert liars. Six of the colonel's surviving sweethearts— now obese and sagging with memories—sat on camp chairs beside the grave of hewn-out granite. The bronze casket lay in the bright western sun. The glass over the colonel's amazingly handsome face began to steam on the inside. You could not see the face after a while, on account of the frosted pane.

"One of the old Camilles[35] rose from her camp chair, with a manner so gracious as to command respect. Then, as though she were utterly alone with her head, and while thousands looked on, this grand old lady walked to the casket and held her antique but dainty black parasol over the glass. She stood there throughout the service, a fantastic, superb figure. It was the gesture of a queen."[401]

These words were said by the Masons over the grave:

"His spirit ascends to God who gave it. His memory we cherish in our hearts. His body we consign to the earth."

At the conclusion of the services, a bugler sounded taps and when the last note had died out a battery fired a salute of thirteen guns and the Stars and Stripes were hoisted from a flagpole over the grave.

Mrs. Louisa Cody (1844-1921) died Tuesday, October 20, 1921, at her home in Cody, Wyoming, and was buried on Lookout Mountain.

Cody's saga did not end there. On August 1, 1948, the Cheyenne, Wyoming, American Legion Post announced they had spent four months on a secret project to return the body of Cody to the town he founded. "Our strategy is a secret, but we are confident of its success….The State of Wyoming has long rankled under the humiliation of Buffalo Bill's enforced absence from his chosen burial spot on Cedar Mountain near Cody, Wyoming. The time has come to correct this unfortunate twist in history. We the American Legion drum and bugle corps, as defenders of the right and champions of the oppressed, have taken a solemn pledge to return the remains….The Cody post promptly… pledged $10,000 cold cash for the return of Cody's founder in time for the Wyoming department legion convention August 15."[402]

The next day the Denver American Legion rallied to defend the grave.

A quartermaster section of the post issued rifles, helmets, boots and

---

[35] Camille - Refers to a Parisian Courtesan from Alexander Dumas novel "The Lady of the Camellias."

other defense equipment. The Legionnaires right-shouldered rifles and marched post around the grave. Years earlier, the vault had been filled in with cement. Cody was going nowhere.

Johnny Baker, the foster son of Cody, and his wife Olive, built a museum called Pahaska (the tepee) at the gravesite and lived there to protect the memory of William F. Cody. Baker died the night of Wednesday, April 22, 1931, at Mercy hospital, Denver. He was cremated and buried in Mount Hope Cemetery, Rochester, NY. His only known instructions to his wife were: "I want you to stay on at Pahaska.... After I'm gone I want you to keep alive the memory of the colonel."

• • •

"C.M. Ercolè, a well known continental music hall agent, with headquarters in Paris, died January 21, 1917, of pneumonia contracted January 18, 1917. At one time the deceased was the European representative for the Barnum-Bailey circus. the business of the late C.M. Ercolè was continued by his widow, with Carron, an American, in charge."[403]

• • •

"Indian fighter and many years' friend and associate of 'Buffalo Bill,' Major John M. Burke (1844-1917), answered the last call and went to join his former chief. Maj. Burke died in his seventy-fifth year early Thursday, April 12, 1917, at Providence hospital, Washington, D.C. Major Burke was left an orphan in New York when he was only two months old, and was brought to Washington, D.C., and reared by an uncle."[404] Some said he died of a broken heart. Members of the Washington Lodge, No. 15, Benevolent and Protective Order of Elks on behalf of New Orleans Lodge No. 30, attended the funeral service on Monday, April 16. Requiem mass was said at St. Aloysius Church. Interment was at Mount Olivet cemetery.

Thomas Oliver the interpreter for the Georgians died in Defiance, Ohio, September 5, 1943. His obituary in the Defiance Crescent-News, September 7, 1943, read in part: "Thomas Oliver, seventy-six, retired circus and vaudeville acrobat, died in Defiance, Ohio, September 5, 1943. He spent his entire life in show business. He was a contortionist and acrobat and traveled with circuses, including Ringling Bros., vaudeville and at one time had his own show, the Oliver Family Shows. Surviving were three daughters, a son, four grandchildren, and a sister."

The known Georgians who remained in the United States from 1917 to the 1920's were:

Barbara Zakareishvili-Imnadze
Christofore Imnadze
Veliko Kvitaishvili
Victor Kvitaishvili
Emily Kvitaishvili
Teopane Kavtaradze
Vaso Tsuladze
Kharitoni Chkonia
Sam Sergia
Kirile Khoperia
Solomon Pataraia
Archial and Babinina Tsereteli

Unfortunately, the records where these men and women worked are unclear in most cases.

BUFFALO BILL & JESS WILLARD SHOW (1917)

What was the Buffalo Bill and 101 Ranch Wild West in 1916 became The Buffalo Bill & Jess Willard Wild West in 1917. This was due to a disagreement between Joseph Miller and Edward Arlington. The show opened April 11, in Norfolk, Virginia. Teophane Kavtaradze and his usual band of Vaso Tsuladze, Kharitoni Chkonia, and Sam Sergia are presumed to be the Georgians working in this show.

On June 13, a telegram informed the public that Jess Willard purchased the entire Buffalo Bill show from Edward Arlington for $150,000.00.

There were 353 performances, visiting 159 towns in 25 states, and traveled 9,657 miles. The newspaper articles late in the season reported the show as being shabby and a poor rendition of a Buffalo Bill Wild West show.

The season ended on November 3, in Jacksonville, Florida, and their winter quarters were in Pablo Beach, Florida.

RINGLING BROTHERS AND HAGENBECK-WALLACE (1917)

Billboard magazine, April 28, reports that "Captain George Georgian has placed for the summer season one troupe of Georgians with the Ringling show and one with the Hagenbeck-Wallace circus. Both troupes figure prominently in the Wild West concerts. Captain Georgian himself will be with the Ringling Brothers."

The known riders with the Ringling Brothers were: Veliko Kvitaishvili, Kaiser Kvitaishvili, Victor Kvitaishvili and Emily Kvitashvili and George Georgian. The Ringling season opened in Chicago, the home town of the Georgian riders, on April 7. The replaced 100 plus horses from fire in late 1916 required much care be taken of the green horses, which were not familiar with the smell of elephants, the band music, and flapping of banners and noise of the crowds.

The police were summoned to Middle Point, Ohio, on Sunday July 8 to question a native of Russia, who wandered into that town and was without military registration papers or others documents to show that he is a lawful citizen. The Russian claimed to have worked up to a few days ago for the Ringling circus and that he was robbed of the his papers and a small amount of money. He was permitted to go on his way.

The Ringling season statistics include 214 show days with 356 performances, visiting 145 towns and traveling 18,115 miles. The season closed on November 5 in Memphis, Tennessee. The Georgians returned to Chicago.

Veliko Kvitaishvili continued riding for the Ringlings until he returned to Georgia in 1920. When Veliko and Maro tried to leave Georgia, the Bolsheviks refused permission.

The Hagenbeck-Wallace circus opened the season on April 18, in Indianapolis, Indiana. The circus had a normal circus program and concluded with Hippodrome contests. It is known the Georgian riders were the No. 4 program in the Hippodrome contests, and were part of the Wild West Frontier exhibition. It is possible Christofore Imnadze, Barbara Zakareishvili, Ilarion Imnadze rode in the Hagenbeck-Wallace circus. There are no reports of accidents to the Georgian riders.

Circus trains were finding it more difficult to meet their schedules as trains carrying war supplies disrupted regular train schedules.

The season ended on October 23, in West Baden, Indiana.

TOMPKIN'S WILD WEST (1917)

The Tompkin's Wild West opened on Saturday, April 21, at Warsaw, Virginia. The No. 17 act was Archil Zescetley's Russian Cossacks featuring Princess Babilina. This show traveled to a lot of County fairs during the season. The records and newspaper articles for this show are minimal.

1918 PROLOGUE

On March 8, the first case of Spanish Flu was reported. It was the beginning of a worldwide pandemic. On May 16, the U.S. Congress passes a sedition act making criticism of the government an imprisonable offense, which impacted the life of Alexis Georgian (Gogokhia). On May 26, 1918, the Menshevik government declared Georgia an independent state, ending 117 years of Russian rule. On November 11 at the eleventh hour the armistice is signed by the allies and Germany ending World War I.

In Georgia the Russians, Germans, Turks and English were all involved trying to gain control and access. The Germans were trying to control the trade route for the shipment of manganese. The Turks were pushing the Armenians out of Turkey. The English had a foothold in Tbilisi. The new Republic of Georgia refused to endorse the peace treaty that gave Kars and Batumi to Turkey.

RINGLING BROTHERS AND HAGENBECK-WALLACE (1918)

There were four Georgian riders in the 1918 Ringling circus. The Ringling opened on April 20, in Chicago and the season closed on October 8, in Waycross, Georgia. It is presume the Georgians were Veliko Kvitaishvili, Christofore Imnadze and Barbara Zakareishvili-Imnadze.

There were three Georgian riders in the 1918 Hagenbeck-Wallace circus. The only record indicates a Victor was the leader of the troupe, presumed to be Victor Kvitaishvili.

June 29, 1918 the most appalling train disaster befell the Hagenbeck-Wallace circus. A speeding empty troupe train crashed into the rear of the second section of the circus train. It tore through four circus cars and demolished the fifth. These were sleeper cars and more than 85 performers were killed. There are no known Georgians killed in the wreck, but they must have experienced it.

1919 & BEYOND

The Ringling brothers in 1919 merged Barnum & Bailey with Ringling, becoming "The Ringling Brothers and Barnum & Bailey Combined Shows, the Greatest Show on Earth," with its debut at Madison Square Garden, March 29, 1919. The only known incident during the season was a train accident in Oklahoma where twelve horses were killed and fifteen mutilated in the third section. The 1919 through 1921 Ringling circus reported having eight Georgian riders.

Georgians refused to be party to any conference with the Bolshevik party since they had set up their own republic. The Washington Herald newspaper reported "Georgian men are the most handsome in the world. Mountain brigands or honest farmers, they are strong, soldierly and chivalrous and good to look upon."

Unfortunately, Georgia's independence was short lived, on February 14, 1921, the Red Army crossed from Azerbaijan into Georgia. In 1924, Iosif Vissarionovich Dzhugashvili (Joseph Stalin) grabbed control of the Soviet Union after the death of Lenin. In the 1930s, Stalin summarily executed his political enemies and declared anyone who had been in America "enemies of the state." Georgian riders in the various traveling shows were persecuted.

Billboard magazine, April 16, 1921 reports, "Chief Tephon (Teophane Kavtaradze) the well known Cossack rider late of the Buffalo Bill and 101 Ranch show paid the Ringling and Barnum boys a visit and left for San Antonio Texas to join the Vern Tantlinger's Tex-Mex Wild West with the Clarence A. Wortham shows."

In 1925, Teophane Kavtaradze (Tephon), Khariton Chkonia, Kaisar Kvitaishvili, and Estan Worsadze were still in the United States working on the Miller Bros. 101 Ranch show.

On January 15, 1925, Solomon Pataraia, age thirty-one, single, arrived in New York onboard the SS California. He listed his agent as Bernard Montague, forty, Shaftsbury Ave. London, and gave his occupation as circus artist. He could have very well ridden in the 1925 Miller Brothers

101 Ranch show.

It was reported that Iorama and Laphier Mshvidobadze died abroad. No record of their death in a show has been recovered.

A film titled "Who is to be blame" produced by Al. Tsutsunava was filmed in Georgia in 1921. Around 300 Georgian riders took part in the races and making the film. Veliko Kvetaishvili and his wife took part. One of the oldest riders, Alexandre Mkheidze tells: "It was fantastic to watch Maro Kvetaishvili riding. Time after time she was taking equipment off her horse and putting it on the ground, on a gallop. Then she would begin to pick up the equipment and after taking the last piece, in able a minute or two, the horse was wholly equipped." She was a woman who could do such things and you can imagine what men could do.

GEORGIAN RIDER BIOGRAPHIES

Ilarion Malakhi Imnadze (1885-1925). In 1910, together with other Lanchkhuti riders, he went to America and lived in Chicago. In 1912 he asked his brother Christopher to come to America and bring with him Veliko Kvitaishvili's wife's sister Barbara Zakareishvili. In 1913 Ilarion came back to Georgia to see his mother. At this time he married Gogola Oragvelidze from the village Shukhuti; a year later their daughter, Shushana Imnadze-Shavdia, was born. Gogola told her daughter that Ilarion never survived the lifestyle of American living and in 1925 committed suicide. Christopher Imnadze took care of Ilarion's family after his death.

Sam Sergia (1884 –1965) reportedly first arrived in 1904. He was married to Christina, but there is no record of children. Sam continued working in the Wild West shows after 1917. In 1938 he was working at the Stockman's Café in Fort Worth, Texas. In 1940 he became the owner of Stockman Café and operated it for several years. In 1950 he had changed the name to the Stock Yards Recreation Club and in 1952 changed again to Sam's Club. The last record has Sergia owner of Sam's Club (recreation) and living at 112 East Exchange Ave., Fort Worth. Sam died on April 4, 1965, at 4:00 p.m. and was buried on April 7 at the Mt. Olivet cemetery. What happened to the cigarette case is a mystery.

Christopher and Barbara Imnadze (Emnadze). Christopher was born on February 1, 1887 and Barbara was born on October 20, 1896. After years working in the Ringling circus, they settled in Chicago. Their address in 1956 was 4403 S. Halsted St. Chicago 9, Illinois. Barbara worked at the Kellogg switchboard in Chicago, and Christopher was employed by W. O. Smith at Union Market. They had four daughters: Evelyn (Martinkus), Marie (Mazeika), Florence (Murphy), and Nina (McGleam). All the girls were married in America. Christopher died October 14, 1953, and is buried in Chicago at a Georgian cemetery. Barbara died January 16, 1988, in Spooner, Wisconsin, with burial in Elmwood Cemetery, River Grove, Illinois.

Jimshet Lomadze was born in the village of Mamati. His parents died when he was little and at the age of seventeen or eighteen he moved to Ozurgeti. He had two wives and eight children. He died in 1951 and his family was in exile from 1951 to 1954. The family lost all their papers and family possessions.

Silovan Kartvelishvili opened a textile and fabric shop in Lanchkhuti with the money he had earned in America. The cotton cloth (calico) was expensive at that time. Here is a story told by his wife to his grandson. "Once a beautiful young lady came into the shop and asked 'What is the price for one meter of cotton?' Silovan answered, 'It is very expensive – one kiss.' The lady replied, "Let me go and ask my brothers." The lady came back shortly with her brothers, who told Silovan to cut 25 meters of the cloth. Silovan could not refuse and gave her 25 meters. The lady started to kiss him on the forehead, eyes, and so on. The brothers were counting." Silovan's business behavior resulted in his going bankrupt.

Panteleimon Tsintsadze was the son of Tarkhan Tsintsadze a tradesman in Lanchkhuti. Panteleimon received a good education and studied foreign languages: English, French and Italian. He was one of the leaders of the Georgian riders, and was known to have used the name Georgian in America. He lived in Chicago and worked as a firm administrator off and on and married the owner's daughter. His wife was a professor at the Chicago University and they had one daughter. Pateleimon returned to Georgia in 1918 and married Elpite Tsheishvili. They had three Children, but two (twins Shalva and Niko) died early. He worked for the local government and started collective farming in Lanchkhuti. Elpite died in child birth to a daughter Tamar. He died suddenly from the flu in 1936 and is buried in Lanchkhuti. Tamar also died giving birth to Ketevan. Ketevan's children Eteri and Aleco Jintcharadze provided this history.

Vaso Tsuladze was born in 1884. He first appeared in America in 1910 with the Buffalo Bill and Pawnee Bill show. Vaso's grandchild told this story. "Some drunk Russian general and his fellows beat up several Lanchkhutian without any reason in Batumi. Vaso heard this story in Lanchkhuti and discovered that the general was supposed to travel through the area by train. Vaso Tsuladze called on some people and armed men who stopped the train near the Lanchkhuti station. They entered the coaches and started looking for the general. Vaso found him, beat him up and took away his golden cigarette case. Vaso went to the United States. After the 1917 revolution he came back to Georgia and lived in Lanchkhuti for three years and when Soviet Russia annexed the Independent Georgia in February 1921, Tsuladze fled to France. He then immigrated to America and by 1930 was a U.S. citizen, at age forty-five. He arrived in Plymouth on September 20, 1930, on the SS Stateman, and was listed as a showman. He lived and died in the United States.

The historical record is silent about many other Georgians who rode in American Wild West shows. Here are the names of Georgians reported as working in American Wild West shows, but unable to identify which show and in what year.

Imnadze Antadze
Serapion Antadze
Malkhaz Antadze
Ivane Avaliani
Iosebi (Dianosi) Baramidze
Silovani Chkhartishvili
Niko Chkonia
Sergia Gvarjalia
Mikhako Imnadze
Nadro Iorashvili (Andro?)
Jimsheri Jorbenadze
Varden Kvitaishvili
Giorgi Maximelishvili
Kote Meskhi

Lauri Mshvidobadze
Raphael Mshvidobadze
Khalampre Murvanidze
Silovan Pataraia
Ioseb Tsintsadze
Siko Tvaladze
Ermile Urushadze
Nipito (first name only)

Teophane Kavtaradze with Dog
Author's Collection
Plate No. 44

BIBLIOGRAPHY

Allen, Charles W. *From Fort Laramie to Wounded Knee in the West That Was.* University of Nebraska Press, Lincoln, 1997.

Blackstone, Sarah J. *Buckskins, Bullets & Business,* Greenwood Press, Westport Conn., 1986.

Buffalo Bill's Wild West, Historical Sketches & Programme, Chicago, IL, 1893.

Bloyd, Levi H. *Campbell Brothers Great Consolidated Shows.* Fairbury, NE, Holloway Pub. Company, 1957.

Brooklyn Museum, The. *Buffalo Bill and the Wild West.* New York, The Brooklyn Museum, 1981.

Burke, John M. *Buffalo Bill From Prairie to Palace.* Chicago, Rand, McNally & Co. 1893.

Burke, John. *Buffalo Bill The Noblest Whiteskin.* New York, G.P. Putnam's Sons, 1973.

Chindahl, George Leonard. *A History of the Circus In America.* Caldwell, Idaho, The Caxton Printers, Ltd., 1959.

Cody, Louisa Frederici. *Memories of Buffalo Bill.* [In collaboration with Courtney Ryley Cooper] New York, D. Appleton & Co. 1919.

Collings, Ellsworth and Alma Miller England. *The 101 Ranch.* University of Oklahoma Press, Norman, 1937.

Coxe, Antony Hippisley, *A Seat At the Circus,* Evans Brothers Limited, London, 1951.

Croft-Cooke, Rupert and Meadmore, W.S. *Buffalo Bill, The Legend, The Man of Action, the Showman.* Sidgwick and Jackson, Ltd., London, 1952.

Croft-Cooke, Rupert & Cotes, Peter. *Circus, A World History.* Macmillan Publishing Co., Inc. New York, 1977.

Croy, Homer. *Jesse James Was My Neighbor.* New York: Duell, Sloan, and Pearce, 1949.

Culhane, John. T*he American Circus, An Illustrated History.* Henry Holt and Company, New York, 1990.

Dean, Frank E. *Trick and Fancy Riding.* The Caxton Printers, Ltd. Caldwell, Idaho, 1975.

Dzhigitovka Book concerning Russian trick riding. No further information available

Edholm, Charlton Lawrence. *Technical World Magazine.* "In Filmland by the Pacific."

Emerson, Edwin, Jr. *Roughriders From Far Frontiers.* Denver Public Library, WH72, Cody Box 6. Unknown publication.

Fellows, Dexter W. *This Way to The Big Show,* Garden City, New York, Halcyon House, 1938.

Foreman, Carolyn Thomas. *Indians Abroad.* University of Oklahoma Press, Norman, 1943.

Fowler, Gene. *Timberline, A Story of Bonfils and Tammen.* Blue Ribbon Books, Inc., New York City, 1933.

Fox, Charles Philip, *Circus Parades, A Pictorial History of America's Greatest Pageant,* Watkins Glen, NY, Century House, 1953.

Friedlaender. *Vaulting*

Gallop, Alan. *Buffalo Bill's British Wild West.* Sutton Publishing Limited, Gloucestershire, 2001.

Gipson, Fred. *Fabulous Empire: Colonel Zack Miller's Story.* Boston: Houghton Mifflin, 1946.

Gollmar, Robert H. *My Father Owned a Circus.* Caldwell, Id: Caxton Printers. Ltd., 1965.

Griffin, Al. *"Step Right Up Folks!"* Henry Regnery Co. Chicago, 1974.

Griffin, Charles Eldridge. *Four Years in Europe with Buffalo Bill.* Albia, Iowa, Stage Publishing Co. 1908.

Hanes, Bailey C., Col., *Bill Pickett Bulldogger, The Biography of a Black Cowboy.* University of Oklahoma, Norman, OK, 1977.

Havinghurst, Walter. *Annie Oakley of the Wild West.* The Macmillan Co., NY, 1954.

Hittman, Michael, edited by Lynch, Don. *Wovoka and The Ghost Dance.* Pg 12-19.

Josephy, Alvin M. Jr. *Wounded Knee Lest We Forget,* Buffalo Bill Historical Center, 1990. Article: Wounded Knee: a History. Pg 10-27.

Koblas, John. *The Great Cole Younger and Frank James Historical Wild West Show,* North Star Press of St. Cloud Inc, Minnesota, 2002.

Lang, David Marshall. *A Modern History of Soviet Georgia,* Grove Press Inc., New York, 1962.

Makharadze, Irakli & Chkhaidze, Akaki. *Wild West Georgians,* New Media, Tbilisi, 2001.

McCoy, Tim & McCoy, Ronald. *Tim McCoy Remembers the West.* New York, Doubleday & co. Inc., 1977.

Miller, David Humphreys. *Ghost Dance,* Duell, Sloan & Pearce, NY, 1959.

Mix, Paul E. *The Life and Legend of Tom Mix.* South Brunswick and New York, A.S. Barnes and Company London: Thomas Yoseloff Ltd. 1972.

Moses, Lester George, *Wild West Shows and The Images of American Indians,* University of New Mexico Press, 1996.

Ogden, Tom. *Two Hundred Years of The American Circus.* Facts On File, 1993.

Parker, Lew. *Odd People I Have Met* (privately printed, n.d.)

Parkinson, Tom and Fox, Charles Philip. *The Circus Moves By Rail.* Pruett Publishing

Co., Boulder CO. 1978.

Paxson, Frederic L. *The Last American Frontier.* New York, MacMillan. 1910.

Poole, Ernest. *The Bridge, My Own Story.* New York, MacMillian Co. 1940.

Posey, Jake. *Last of the 40-Horse Drives,* New York, Vantage Press Inc. 1959.

Reynolds, Chang. *101 Ranch Wild West 1907-1916.* Bandwagon, Vol. 13, No. 1 (Jan-Feb), 1969, p. 4-21.

Robinson, Josephine DeMott. *The Circus Lady.* New York, Arno Press, 1980.

Rosa, Joseph G & May, Robin. *Buffalo Bill and His Wild West: A Pictorial Biography.* University Press of Kansas, 1989.

Russell, Don. *The Wild West: A History of the Wild West Shows.* Fort Worth, Amon Carter Museum of Western Art, 1970.

Sayers, Isabella S. *Annie Oakley and Buffalo Bill's Wild West,* Dover Publications, Inc., NY 1981.

Sell, Henry Blackman & Weybright, Victor, *Buffalo Bill and the Wild West,* New York, Oxford University Press, 1955.

Seymour, Forrest W. Sitanka, *The Full Story of Wounded Knee,* The Christopher Publishing House, W. Hanover, Mass. 1981.

Shirley, Glenn (ed). *Buckskin Joe.* Lincoln: University of Nebraska Press, 1966.

Shirley, Glenn, *Pawnee Bill.* University of New Mexico Press, Albuquerque, 1958.

Tsamtsishvili, Amiran, *The Georgian Riders Abroad,* Tbilisi, U.S.S.R., 1958, translated by Nana Khizanishvili.

Tatler, The. London. Various Issues

Tompkins, Charles H. *"Gabriel Brothers Wild West,"* The Westerners Brand Book, [Chicago] XIII (October, 1956)

Walsh, Richard J. *The Making of Buffalo Bill.* A.L. Burt Company, New York, 1928.

Wetmore, Helen Cody. *Last of the Great Scouts.* New York, Grosset & Dunlap. 1899.

Willson, Dixie. *Where the World Folds Up At Night.* New York, D. Appleton & Co., 1932.

Wilson, Robert Lawrence. with Martin, Greg. *Buffalo Bill's Wild West An American Legend,* Random House, New York, 1998.

Winch, Frank. *Thrilling Lives of Buffalo Bill, Colonel William F. Cody, Last of the Great Scouts, and Pawnee Bill, Major Gordon W. Lillie, White Chief of the Pawnee.* New York, S.L. Parsons & Co., 1911.

Yost, Nellie Snyder, *Buffalo Bill his Family, Friends, Fame, Failures and Fortunes,* The Swallow Press Inc., Chicago, 1979.

SOURCE NOTES

1. The Cossack Counter Revolution, The New Times, Minneapolis, Minnesota, December 29, 1917.
2. Dee Brown, The American West, A Touchstone book, Simon & Schuster, New York, p. 388.
3. Amiran Tsamtsishvili, The Georgian Riders Aboard, Tbilisi, 1958.
4. Indians Must Stay at Home. New York Times, October 1, 1890, p. 8 col. 4.
5. Georgian Riding Games, Kapiton Nachkehia, pps 45 and 46.
6. Amiran Tsamtsishvili, The Georgian Riders Aboard, Tbilisi, 1958.
7. Interview with Alika Jorbenadze, Batumi, Republic of Georgia, 7 and 8 November 2002.
8. News from Batumi. Iveria, No. 127, Friday, June 19, 1892, p 2.
9. Our Interviews. The Red Man "On Tour." The Oracle, May 28, 1892, p. 12.
10. New York Clipper, April 20, 1889, p. 97.
11. Buffalo Bill's Wild West. Omaha Daily Bee, June 19, 1892, p. 12 col. 1.
12. Frederic Remington, "Buffalo Bill in London," Harper's Weekly, Vol. XXXVI, No. 1863, Saturday, September 3, 1892.
13. Alan Gallop, Buffalo Bill's British Wild West, (Sutton Publishing), Thrupp, England, 2001.
14. Nate Salsbury, "Wild West at Windsor," The Colorado Magazine, volume XXXII, July Cossacks, Indians & Buffalo Bill / 1955, pp. 208- 211.
15. Exhibited Before Queen Victoria. Brooklyn Daily Eagle, Sunday, June 26, 1892.
16. Court Notice. The London Times, Monday, June 27, 1892.
17. Joseph G. Rose and Robin May, Buffalo Bill and His Wild West, A Pictorial Biography, University Press of Kansas, p. 156.
18. Advance of the Plague. The Brooklyn Daily Eagle, August 26, 1892, p. 1.
19 Last of the Wild West. The New York Times, October 13, 1892, p. 5.
20. The Forepaugh Show Sold. New York Times, January 14, 1892, p. 1.
21. Abstract from Paris Journal, Petit Journal. Iveria, No 36. February 19, 1893, p 2 col. 4.
22. Towed Into Port, Her Shaft Broken, New York Herald, Thursday, March 30, 1893, p. 14 col. 1.
23. From the Russian Frontier. The New York Daily Tribune, Thursday, March 30, 1893, p. 7 col. 4.
24. The Circus Cossacks, New York Times, Friday, March 31, 1893, p. 8 col. 5.
25. Interview with Tsutsuna Jincharadze, Onchiketi, Chokhatauri, The Republic of Georgia, May 19, 2002.
26. Under the White Tent. New York Clipper, April 22, 1893, p. 100 col. 2.
27. Forepaugh's Circus, The Philadelphia Inquirer, Sunday, April 9, 1893.
28. Last Evening's Entertainments, The Philadelphia Inquirer, Tuesday, April 18, 1893.
29. Dramatic Doings, The Pittsburg Dispatch, Sunday, April 30, 1893, p. 18, col. 2.
30. The Circus Comes to Town. The Washington Post, Monday, April 24, 1893, p. 5, col. 2.
31. Pass On Into The Big Show, The Washington Post, Tuesday, April 25, 1893, p. 2 col. 5.
32. Circus World Museum, Forepaugh collection, Adam Forepaugh 1893 Route book, p. 51.
33. Cossacks at Church. The Pittsburgh Post, Monday, May 1, 1893, p. 2, col. 2.

34. The Circus. The Pittsburgh Post, Tuesday, May 2, 1893, p. 2 col. 4.
35. Circus World Museum, Forepaugh collection, Adam Forepaugh 1893 Route book, p. 60.
36. Circus World Museum, Forepaugh collection, Adam Forepaugh 1893 Route book, p. 64. And p. 70.
37. New York Clipper, June 24, 1893, p. 249, col. 2.
38. The White City. The Cleveland Plaindealer, Monday, July 10, 1893, p. 8, col. 1.
39. Four Cossacks. New York Dramatic Mirror, July 29, 1893, p. 8, col 4.
40. Circus World Museum, Forepaugh collection, Adam Forepaugh 1893 Route book, p.76.
41. Ibid., p. 78.
42. How Circus People Live. Topeka State Journal, Tuesday, August 29, 1893, p. 1, col. 4.
43. In and About the Circus. The Kansas City Star, Monday, September 11, 1893, p. 5, col. 1.
44. National Archives, New York Passenger List, M237, Roll 606, SS Persian Monarch.
45. Thousands See the Wild West. Chicago Tribune, Monday, May 8, 1893.
46. President Palmer Resigns. Brooklyn Daily Eagle, July 1, 1893, p. 4.
47. Caravels Reach Chicago. New York Times, July 8, 1893, p. 8.
48. Girt by Flames High in Air. New York Times, July 11, 1893, p. 1.
49. My Fine Buffalo Bill, The Omaha Bee, Sunday, July 23, 1893, p. 16 col. 3.
50. Interview with Ketino Vashalomidze, Anaseuli, Ozurgeti, Guria, Republic of Georgia, August 4, 2001.
51. Interview with Givi Mskhaladze, Makvaneti, Ozurgeti, Republic of Georgia, August 15, 2001.
52. Interview with Dali Avaliani, Ozurgeti, Guria, Republic of Georgia, August 27, 2001.
53. Bridgeport Public Library, Historic collection, Box McCaddon materials 1987.15, Bailey's History.
54. Miscellaneous. New York Clipper, March 9, 1894, p. 7 col 3.
55. Chief of The Steppes. San Francisco Chronicle, Tuesday, January 23, 1894, p. 12 col. 5/6.
56. Mail and Sailing. The London Times, March 12, 1894, p. 10 col 4.
57. Marine Intelligence. New York Times, Wednesday, March 21, 1894, p. 6 col 5.
58. Hertzberg Circus Museum, San Antonio, TX, Box 3A133, Barnum & Bailey 1894 Program.
59. Hertzberg Circus Museum, San Antonio, TX, Box 3A134, Courier Collection, Barnum & Bailey 1894. p. 4.
60. Hertzberg Circus Museum, San Antonio, TX, Box 3D4, Route Book, p. 43.
61. Wonders of Barnum. The Washington Post, Tuesday, May 8, 1898, p. 8 col 3.
62. Hertzberg Circus Museum, San Antonio, TX, Box 3D4, Route Book, p. 45 & 46.
63. World's Riders with Buffalo Bill. New York Times, Wednesday, May 2, 1894, p. 8 col. 2.
64. Mail and Sailing. The London Times, April 23, 1894.
65. Marine Intelligence. New York Times, Wednesday, May 2, 1894, p. 6 col 1.
66. In and About Wall Street. New York Times, Thursday, May 3, 1894, p. 10.
67. Expert Rough Riding. The Brooklyn Daily Eagle, Thursday, May 10, 1894.
68. Daring Feats by Horsemen. New York Times, May 10, 1894, p. 9 col. 2.

69. Delighted Twenty Thousand. New York Times, May 13, 1894, p. 2.
70. Life at the Wild West Show. New York Times, Saturday, June 9, 1894.
71. Close of the Wild West. New York Daily Tribune, Sunday, October 7, 1894, p. 8 col. 1.
72. Under the Same Business Management. New York Times, Sunday, January 6, 1895.
73. McCaddon Memoirs, McCaddon Papers, 1987.15, Bridgeport Public Library, History Collection.
74. Marine Intelligence. New York Times.
75. Marine Intelligence. New York Times, Sunday, April 14, 1895, p. 7 col 3.
76. The Sunday Item, Philadelphia, April 28, 1895.
77. The Wild West Show. The Orange Chronicle, Orange NJ, Saturday, September 28, 1895, p. 4 col. 3.
78. New York Clipper, May 18, 1895, p. 165 col. 2.
79. New York Clipper, May 25, 1895, p. 179 col. 3.
80. Miscellaneous. New York Clipper, August 17, 1895, p. 374 col. 4.
81. Buffalo Bill's Discipline. New York Dramatic Mirror, September 28, 1895, p. 3 col. 4.
82. Thought He was in Russia. New York Times, Tuesday, September 24, 1895, p. 10.
83. Horsemen of the World. The Sun, Baltimore, Monday, September 30, 1895, p. 10, col. 3.
84. Cowboys and Indians. Baltimore American, Monday, September 30, 1895, p. 8, col 6.
85. All Are Rough Riders. The Washington Post, Thursday, October 3, 1895, p. 4 col. 1.
86. The Wild West Show. The News and Observer, Raleigh, NC, Thursday, October 10, 1895, p. 5 col. 2.
87. Marine Intelligence. New York Times, April 12, 1896, p. 14 col 3.
88. Ready For The Big Show. Chicago Tribune, Monday, June 1, 1896.
89. Chicago Evening Post, June 6, 1896.
90. Sixteen Thousand. Daily News-Tribune, Muscatine, Iowa, October 3, 1896.
91. Stopped The Show. Daily Chronicle, Wednesday, August 12, 1896.
92. Great Performances. Saturday Times, South Bend, Indiana, Saturday, August 15, 1896.
93. Col. Cody's Motley Crowd. The Times, Kansas City, October 19, 1896.
94. Buffalo Bill's Return. Brooklyn Daily Eagle, Saturday, March 27, 1897.
95. Village Mamati Charity. Cnobis Furceli, #91, January 21, 1897.
96. Weather. London Times, March 27, 1897, p. 13 col 3.
97. Marine Intelligence. New York Times.
98. Weather. New York Times, Sunday, April 5, 1897, p.1 col 1.
99. From Caucasus. Boston Journal, Sunday, May 23, 1897.
100. Buffalo Bill's Show. The Evening News, Toronto, Canada, Tuesday, July 6, 1897, p. 2 col. 2.
101. Worship The Colonel. The Herald, July 23, 1897.
102. Warrant for "Buffalo Bill." New York Times, August 8, 1897, p. 1.
103. The Wild West's Shows. The Indianapolis News, Saturday, August 28, 1897.
104. Buffalo Bill's Big Parade. The Dispatch, August 31, 1897.
105. The Nashville Banner, October 8, 1897.
106. Shipping and Mail. New York Times, Wednesday, October 20, 1897, p. 4 col. 6.
107. Buffalo Bill in the City. Lebanon, Pennsylvania, Daily News, June 22, 1898.
108. Port of New York, Arrived. New York Herald, Saturday, March 19, 1898, p. 12 col. 3.

109. Rough Riders At The Garden. New York Daily Tribune, Thursday, March 31, 1898.
110. Behind The Scenes at a Wild West Show. Harper's Weekly, April 30, 1898, p. 422.
111. Crowds See Show Arrive. Virginian-Pilot, Norfolk, Virginia Monday, May 26, 1913, p. 9 col. 3.
112. Wild, Wild, West. Philadelphia Inquirer, Thursday, May 5, 1898.
113. 15,000 People Applaud the "Wild West." The Item, Thursday, May 5, 1898.
114. Wild Western Life. The Evening Telegraph, Thursday, May 5, 1898.
115. Big Pow Wow at the Continental. Newark Daily Advertiser, Saturday, May 21, 1898, p. 3 col. 6.
116. Stuck in the Mud. The Hartford Daily Courant, Saturday, May 28, 1898.
117. Col. Cody's Cossacks. Friday, June 3, 1898. BBHC scrapbook.
118. The Evening News, Detroit, Thursday, July 14, 1898.
119. Two Large Audiences. Wheeling, Intelligencer, Tuesday, July 5, 1898.
120. A Few Plain Questions. The Brooklyn Daily Eagle, October 23, 1898, p. 33.
121. Interview with Magnolia Cheishvili-Lomadze, Ozurgeti, Guria, Republic of Georgia, November 2001.
122. Legal Notices. New York Times, November 18, 1898, p. 10.
123. The New York Dramatic Mirror, April 1, 1899, p. 17 col. 2.
124. Along the Water Front. Boston Sunday Post, March 26, 1899, p. 6 col .7.
125. Chat With Cody. The St. Louis Star, Wednesday, October 4, 1899.
126. Boy's Skull Fractured. The Morning Herald, Baltimore, Tuesday, April 18, 1899.
127. Panic After Crash. The Commercial Tribune, Wednesday May 8, 1899.
128. Two Showmen were Burned. The Weekly Tribune, Beaver Falls, PA., Wednesday, August 2, 1899, p. 5 col. 5.
129. Col. Cody Is Here. The Evening News, Detroit, Michigan, August 12, 1899.
130. Gossip. The New York Dramatic Mirror, Saturday, October 21, 1899, p. 17 col. 1.
131. Port of New York, Arrived. New York Herald, Sunday, April 15, 1900. p. 10 col. 1.
132. Buffalo Bill The Man and the Horse! Lewiston Saturday Journal, June 9, 1900.
133. Wild West Wreck. The Detroit Free Press, Monday, July 30, 1900, p. 1 col. 3.
134. Preached To Cowboys. The Minneapolis Tribune, Monday, August 13, 1900.
135. An Odd Crowd. The Minneapolis Tribune, Monday, August 13, 1900.
136. People Of All Nations. Louisiana Missouri Press, September 27, 1900, p. 10 col. 6.
137. The Friesland In Port. The New York Times, Thursday, November 22, 1900, p. 6 col. 7.
138. The Wild West. The Daily Pantagraph, Bloomington, Ill, August 20, 1900, p. 3 col. 2.
139. Editorial. The Messenger, Phoenixville, PA., Thursday, May 10, 1900, p. 2 col. 1.
140. Wild West Attack on a Saloon. The Philadelphia Inquirer, Tuesday, May 15, 1900.
141. Indians From Wild West Show Engaged Italians in a Riot. The North American, Philadelphia, Tuesday, May 15, 1900, p. 4 col. 4.
142. A First Rate Exhibition. The Jackson Daily Citizen, Friday, July 20, 1900, p. 6 col. 4.
143. Ticket Seller was Arrested. Lansing Journal, Friday, July 29, 1900, p. 1 col. 4.
144. Mt. Clems Monitor, July 27, 1900, p. 1.
145. Pawnee Bill's Wild West. The Clare Sentinel, Friday, August 3, 1900, p. 1 col. 5.
146. From Saturday's Daily. Semi-Weekly Iowa State Reporter, Tuesday, September 18, 1900, p. 8 col. 2.
147. Interview with Tsutsuna Jincharadze, Onchiketi, Chokhatauri, The Republic of

Georgia, May 19, 2002.

148. Buffalo Bill is Here. The New York Times, April 1, 1901, p. 7 col. 2.
149. Prince Lucca Hurt. The St. Louis Star, Tuesday, May 14, 1901, p. 3 col. 3.
150. Buffalo Bill's Historical Center, Cody Wyoming, Microfilm scrapbook, 1, 1901.
151. Buffalo Bill Here. The Battle Creek Moon, July 9, 1901, p. 8 col. 3.
152. Wordy War in the Camp. The Chicago Record-Herald, Monday, July 15, 1901, p. 4 col. 3.
153. Buffalo Bill's Train Wrecked. Charlotte News, Tuesday evening, October 29, 1901, p. 1.
154. Ninety-Two Horses Killed. Charlotte Daily Observer, Wednesday, October 30, 1901, p. 1.
155. Did you hear about Buffalo Bill's Wild West Show? by Franklin Scarborough, Salisbury Post
156. The Wild West Show. The Evening News, Kenosha, Ill., Wednesday, May 29, 1901.
157. Season 1901, Official Route Book of the Pawnee Bill Wild West Show. p. 33.
158. Rain Stopped Wild West Show. The Minneapolis Times, Saturday, 29, 1901, p. 7 col. 4.
159. Circus Tents Blown Down; But One Child is Injured. The Minneapolis Tribune, Saturday, 29, 1901, p. 2 col. 2.
160. Cossack who Fell. The Arkansas Democrat, Monday, October 21, 1901.
161. Ninety-two Horses Killed. Charlotte Daily Observer, Wednesday, October 30, 1901, p. 1.
162. 74 Horses Saved. Charlotte News, November 1, 1901.
163. Tent Shows. Billboard, January 3, 1902, p. 4.
164. David Marshall Lang, A Modern History of Soviet Georgia, New York: Grove Press, Inc., 1962, p. 142.
165. Thirty Rioters Killed. The Nebraska State Journal, Monday, March 24, 1902, p. 1 col. 3.
166. When Lemonade was Pink. The Montgomery Advertiser, Sunday, October 13, 1912, p. 7 col. 1.
167. Tent Troopers, Buckskin Bill. Billboard, May 10, 1902.
168. Had a Real Joint. The Emporia Gazette, Tuesday, August 19, 1902.
169. Buckskin Bill Suffered. The Paducah Sun, April 26, 1902, p. 5 col. 4.
170. The Paducah News-Democrat, May 16, 1902, p. 3 and May 22, p. 4.
171. Tame Wild West. The Messenger, Owensboro, KY, Saturday Morning, May 10, 1902, p. 6 col. 3.
172. Will Probably be Cleared. Portsmouth Times, Ohio, Saturday, June 28, 1902, p. 5 col. 1.
173. Throngs Witness Performance of Buckskin Bill's Troupe of Rough Riders. The Washington Post, Tuesday, July 1, 1902, p.2.
174. Accident. The Newark Advocate, Saturday, July 12, 1902, p. 6 col. 4.
175. Word with Bill. Topeka State Journal, Friday, August 15, 1902, p. 5 col. 1.
176. Sheriff Shot First. Idaho Daily Statesman, Wednesday September 10, 1902, p. 2 col. 3.
177. Many Saw Wild West Show. The Arkansas Gazette, Tuesday, October 28, 1902.
178. Buffalo Bill's Show Coming. The New York Times, Sunday, April 13, 1902, p. 15 col. 3.
179. With the Wild West Show. New York Daily Tribune, Sunday, April 20, 1902, p. 12 col. 1.

180. A Fight at the Wild West. Brooklyn Daily Eagle, Tuesday, May 6, 1902, p. 1 col. 5.
181. The Wild West Here. Philadelphia Inquirer, Sunday, May 11, 1902.
182. Breezes. New York Clipper, Issues June 28, July 5, and July 19, 1902.
183. Buffalo Bill Here. Minneapolis Journal, Saturday, July 26, 1902.
184. Buffalo Bill's Fist Settles The Dust. Los Angles Daily Times, September 25, 1902.
185. Buffalo Bill Has Drawn on Many Lands. The Daily Picayune, New Orleans, November 2, 1902.
186. Jake Posey, With Buffalo Bill in Europe, Bandwagon, October, 1953 p. 4-6. 565.
187. Nathan Salsbury's Funeral. New York Times, December 29, 1902, p. 7.
188. Alan Gallop, Buffalo Bill's British Wild West, Gloucestershire, Sutton Publishing Ltd., 2001. p. 213.
189. 7000 Saw Wild West Show. Blue Ridge Zephyr, Waynesboro, PA., Saturday, May 24, 1902, p. 3 col. 3.
190. Pawnee Bill's Show. Delaware County Democrat, Chester, PA., May 8, 1902, p. 3 col. 3.
191. Pawnee Bill. The North Carolinian, Elizabeth City, Thursday, May 15, 1902, p. 3 col. 3.
192. Wild West Here. The News, Frederick, Maryland, May 20, 1902, p. 2 col. 2.
193. Pawnee Bill's Show. The News, Frederick, Maryland, May 21, 1902, p. 3 col. 3.
194. Pawnee Bill Came to Grief. Shenandoah Herald, Woodstock, VA, October 24, 1902.
195. Big Circus Combination. New York Dramatic Mirror, July 26, 1902, p. 3 col. 3.
196. New York Dramatic Mirror, October 4, 1902, p. 17 col. 3.
197. A Letter from Paris. Tsnobis Purtseli, (Newsletter) No. 2124, April 16, 1903 (Julian old style), p. 3.
198. Circus Men to Harvest Fields. The Daily Nonparcil, Council Bluffs, Friday, July 17, 1903, p. 1 col. 2.
199. Letters from London. Tsnobis Purtseli, (Newsletter) No. 2120, April 12, 1903, p. 2.
200. Lady Colin Campbell, A Woman's Walks. The World, London, January 6, 1903.
201. Royalty at Wild West Show. New York Daily Tribune, Sunday, March 15, 1903, p. 3 col. 3.
202. The Wild West, [unknown newspaper from Manchester], April 26, 1903, Buffalo Bill. Historical Center microfilm scrapbook.
203. Jake Posey. Last of the 40-Horse Drivers, New York, Vantage Press, Inc., 1959, p. 56.
204. John Koblas. The Great Cole Younger and Frank James Historical Wild West Show, St. Cloud, Minnesota, North Star Press of St. Cloud, Inc., p. 75.
205. Tantlinger Diaries, 1903, The University of Oklahoma, Western History Collection, No. 886. p.15.
206. Bandits in Days Gone. The Louisville Herald, Tuesday, August 18, 1903, p. 10 col. 3.
207. Cole Younger in Jail. The Humeston New Era, Wednesday, September 30, 1903, col. 2.
208. Must be Pretty Bad. The Paducah Sun, September 23, 1903, p. 2 col. 4.
209. Struck for Pay. The Daily Oklahoman, Wednesday, September 30, 1903.
210. The Wild and Wooly West. The Bowie Blade, Friday, October 9, 1903, p. 3 col. 1.
211. Cowboy Tried To Stop A St. Louis Street Car. St. Louis Globe Democrat, Saturday, April 18, 1903, p. 16.
212. Alexis A. Georgian v. Demetri Dcinsadze (Dimitri Tsintsadze), 107614, 4th Judicial District, State of Minnesota, (Jan 9, 1909).

213. The Luella Forepaugh-Fish Wild West show. The Chillicothe Daily Constitution, Missouri, Thursday, May 7, 1903, col. 3.
214. Hard Luck for Circus. The Daily Nonpareil, Council Bluff, Iowa, Thursday, May 28, 1903.
215. Show Car is Burned. Ashland Daily Press, Tuesday, June 23, 1903, col. 2.
216. Reminiscences of George Leonard, Minnesota Historical Society, Manuscript #185, dated 1954, p 24, Box 11.
217. Cossack is Arrested. Evening Times-Republican, Marshalltown, Iowa, Tuesday, July 14, 1903. p. 7 col. 5.
218. Indian wants to Kill Whiteman. The Janesville Daily Gazette, Monday, July 27, 1903.
219. Indians Await Transportation. The Janesville Daily Gazette, Thursday, July 30, 1903.
220. Mr. and Mrs. Fish. The Janesville Daily Gazette, Wednesday, August 5, 1903, p.2 col. 3.
221. Bad Luck for Wild West Show. The Janesville Daily Gazette, Monday, August 3, 1903.
222. In Hard Straits. The Daily Mining Journal, Marquette, MI, Friday, August 14, 1903, p. 6 col. 3.
223. Cossack Wants his Cash Bad. Janesville Daily Gazette, Monday, November 23, 1903.
224. Explosion. Billboard, June 6, 1903, p. 7 col. 1.
225. Pawnee Bill Brings a Trend of Events. The Xenia Gazette, Tuesday, May 26, 1903, p. 8 col. 1.
226. Local News. Franklin Evening News, Tuesday, September 1, 1903, p. 2 col. 4.
227. Was a Great Storm. The Semi-Weekly Enterprise, Cambridge Springs, PA, Tuesday, September 1, 1903, p. 1 col. 3.
228. The Wild West in Great Shape. The Evening Times, Cumberland, Maryland, Tuesday, 9, 1903, p. 1 col. 4.
229. Edwin H. Low Drowned. New York Times, Sunday, July 19, 1903, p.1 col 5.
230. Alex Georgian's Ideas of the War. The Janesville Daily Gazette, Saturday, March 5, 1904, p.2 col. 3.
231. Greater Foe Than Japan. Winona Republican Herald, March 23, 1904, p. 2.
232. J. Delmar Andrews Leaves Tuesday for Fort Worth. The Perry Daily Chief, Sunday, April 3, 1904, col. 2.
233. Russia Has Her Troubles. The Daily Times, Oklahoma City, Wednesday, April 20, 1904, p. 1 col. 1.
234. Russian Officer. The Daily Oklahoman, Thursday, April 21, 1904, p. 1.
235. Alan Gallop. Buffalo Bill's British Wild West, Gloucestershire, Sutton Publishing Ltd., 2001, p. 237.
236. From Buffalo Bill's Wild West. Billboard, September 24, 1904 p. 19.
237. Alan Gallop. Buffalo Bill's British Wild West, Gloucestershire, Sutton Publishing Ltd., 2001, p. 239.
238. Happy Day for Small Boy. The Sioux City Journal, Thursday, May 19, 1904.
239. Ibid.
240. Cossacks are Cruel. The Sioux City Daily Tribune, Thursday, May 19, 1904, p. 2 col. 3.
241. The Circus. The Neola Reporter, Thursday, July 7, 1904, p. 5 col. 6.
242. Campbell Brothers' Circus. Fairbault County Register, Blue Earth, MN, Thursday,

July 28, 1904, p. 1 col. 3.
243. Gorilla Runs Circus Train. El Reno Daily Globe, September 28, 1904.
244 Day by Day with Barnum & Bailey. April 20, New York City, p. 65.
245. Hisses for Show Cossacks. The St. Louis Republic, June 5, 1904, Part II p. 15.
246. The Show. The Daily Republican, Phoenixville, PA, May 23, 1904, p. 1 col. 5.
247. Tent Shows. Billboard, June 4, 1904, p. 6.
248. Pawnee Bill's show. The Evening Star, Thursday, June 2, 1904, p. 3 col. 2.
249. Pawnee Bill's Wild West Show. The Washington Times, Thursday, June 2, 1904, col. 1.
250. Poole, Ernest. The Bridge, My Own Story, New York, Macmillan Co, 1940, p. 160.
251. Wild West in Paris. The New York Herald, Paris Edition, Sunday, March 5, 1905, p. 6 col. 3.
252. Buffalo Bill's Divorce. The New York Herald, Paris Edition, Friday, March 10, 1905, p. 1 col. 2.
253. The Russian Labour Troubles. The Times, Friday, February 24, 1905, p. 5 col. 3.
254. Wild West Cossacks' Strike. The New York Times, Wednesday, May 10, 1905.
255. Wild West Provincial Tour. The New York Herald, Paris Edition, August 19, 1905.
256. Circus Gossip. Billboard, December 16, 1905, p. 16.
257. Wild West Minus Horses. New York Times, December 8, 1905, p.1.
258. Circus in Town. Nebraska State Journal, Thursday, May 11, 1905.
259. Local Interest. Austin Daily Herald, June 22, 1905, p. 2 col. 1.
260. Local Interest. Austin Daily Herald, June 23, 1905, p. 2 col. 1.
261. Tent Shows. Billboard, November 8, 1905.
262. Animals did not Escape. Galveston Daily News, Friday, November 10, 1905, p.7 col. 4.
263. John F. Polacsek. Seeing the Elephant: The McCaddon International Circus of 1905. Bandwagon, September-October 1982, p. 13-19.
264. Grafting French Officials Ruined the McCaddon Show. New York Telegraph, September 2, 1905.
265. Bearded Lady's Sad Story. August 1905, Princeton University Library, TC040, Scrapbook #14.
266. May 4, 1905 Telegram. Princeton University Library, TC040, Box 7, folder #4.
267. To the Editor of the Herald. The New York Herald, Paris edition, Wednesday, August 30, 1905, p. 7 col. 3.
268. Grafting French Officials Ruined the McCaddon Show. New York Telegraph, October 2, 1905.
269. My Darling Wife...Devotedly your love, Joe. Circus World Museum achives.
270. Bearded Lady's Sad Story. August 1905. Princeton University Library, TC040, Scrapbook #14.
271. Vicissitudes of the Professional Showman. New York Herald, Paris Edition, Sunday, September 3, 1905, p. 2 col. 2.
272. Unlucky Showman Comes Home. New York Daily Tribune, Saturday, December 9, 1905, p. 7 col. 5.
273. Storm Wrecks Circus. Decatur Daily Review, Tuesday, September 12, 1905, p. 2 col. 7.
374. David Marshall Lang. A Modern History of Soviet Georgia, Grove Press Inc. New York 1962, p. 152.
275. Situation in the Caucasus. London Times, Monday, March 5. 1906, p. 5 col. 5.

276. Vice-Consul Murdered. The Wall Street Journal, May 22, 1906, p. 2.
277. The State of the Caucasus. London Times, Saturday, June 23, 1906, p. 9 col. 4.
278. Jake Posey, "With Buffalo Bill in Europe," Bandwagon, October 1953, p. 4-6.
279. Order Against the Wild West Show. The New York Daily Tribune, Sunday, March 18, 1906, p. 3 col. 3.
280. Cody Not Permitted to Pitch Tents in Pisa. Lincoln Daily Evening News, Monday, March 19, 1906, p. 1 col. 5.
281. Charles Eldridge Griffin. Four Years in Europe with Buffalo Bill, Stage Publishing, Co, Albia, Iowa, 1908, p. 71-87.
282. The Great Day is Coming. Fairbury Journal, NE, Friday, April 27, 1906, p. 1 col. 5.
283. 2500 People see the Circus. The Wakefield Republican, Dixon Co., NE, Friday, June 8, 1906, p. 1 col. 2.
284. Arendt Catches Rape Fiend. The Lemars Globe-Post, June 13, 1906, p. 1 col. 1.
285. The Circus. The Daily Independent, Chippewa Falls, June 16, 1906, p. 3 col. 4.
286. Good Crowds. The Repository, Canton, Ohio, Sunday, April 29, 1906, p. 13 col. 4.
287. Cossack Riders Hurt at Brighton. New York Daily Tribune, Friday, June 22, 1906, p. 2 col. 2.
288. Storm. The New York Herald Tribune, Wednesday, July 18, 1906, p. 2 col. 3.
289. Two Killed by Lightning during Terrific Storm. The Patroit, Harrisburg, PA, Tuesday, August 7, 1906, p. 1 col. 1.
290. Jule Keen. The New York Times, November 1, 1906, p. 9 col. 5.
291. Indians Invade Brooklyn. New York Press, May 6, 1907.
292. Dashes Into Town with Wild Indians. The Indianapolis Star, Monday, August 26, 1907.
293. Big Show Pleases Many. The Indianapolis Star, Tuesday, August 27, 1907.
294. Buffalo Bill Here to Give us a Few Thrills. The Morning Herald, Uniontown, PA, Tuesday, September 10, 1907, p. 2 col. 1.
295. Everybody Interested. Alliance Semi-Weekly Times, May 14, 1907, p. 8 col. 1.
296. License Fees. Bismarck Daily Tribune, Tuesday, August 20, 1907, p. 5 col. 4.
297. Billy Hall Buys Circus. Chillicothe Constitution, Monday, September 30, 1907, p. 1 col. 3.
298. To Rival the Circus Trust. New York Times, January 25, 1907, p. 9.
299. Cosmopolitan Golf Club along with Pawnee Bill. St. Louis Daily Globe-Democrat, Sunday, May 5, 1907, p. 15 col. 2.
300. Pawnee Bill is Here. Minneapolis Tribune, Sunday, June 16, 1907, p. 7 col. 2.
301. Wild West Show Can't Keep Men. The Minneapolis Journal, Monday June 17, 1907, p. 8 col. 3.
302. Wild West Show. Houston Daily Post, Tuesday, October 29, 1907, p. 5 col. 1.
303. A New Wild West Show. New York Times, May 3, 1907, p. 7.
304. Buffalo Bill Interview. San Francisco Chronicle, Sunday, October 11, 1908.
305. Buffalo Bill Comes to Town. The Detroit Free Press, Monday, August 3, 1908, p. 5col. 4.
306. Tomorrow the Circus. St. Joseph, News-Press, Tuesday, August 18, 1908.
307. Daring Cossack is Hurled to Ground. The Muscatine Journal, Thursday, September 17, 1908, p.2.
308. Circus Gossip. Billboard, November 28, 1908.
309. Daring Rider Falls in Arena. The Saint Paul Pioneer Press, Tuesday, June 16, 1908.
310. Great Crowd Came to See. The Hutchinson Leader, July 24, 1908, p. 1 col. 6.

311. Wild West Show. The Bay City Times, Michigan, Monday, August 10, 1908, p. 4 col. 5.
312. Cowboys in Thrilling Work. The Bay City Tribune, Tuesday, August 11, 1908, p. 5 col. 3.
313. Wild West Shows Rehearse in Mud. The New York Times, Sunday, April 25, 1909.
314. Col. W.F. Cody Not Dismayed. Every Evening, Wilmington, Delaware, Friday, June 4, 1909, p. 5 col. 3.
315. The Wild West Show is Here. Kansas City Times, September 13, 1909, p. 2 col. 2.
316. Great Crowds Gather at Wild West Shows. The Daily Times, Chattanooga, TN, Monday October 18, 1909.
317. Many Victims of Circus Sharpers. The Sacramento Union, Saturday, April 17, 1909, p. 2 col. 1.
318. Circus Day. River Falls Journal, July 8, 1909, p. 5 col. 5.
319. Notes From the Greater Norris & Rowe Circus. Billboard, July 17, 1909.
320. Norris and Rowe circus 1901, by Bill Low, Circus World Museum GT File (Norris and Rowe), June 1946.
321. Miller Bros. "101 Ranch." Variety, July 24, 1909.
322. Cossack is Badly Injured in Fall. The Daily Times, Davenport, IA, Monday, August 30, 1909, p. 10 col. 3.
323. Miller Brothers. Billboard, October 30, 1909.
324. Circus News. Variety, November 20, 1909, p. 16.
325. The Wild West Show. Buenos Aires Herald, Sunday, December 5, 1909, p. 7 col. 3.
326. The Last of the IXL Ranch in Buenos Aires. Buenos Aires Herald, Sunday, January 23, 1910, p. 9 col. 3.
327. I.X.L. Show Returns. Billboard, July 2, 1910, p. 20 col. 1.
328. Foreign Artists and the Custom Service. Variety, December 11, 1909, p. 4 col.1.
329. Employee of Circus Sues to get Wages. The Wilkes-Barre Times-Leader, Tuesday, May 24, 1910, p. 19 col. 2.
330. A Campbell Act Arrives. Billboard, March 5, 1910.
331. Great Railway Wreck. Wisconsin Valley, August 18, 1910, p. 1 col. 1.
332. Circus Gossip. Billboard, October 22, 1910.
333. Robinson Ten Big. Billboard, May 7, 1910.
334. Many Injured by Falling at Circus. The Richmond Climax, Kentucky, Wednesday, August 3, 1910, p. 5 col. 8.
335. Jones Show Framed Up. Variety, April 9, 1910, p. 18.
336. Thomas O'Donnell. The Agitator, Wellsboro, PA, Wednesday, May 18, 1910, p. 5 col. 4.
337. Circus Gossip, Billboard, July 16, 1910.
338. Gate Shut Off Horses Drawing Steam Calliope. The Coshocton Daily Age, Ohio, Wednesday, August 17, 1910, col 5.
339. Runaway Girl is Deserted at Canton. The Coshocton Daily Age, Ohio, Friday, August 19, 1910, col. 3.
340. Circus News, Variety, April 23, 1910, p. 17.
341. Makharadze, Irakli & Chkhaidze, Akaki. Wild West Georgians, New Media, Tbilisi, 2001, p. 32.
342. Feeding the Show People. State Journal, Lincoln, NE, Sunday, September 18, 1910, p. B-3 col. 2.
343. The Bijou's Show Last Night. The Greenville Times, Friday, October 7, 1910, p. 1 col. 2.

344. Vernon Seaver Jr., Young Buffalo Wild West Young Buffalo Jr. White Tops, November-December 1967, p. 48.
345. Show is Called Off. Kenosha Evening News, Monday, June 20, 1910, p. 1 col. 5.
346. Troop D's Games. The Syracuse Herald, Tuesday, February 14, 1911. p. 9 col. 1.
347. Wild West in Capital. The Washington Post, Sunday, April 16, 1911.
348. Buffalo Bill Here Today. The Indianapolis Star, Tuesday, July 11, 1911, p. 3 col. 3.
349. Wild West Show Tent Blown Down. The Syracuse Herald, Sunday, July 16, 1911, p. 1 col. 7.
350. Dover Girl has a Narrow Escape. Middletown Times-Press, Monday, May 29, 1911, p. 1 col. 2.
351. Tent show Gossip. Billboard, June 10, 1911.
352. Circus Gossip. Billboard, July 22, 1911, p. 26.
353. Killed by Elephant. The Mansfield News, Ohio, Saturday, April 29, 1911, p. 2 col. 5.
354. Lynx Kills Monkey. Colorado Springs Gazette, Friday, May 19, 1911, p. 6 col. 5.
355. Milton David Hinkle, Kit Carson's Buffalo Ranch real Wild West Big Three Ring Wild West circus, The Bandwagon, Part I September-October 1963, p. 4-10, Part II November-December 1963 p. 17-21.
356. Milt Hinkle, The Kit Carson Wild West Show, Frontier Times, April-May 1964, p. 6-11, 57-58.
357. Brothers Reunited. The Sandusky Register, Monday, April 10, 1911, p. 1 col. 2.
358. Newsboys have Own Circus while Big Show Goes On. The Sunday Repository, Canton, OH, May 28, 1911, p. 17.
359. The Fourth of July. The Union City Times, Thursday, July 6, 1911, p. 1 col. 3.
360. Robinson's Circus is Hit by Tornado. The Evening Telegram, Elyria, Ohio, Thursday, July 13, 1911.
361. Prairie Joe's Wild West. The Bee, Phillips, WI, Thursday, May 25, 1911, p. 1 col. 3.
362. Circus Notes. Bethany Republican, May 11, 1911, p. 1 col. 1.
363. Coulter's Circus. The Daily Chronicle, Macon, MO., May 15, 1911, p. 2 col. 2.
364. Indian Pete's Wild West Show in Our City. Wood County Reporter, Grand Rapids, WI., Thursday, July 20, 1911, p. 4 col. 7.
365. Circus Brings Eggs. The Evening Times, Cumberland, Maryland, Friday, May 24, 1912.
366. Buffalo Bill Champion of Woman's Vote. The Lima Daily News, August 9, 1912, p. 13 col. 1.
367. Circus Quits. Fairbury Journal, Friday, August 16, 1912, p. 1 col. 1.
368. Bandwagon, 1957
369. 101 Spends five days in Frisco. Billboard, May 11, 1912.
370. 101 Ranch Wild West. Billboard, November 16, 1912.
371. Tent show Gossip. Billboard, March 2, 1912.
372. Young Buffalo. Evening Times, Cumberland, MD, May 2, 1912, p. 10 col. 2.
373. Show Train Wreck. The Bay City Times, Saturday, May 11, 1912, p. 8 col. 5.
374. Cossack Rider's Skull Fractured. The Evening Times, Cumberland, MD, Saturday, May 25, 1912, p.3 col. 1.
375. Two Russians Buried. The Evening News, Cumberland, MD, Monday, May 27, 1912, p.9 col. 3.
376. A Correction. Billboard, July 20, 1912.
377. Gene Fowler. Timber Line, Blue Ribbon Books, Inc. New York City, 375-377.

378. Wild West Show has Much Trouble. Ashtabula Beacon, Thursday, August 8, 1912, p. 2 col. 5.

379. News Items. Poverty Bay Herald, volume XXXX, Issue 12974, 5 February, 1913, p. 4.

380. Australian Rain too Much for Wyomingites. The Hawaiian Gazette, May 6, 1913, p. 6 col. 5.

381. Stranded Red Indians. The Sydney Morning Herald, Thursday 17 April 1913, p. 8.

382. Crowds See Show Arrive. Virginia Pilot, Monday, May 26, 1913, P. 9 col. 3.

383. Buffalo Bill, In Atlanta, Denies Knoxville Reports of His Dangerous Illness. The Atlanta Constitution, Monday, June 9, 1913, p. 2 col.3.

384. Sheriff Gets Buffalo Bill Show Money. Daily News, Denver, Wednesday, July 23, 1913, p. 1 col. 2.

385. Buffalo Bill's Show Hard Hit. Daily News, Denver, Thursday, July 24, 1913, p. 3 col. 7.

386. The Kit Carson Show in Hard Luck. Wisconsin Tobacco Reporter, Friday, July 18, 1913, p. 5.

387. Circusy Circus is Offered by the Ringlings. The San Francisco Examiner, Sunday, August 31, 1913, p. 66 col. 1.

388. Shot 48 trained Horses. The New York Times, March 30, 1914, p. 18.

389. Cossack killed here Saturday. Big Sandy News, Louisa, Kentucky, October 16, 1914.

390. $3000 Bail for Nathan C. Day. Big Sandy News, Louisa, Kentucky, October 23, 1914.

391. 101 Wild West Good. The News, Lynchburg, VA, September 24, 1914, p. 10 col. 3.

392. Iowa City Daily Press, Friday, August 14, 1914, p. 2 col. 5.

393. Capture of Batoum (sic) Imminent. Wall Street Journal, November 20, 1914, p. 4.

394. Revolt Against Russian Rule. Wall Street Journal, November 24, 1914, p. 7.

395. Big Judgment Entered. The New York Sun, Friday, December 18, 1914.

396. Billboard, October 23, 1915.

397. Makharadze, Irakli & Chkhaidze, Akaki. Wild West Georgians, New Media, Tbilisi, 2001, p. 38.

398. Buffalo Bill Show in Wreck. The Daily News, Frederick, MD, Tuesday, October 10, 1916.

399. Ringling Bros. Show Crippled by Flames. Waterloo Evening Courier, October 31, 1916, p. 12 col. 4.

400. Buffalo Bill Bids A Last Farewell. The Hartford Daily Courant, Friday, May 12, 1911, p. 6 col. 1.

401. Fowler, Gene. Timberline, A Story of Bonfils and Tammen. Blue Ribbon Books, Inc., New York City, 1933, p. 43.

402. Legionnaires Seek to Transfer Cody's Body to Cedar Mountain. The Billings Gazette, Sunday, August 1, 1948, p. 18 col. 1.

403. Variety, February 16, 1917 and Variety February 23, 1917, p. 4.

404. Maj. Burke, Friend of Col. Cody, Dead. The Washington Post, Friday, April 13, 1917.

Alexis Estate Georgian (Gogokhia), ca 1919
The Author's inspiration for this book.
Noe Zhordania in 1919 asked Alexis to be Georgia's first ambassador to the United States.
Alexis had to decline due to pending legal issues.
Author's Collection
Plate No. 41

www.ingramcontent.com/pod-product-compliance
Lightning Source LLC
Chambersburg PA
CBHW032030090426
42733CB00029B/69